RELOCATIONS

OF THE

S P I R I T

Other books by
Leon Forrest

There is a Tree More Ancient than Eden

The Bloodworth Orphans

Two Wings to Veil My Face

Divine days

RELOCATIONS

OF THE

S P I R I T

Essays by

Leon Forrest

ASPHODEL PRESS

MOYER BELL

WAKEFIELD, RHODE ISLAND & LONDON

Published by Asphodel Press

First Edition

LIBRARY OF CONGRESS
CATALOGING-IN-PUBLICATION DATA

Forrest, Leon.
Relocations of the Spirit / Leon Forrest—1st.
ed.

p.   cm.

1. Afro-Americans. I. Title.
E185.F595   1993
973'.0496073—dc20   92-42600
ISBN:1-55921-068-0 (cl-1994)
      1-55921-080-X (pb-1995)
                                    CIP

Printed in the United States of America
Distributed in North America by Publishers Group
West, P.O. Box 8843, Emeryville, CA 94662, 800-788-
3123 (in California 510-658-3453), and in Europe by
Gazelle Book Services Ltd., Falcon House, Queen
Square, Lancaster LA1 1RN England.

To the memory of Ronald Williams (1927–1985)
. . . and in salute to the Mississippians:
Uncle Eddie Richardson (1911–1992),
and Perrin Holmes Lowrey (1924–1965).

CONTENTS

AT HOME IN
THE WINDY CITY

IN THE LIGHT OF THE
LIKENESS—TRANSFORMED

> "Mother of mine, why do you object
>   to our trusty singer
> giving delight in whatever way his
>   mind inspires him?
> The poets are not responsible for
>   their subject matter but Zeus
>   rather
> who gives to each man what he will.
> So attach no blame to this man for
>   singing of the Greeks' sorry fate.
> For men much more praise which-
>   ever song comes newest to their
>   ears."
>
> —Telemachus to his mother,
>   Penelope, in Homer's *Odyssey*

I was raised by a magical seamstress, a lady who was always transforming life: first the cloth, now the body, and then the very spirit of the re-created person before our eyes. Like any good beautician or barber, my Kentucky "aunt" knew what her clientele said they wanted, and she knew what would "work wonders" on her *characters*, transforming them into new ladies. She kept hundreds of old patterns in her room, and scores of contemporary fashion magazines from around the world. She received many of these magazines from a Negro woman, who traveled throughout Europe as the maid for a famous and wealthy white woman. These magazines formed the "literature" of her seamstress art; the human form, her springboard.

3

When Lenora Bell got going on a dress, something new, something magical, happened to that material once the new apparel was fitted upon the lady's form. Magical, too, in the sense of character, because she not only tailored the pattern to the fit of the woman's bodily form, she also revealed the best of the lady's soul and personality. "Aunt" Bell's clientele suddenly appeared radiant in their new dresses and suits, as if touched by the wand of a goddess. But she also remade these women—into ladies, in the light of Lenora Bell's own lyrical image. Thus my seamstress "aunt" put her stamp or style or reinvention upon her inspired art: here indeed was the body and the spirit transformed.

Now long before I ever dared dream of making any woman, long before I discovered the divinity of the female form, with my own shape-adoring hands in the dark, I dreamed deeply of re-creating women (and men) in not only the likeness of God, and Zeus, but in the light of the likeness—transformed. And the possibilities for unleashing and making new transformations were all around me as I grew up in Chicago.

I remember the great blues singer Big Bill Broonzy once saying that all he needed to create a blues was some essential item (ethos-bearing, he probably meant). "Take a knife," he said. "There you have five verses right there. A man on the run takes a knife and he shaves with it; he cuts his corns off his feet with it; he washes it off and carves up a chicken with it; he cuts branches of a tree with it for fire by night; and he slices the throat of a pursuer with it." Five verses indeed, with much inherent conflict possibilities for character-in-process transformation. Note too Broonzy's shape-singing of his character's personae: transformed into something heightened and different with every slicing of the knife, even as the knife itself becomes a more celebrating and menacing ritual instrument of thematic power; each new carving connected to the theme of the larger blues he's creating. For me, theme means the intelligence of a given work and the paths of lucidity it provides.

Now my point is that only the knife—in the right hands—was necessary as ethos image to spring Broonzy's imagination and, from this, to carve out a character buried within the consciousness of his imagination. Just as, in a different dimension, it is the handkerchief of the Bard's Othello that comes knotted too, then unfolded, within our imagination, whenever we think of the Moor's public and private soul, as *the* cultural core source of his keening, tortured, sorrowing spirit. And in act 3, scene 4, the nostalgia so layered within his unravelled soul, but now evoked by the missing handkerchief, is made even more painful for Othello, because he has begun to believe Desdemona has lost the heart of her love for him, and replaced him with Cassio. In this scene, Desdemona has momentarily lost the handkerchief given to Othello's mother by an Egyptian charmer, who "could almost read / The thoughts of people." (She sounds something like evil Iago.)

> She told her, while she kept it,
> 'Twould make her amiable, and subdue my
>   father
> Entirely to her love; but if she lost it,
> Or made a gift of it, my father's eye
> Should hold her loathed, and his spirits
>   should hunt
> After new fancies. She, dying, gave it me,
> And bid me, when my fate would have me
>   wiv'd,
> To give it her.

And when the Venetian lady, Desdemona, expresses her awe and doubt, the Moor says:

> 'Tis true; there's magic in the web of it.

This scene with the handkerchief hurls our memories back to Othello's first gift of wooing; back to the whirlwind courtship between the Moor and Desdemona; flirts with her Venetian refinement of layered sophistry in courtship, even more ironic and pitiable since whenever was there a heart so true, so innocent, so gullible. This same handkerchief is brought low, even as the majestic Moor is brought so low—in act 4, scene 1, set in motion by that truth-whore, Iago—when Othello sees Cassio's delightful whore, Bianca with the handkerchief. Othello's soul, so yeasty with transformational possibilities, is here driven to a furious pitch, through the roles the handkerchief plays and evokes, within his soul. In the larger sense of the work, every character of major importance touches the handkerchief but is only touched by one aspect of its power. But for Othello, this handkerchief possessed mythic powers:

> A sibyl, that had numb'red in the world
> The sun to course two hundred compasses,
> In her prophetic fury sew'd the work;
> The worms were hallowed that did breed the
> silk,
> And it was dy'd in mummy which the skillful
> Conserv'd of maidens' hearts.

The handkerchief comes to stand for the stages of Othello's transformation: his gullibility, his hidden self, his Moorishness, his romantic nature, his spiritual otherness, his loyalty, his divided soul, etc. The handkerchief's core cultural symbolism is the nostalgic talisman, which metaphorically provides, at least in part, Othello's warring mind with a web of self-definition; and helps this man of action to forge the reflective, eloquent language of Myth, attendant to the Ritual act of suicide in the final scene of the play.

This kind of transformation was also true of Faulkner's works again and again. Take Caddy's muddy drawers in *The Sound and the Fury*. Faulkner simply began with this image—connected to that of some children being sent away from the house during the grandmother's funeral. Then he added that precocious little flirt of a girl, Caddy, climbing up into the tree to look in the window to see what was going on inside; with her brothers and some of the black kids looking up at her; and her drawers were viewed as muddy. The girl with the muddy drawers confusing Damuddy's funeral with a party; a symbol which becomes as powerfully implanted in the reader's memory bank, throughout the work, as Othello's handkerchief, or Amanda's glass menagerie of animals in Tennessee Williams's *Glass Menagerie.*

As a writer who comes out of a culture steeped in the eloquence of the Oral Tradition, I've come to see the Negro preacher as the Bard of the race; and throughout my novels, that rich lodestone of eloquence has provided me with an important springboard. I once heard an illuminating South Side preacher in Chicago explaining the Easter Resurrection of the Redeemer concerning his processing, this transformation of the light of the likeness. He said of the arisen Christ: "Jesus was the same man he was on the Friday of the crucifixion, but now he was also different." Or, put in another way: "For now we see through a glass, darkly; but then face to face." Engagingly enough, it was a Mississippi white man, a professor of English and humanities at the University of Chicago, who first suggested, quite indirectly, the possibilities of exploring this richness of the preacher's art, when he was lecturing on (two seminal works in my own development) William Faulkner's *Sound and the Fury,* with a particular emphasis upon the Reverend Shegog's sermon, and Ralph Ellison's *Invisible Man.*

My professor, and mentor, the late Perrin Holmes Lowrey, was an authority on Faulkner's works. He was quite taken by one particular South Side minister, the Reverend Louis Boddie, whose sermons were broadcast over radio, and Professor Lowrey often wondered if anyone was taping these sermons and sermons like them. I had been listening to sermons all of my life; but at the time, I was overwhelmed by so many art forms of performance and celebration in the black community, and had little confidence in my abilities to make something magical of the overpowering voices I heard all about me.

Indeed, at the time, Professor Lowrey did not know of my interest in becoming a novelist—that came near the tragic end of his life. But his remarks, combined with James Weldon Johnson's *God's Trombones;* Faulkner's Negro preacher, Reverend Shegog (named for a Southern white general); Ellison's uses of the form both in his magnificent novel and works in progress; the sermons in Joyce's *Portrait of the Artist as a Young Man;* John Donne's sermons; and Reverend Mapple's sermon in

Moby-Dick, finally got me energized into the possibility of seeing my way into the texture of the sermon as a seminal source, not only to my culture, but into my own fledgling art. And as the very source for reinvention and transformation of the self, in character.

That Professor Lowrey's timely but indirect salute should have set loose such an avalanche of sermons (over the course of three novels, with more to come, Lawd-God) seems all the more remarkable to me, not because I've mastered the form, but rather it recalls how furiously I was looking for clues to cultural exploration, when lo and behold here was a quite obvious one—the Negro sermon. The clue came from a Southern white man to a Negro Catholic whose autobiographical vitae of options were so scattered and scatterbrained at the time that I thought I'd never write anything solid. Never achieve wholeness, or the transformation I sought so dearly as my way home, as I essayed to sing of the sorry fate of my race.

Professor Lowrey was also a superb short-story writer, so that his hints, tips, or sidebars into the literary text, as professor, also had a kind of doubleness for my hunger-hearted imagination. His insights into Ellison's *Invisible Man* were deeply illuminating. That he knew this Negro author who had achieved the kind of thing I wanted so much for my own work—transformation of oral eloquence into literary eloquence—was all the more intriguing and instructive to me. How was I to know then, when I took classes with Professor Lowrey, and questioned him about the works of his friend, that my own published eulogy to Lowrey would form my initial tie with the celebrated novelist years later. How was I to know, that late May morning in 1965 when I sat in on Lowrey's class on the novel, that this, his last lecture for the quarter, on *Invisible Man,* would be his last at the University of Chicago, and that within a month I would hear of his tragic automobile accident at Sweet Briar, Virginia.

I often remember what Tennessee Williams said when he took his mother to see the opening performance of his play *The Glass Menagerie.* This memory play contains within its fragile soul many recollections of

8

life and a Southern mother who was something like Tennessee's own mother. That excellent critic Claudia Cassidy described Laurette Taylor's portrayal of The Mother, Amanda, as the "role of her maturity" when the play was staged in Chicago's Civic Theatre, December 26, 1944. Miss Cassidy wrote:

> As a bedraggled southern belle who married the wrong man, living in a near-tenement, alienating her children by her nagging fight to shove them up to her pathetically remembered gentility, she gives a magnificent performance. The crest of her career in the delta was the simultaneous arrival of 17 gentlemen callers, and her pitiful quest in this play—as often funny as sad—is the acquisition of just one gentleman caller for her neurotically shy daughter, the crippled girl played by Julie Haydon.

Now at the end of the evening, Mrs. Williams herself announced, to Tennessee's heightened fears of self-revelation, that she indeed did want to go backstage to meet this actress, Miss Laurette Taylor, who was so powerful as Amanda. Tennessee was now in a state of shock at what he had done to his mother or, should I say, what he had vaulted out of and re-created from his mother's pattern and form. After Mrs. Williams was introduced to Miss Laurette Taylor, Tennessee's real-life mother exclaimed, "You were so believable; I know Southern women just like the woman you played." It was then that Tennessee knew that his magical web had worked. He was saved—if not redeemed. Both of his mothers were transformed. Transformed in the light of Tennessee's own artistic likeness, to be sure.

In characterization, it seems to me, we have the dramatized re-creation and reinvention of deeply felt immemorial traits, within not only our conscious heritage but our underground, perhaps even unadmitted, sense of life, recombined with the written heritage of the tongue. Out of this, the writer is able to create something new, something different, from character patterns observed over and over again until he astutely knows these patterns as assuredly as the palm of his hand, or with the assuredness of his sexual backstroke, his prayers to God, his knowledge of the use of a knife. He may also have the common lack of confidence concerning how well he is adept at any of this. Yet with this foundational springboard knowledge—this "two boards and a passion"—he is able to forget about the springboard completely because he or she is so well grounded in the materials of "felt-life," and then he can go on to transform life into new life, even as he is transformed by his creation, as a preacher is transformed, as he seeks a collective transcendence at the height of his sermon—and stands convicted. Or, for us Catholics, that moment of a miracle when the bread becomes the Body of the Redeemer, and the wine, His Blood—all offered up in a most unbloody manner. And what do I mean by re-creation and reinvention? I mean the powerful use of the imagination to take a given form and make something that appears completely new of it—that creates within the reading or listening audience a sense of the magical meaning of life transformed.

But it is this difference, physical, emotional, intellectual, spiritual—this transformation in which the writer takes the body of his character materials up to the high place—that has so bedeviled and intrigued the brooding artist within us, from the springboard and through the launching powers of his imagination, he vaults the swimmer's body and soul out of her living body into the air. Suddenly the swimmer is no longer your daughter or my sister; she is a fictive creation of body and spirit transformed into an Olympian spirit, now doing unbelievable flips and somersaults in the physical and spiritual space of the text—vaulting off the page—light-years beyond your loins or my brotherly beholding arms of love. In a real sense she is out there skywriting her own autobiography, even as she is creating it, in mythical space. And as we watch her? I, her author (if I am supremely lucky) am almost as amazed as you are. The novelist Elizabeth Bowen's admonishment seems applicable here:

> The term "creation of character" (or characters) is misleading. Characters pre-exist. They are found. They reveal themselves slowly to the novelist's perception—as might

fellow-travellers seated opposite one in a very dimly-lit railway carriage. The novelist's perceptions of his characters take place *in the course of the actual writing of the novel.* To an extent, the novelist is in the same position as his reader. But his perceptions should be always just in advance.

And as we watch her further? The wonder of it all too, that she has found a place for chaos (and a way to transform a daredevil need to tempt death, the Fates, the Gods into a work of art) within her own two boards and a passion. Or that she has found a way to shape a contour of her life, in facing death, not defeated by Death, even as she is struck down, perhaps by lightning, or some failure in judgment, or by her Icarus-like thrust to experience flight beyond human knowledge. She's gone beyond anything we've ever known of this life. Surely this must have been the case for the greatest of novelists, Leo Tolstoy, when the totality of the character Anna Karenina materialized out of his imagination. And as Miss Bowen says, in her very useful essay *Notes on Writing a Novel:*

> By the end of the novel, the character has, like the silkworm at work on the cocoon, spun itself out. Completed action is marked by the exhaustion (from one point of view) of the character. Throughout the novel, each character is expend-ing potentiality. This expense of potentiality must be felt.

This is an imperative: the writer must be a constant reader; and he must be scholarly about what he reads, though not necessarily a scholar in the way this word is defined in the Academy. I was stimulated at an early age into writing because of my reading. That's true with almost any writer you'll meet. I came from a lower-middle-class Negro household on the South Side of Chicago. My father was a bartender on the Santa Fe Railroad and Daddy would read to me and my mother when he was at home. My mother read to me constantly. My great-grandmother lived with us until I was ten; and I used to read the Bible to her, mainly the Old Testament. Her formal schooling stopped at the

11

third grade; I was thirty-two when she died. Her mother had been a slave.

On my mother's side, I had the task of going to my great-aunt's house after mass on Sundays and reading the Epistle and the Gospel for that week. She was an invalid. This is on the New Orleans side, the Catholic side of my family tree. My grand-uncle on my mother's side was a great storyteller and he was a banjo player; he had gone to school with Louis Armstrong in New Orleans. He was also a barber and his story-telling patterns have enriched my memory bank, in the oral tradition. He knew a lot about early New Orleans Jazz, Negro baseball, and black boxers. One of my most vivid memories of his stories springs from his account of hearing Sam Langford, the Boston Tar Baby, extol the great defensive skills of Jack Johnson one might in a New Orleans bar. My uncle George Dewey White had a wonderful comic sense, and he enjoyed imitating the voices of people he spoke of, such as Sam Langford, even as he told stories about them. He also enjoyed dubbing family members with nicknames. These coinages were invariably more effervescent, or telling, than the given names, because these pseud- onyms were *stage names*, given to the individuals after observing their *performances*, their acting out, or their innocence, or their capacity for lying over a period of years. The earned titles were ritually handed along by my uncle as patriarch, because the family member had transformed the individual life, and the given name, into something new . . . and always something else, and now needed to be christened with a secular stage-name. Sometimes these names could be more epithet than halo, and often a combination of both, as my uncle George Dewey White played out his ironic role of high priest, vaudeville cum picnic, and delightful trickster. We family members often as not missed the wit and the vital comment of these uncle-inspired pseudonyms because of the old man's humor, his spontaneity. Perhaps we believed with Telemachus that "the poets are not respon-sible for their subject matter." And that the gods give "to each man what they will." These coinages, however, are no more vivid in my imagination than his stories of scenes at the Funky Butt bar in New Orleans.

I was apparently deeply impressed by the ritual service in the Catholic church, as I saw it expressed at St. Elizabeth's in Chicago, from my mother's side; and from my father's people, the Mississippi Protestant side, I learned to love the art of the folk preacher and particularly the spirituals and gospel singing. My father was once a singer in the choir at Pilgrim Baptist Church on Chicago's South Side. The pastor there, the Reverend J. C. Austin, was once acclaimed by that great orator President Franklin Roosevelt as having the greatest speaking voice of any public man in America. Pilgrim Baptist Church, Thirty-third and Michigan, was a former Jewish synagogue. Thus, too, the linkage between the Negro spiritual and the struggles of the Jews, as a way of transforming the light of oral eloquence into illuminating oracles of elegance, was vivid in my imaginative springboard long before I ever dreamed of becoming a writer. Just as sermons by Reverend Austin and others were vivid in my memory bank long before I thought of calling upon them as a resource for my own art.

This church is also known for the pioneer of gospel music, Reverend Thomas A. Dorsey. Reverend Dorsey has been connected with Pilgrim for decades, and was the director of the choir. His own life story of going in and out of the church has been revealed in several magazine articles; apparently he went through several transformations. He was a blues pianist and a composer for a long time; and this base enriched and deepened the kind of gospel music he composed, as he transformed the refinements of the spiritual into a music that fitted the more angular needs of an awakening people, hungry-hearted for a dialogue in song which captured both their secular and their spiritual sense of life, as agony and wonder. This marriage of blues and spiritual seemed far too rowdy an intermarriage for most middle-class Negroes for a long time.

Dr. Dorsey is of course known for "Precious Lord Take My Hand," which was made famous by Mahalia Jackson (one of several of the chosen for whom he composed). The song seems now enshrined upon our national consciousness, born out of Dr. Dorsey's own private turmoil, even though the actual lyrics sought a personal healing. It was this song that Martin Luther King longed to hear (in his own need for healing) that fatal night, from the balcony of the Lorraine Motel. Seconds after he called out to the Chicago saxophonist Ben Branch to play "Precious Lord take my hand . . . lead me on . . . let me stand" at the railing where he stood, a rifle blast took Dr. King's life.

I have mentioned that I was raised by a seamstress who was an Afro-American Victorian lady from Kentucky, and this spinster was also a Republican who remained a Republican, Roosevelt be damned; and I remember a placard on the sewing machine of a colleague of hers which stated: "What? No Goddamn fourth term," referring to FDR's bid at winning a fourth term in office as President. The seamstress friend of my "aunt" Lenora Bell's was also the precinct captain for the Republicans. By the mid to late 1940s, this was a most lonely job for a Negro—almost as lonely as that of the fabled machine repairman in the Maytag ads. These two ladies were the only Afro-Americans I knew who remained staunch and true to the party of Mr. Lincoln. The whole of the black community may have been transformed into Democrats by President Roosevelt, but damned if these two ladies were to turn from the party of the man who had transformed their ancestors from slave to free. Indeed we often thought that Lenora Bell was so old that she had actually seen or even sewn buttons on the shirts of the vaulted Redeemer. As it turned out, my seamstress aunt (by the way not related to me by blood, but rather another vestige of the extended Afro-American family) remembered seeing, as a very young girl, not the great Emancipator, but rather President Rutherford B. Hayes. It was upon this memory alone that we were able to ascertain general guidelines for her age, for although Aunt Bell never married, she embraced the mirror of female vanities and fought hard to let no man know her age. The fact that she slipped up and told us about seeing Hayes always seemed most human to me. Upon three glasses of Fox Head 400 beer, she would often tell me of her handsome old beaus.

She would read to me, and I would read to her; she lived with us all of my growing-up years. She taught me how to tell time, helped me with my multiplication tables; she introduced me to brains and mackerel for breakfast and eggplant for dinner. In my own growing-up years there were three cuisines to feed my appetite: the Mississippi soul food, the New Orleans creole dishes, and this border-country cuisine of Aunt Bell's.

That there were limited cross-encounters between the two sides (factions really) of my family tree helped me, probably, to see each clan quite separately and individually. Each side for me surely represented but two of the many which compose the Afro-American diaspora. The two aunts to whom I dedicated my novel *Two Wings to Veil My Face* were as clearly different for me as oil and water. One is from Greenville, the other from New Orleans. I doubt if they ever met more than three times in my growing-up years. And because I am an only child, of two only children, I formed my opinions and visions of them undisturbed by sibling rivalry. They were both named *Maude*, but that is about as close as they come to one another. Yet in my imagination, they were as vivid to me as healing waters and ritual soothing oils, but in juxtaposition, and long before I ever thought of what a character spectrum in a novel meant.

My aunt Maude Richardson, on my father's side—now in her mid-eighties—played godmother for many neighborhood children. She still does. I often spent weekends with Aunt Maude and her very stable and devoted husband, Eddie Richardson. She is my father's aunt; and she taught Bible class in the Protestant tradition, which in her ethos was something of a commingling of Baptist and Methodist interpretation, recombined with Negro peasant savvy. She and her husband maintained the ethos of the South, and the Negro values of genuine effort, and God-fearing connections. But she never worked once she came north with her husband. This migrant from Greenville, Mississippi, never let the ethos of Chicago get into the bloodstream of her values. Thus, in the very heart of the slums, where they live, you will find a little Southern patch of vegetables growing in the backyard and

Uncle Eddie's flower garden growing in the front—untouched, and even respected, by winos and lost souls of the neighborhood.

My aunt Maude on my mother's side ran the cafeteria at St. Elizabeth's Catholic High School. She worked long hours; but she was also rarely without her rosary beads; she took in many orphans from the Catholic Home Bureau. She attended the earliest mass, each morning, and took Holy Communion regularly, throughout the week. In the last years of her life, I used to write her Christmas cards for her. I enjoyed this task, too. Often as not, one-third of the cards went to retired priests and nuns; and special messages of remembrance went out to them.

These "three women in my life," Lenora Bell, Maude Richardson, and Maude White (each an aunt-figure of a different kind), were linked in their love for children and Christian mission, but little else. In short, Negro character, as it came to me, early on (with its great diversity, complexity, individualism, and variety), was clearly rich and riddled with angularity long before I started writing. But this blessing found me up a tree, indeed, as to how I might employ my gift to transform it all into art. Or how I might do justice to a people who were so often presented as nondimensional.

As a kid I loved to play baseball, and I played with Ida B. Well's grandson Troy Duster. (He is now a professor of sociology at Berkeley). I remember when they broke ground across the street from where I lived for the Ida B. Wells Project. She was the lady who had fought lynchings in the South with her speeches and her journalistic efforts. I was in contact with her daughter, Mrs. Alfreda Duster, until she died in 1983.

My father not only read to us when he was home from the railroad, but he brought home stories from this experience. Serving and talking with men as varied as Bing Crosby or Cootie Williams, the great trumpet man with Duke Ellington, Daddy picked up on many interests and engaging conversations and stories and relayed them to me.

My father took motion pictures of my graduation from Wendell

Phillips Grade School. He was a lyricist; and he had a few songs published. He had a good singing voice and he recorded several of his songs. We often looked at movies Daddy had made of family times in the evening. And we watched boxing matches and sporting events projected upon the screen. He was always thinking of how he might transform life into something higher, and more intellectually engaging. He converted to Catholicism when he was about thirty. In his mid-thirties, my father became an ardent devotee of the Rosicrucian philosophy. This philosophy gave him the kind of leverage over life that he needed. "The kind of cosmic consciousness" that he was looking for. My father was a hypersensitive, talented, Mississippi mulatto, who did not know his white father, Archie Forrest, so that compensating for his lack of a father and a family unit became everything to him. I remember quite vividly when my mother gave him twenty-nine gifts for his twenty-ninth birthday, as a surprise upon his return from the railroad. Daddy's reaction was like that of a schoolboy brought in from the rain and showered with love and warm clothing. He could be extremely spontaneous and affectionate; he was also a very volatile man. He had a very quick temper as a young man. But he never held a grudge. My father had a wonderful flair for the language. On this occasion, when tears flowed from his eyes, it was touching, and I thought I understood some of his need and his momentary happiness. Upon his twenty-ninth birthday, my fatherless father was lost for words, due to the thoughtfulness of my mother's gifts. She had grown up with everything in the way of material comforts and familial adoration. Daddy had been working since he was six and, with the exception of his grandmother, he had known little affection and material security and spontaneity.

Stage shows were big then in Chicago and while I was reading Edgar Allan Poe and falling in love with his terrorizing story "The Tell-Tale Heart" I was transfixed and transformed by several memorable readings of Poe's tale of horror, by none other than Peter Lorre himself, pitched into the dark with a dwindling light, where he tossed his voice on the stage of the old Chicago Theatre and read in that eerie voice of

17

his: "It was not the old man who vexed me but his Evil Eye." Or again, seeing at the age of eleven the magnificent Josephine Baker, one of her infrequent trips back to the U.S., on that very stage. She sang twenty-five songs in English and French. She dressed and redressed in fabulous gowns—far beyond my imagination, and I suspect even that of Lenora Bell's. All of the children in the audience were brought up upon the stage and given a flower from the very hand of the majestic, sexually divine, grand lady, who had emerged from the slums of St. Louis to become an important symbol of vaulting freedom over oppression and a freedom fighter in the French resistance during World War II, against Hitler's armies of occupation. Nothing I had seen on the stage of the Regal Theatre on the South Side could match her; ah, here indeed was the body, mind, and soul transformed there upon that stage by this Afro-American turned citizen of France.

But this sense of personal artistic vision, as a public matter rather than the reverse, was deep within me, growing up from my mother's interests in, and intelligence about, the great Negro vocalists and jazz singers—my parents had gone to high school with Nat King Cole, indeed he was kind of sweet on my mother, or so I was told—and our apartment at 3704 South Parkway (now King Drive) swung out with artistry of the great story-tellers like Billie Holiday (mother's favorite) and Billy Eckstine, Sarah Vaughan, and Ella Fitzgerald, as well as that of the great white singers, who were in the great traditions, like Frank Sinatra, Peggy Lee, and Anita O'Day.

I learned very early, then, that men "much more praise whichever song comes newest to their ears" from these ethos-bearing, reinventive songsters of the soul. Ironically enough my father (who was an amateur lyricist) knew more about what the instrumentalists were doing. And my mother, who sent off several stories to magazines, but none were published, was closer to the story-telling vocalists. My parents made me aware that in jazz the vocalist is always trying to get back to the purity of the instrument, and the instrumentalist is always trying to get back to the purity of the vocalist, like Fitzgerald, Sarah Vaughan, and Lady Day.

All of this became a kind of standard for me when I started to write in terms of the transformation of Oral Eloquence, and in my fitful attempt to capture the "voices" I heard within my evolving literary and artistic consciousness.

But all of these artists, along with the writers I was to read and was reading, affirmed what André Malraux said about the coming of powerful personalities into Western Culture, who have indeed transformed their chosen artistic mediums. Malraux said:

> I regard the weakening of the importance given to objects as the capital transformation of Western Art; in painting, it is clear that a painting of Picasso's is less and less a "canvas" and more and more the mark of some discovery, a stake left to indicate the place through which a restless genius has passed.

This statement spoke to me, and still speaks to something deep and abiding within my soul, about a range of American heroes I took to the very core of my imaginative being, from Poe to Holiday, from Faulkner to Charlie Parker, from Melville to Ellison. But what also finally ties the reader and writer is a library of ever-transforming light. For it is only through the possession of an ever-illuminating library that we can come to recognize and understand the horror and wonder of the human family's *Odyssey* and its quest for wholeness, freedom, salvation, love, and dominion over fire, flood, suffering, and even disease and death—from the river Styx to space. Without reading as an essential resource for survival in our everyday experience, the individual exists in a no-man's-land of spiritual meanness and intellectual poverty, where fallacious politics, TV fad, stock-market flux, and commercial joke continue to possess and mock the intellect and the soul with gaseous gods of glut, and the individual swings in the orchard of time, an empty-headed scarecrow—gleeful in his wilderness. But for me this attitude gets started in the beginning, back at Wendell Phillips Grade School, with a black teacher by the name of Mrs. Lucille H. Montgomery. During the 1940s, when I was a student in this elementary school—named for an abolitionist—in order to pass Lucille H. Montgomery's English class, students in the sixth through eight grades had to turn to a Negro history notebook during the second week of February. We learned about Paul Laurence Dunbar, Langston Hughes, and W.E.B. Du Bois, along with the traditional classics of our literary library. Because my mother had taught me to use the typewriter, I always turned in my notebook typed.

While encouraging us to be proud of our heritage, Mrs. Montgomery stressed the totality of that African-American expression—seeing our Negro-American culture as varied, complex, black/white; and she stood absolutely for a desegregated library, as *her* ancestral imperative, and as the only way to forge the intellectual tools to free our people. Indeed the general date of what was then called Negro History Week's "birthright" fell between the birthdays of two great Americans who had complex visions of the shape and direction of black freedom, Frederick Douglass (ca. February 7, 1817) and Abraham Lincoln (February 12, 1809).

Black scholar St. Clair Drake expressed it best a decade ago, while paying tribute to the influences and imperatives he received from one of his mentors, the scholarly giant Allison Davis:

> While rooting oneself in fighting for one's people, one also tried to make a contribution at the highest . . . level of scholarship.

From the beginning, my Northern-based Black characters emerged from a labyrinth of several worlds. The novels were set in a Northern city (suggestive of "Chicago"); but the characters and the scenes of my Forest County were fundamentally rooted in a kind of mythical city of body and soul, where the memoirs of the South migrated up to the North. Of my second novel, *The Bloodworth Orphans*, a critic for *Chicago* magazine observed: "Forrest's novel is *Roots* as James Joyce might have approached it. The setting is Chicago, but it bears the same relation to Chicago as Bloom's Nighttown does to Dublin."

Even my characters who were cut off from past havoc, directly (born unto the second or third generation in the Northern Kingdom), were reconnected to the backbone of memory by Oral Tradition. In reviewing my most recent novel, *Two Wings to Veil My Face*, for the Grand Rapids Press, the critic Herbert L. Carson stated the following about Sweetie Reed, the main character, as she relives her saga to the grandson, Nathaniel Witherspoon, in a Forest County building:

> The story is told mainly by Sweetie as she rapturously recalls the terrible events of her childhood and of her youthful marriage to Jericho (Witherspoon) and of those difficult later years when she could not produce for him a single living child . . . This is a musical novel, with echoes of the spiritual and or prayer (for Sweetie was a youthful preacher, as well). It provides insights into the plight of the slave, the early post-bellum years in the South, the struggles of blacks seeking freedom.

Now the Mother Country—Lodestone for all of this—is Mississippi on the one hand and New Orleans (a kind of state unto itself, in terms of its layered creole ethos) on the other. Undergirding my vision of characterization in the novels is a will to re-create the complex layers of the Afro-American memory, and the impact of history-as-memoir upon the contemporary experience. My characters are a consequence of varied stocks and sources, motifs, ideas, religions, and relationships to the American Dream. The spiritual agony and the quest for wholeness seem to be at the backbone of my novels and the new stories: a central measure for my pilgrim's progress.

The Black church, the Negro spiritual, gospel music, sermons, the blues, and jazz appear to be both the railroad tracks and the wings for my imagination and the migrating train of my Southern-turned-Yankee sagas. One character, for example, in *The Bloodworth Orphans* delivers an important conversion sermon in that novel and he reappears in *Two Wings*.

In *The Bloodworth Orphans*, we are imaginatively relocated with this preacher's spirit, when it is revealed that at one time, Reverend Packwood was a blues singer; he went in the church, came back out, and reentered—finally relocating his spirit. This entry, leavetaking, and going back—Southern and Northern—touches upon the spiritual dream rooted in the Christian interpretation of Life, Death, and Rebirth, and upon the question of spiritual agony, death, and rebirth, and the theme of transformation of the self. In *Two Wings*, this transformation of the self is based on the impact of whites and blacks upon each other, sexually, culturally, intellectually, and spiritually; the making of a new people, in a new land, eternally seeking an internal wholeness for the migrating spirit; integration of the spiritual whole is important here.

An image of connecting the continuities and the discontinuities of migration from the South to the North is enough to spring the imaginative reinventive gestalt within me. For example, in *The Bloodworth Orphans* the blind prophetess, Sister Rachel Flowers, is calling out all forms of demons—particularly those within the obese body of her husband and from the living room, which she has turned into a prayer room of possessed rugs adorned by Old Testament scenes and stapled fast from the upper window-panes down to the bottom of the floor. And then we hear the sweep of her genesis story.

But while I was writing this section, I was reinspired by the Alvin Ailey Dance Theater's Judith Jamison and her soul-stirring dance called *Cry*—a tribute to the black woman. Miss Jamison employed a huge cloth as the symbolic agency in order to reenact—through ceremonial stages—this migration of the soul, this epic story of the black woman in the Western experience. With a section of her cloth pressed into service—*durante vitae*—we see Jamison as the black scrub woman; then again, using her cloth as "carriage" for the nursing of everybody's babies; then as a shawl of adornment; now as a cotton sack; later as a wraparound, Northern Muslim woman's headgear, etc. Jamison's tribute is accompanied by Coltrane's music. Well, since I listened almost religiously to all kinds of Black music, while I was writing and incorporating every sound I could set my ear to into my fiction (including of course the spiritual incantation of "A Love Supreme" by 'Trane), I now attempted to incorporate Jamison's episodic cloth, as a springboard of relocation, into Sister Rachel Flowers' genesis saga of transformation and reinvention of life.

One of the literary constants of Afro-American literature is the Reinvention of life. Or, the cultural attribute of black Americans to take what is left over or, conversely, given to them (either something tossed from the white man's table . . . or, let us say, at the other end of the spectrum, the Constitution, or basketball) and make it work for them, as a source of personal or group survival, and then to place a stamp of elegance and élan upon the reinvented mode; to emboss, upon the basic form revised, a highly individualistic style, always spun of grace, and fabulous rhythms . . . a kind of magical realism. Of course the improvisational genius of jazz is the epitome of what I am getting at here. This is central to the art of Ellington, Armstrong, Lady Day, Sarah Vaughan, Ray Charles, Muddy Waters, Alberta Hunter; I could of course go on. Or in athletics Doctor J, Jackie Robinson, and Willie Mays, to name but a scant few.

I believe that in Afro-American literature, *reinvention* has been the basic hallmark of the transformation of those black novelists coming after Richard Wright: Ralph Ellison, Toni Morrison, and Leon Forrest. I am thinking here of these writers' capacity to celebrate life out of the wrenching aspects of the experience, because of their appreciation for the angularity of the cultural expression and the existentially rugged independence of their oppressed but not destroyed characters, and their abilities to see the story of migration or life in exile, on chain gangs or in prison, as having a continual significance and metaphorical importance.

Each of these writers sees the authorial voice of the migrating ancestral community as both that of high priest and high priestess—warning of demons and extolling virtues to be fostered from the past, thereby offering the writer a way into the angularity of the contemporary experience, and a way station for the relocation of the spirit.

But before Ellison, Morrison, and others, there was Jean Toomer;

and his pilgrimage to Georgia resulted in the creation of the finest novel to come out of the Harlem Renaissance—*Cane.* Relocation of the spirit and the myth of return and rupture are at the heart and soul of *Cane,* as a hypersensitive soul filters through cycles of baseness and refinement within Negro culture. "When one is on the soil of one's ancestors," Toomer's narrator observes, "most anything can come to one." And later Toomer's fear of the parting soul of slavery, the discontinuities, is expressed:

> for though the sun is setting on
> A song-lit race of slaves, it has not set;
> Though late, O soil, it is not too late yet
> To catch thy plaintive soul, leaving, soon
> gone.

Perhaps the prime source of this continuum, for the relocation of the spirit and contemporary possibility, is seen in the art of the folk preacher, and the constancy of the Negro Spiritual over time and place, as a deep river oracle of what we are and who we are as a people.

If the preacher stood as the linkage and the oracle from Mississippi to St. Louis to Chicago, let us say, how much does the substance of his sermon now renew the sons and the daughters of the great migration—now unto the fifth and sixth generations? These questions and issues bedeviled me in the old works, but in a particularly different, updated way from the manner in which they intrigued me and played at the center of my consciousness in the new novels. For if my father sought a "kind of cosmic consciousness" from the Rosicrucian philosophy, his novelist son found a kind of cosmic totality within the monologue of the Negro preacher, which might, in turn, lead to a cosmic consciousness of the race. Take for example the sermon by Pompey c.j. Browne "Oh Jeremiah of the Dreamers," which comes at the end of a new section, entitled *Transformation,* in the reprint of *There Is a Tree More Ancient than Eden.*

The setting for the sermon is the Crossroads Rooster Tavern (a famous after-hours blues bar on the South Side of Forest County), where a group of embittered city dwellers are gathered to assess the meaning of Martin Luther King's life on the twelfth anniversary of his assassination. But the evening breaks up into a wild talkfest, filled with curses and moments of celebration, hyperbole, wild political jokes, laconic spiel, tall tales, horror stories—moments when the slain King is both eulogized and in the next breath scandalized. Finally, at five thirty in the morning (and before the cock crows), the man who called the gathering, who earlier gave the invocation, now rises to give what he terms "the principal sermon-address obsequies and the benediction." This wild sermon is rendered up by the six-foot, seven-inch Negro minister, Pompey c.j. Browne, whose art seems influenced by that of Adam Clayton Powell, Martin Luther King, Leon Sullivan, and Richard Pryor, for starters. Other readers will, I hope, recall Reverend Browne's sermons in *Two Wings to Veil My Face* and, earlier, a brief vignette about the odyssey-singing preacher in *There Is a Tree More Ancient Than Eden.*

This last section of *Transformation* takes place in a tavern—where the blues is normally heard throughout the week. The blues is yet another form open to the black writer, or any writer—as a way into the fiber, texture, and soul of Afro-American consciousness. And as a native son of the blues, second major home—Chicago—I am deeply interested in the many wonders and haunts of the blues; specifically, the Reinvention of life, renewal of language, and transformation of character. How better to trace the genesis of black consciousness—and the migration of the spirit—from the lip of the Delta to the packing-houses, than through the rowdy eloquent long tongue of the blues.

The eternal search for the Blues Singer is quite similar to that of the working novelist: to try to find true words to capture the ever-changing conditions of life upon the highly vulnerable heart. A life which is essentially tied to rupture, chaos, celebration, agony, humor, and always trouble. The migrating scenes often lived out by the wandering blues men and women can be heard of course in their music. Oftentimes these were men who supported themselves in a variety of odd jobs, as they looked for work continually, on the farms or plantations of the South.

For the blues singer, personal, existential experience always out-weighs handed-down wisdom. He is always after true feeling, which must be expressed rawly and sincerely; at its base the blues is always about how to deal with trouble. Blues people seem to accept the idea of trouble as the condition for initiation in the gospel of the good news of the blues. This angle of vision is perhaps comic at base, and is probably why there is so much wicked humor in the blues. We might say, then, that Trouble is always at your back door and, if you would but look, at your front door as well. Out of this you can recreate your life, by constantly crafting out new side doors in the menacing mansions and old houses of life. The lyrics of the blues are often highly evocative and filled with oracle-like secular street wisdom, culled from the essence of existence, at the very cutting edge of life (surely Big Bill Broonzy's image of the many uses of the knife comes back to haunt us here). Indeed the worst thing that can happen to you, if you are a blues believer, is the loss of the blues. It is an eternal education. You lose the blues at the risk of losing your hold on existence. You lose your tragic sense of life, in other words. Ellison's classic definition is most useful here:

> The blues is an impulse to keep the painful details and episodes of a brutal experience alive in one's aching consciousness, to finger its jagged grain, and to transcend it, not by the consolation of philosophy but by squeezing from it a near-tragic, near-comic lyricism. As a form, the blues is an autobiographical chronicle of personal catastro-phe expressed lyrically.

The very first scene that I wrote for the novel *The Bloodworth Orphans* evolved a blues man—Carl Rae. I was quite swept up with the lines from Lightnin' Hopkins's blues song "I've Had My Fun." I found particularly haunting the lines "On the next train sound / You can look for my clothes home . . . But if you don't see my body, Mama, all you can do is mourn." These lines unleashed within me the saga of an aimless drifter who gains a species of honor on his deathbed, wailing his monologue as odyssey home: this becomes his attempt at transformation of the self, as it were, even as it is rendered up from a garbage heap.

But this outlaw spirit, this anti-hero, as hero, marks so much of American literature, as well as Afro-American literature. The migration of the spirit is no segregationist at heart, of course—rather each group enriches the whole, if we would but listen and read each man's and woman's history and literature, as yet another route to our way home.

It was the mid-1960s. I was down and out. Jobless. And I was trying to make one last-ditch effort at becoming a writer. But I couldn't seem to turn the corner without running into a slew of dead-end corridors. Spiritually, I was like a man lost in an elaborate cave, trying to inscribe the name of God on the walls of eternity, but confusing way stations with the Stations of the Cross; lost in a labyrinth and running out of time and confusing nostrums with nostalgia. Trying to write scripture on the walls of eternity. But I couldn't find the right words. I was speechless and tongueless before the altar of the great writers of the past. My patron saints . . . and those gods I loathed—*Lawd*, left me lost for words. I'd go mad at my typewriter, like the dervishes dancing before the Lord.

Depressed and defeated like a man on New Year's Eve without a girl friend; no place to party and a thimble of Heavenly Hill. My condition, in my own mind, was worse than Wright's *Man Who Lived Underground*, for I was down to a crawl space in the marginality of time. I was also going through the last throes of daydreaming my artistic heroism, as outlaw—therefore many of my heroes and heroines had lived fast, mercurial, brilliant, but brief flings in the noonday sun, artistically.

The death of my mother—an anchor and a rock, a source of worship and agony—had left me riddled and confused earlier that year. Now I was jobless again. Living in a one-room "flat" for forty dollars a month, in a building on South Dorchester called the Avon (believe it or not). Trying to pick up my troubles and ruins at the high altar—too high for my bleary talents? Was there anything in me worth the attempt to make something new—to improvise upon?

Each evening after another failed job attempt, I'd come home, fix another can of beans or sardines, pray that I could find a way out of no way at my typewriter, and try again. And, I'd listen to Mahalia Jackson on a small record player. I had friends. Intellectual friends and a few who were also trying to write. But none cared for the life of the spirit—or the spiritual questions. And so there was a great part of my mind that could not speak of my soul agony. I found it the most difficult aspect to write of these things of the spirit. Spiritual agony was an unspeakable condition amongst the politically "saved"—far worse than failed and even gutted affairs of the heart, in this most inhospitable season for the hypersensitive soul; though politically, most of my friends were out to *save the world, baby,* in a moment of some patched-up ideological miracle. My soul was a crownless, wingless wonder. I was disconnected at the skullbone—and my backbone was in dire question. Even in my own eyes I was dispossessed of my rusty ole halo . . . I was a secondhand soul—full of almighty patches.

But in the heartless days of winter, in that odd old building, Mahalia's soul visited me on several occasions. She didn't try to convert me; even Mahalia, in all of her burnished brown glory, knew better than this. Her scripture of song was enough; she seemed to reach me in a profound way as I raced around my labyrinth of dislocation, through her song "How I Got Over." She spoke to my running notes to God, in my profound lostness for words—addicted as I was to literature as my religion and as my soul's skullbone connection to a Divine Maker. My inflated afflatus. Mahalia seemed to move over mountains and reintroduce me to the motherlode and the mother tongue of the folk culture, transformed into a memorial art. She spoke not so much to affirm my talent, in its nakedness, body and soul; yet Mahalia's music seemed to evolve me out of my condition. *Mea culpa?* She would not stand for it. She seemed to underscore—in her proud peasant's soul in her powerfully forged art—what I had admired in the great literature that was my heritage (the Bible, Dostoevsky, the Greeks, Shakespeare)—that all great literature at its backbone was and is and ever shall be, world without end, amen, about man's spiritual agony and ascendancy. A spiritual agony that I seemed steeped in, like a child baptized in the chilly waters of the Jordan. But I couldn't find a way out of no way, that was my labyrinth and my burden—and then she left me, all alone to wonder. Saying I just couldn't will what I wanted to be by faith alone. I was shocked.

The next night Mahalia seemed to return to me in a visitation out of a whirlwind—did she know my soul was caught up in the eye of the storm—deboozed out of my bourbon—in the crawl space beneath the altar of my typewriter? I tried to hide my spirits. (I did not want her to know that I was a hundred-proof liar.) But now as her haunting voice spun out "Didn't It Rain?" Mahalia was saying that I was lucky to have a spiritual embattlement to write about . . . to sing about. But how did she know that I wanted to be a singer of the language—in the tradition of her majestic self and the Negro Preacher. Had she read a draft of one of my ranting revisions—in a language not even a mother could love.

Her way into all of this, leading me by the hand, made me understand what was missing in the work of my contemporary fellow writers—no spiritual agony at the core. I didn't have an art to crow about. No finished book, no finished manuscript. But I had something of that anguish at the core, and the outcrying heart of an artist; but I had to find my tongue, and my speech, my voice.

And that was the exact moment when Mahalia told me that the world would hate me if He changed my name. And did I have the backbone for the journey up the mountain? Because I didn't appear to be wrapped too tight much of the time. But then she smiled upon my condition, making me think of Dilsey's commentary on God's possible role for the least of these, when she says of the insignificant-looking visiting Black preacher for the Easter Service, "I've knowed de Lawd to use cuiser tools dan dat."

No, Mahalia didn't visit me in the "Upper Room" but her art made her presence reveal what the old minister who used to travel up and down the "el" train coaches meant when he cried, "Everybody wants to go to Heaven, but don't nobody want to die." For now I saw what I had not wanted to see—that if I wanted to climb that mountain, I'd have to "die" in terms of the materials the world worshipped most. In a secular sense I was paying my dues, as Yardbird had warned all striving artists.

"O for a Muse of fire, that would ascent / The brightest heaven of invention," but Mahalia's presence gave me warmth and radiance in the loneliness of my little room, gave me a hint of the Promethean fire and the Word, woke me up to a task and an employment—not made of hands, but surely written with them—and a burden. She showed me one meaning of a mountain I'm still trying to climb. Told me I would have to stand all alone by myself; for in the end the artist is constantly transforming himself again and again out of the chaos of his soul; he must be reborn again and again if the moment of a miracle is to have any meaning for us, the living (O Lord).

My only problem was—to find a brand new way of singing.

SOULS IN MOTION

Baptisms at the West Point Baptist Church, at 36th and Cottage Grove in Chicago, are conducted in a pool plainly in view of the congregation, in a small, glass-enclosed room high above the heads of the choir. The candidates—wearing a white cap and white linen blouse or shirt and white slacks, recalling a swimmer's outfit of the late nineteenth century—are ushered up a short flight of steps to the left of the altar, one by one. As the choir and the congregation sing out in a call and response, the Reverend Carroll J. Thompson conducts that ritual of baptism, calling forth—so that the microphone pitched just above the pool picks up his words of affirmation—"I do baptize you, my brother [or sister], upon the profession of your faith . . ."

The call and response continues as the candidate's body is deftly lowered into the tank of water:

Choir call: "Have you got good religion?"
Congregation: "Certainly, Lord. Certainly, Lord."
Choir call: "Have you got *good* religion?"
Congregation: "Certainly, Lord. *Certainly*, Lord."

This is a dramatic moment of witness bearing and conversion, and the congregation's role in the ritual is participatory, like that of the chorus in Greek drama. Each time the body of a baptismal candidate is carefully lowered and swiftly raised by Reverend Thompson, a throb of rapture and confirmation is heard charging through the more than 300 members present at this service. It is an ecstatic moment for

31

many as they recall their own spiritual awakening—"I was blind, but now I see." Embossing the panel behind the tank of water is a landscape of the Holy Land, a view to paradise on this Sunday morning as the October light streams through the stained-glass windows of the church.

When the last of the four candidates is brought forth, a woman in the pew in front of me cries out, "My boy, that's my son!" He is a heavyset fellow, a rich, dark mahogany brown; he wears a jeri-curl. As Reverend Thompson holds the young man's slowly descending body in his arms, the candidate cooperatively tilts his full-back's frame; their movements are ever harmonious, recalling for me the Alvin Ailey dancers' performance of *Wade in the Water.*

Out of the corner of my eye, I observe the mother's face all aglow as her son goes under, ever so nimbly. Her hands reach out and tremble as he begins to emerge, and there is a sudden shout from the congregation as he is brought forth, drenched from head to toe. I hear the old Negro spiritual echoing through my soul: "Jordan river chilly and col', chills the body, not the soul."

The question at every turn in the service is how to keep the fire and the zeal up-tempo, how to let neither the body nor the soul cool off. The service is always bound up in a keening relationship between great solemnity and the furious rhythms of body and soul. There is a place here for the commingling of the sexual and the spiritual.

As the choir sings "Your Labor Is Not in Vain," all of the newly baptized souls have returned to their seats, except for the son of the woman in front of me. The choir and the congregation trumpet forth again and again:

Choir: "Your labor . . ."
Lead singer: "Hang on in there . . ."
Choir: "Your labor . . ."
Lead singer: "Hang on in there . . ."
Choir: "Your labor . . ."
All: "Your labor is not in vain."

Each round pitches us higher, so that when we reach the fiery climax of the last winging round, Reverend Thompson can exclaim, just before delivering his sermon: "Our choir sounds like it came to church, for church today."

The newly baptized son of the woman in front of me returns dressed in fashionable street clothes and touches his mother's hand. I see fresh pride in her burnished, autumn-brown face, the baptismal light still incandescent in her eyes.

At Mount Pisgah, at 46th Street and King Drive, the choir enters, singing along with the congregation "We Came This Far by Faith." Each member of the congregation clasps hands with the person on his left, and the service begins with the singing of The Lord's Prayer.

The choir looks like a delegation from the United Nations, culled from the bloodlines of Africa, Europe, and Native America. As the choir sings of a "new way of walking and a new way of talking," they rejoice that if you have the Lord, "it's wonderful, really wonderful." And you realize that this group, this remnant of the race, in this place on Sunday morning feel that they are a new kind of people "who came this far by faith." In this former Jewish synagogue, choir and congregation feel that *they* are the newly chosen people.

Lead singer: "I've got a new walk . . ."

Choir: "Over in glory."

Lead singer: "I've got a new talk . . ."

Choir: "Over in glory."

At Mount Pisgah the choir is directed by a young woman whose lightning-rod motions seem to be those of a winging eagle caught up in a sudden storm: calm, trembling, then vaulting into space. "I'm going to wear this world—I don't believe you know what I'm talking about—I'm going to wear this world like a loose garment," she sings, raising her arms and the balloon-like sleeves of her robe in a sweeping arc. Her very body seems disconnected from her backbone, superruled by her skullbone . . . "oh, hear the world of the Lord." In her declaiming, redeeming, recalling command over the choir, she appears to have more moves in her repertoire than Dr. "J." on one of his better nights in the NBA. The song is "Move Mountain."

Now the first lead singer and a second lead are having a battle of "antagonistic cooperation" as they wing it out over a mountain. They call and respond and then each outdoes the other in escalating rhythms with the church organs racing them on and the younger members of the church following in an avalanche of sound:

> Let me tell you how to move a mountain
> that's too hard for you to climb.
> Let me tell you how to move a mountain
> one that hides the bright sunshine.
> When your hands are bleeding and torn,
> and your feet are weary and worn;
> when you try to climb up,
> but the rocks and reels makes the
> going tough,
> just say move mountain, move mountain,
> mountain get out of my way.

> Let me tell you how to move a mountain
> when the climbing gets you down.
> Let me tell you how to move a mountain
> when you've traveled your last round.
> When your friends have left you behind,
> and your way you cannot find;
> when your prayer is for help,
> but you stand alone feeling by yourself
> just say move mountain, move mountain,
> mountain get out of my way.[1]

Not all of the members are caught up in the frenzy, but many of the young people appear to be going through a religious moment, a

---

[1]From *Move Mountain.* Copyright © 1983 by Margaret Pleasant Douroux. Reprinted with permission.

seizure that is fitfully sexual and spiritually elevating, that lifts them to some imagined mountain. At this point we can see the importance of the church's nursing cadre.

These soul-soothing sisters move in to aid the spiritually seized members, whose bodies leap forth in convulsive spasms. Dressed in hospital white, the nurses attempt to revive, but not cool off, these swirling, mountain-moving souls. One young man proclaims, "In the Lord's good time"—and I recall that the precursors of the prophets were often wild, spinning dervishes caught up in the perceived moment of a miracle, in the revelation of radical faith.

This sets the stage for the Reverend Joseph Wells, who has just announced his text. He has a rich voice full of Negro grain and timbre—a rugged grain, fermented, it would appear, in the South. His voice is husky, vibrant, and gruff one moment and mellow the next, like the combined voices of Jimmy Rushing, Louis Armstrong, Ray Charles, and James Brown—all blues-brooding, full-bodied voice.

But Reverend Wells can't get started yet, because the nurses are still fanning several of the felled faithful, who have apparently moved that mountain out of their way but are drained by the action . . . *but coming through* . . . and trying to rise. After the first lead singer comes back for yet another chorus of the song, Reverend Wells is at the microphone and ready to preach. He says, "If it weren't for the grace of God, I don't know where I'd be." This works in beautifully, because it identifies him with what the fury-charged souls of the congregation are feeling—heelbone to backbone to skullbone.

Throughout his sermon Reverend Wells relates everything that has happened on this Sunday to the larger interests of his text, which is based on God's protection of the Israelites in Egypt in the Old Testament: "Going down the Dan Ryan—thinking about a mountain in my life and suddenly God moved it. I got happy in the car . . . Did the Lord bring you from somewhere, church? God brought me from the cottonfields of Mississippi, from behind the plow. What the Lord did for Israel—moved that mountain and protected them. The Lord brought us through . . . Some of you worrying about Reagan. Lord brought us through Hoover.

". . . But Israel had forgotten that God had worked in their interests. Israel had forgotten that God had divided the Red Sea."

The structure of a black Baptist sermon is orchestrated, with highly associative links to group memory, the Bible, Afro-American folklore, Negro spirituals, secular blues phrases, politics, and personal testimonial. A sermon is open-ended, allowing a preacher to expand new ideas or to cut out sections if they aren't working. The role of the congregation during a sermon is similar to that of a good audience at a jazz set—driving, responding, adding to the ever-rising level of emotion and intelligence. Ultimately, the preacher and the congregation reach one purifying moment, and a furious catharsis is fulfilled.

Several years ago at a Christmas party, I met the Reverend Morris Harrison Tynes. We had a brief but memorable exchange, and I was delighted and instructed by his many-sided intelligence. Reverend Tynes is a man who believes that all things happen for a deeper purpose, so I am certain that he felt our first conversation was fortuitous when I turned up late last fall at the Greater Mount Moriah Baptist Church, at 214 East 50th Street, where he is the pastor, and again the following week at his home for an interview.

Reverend Tynes is gifted with an exceptional flair for language, story-telling, and ideas, and he has an excellent singing voice; he is a powerful orator in the pulpit. He holds several degrees, including a Ph.D. in philosophy and ethics, and he is one of the most articulate men of the cloth in Chicago. As he speaks, one hears a preacher's voice ascending in layers of rhetorical eloquence.

FORREST: How is the divine moment of spiritual and emotional ecstasy that a preacher feels as he builds toward the climax of a sermon different from what an artist or composer feels during profound moments of creativity?

TYNES: I think that each man's historical perspective determines his response to this divine encounter. There is something in his life that exalts him to great inspiration. Take Handel writing the *Messiah* in less than 30 days. He must have ascended to heaven! There is no way possible that a human being could have written that alone.

FORREST: Is it the moment of a miracle?

TYNES: I think the same thing happens in preaching at its zenith; and, yes, I do think it is the moment of a miracle. I think that any time man can discover God, or God discloses to man, that's a miracle.

FORREST: What about the man in the street who doesn't go to church but who has developed a certain grit and fiber to deal with life, or so he thinks? Doesn't he feel he needs the support of the church?

TYNES: These street people have often told me that they'll be in church next Sunday, and I'll say, "You've been telling me that for two years." Then I'll pose this question: "Are you happy with your life the way it is? Because every time I see you, your eyes are full of whiskey and dissipation. Do you think that this is the highest fulfillment of your life?" Time and again the man or woman will say, "No, Doc, I'll tell you the way it is—I'm not happy with my life. To be frank with you, Doc, I'm not satisfied with myself."

FORREST: Those street people probably speak for a lot of lost souls at some very effete levels.

TYNES: You know St. Augustine said, "My soul shall not find fulfillment until it rests in Thee." He was alluding to this spiritual hunger.

FORREST: How do you deal with the mystery of iniquity and the absurdity of human misfortune? I'm thinking here of the high-school basketball player Ben Wilson, who was murdered by three young black men.

TYNES: Man's freedom is his glory and his shame, because God gave man the freedom to become like the God in whose image he was created or to sink to the level of the worst beast, the worst criminal on earth. In other words, man can be either a marvelous musician or a monster. Where does suffering come in? Where does pain come in? Job raises this question, Why do the righteous suffer, instead of the wicked? My simple answer is that since we are made in God's image, He wants us all to be like Him. If I share in the benefits of an illumination that I had nothing to do with creating, then I must also share in the consequences of an evil that I had no part in creating. When an airplane goes down, the nun and the gangster die together. That is the collectivity of man's basic freedom. That is the price we pay for freedom.

FORREST: But what would you say to Ben Wilson's mother if she were sitting across from you at this moment?

TYNES: I would say that your son—very precious in your sight and in God's sight—was caught up in the ambiguity of personal option. He did not have to be walking on that street, at that time of the day. He could have been in another place. But he chose to walk down that street. So I would say to her what the prophet Gibran; I think it was, said, "Your children are not your children. They come through you but not from you." That son of yours, though he was to be a great basketball star, perhaps shines more brightly now through the tragedy and the ambiguity of his untimely demise than he would have if he had been a basketball star *only*. Because his murder has highlighted another aspect of the human condition—black-on-black crime, which could not have been highlighted as effectively, nor more dramatically, than by seeing his beautiful, handsome face and body sacrificed on this altar of senseless, brutal killings in the black community. And since he was so great and so good, God said, I'm going to let you do this. But in the other life, in heaven, you will shine more brightly than you ever would have on the basketball court. There, you would have shined for only eight or ten years, but in eternity, in heaven, you'll shine with ever-increasing illumination.

FORREST: What would you say to the kids at Simeon High School if you were lecturing them about the punks who killed their star?

TYNES: There are two ways to look at those punks. Look at them as misguided children of God, who need sympathy, love, and forgiveness—just as Martin Luther King forgave that black woman who stabbed him. He said, Don't treat her harshly; Christ will forgive her. That is the ultimate Christian response. The other response is the human reflex: "Let's string them up. Let's have a public execution." But I believe the finality of death would be to them a blessing. They would be released from the agonizing shame and frustration that they will have to go through for the rest of their lives. As they get older they will see the dimension of what they've done, more than they do now in their little 19- and 20-year-old minds. And if they are in prison they are going to have a long time to think about their deeds. And the awesome dimension of that may turn them into saints.

So it could have been a two-edged sword of goodness. God using this boy, Ben Wilson, to highlight the many sons who have been lost and murdered, and then God using those other boys—ignominious as their crime was—to say what can become of two hideous individuals 20 years hence. Because Christ always looked at an individual as if he were what he ought to be so that he might become what he should be.

FORREST: But, Reverend Tynes, what can the church do about these gangs?

TYNES: Most of these gang people are peripheral to the church, at best. They know that the lives they are living are sordid and criminal, and they don't want any part of the church. I believe that the gang phenomenon is the manipulation of these teen-agers by older men, 27 to 35 years in age, who send these teen-agers out to sell dope. Then they bring the bounty back and give it to these bosses. So I believe that these boys, like the ones who killed young Wilson, are manipulated. You look in these kids' eyes and they look frightened. That's the way the bosses enforce; that's the way they control. They control them through fear. They have enforcers who beat the teen gang members with baseball bats.

The question of spiritual alienation from the Christian community surges through at central moments in *Native Son*, Richard Wright's Chicago-based novel. Published in 1940, it seems so prophetic now. Wright's Bigger Thomas is a gang member, a manchild deteriorating in the wasteland of the city slums. For Bigger Thomas, violence became the one symbolic action in which he could feel a sense of creative elevation, could attain a profane spiritual high. Bigger's brief life of murder suggests the sort of wayward behavior that is open to a closed-off contemporary youth who is black, fatherless, undereducated most of his life, and churchless.

After Bigger's arrest for the murder of a white girl, he is visited in prison by a black minister. This scene isolates the growing cleavage—even then—between the unemployed slum dweller and the Negro church. The minister's words about moral redemption and the kingdom of God are hollow sounds that have lost all of their resonance for Wright's emptied-out Underman.

The Chicago-born playwright Lorraine Hansberry believed herself to be almost as far to the left ideologically as Richard Wright. She grew up in a complex black middle-class family but chose a Chicago working-class family emboldened by visions of the American Dream as the subject for *A Raisin in the Sun.* Hansberry's play introduced at least four black characters previously invisible upon the mainstream American stage: an intellectual African, meaning an African without a bone in his nose; a young female college student engaged in spinning out her identity; a chauffeur, who suggested the frustrated ambitions of an energetic black man—a long way from Wright's Bigger—who wants out of the slum mentality but whose options are limited to buying a liquor store in those slums. But none of the characters is more memorable than Lena Younger, the matriarch, whose spiritual core dominates the stage like Mahalia Jackson singing "How I Got Over."

At one point in the play, Lena Younger slaps her daughter, Beneatha, for saying, "There simply is no blasted God—there is only man who makes miracles!" Then she demands: "Now—you say after me, in my mother's house there is still God. . . . In my mother's house there is still God." Indeed, it is Lena Younger—created by an agnostic—who asks the central question of the play and perhaps the primary question that could be asked about the materialistic ambitions of some of today's young blacks, as well. In an exchange with her chauffeur son, Walter, Lena Younger finds an answer to that question:

> MAMA: Son—how come you talk so much 'bout money?
> WALTER: (*With immense passion*) Because it is life, Mama!

MAMA: (*Quietly*) Oh—(*very quietly*) So now it's life. Money is life. Once upon a time freedom used to be life—now it's money. I guess the world really do change. . . .

WALTER: No—it was always money, Mama. We just didn't know about it.

MAMA: No . . . Something has changed. (*She looks at him*) You something new, boy. In my time we was worried about not being lynched and getting to the North if we could and how to stay alive and still have a pinch of dignity too . . . Now here come you and Beneatha—talking 'bout things we ain't never even thought about hardly, me and your daddy. You ain't satisfied or proud of nothing we done. I mean that you had a home; that we kept you out of trouble till you was grown; that you don't have to ride to work on the back of nobody's streetcar—You my children—but how different we done become.

There are several major black Baptist churches between 35th Street and 51st and King Drive, and each Sunday inner and outer traffic lanes in the area provide extra parking for a multitude of worshipers. And, oh, those ladies' hats. They are something of a fashion show on parade. Some are too outrageous to be audacious; others are too bodacious to be missed on Sunset and Vine. Take the gushing rainbow of a bonnet before me, climbing to God's kingdom in a babbling tower of colors. Many designer hats—and some redesigned by virtue of Afro-American reinvention—send the observer's head spinning, as when one tries to let the eye follow the layers of a wraparound turban. Rarely simple, these hats can often be as dazzling as the crack of daybreak on Lake Shore Drive.

If you want a prediction for the coming fashion season, you might drop in at the Liberty Baptist Church, at 49th Street and King Drive. The hats the ladies wear there are something to behold. The church is also deeply involved in a range of self-help and service programs, and on the Sunday of my visit, Liberty is getting an award for its donation to the relief effort in Ethiopia. Spencer Leak, one of the leading morticians on the South Side and a church activist, leads a group of members to the altar for this homage.

The black middle class, recalling the heightened consciousness of upwardly mobile Poles, Jews, and Irish, is reaching a growing awareness of those brethren left behind—of the underclasses in this country and in the motherland as well. Later, in his sermon, Chester Baker, a young visiting minister, will address this attempt at spiritual linkage with, and obligation toward, Africa. He tells the congregation, numbering more than 750: "These people who are oppressed in Africa *are our people.* And those who don't see this unity lack ancestral integrity. They are our people. For if you think of yourself as white, then you are going to treat our people like the racists treated us."

Yet how much the congregation knows of Africa is worthy of contemplation. More than likely, the thinking would go something like this: There are oppressed, poverty-stricken people over there; they are black and we are black; they have been oppressed and so have we. Wherever the black man is in the world, he is catching hell. We came from Africa; therefore, we must help them. And it is in this sense that the black man here identifies with the heartaches over there.

Many Chicago Poles have relatives in Warsaw, and many who live here speak Polish; there is a Polish-American newspaper in Chicago. Mayor Daley was only two generations removed from Ireland; and the Jews have myriad ties to Israel—language, direct Biblical linkage, and physical presence there. Black Americans can share little of this kind of linkage with their motherland.

But before Reverend Baker turns to this issue, he takes a good look at the congregation and apparently decides that he has a lot to say about what he sees now and about what he has seen on the streets. He denounces unisex fashions as a craze, claiming, "We are trapped in a gender twilight zone, somewhere between male and female." Given the growing role of gays in choirs at many black churches, one wonders whether someone should warn this young preacher to exercise some restraint. But Reverend Baker is witty, and the idea of castigating the congregation for giving in to wayward influences has an ancient heritage.

"You can stand on the el platform and see women wearing hats like Indiana Jones," he shouts. "You see men wearing pants so tight you can almost see the label of their underwear." (This unleashes much lighthearted laughter from the membership.)

"Christmas is not the time for us to parade under some illusion that we are a part of the cast of *Dynasty*." (How well this sits with the beauties here who are bathed in finery *à la* Joan Collins or Diahann Carroll can only be left to speculation.) The minister warns the flock: "If Jesus had wanted us to celebrate his birth, he would have told us so. We need an internal confirmation that we don't get from outside the church. We need to be asking ourselves what can we do to be saved."

The choir of 100 voices at Liberty is one of the more impressive on the South Side. The members follow closely the Biblical edict "Make a joyful noise unto the Lord." Their first song for the service—"Jesus Is the Light of the World"—was at one time the signature song of the famous First Church of Deliverance, at 4301 South Wabash Avenue. One of the most profoundly influential institutions on black church tradition in Chicago, it was not Baptist, but rather nondenominational.

In the old days, if you were out driving on the South Side on a Sunday night, you might set your radio dial for the 11 P.M. services emanating from the First Church of Deliverance to hear its monumental choir commence the evening to God with a heaven-ascending version of The Lord's Prayer and then lead into a driving, stomping rendition of "Jesus Is the Light of the World." The choir toured the world, and it was celebrated for the range of its magnificent voices.

Equally well known for his way of weaving the Word in and out of the flesh, in and out of this world, was the Reverend Clarence H. Cobbs, the church's preacher from the late 1920s until his death in the late 1970s. His style in the pulpit was in sharp contrast with that of the huge, high-spirited choir. Yet they complemented each other to form a path-breaking service. Reverend Cobb's delivery was low-key, urbane, naughty, and layered with pithy insights. Intimate as a ballad sung by

Nat King Cole, his conversational sermons were constantly punctuated, accented, and underscored by the church organist. The large, romping rumble of the organ actually took on the role of the chorus. Cobb's singing voice was a sweet and sassy high tenor, sometimes swooping to an alto register akin to that of the Ink Spots' lead singer, Bill Kenney. His normal speaking voice recalled Cole's or Sam Cooke's or perhaps, in our time, Marvin Gaye's.

Reverend Cobbs spun his sermons out of vignettes from life and from the Bible, out of epiphanies from spiritual witness, out of coined aphorisms and stories of people who called on him for advice (often prisoners wrote to him). Cobbs was in the tradition of the stand-up monologist who spoke off the cuff and from the heart during the frontier makings of this country. His delivery was that of an intimate friend you might call in the still of the night when your woman left you, when your younger brother got stabbed in a South Side bar, or when you couldn't make groceries. He would save a bit of hyperbole for a key moment, and like the great entertainers of the American stage, he knew that timing was everything.

Like the best of James Baldwin's rambling essays, Reverend Cobb's sermons seemed to be running notes to man and God; they had the structure of a crazy quilt, and yet they worked beautifully. Indeed, his sermons were rendered up in a street-corner rapping voice; listening to them was like opening up a telephone booth on, say, 39th Street and King Drive and falling in on an envoy from God whose feet hurt and who was telling his best friend's story to the Maker. There was no slaughterhouse oratory in his sessions. He was something of a brother-confidant, as opposed to the preacher as father over his flock.

Not only did Cobb's style of preaching and the expanded role that he allowed the choir influence other churches but he also was one of the first church leaders in the Negro community to use a regular radio broadcast as a major religious voice. Cobbs knew that many people wouldn't be caught dead in church but that they still found moments of ecstasy in spirituals and gospel music. When you listened in on the radio, you didn't have to pay to pray. These broadcasts greatly enlarged

Cobb's audience, and his influence.

One night at a bar, just before leaving to catch Cobbs on his car radio, a man told me, "Reverend Cobbs may believe that Jesus is the light of the world, but 'Preacher' don't try to blind you with that light."

The service at Christian Tabernacle, a Baptist church at 4712 South Prairie Avenue, reflects the influence of First Church; and the Reverend Maceo Woods is very much in the tradition of Cobbs. Like Cobbs, Woods is clever, stylish, and soft-spoken. He is a dapper dresser and youthful in appearance, although he has been pastor of this church for 25 years. Woods also hosts a popular radio show: *The Good News*, on Sundays at 5 P.M. on WCFL.

The role of the choir at Christian Tabernacle is even more expansive than that at Cobb's church in the old days. They back Woods and two organists, a drummer, and a tambourine player. In this church, the music seems to set the stage for the performance in the pulpit, and Reverend Woods cunningly blends into the fabric of the moment. This freedom from domination by the personality of the minister makes Christian Tabernacle, a former theatre, a popular place to worship. It draws young people with a feel for music, as well as those who need to act out, or jam with joy, for Jesus.

The choir here is professional and solemn in the beginning, and then all holy hell breaks loose. On this Sunday, tenor Melvin Smothers leads in a voice of power and fire heading toward furor. The song is "He Walks with Me," and when Smothers disengages himself from the body of the choir—"Got a new walk . . . got a new talk"—and begins to speak in a witness-bearing, singsong voice, I'm reminded that theatre emerged from religion.

It is the force of the music—the obsessive and repetitive rhythm—tied to lyrics suggesting a reordering out of chaos that leads one from a state of self-possession to a momentary state of blessed assurance, when you "take hold of your life through Jesus Christ." The singer—as caught-up spiritual performer—is in control and then loosens control over his spirit. When he appears to be on the verge of losing control, he is actually opening himself up to be taken over by the Holy Spirit. And that is why

Melvin Smothers and the others can "get happy."

Just now two young men become so enraptured that they can't break the spell. Nurses move quickly to the rescue, but the lads are starting into a holy jumping, stomping dance to Jesus, and they are babbling in tongues. During these seizures, the anklebone and the hipbone, the hipbone and the backbone seem almost disconnected, so violent is the shock of the rhythm. One can only wonder about the polyrhythms of the blood flow to the chambers of the heart during these fitful flurries. And one can't help but reflect on how these holy dances have influenced popular dance patterns. For under the cover of the church and in the name of God, you might act out dance steps that you would not show at home, nor even think to attempt. But here the creative juices are up; you are encouraged to let the mind and spirit romp, roam, and reinvent. And if you are high in your ecstasy for Jesus, who knows what the body might tell the soul to reveal? So much of James Brown's act came out of the church, particularly those moments of ecstasy, seizure, death, and rebirth that he brings to his stage performances.

At every stage of the service at the Antioch Missionary Baptist Church, at 6248 South Stewart Avenue, the Reverend Wilbur N. Daniel is a mighty presence—and he is an awesome anchor for his people.

Every Sunday the church has a responsive Scripture reading; and because we are two weeks from Christmas, Reverend Daniel's selection is taken from Matthew 2:1–11, which covers the birth of Jesus in Bethlehem; the troubling of the evil King Herod over the star—implying his downfall—so luminous in the East, with the miraculous shock of the Savior in its fierce light; Herod's calling of the wise men to inquire when the star appeared; his command that they go search for the infant and report back to him, "so that I may come and worship him also." Reverend Daniel's dramatic rendering—coupled with his radio announcer's voice and his romance with language—turns this story into a kind of mini-sermon, as well as a call-and-response recitation for pastor and congregation.

A powerful singer, Reverend Daniel now leads the congregation and the choir in one rousing chorus of "O Come, All Ye Faithful," immediately followed by a sober performance of "The Lord's Prayer." Then Reverend Daniel breaks that mood, as if suddenly caught up in the scale-rippling spirit of the pianist. He announces:

"Jesus didn't come to bring sadness into the world. If you are gonna be sad, don't put out any Christmas tree, don't wrap any presents. There is nothing about Christmas that is designed for sadness." He proceeds to do a parody of "O come, All Ye Faithful":

"Oh come, all ye doubters, sad and defeated. Oh come ye to Mississippi. . . . Oh come and behold him from skid row. Oh come let us weep and mourn for Joe, the drunkard." Reverend Daniel warns his congregation, "The Lord was not born for you to be sad. You may not get all you want for Christmas, but you can have all the joy you want." He says that he's so happy with spiritual joy that he might even fly: "How would you folks in the balcony feel if on this Sunday I would fly into the balcony? Would that frighten you? . . . The kind of joy I'm talking about doesn't depend on what you have, because if you don't have joy with that rabbit coat, you won't have any with that mink."

In calling for the benevolent offering, however, Reverend Daniel is all seriousness. A young deacon, his head bowed, gives the prayer over the collection. Much of what he has to say is predictable; yet what gets the attention of the membership—the "Amens" and the "Yes, Lords"—are the stock phrases, some from the Bible, others with an oracular cast that speaks to the group ethos:

"We know You [Lord] love a cheerful giver. We stand in need of Thy divine blessing, Father. We want to thank You for waking us up this morning. For when we awakened we found that You had left watch angels to guard us while we slept. We thank You for touching us this morning with love, so that our eyes flew open and we beheld a sunlight and a day that's been coming since creation. . . ."

Then, sounding like a blues singer, the deacon cries forth: "We need You . . . can't get along without You. Hold our hands while we run this race." One of the elder deacon rises, and he and Reverend Daniel do a variation on a call and response in which a member, usually a

47

deacon, "lines the pastor out": The deacon provides the pastor with lines from the Bible that he either repeats or uses as the basis for improvisation. After he has absorbed the lining out and repeated it or exhausted his improvisation of the Word, the pastor will usually say, "Line me out some more"; and the deacon will provide him with more text.

After the collection has been blessed and prayed over, Reverend Daniel announces that the choir will sing "Move Mountain." The lead singer, Paula Williams, gives such a surging rendition of the song that I can't help but think she might well do battle with and win out over those two divas at Mount Pisgah. The choir here at Antioch is better than average, and this young woman—with an angel's wing touched to the harp of her throat bone—*can* move mountains. You can hear the influences of Mahalia Jackson, Rosetta Tharpe, and Clara Ward in Paula Williams's voice. But her interpretation of the song puts power behind the phrases, that celebrate the will of the individual—not only those that honor spiritual fiber but also the lines rooted in the secular ruggedness of grit and guts. Now I know what the old folks meant when they told me that to make it in life you needed "grit, shit, and mother wit." And I am now one with the congregation as we all unleash a thunderous shout when Paula Williams flies us to the mythical mountain.

> When your friends have left you behind,
>   and your way you cannot find;
> when your prayer is for help,
>   but you stand alone feeling by yourself
> just say move mountain, move mountain,
>   mountain get out of my way.

Later, in a calmer mood on this Sunday so close to the birth of the Redeemer, I feel a renewal of faith and intellect as I reflect upon Williams's anchoring interpretation for all of us who must stand alone before that mountain of ascendancy.

—To Peggie

Because we had the advantage of not being obsessed with the scholarly fact that we were disadvantaged (although we knew we were segregated), we developed certain advantageous schemes and strategies for survival and erected institutional support systems behind the walls of residential segregation. More than anything else we believed that the individual had to find something within himself, some talent, moxy, intelligence, magical nerve, swiftly developed skill, education, knack, trade, or underground craft and energize it with the hustler's drive. We could not move outside the so-called ghetto, but we could move up and around within the ghetto. Many of the life supports, or the specific individual role models were there all about us to see, to partially emulate, or to spurn within the neighborhood, from the working class, lower middle class, and the middle class. Indeed some of the most suave and sophisticated men I have ever known were waiters and doormen who one met in the barbershop. No sociological definition fits the royal ruggedness of these men. I can only think of them as the cultivated working-class aristocracy, especially when one heard them talk about politics, art, racism, religion in the barbershop; or watched them on the dance floor, or overheard them rapping to a lady at the bar. They set dress-horse-standards within the community; they embossed high style on everything they touched; they drank the best bourbon.

One key to self-transformation was this: take something from the hustler, but split away from other aspects of his world; take the attributes of guts and self-discipline from the many coaches of sports' teams, but spurn other qualities. Take on the imaginative soaring of the jazz musicians as one definition of the meaning of life, through the potential powers of the imagination; but avoid the drug scene that festered about their world.

Even the middle-class blacks were not that far removed from our immediate world; and they were highly visible. In contrasting today's middle class and the middle class of the 1940s and 50s, William Julius Wilson has stated in *The Truly Disadvantaged*: "Whereas today's black middle-class professionals no longer tend to live in ghetto neighborhoods and have moved increasingly into mainstream occupations outside the black community, the middle-class professionals (doctors, teachers, lawyers, social workers, ministers) lived in higher-income neighborhoods of the ghettos and serviced the black community."

Several of our grade school teachers at Wendell Phillips lived within the immediate neighborhood and not far from the hustlers and policy men, the waiters, barbers, janitors, and railroad men.

For me one of the main fallacies behind our current obsession with the idea of projecting so-called picture-perfect role models for our youth is this: it sets in motion a blissful prescription about human nature and diminishes the jagged-edged complexity of African-American character, when actually there are often many qualities about the most powerful role models, or even saintly church souls that one would want to spurn, if one is to deal in the real world and truly transform one's character.

The best-read man in our community was a fellow who ran on the Sante Fe Railroad with my father. He had a wonderful library and lived with his wife only two blocks from our apartment, on 37th and South Parkway (now King Drive) in Chicago. He was a fourth cook, which meant that he was dishwasher. Although he had waited tables in college, this most fundamentally responsible man refused to take any promotion—to waiter or dining car attendant—because those duties were beyond his immediate interests which were books and personal improvement through continual self-education. Not only were the ambitions and energies of this fourth cook, this dishwasher caught up with the life of the mind, he plainly did not want to be looked upon as a hustler; and man you really had to hustle to make those tips on the railroad. I remember standing in awe of the shelter of his book collection, and this dimension of his life style spun out in solitude.

It also happened that he was married to a woman who ran a dance school, so that he didn't have to worry about making a lot of money. Obviously a man who didn't work himself to death at the hang, yet had a reverence for books and learning, with a wife who had a good business sense, possessed strong appeals to an imaginative child, who had dreams even then of transforming himself into a writer. Yet while I was enchanted by this gentleman and received tips for learning and living from him, there was something of the hustler's drive and style that I also admired, that my fourth cook didn't possess. If I were ever going to make anything of myself—transform my dreams—I found myself energized by all kinds of hustlers, who were always bent on reinventing themselves, always attempting to remake their several worlds. Actually my father who was a bartender on the railroad thought of himself as a hustler. My childhood sweetheart's father was an underground hustler, an ambulance chaser by night (now that's a real hustle) for several white lawyers downtown. He was also a part owner of a bar.

Certainly my uncle, who was a body and fender man, was a hard-driving hustler. Going from several auto dealers' body shops over the years, when his skills were manipulated and he was directed to teach white men his craft, and soon enough management gave the whites, whom he had trained, the best jobs to work on. Uncle T. D. would then pick up his tool bag, split the scene, and find a new job; but always warning me to learn a trade or get a good education. Then Uncle T. D. would adjust this survival bulletin to a line from a song, "No, no they can't take that away from me."

My Uncle T. D. also took me out to the prize fights at the old Savoy Ballroom at 47th Street on Tuesday nights, where for years we would see male hustlers, young black fighters representing tough towns like the steel-driving communities of Gary or Akron come to the city to fight our Chicago boxing team. Some of these amateur boxers eventually fought their way up into the pro ranks, and a few went on to title shots. In my growing-up years—from eight to twelve—we went out to the Savoy regularly. Early on the idea of life being a fight for survival was riveted in my imagination from the battles I witnessed in the ring at the Savoy.

In terms of style and intelligence, this range of possibilities for self-transformation within the Negro community was capsulized in the following scene, which occurred in a barbershop years later, where there was still a chance to see and hear a wide spectrum of black men gathered in one place. One of the most distinguished and renowned black professors in America had been talking to an enterprising, oily-tongued fellow who had a cunning suaveness and a reflective angularity concerning his overview of the world, and the vicissitudes of the human condition. When finally this dressed-down-dude left the barbershop, opened the door to his baby-blue Cadillac, then drove off, my dear professor friend asked the barber, *Who was that man?* And the barber, who delighted in bringing together a collectivity of black men under his roof and beneath his scissors, said, sounding very much himself like an academic: "Professor, I just had the high honor and personal privilege of hearing for over half an hour in my establishment the world's greatest professor, in heavy conversation with the world's greatest hustler and pimp."

At least four attributes informed the awakening consciousness of black Chicago during the period of 1940 through 1960, from behind the walls of segregation. First that it was a hustlers' town, where there weren't the rigid restrictions on who you were and what you were; and which school you had attended and what were the specifics of your family lineage. It was a town where you could get busted, broken down, and defeated, but not necessarily destroyed—you could always get off the canvas and make a come-back. The word was if you couldn't make it in Chicago you couldn't make it anywhere. Patterns of intra-group color bar, caste designation, and high-class status weren't nearly as fixed and formidable in Chicago as they were in other cities.

The second attribute generally epitomized in the black Chicago ethos was the idea of Reinvention. This is the improvisational genius of jazz and it is in an attribute central to the art of blacks in the dance, dress styles, athletics, and in all forms of life's celebrations. It is not accidental that the great Southern art forms of the blues and Gospel music not only flourished in Chicago, but also these forms were reinvented, mainly in Chicago. Surely we began to see this reinvention in the mid-1950s when black basketball teams started to dominate the sport by reinventing the hoopsters' art here in Chicago.

The third dimension of this evolving consciousness behind the walls of segregation? We declined to think of our ethos as symmetrically consummated. We were a people in process, even in metamorphosis. We did need intellectual encounters with other cultures, in order to truly transform ourselves. Our ultimate growth as a people depended upon the achievement of an open society. We needed to carve out a desegregated Chicago (in housing, jobs, and education), where our larger ambitions and dreams of freedom could flourish. Here I am talking about desegregation, not integration.

In the quite contemporary mood of cultural and intellectual reseg-regation, which so grips the life supports of our African-American ethos, we've come to think of ourselves as not needing this intellectual encounter with other cultures. If an intellectual concept isn't rooted in some species of black nationalism, then forget it. It's as if we've come to think that by engaging a cultural value or a desegregated idea from other ethnic groups that we will drain off our cultural blackness; that an assimilationist blood-letting will occur, and we will be bled white. Ironically enough, the blacks in this city we most often admire, like the late Harold Washington, have been able to achieve this intellectual and cultural balance. Mayor Washington best revealed a desegregated mind-set and a layered consciousness; certainly a ranging library of books and ideas ordered his intellectual development, forged in the furnace of Chicago politics and radical protest political vision. His life was a study in the constant possibilities for the transformation of the self. So, I personally reject all forms of intellectual segregation.

And yet this will to separateness amongst blacks has a genesis and a history rooted in a deep sense of racial rejection, on the one hand, and a will to celebrate the strengths within the culture, on the other. It springs from direct experience; the city wasn't opening up fast enough to accommodate our dreams of fulfillment, in housing, jobs, education, and power sharing. All of which brings me to the fourth dimension of this evolving consciousness. For once we began to look at where we were as a people there were strangle holds in place, at every turn. We were uncovering concretely (what we knew or had known in a general, yet underground subconscious manner all along) that the axiom from the barbershop was correct: *In this man's town everything is politically fixed, except fishing*; and this unveiling was a metaphor for our entrapped larger condition, as a people. We were alive to the fact that there were two economies within our community. The jobs from the packinghouse to railroading were drying up or dying out. On another level, there was teaching or the post office and social work; and then there were the professions. Or, the varied world of the underground economy, the numbers racket, the ambulance chasers, the thriving and growing clusters of bars and taverns; but these jobs offered no healthy growth routes for the future. (Even my father's route to semi-security on the railroad represented a work-a-day world that was swiftly declining as a way for a young black man of my generation to make a livelihood in the latter portion of this century.)

Now more and more we were becoming aware of an advancing economy of destruction, the welfare world which fed off of an increasingly undernourished family life; pitched forth for our detainment, like the rising projects all about us, in the mid-1950s and 1960s, which brings us to an overview of the ways in which segregation and racism were condoned and exploited at the highest levels, politically and morally in this city, and how blacks came to a breaking point in their faith in freedom within the structures of this life.

We were carefully taught in school that there was a separation between Church and State, but we knew better. The political, economic linkage from Church to city hall down to the grassroots white ethnics (all a part of the white power institutions) was obvious and deeply embedded in Chicago throughout the life of this century. The leader of Chicago's Archdiocese for years, George Cardinal Mundelein, used the phrase "parochialism" as a way of not only celebrating his own vision of the power of inwardness; but also as a code word for condoning and encouraging residential segregation. The powerful Cardinal of the universal church in Chicago often said that Slovak, Italian, Irish, German, and yes Negro Catholics in this city should "stay in your backyard." His oral doctrine was issued to encourage the idea of national parishes *and* residential segregation.

I remember when I was twelve years old, about ten of my neighborhood buddies (from eleven to fourteen years of age) accompanied by my father and another adult struck out one Saturday for our usual baseball site at a playground near Wentworth. But this noontime the field was just too crowded; and so we strayed over into a park area very close to the old Comiskey Park. We had been out there about fifteen minutes, when suddenly a group of forty white ethnic males, between the ages of twenty and thirty-five, commenced to gather with broken bats, brick-bats, broomsticks, and broken bottles, and they were definitely looking our way in a venomous manner. Soon they had us surrounded and they were demanding that we get off of their field—as if they held deeds to city property. First they said we were messing up their grounds; they had a game there that night; next they were claiming that one of our guys had tried to molest one of their girls recently. Recalling this scene many times down the years, I was often reminded of a refrain from a poem by Sterling Brown—culled from sagas of white mobs coming after blacks in the South—"They don't come by ones /They don't come by twos . . . They come by tens."

We left the playing field of course; but I'll always remember that my father told the leader of this mob that he had a responsibility to the youths with him; we weren't there for trouble but that we were going to file letters of protest. This last rejoinder to the mob's demand allowed my buddies and me to maintain some sense of manliness before the fires of our tormentors . . . that we would protest. It was the first time I had actually witnessed the loathsome hatred of Racism; the looks in the whites of these ethnics' eyes were shot through with a loathing for us that I hadn't seen before. But the whole experience introduced into my consciousness the difference between the mean, cruel looks and treatment represented by discrimination, and the icy razors of racism, and the overkill of the numbers, brought down upon us, I can tell you that. Before the eyes and power of those white males, we were viewed as an abomination. A few years later, when I was reading Wright and William Faulkner, where mob hostility in the South against blacks was an understood and almost expected form of tragic theatre, I thought back on that experience of an afternoon in Chicago, near the Bridgeport area. Robert Frost's satire of "good fences make good neighborhoods" seems but a mild bromide when compared to the trouble we saw brewing that day.

In the early 1950s, dope had commenced to work its evil way into the black community in Chicago and other big cities, with an unseen hand doing the larger than life dealing. My best friend's brother had beaten their mother nearly to death in order to get money for his heroin habit. My own mother started taking me around to "Dope Must Go" meetings within our community. There we were confronted with the paraphernalia that drug addicts used. It may well be that this growing spread of life-destroying drug addiction caused the sharp rise in the Black Muslim's faith, as a possible form for rebirth in this life (not the next). Certainly the Muslims were on to something about the kind of spiritual-shock therapy seeded in group nationalism, that these most dislocated and deadened people needed in order to awaken. And if you'll remember, it was about this time that the Nation of Islam (headquartered in Chicago) suddenly became quite visible.

The word in the barbershop was this: that there was absolutely no way in the world that the white power structure did not know what was going down . . . as long as dope didn't become a heavy trade and problem in the white areas . . . *then let the niggers go down dead.* And furthermore, The Man was pouring dope into the ghettoes to destroy us as a people.

Then there was the impact of the hideous murder of a fourteen-year-old Chicagoan by the name of Emmett Till, down in Money, Mississippi. His mutilated body over at Rayner's Funeral Home still haunts the collective memory of black Chicago's ethos, like the huge tree of slavery's lacerating disfigurement upon the back of Sethe, in Toni Morrison's novel, *Beloved.*

In African-American literature three of our finest modern writers had warned us of what was brewing in ghetto life in Chicago: the psychological entrapment of slum conditions upon the dislocated males of the underclass and the working class. Richard Wright's *Native Son* was set on Chicago's South Side. This novel, published in 1940, prophesied the rage of the coming manchild our slums were shoveling forth, in the outlandish form of Wright's anti-hero Bigger Thomas, and the specifics of his rat-infested apartment; and the growing impact of white power upon his mind, not only within the world of the slums, but also as a controlling agency, once he left the immediate world of the black South Side. Why Bigger Thomas commits murder twice without any sense of guilt or remorse should be one of the central concerns of our city and our nation today as we attempt to deal with the psychological rage and the spiritual nothingness of alienated young black males merely existing upon the reservations within our crack-infested slums.

No less tragic, and perhaps as eloquent as Wright's novel, are the two poems Pulitzer Prize-winner Gwendolyn Brooks is best known for during this period. These poems speak to the unraveling of solid values, the spiritual lostness, and the desperate attempt on the part of young Chicago black males to cling to mercurial symbols, and slippery, mesmerizing touchstones of affirmation behind the narrows of the closing wall of segregation. Each poem is about the death or dying of young black men. *of de Witt Williams on his way to Lincoln Cemetery* is a muted, taps-like eulogy for a young man who lived fast and died young. In *We Real Cool,* the young men are on the way to a fast and early grave.

The Pool Players

Seven at the Golden Shovel

We real cool. We
Left school. We

Lurk late. We
Strike straight. We

Sing sin. We
Thin gin. We

Jazz June. We
Die soon.

Nearly twenty years after *Native Son* was published, Chicagoan Lorraine Hansberry's play, *A Raisin in the Sun*, projected the saga of a working-class family with middle-class aspirations, driven to get out of the slums and buy into a better neighborhood, as an expression of their rage for freedom. But the family is also very divided concerning how to best use the money from an insurance policy left by the death of Walter Lee Younger, Sr. The ambitious sister in the family wants a portion of the money used for her medical school education. Walter Lee Younger, Jr., the ambitious son of Lena Younger, rages against the confines of the slums, and the lack of opportunities outside the ghetto in the white man's world. He wants to employ the insurance policy money to launch a tavern on the South Side, in partnership with an improbable chap, who turns out to be a hustler-as-trickster. Here Hansberry is satirizing black values, too. For the last thing Blacks need is yet another tavern on the South Side; but Hansberry was also very aware of the lack of opportunities for Walter Lee. She understood the world he was attempting to craft for himself behind his limited options, within the walls of segregated Chicago.

The dearer American Dream that Mama Lena Younger stands for is that the insurance money should be used to get a home for the family.

The play explores the racists' attempts to keep the Younger family from the South Side, cut off from fair-housing opportunities. Hansberry's own father had fought against restrictive housing covenants for years before winning a Supreme Court decision against this form of hidden but real stranglehold on black housing upward mobility.

By the 1950s kitchenettes were spawning everywhere; apartments carved up to keep blacks piled up. We could indeed move up as long as we moved higher and higher on top of each other. These were butchered up apartments sliced down (like bad meat upon a slum butcher's chopping block), supplied with a hot plate, a small ice box or refrigerator, and a common john on each floor for several families. Through half the twenty-year reign of Mayor Richard J. Daley, the projects flew up and became festering Bantustans of black entrapment and flourishing gang activity, thereby reproducing lost, aimless, tragic outlaw characters like Bigger Thomas.

As part of the political fix in the 1950s between official Washington and Chicago, CHA (Chicago Housing Authority) built high-rises with the unspoken edict to keep the huge migration of blacks pouring from the South *running* on top of each other in the high-rises and absolutely segregated from the white ethnics. Certain middle-class blacks who made an attempt at a jail break out of the slum imprisonment often faced something infinitely more savage than what happened to the Youngers in Lorraine's play. Mobs greeted blacks in the summer of 1951 in Cicero; or I recall how the families that moved into Trumbull Park Homes, the CHA project on the far South Side, caught hell, as the late Frank London Brown revealed in a fine documentary novel about his family's experiences there entitled *Trumbull Park.*

Martin Luther King's 1966 drive for equal rights in Chicago was primarily directed toward fair and open housing. The thematic title for his Chicago campaign was "End Slums." When Dr. King's freedom movement soldiers marched in white neighborhoods to protest housing discrimination, they were tackling one of the deepest-held hostilities within the eyes, the power and the ethos of the white ethnic working class and the lower middle class—head on—the racism of tribal turf transformed into a violation of "their" grounds, which were suddenly sacred, when the blacks and their integrated numbers appeared. The idea of blacks moving next door was tantamount to the acceptance of rape by a dark stranger, upon the floor of their religious temple, in the spiritual-imaginative economy of these protesting white ethnics; it was as if they held the spiritual covenant to the city's soul. And who can forget the trouble the integrated troops of foot soldiers faced—the rocks hurling in the air that they witnessed. Dr. King was struck in the head, by a rock, on August 5, 1966, as the march in Marquette Park began. He remarked later that he had witnessed an icy loathing in the eyes of the white ethnic mob in Chicago, unparalleled by any racists' fury he had endured in his Southern campaigns for equal justice.

During the late 1960s we became aware of not only the crisis in the high-rise projects, but how the administration's officials and other members of the white power structure intended to handle housing matters. This problem only became an advertised blight on the city—but not its conscious—when Mayor Daley cordoned off the Robert Taylor Homes area, which runs from Thirty-fifth Street to Fifty-fourth Street, from the view of the delegates to the 1968 Democratic Convention, as they went down on the Dan Ryan Expressway in auto or on the public transportation system. Of course this barrack didn't prove that good fences make good neighborhoods; rather it only revealed a gross hoax of racial regression, being played out by Dick Daley. His Honor had a lot more to be worried about in the way of an immediate embarrassment from other sources of police state tactics at this convention, and as it turned out the Mayor had only himself to blame as the police created a barrack against the marchers and protestors to the convention. For earlier that year, after Martin Luther King was assassinated, and rebellion spawn of the growing crisis and hopelessness of slum living erupted, Mayor Daley gave unforgettable and unforgiveable orders that really let loose a license-to-kill mentality on the part of white cops against blacks. The mayor of all the people of Chicago said:

I have conferred with the superintendent of police this morning and I gave him the following instructions: I said to him very emphatically and very definitely that an order be issued by him immediately and under his signature to shoot to kill any arsonist or anyone with a molotov cocktail in his hand because they're potential murderers, and to issue a police order to shoot to maim or cripple anyone looting any stores in our city.

What was also not discussed openly in public until the early 1970s was the growing crisis of the hundreds of buildings, which were ready to go up in flames on the West and South Sides and which threatened the lives of poor blacks. In the condemned buildings lived the poorest of black Chicago's citizenry. Hundreds of these condemned families were either jobless, on welfare, or underemployed. They couldn't move because they didn't have the money for housing; landlords said that it was risky business renting to these people. In 1971, these citizens faced a winter without heat, water, or electricity. Because many were on welfare, they faced the possibility of having their general assistance payments cut by some 60 percent because of a "tax saving" directive from the Governor of Illinois, at that time, Richard Ogilvie. During this year over 160 buildings were placed under receivership by a Housing Court Judge, Franklin Kral. These abandoned and condemned buildings revealed the tragic hopelessness and the cycle of powerlessness poor people faced in Chicago. For when a landlord abandons a building, the utility bills become delinquent. The city shuts off the water, the gas company the boiler and the heat, the electric company the lights. There is no janitor. The absentee landlord gets off scot free.

I remember the response of the Chairman of the Chicago Dwellings Association, James Downs when he was asked what was to become of the poor locked away in this situation. He said: "Every place in the world has some families living in shacks and caves. They've always existed and they always will. There simply isn't a solution for every problem. We are in the business of providing housing units, not welfare. We will supply heat for families on an emergency basis, but we can't rebuild heating plants for all of the buildings. This winter if the emergency is bad enough, we'll put them in a hotel. New York has hundreds of families living in hotel rooms."

Downs went on to excuse the landlord's decisions not to rent to welfare recipients from these condemned buildings with the line that they "fear the welfare recipients will destroy the property." Not a lot has changed since then in terms of the dangers slum dwellers face who live in an intimate climate with these abhorrent conditions, with no way out, and no political voice to speak for them. Nor has much been accomplished in the area of relocation, because middle and upper-income families, both white and black, are constant in their disdain for the destitute, when the poor's physical presence is presented near the doorsteps of their well-to-do reality. These same successful American citizens are constant in their intellectual vigil, and armed with piercing verbal arguments supporting an "Open City" and "Open Housing." This problem of abandoned buildings haunts us today, more than ever because these empty structures provide shelter for troupes of lost drug addicts, lost souls strung out in the slums, where a carnival of self-slaughter occurs, with their pushers in these crack houses of the night.

Meantime, between 1960 and 1970, welfare rolls expanded nationally from 3 million to 6.7 million, to 10.9 million in 1972. In 1964, 29 percent of single mothers were on welfare; by 1972, 63 percent were on welfare.

The rescue mission needed for our cities in the areas of jobs and fair-housing implementations must be predicated upon the ideal of the American genius; that you can be what you want to be and that you ought to be able to move about freely and live where you want to live, without restriction, in order to manifest your highest potential. Actually this was part of the dream that drove and fired my African-American ancestors and the waves of black migration to Chicago. Indeed as Justice Steward Potter wrote, in stating the majority opinion for the Supreme Court, in 1968, in Jones v. Alfred H. Mayer Co., "At the very least, the freedom that Congress is empowered to secure under the Thirteenth Amendment includes the freedom to buy whatever a white man can buy, the right to live wherever a white man can live. If Congress cannot say that being a free man means at least this much, then the Thirteenth Amendment made a promise the nation cannot keep."

I can think of few more important gauges of our growth as a city than in the area of opening housing, fair housing, that the city cannot replenish its soul without finding ways to make common ground between the white ethnics, blacks, and Hispanics. Actually these groups in the lower middle class have many of the same problems—poor schools and a crumbling infrastructure; their politicians are equally duplicitous and corruptible.

No matter how far we in the middle and upper middle class (white or black) leap forward materially, we won't be a city that truly works until we learn something from the old folklore adage "that it makes no difference how far ahead of himself a turtle extends his two front feet, he cannot move his body until he moves his hind legs." We must always be about bringing up the rear. We not only need a Marshall Plan for our cities and a Peace Corps working within the communities, we also need on an individual basis to extend back to our young people a sense of private and public morality—that I shall be judged solely on my merit—and that I will have something meritorious to offer. We need to force industry to live up to this moral charge. We are in dire need of the muscle of government where the conscious of industry goes blind when the applicants are black.

Our kids don't see in the immediate environment enough ranging character options to emulate. They either see huge success stories wrought from violence or massive duplicity, or opulent splendor without a soul, on television. They witness the failures of life supports on every floor of their psychological prisons within the housing projects. They witness and even participate—first hand—in the economy of the new enslavement, spawned from the world of drug addiction.

This false economy, in all of its terribleness, conveys a false creation of the mind, even as the actual intellect and soul of the addict, like the will of the community is under siege, and is dreadfully diminished, before our very eyes. In this world of the new enslavement, examples of self-transformation seem dedicated to the destruction of inner-city dwellers, not devoted to their uplift. The savagery of the new street royalty offers absolutely nothing for young people to emulate. And the bitterest words from the barbershop of my youth concerning the continual profit made off dope and the lack of will power by the white power structure to stop the flow of narcotics into the slums seems infinitely more troubling, and truthful today.

Yet nowhere is the faith for an open society more charged with possibility than in the ideal of fair housing. Upon these grounds Democracy's dreams face their greatest challenge to see if our people in this city can live in proximity to each other in a laboratory where the quest for liberty is erected and respected. It is a final testing ground, here on earth. In fair and open housing we can learn the art of political power sharing, compromise, and democratic possibility, at the local, or grass roots level, through community forums, spun out of these intellectual encounters between the different groups of the city, as they rankle and jocky for power. As this century winds down, Chicago will be something like 30 percent black, 30 percent white, 30 percent Hispanic, and 10 percent Asian.

We will be forced to discover whether, in fact, we love liberty in an open, free society enough to share common ground in a spirit of antagonistic cooperation, with our neighbors, and thereby prove ourselves a better people than the racial chauvinists who were also the planners of our city and the founding fathers of our Republic ever dared to dream we, as a people, might dare to become, as a nation . . . *where the minorities were the majority.* Or we may go down dead.

Nor is this issue of a passionate drive to live where one wants to live locked in historically to the racial confrontations of Chicago, alone. For example, in 1925, when Dr. Ossian Sweet, a black, moved into a white neighborhood in Detroit, a raging white mob surrounded and stoned his house. He in turn had armed himself. Shots rang out. One white man was killed. Dr. Sweet and several friends who were visiting him were arrested. The famous lawyer Clarence Darrow was secured by the NAACP to defend Sweet and his friends. Initially the first jury called could not reach a verdict. In the second trial, Sweet's son, Henry was acquitted; in addition, the charges directed against the ten friends of the Sweets were thrown out of court. Clarence Darrow's words in his summation to the jury in the Sweet trial speak to this personal issue of people working together in the pursuit of liberty: "Every human being's life in this world is inevitably mixed with every other life and, no matter what laws we pass, no matter what precautions we take, unless the people we meet are kindly and decent and human and liberty-loving, then there is no liberty. Freedom comes from human beings, rather than from laws and institutions." The needed intellectual encounters with other cultures in order to be truly transformed into a first-class citizen of the whole city can come from a community where fair housing is encouraged.

Chicago is, of course, our shaky, rowdy, violence prone, beloved city—our only home, this side of Paradise. We are not Dubliners, nor are we Warsawians; nor are we Ghanians. It's our city to have and to hold, in all of its sickness and in all facets of its health and its wealth, its homelessness and its mighty mansions.

My own hate/love relationship with Chicago is best revealed not in the lines of any particular writers but rather in the words of Reverend Louis Rawl's son, when he sings: "I despise you cause you funky—but I love you cause you home. . . ."

ELIJAH

It was the whiteness of the whale that above all things appalled me . . . Bethink thee of the albatross: whence come those clouds of spiritual wonderment and pale dread, in which that white phantom sails in all imaginations?
—From Chapter 42, "The Whiteness of the Whale"
Moby Dick by Herman Melville

"Brothers and sisters, my text this morning is the 'Blackness of Blackness.'"

And a congregation of voices answered: "That blackness is most black, brother, most black . . ."
"In the beginning . . ."
"At the very start," they cried.
". . . there was blackness . . ."
"Preach it . . ."
". . . and the sun . . ."
"The sun, Lawd . . ."
". . . was bloody red . . ."
"Red . . ."
"Now black is . . ." the preacher shouted.
"Bloody . . ."
—From the Prologue to
Invisible Man by Ralph Ellison

ELIJAH'S MIRACLE DRUG

Elijah (Poole) Muhammad was on to something quite powerful, deeply troubling, yet dangerously electrifying concerning the condition of American blacks in general and disadvantaged African-Americans, in particular. For Elijah (who referred to himself as the Messenger of Allah) this bottomed out, "so-called Negro," so dislocated from all true moorings of spiritual support, all keening touchstones of *trueblood* direction toward clean-cut identity, really hungered for a new birth of freedom; thirst for a new species of meaningful rituals and myths. Elijah believed that the way to create the new was really through a cunning transformation of the old. He believed that the way to fashion up the new Black Muslim man (and woman, too) was to completely reverse certain Judeo-Christian myths; or in certain cases to simply relocate the spiritually famished flock of lost/found through the Black Muslim mask of Mohammed, that this Messenger as new world prophet wore. So profoundly dire and fitfully destructive were the lives of this lost-found tribe of Shabazz in the wilderness of North American, that they needed a great awakening, which must take the form of a spiritual shock therapy. A wonder drug compounded from nationalistic, spiritual and ideological properties into a serum, which surged forth from the hypodermic needle to the body and soul of the so-called Negro, with side effects, which helped in a practical self-help way for dealing with the daily grind, and counteracted against the dosages of racism, which insulted the blacks at every turn of their three-hundred-year existence, in "the wilderness of North American." Of that remembered history, James Baldwin has stated in his furious essay, *The Fire Next Time.*

> This past, the Negro's past, of rope, fire, torture, castration, infanticide, rape; death and humiliation; fear by day and night, fear as deep as the marrow of the bone; doubt that he was worthy of life, since everyone around him denied it; sorrow for his women, for kinfolk, for his children, who needed his protection, and whom he could not protect;

rage, hatred, and murder, hatred for white men so deep
that it often turned against him and his own, and made all
love, all trust, all joy impossible. . . .

A master of reverse psychology concerning the self-perceived negatives of the Negro ethos, Elijah believed that in order to awaken the
"dead" so-called Negroes to some semblance of humanity, spiritual
health, and productive living, this radical serum of an experimental
kind was obviously needed, if African-Americans were ever to be
roused into responsibility from the many kinds of nightmares—devised
into being by the whites—that Baldwin cites in his litany of the group's
suffering ethos. But Baldwin also went on to say of the blacks'
remembered history:

> . . . this past, this endless struggle to achieve and reveal
> and confirm a human identity, human authority, yet con-
> tains, for all its horror, something very beautiful. I do not
> mean to be sentimental about suffering—enough is cer-
> tainly as good as a feast—but people who cannot suffer can
> never grow up, can never discover who they are. That man
> who is forced each day to snatch his manhood, his identity,
> out of the fire of human cruelty that rages to destroy it
> knows if he survives this effort and even if he does not
> survive it, something about himself and human life that no
> school on earth—and indeed, no church—can teach.

Elijah would never make this kind of statement publicly, nor hold
out the possibility for the blacks to achieve beauty on an individual
basis in this nightmarish land. Stripped as the new-world Africans were
of their cultural and religious life supports, during the early stages of
their enslavement, Elijah believed that they must now be further
stripped again, but this time of all of the impure materialities and
properties they had gathered in consciously or unconsciously through
their three-hundred-year encounter with the value system of the white
West. Possessed as the blacks were now by a white-washed mask of the
white man's civilization, which had been grafted upon their conscious-

ness, the Negro preacher's worship of the white man's interpretation of the Bible was but one of Elijah's examples. The ultimate step in this evolutionary process, for "the Original man" as Elijah called the Blackman, would be for the *Asiatic Blackman* to be personally empowered with the knowledge that they were the kings of this earth, a superior form of human life and that they had a special relationship with Allah (perhaps recalling the relationship the Chosen People of the Old Testament, the Jews, had with Yahweh).

Elijah absolutely believed that if the tribe were ever to awaken from the nightmare of wearing the white man's mask over their consciousness, the blacks must not only drop this mask but must be disembodied of the poisonous fluids and properties of Negro Culture and consciousness: the blues; the premium placed upon rhythm; all forms of the dance; the rowdy power in jazz (mild forms of jazz strains were all right at the Black Muslim restaurants, as played by converts, or admirers of Islam, and threaded with influences of Eastern music). Also on the hit list were: all species of unbridled laughter of the cracking-up variety; hyperbole of expression, and signifying; much of the folklore; novels and literature, because all of these forms were made-up stories, when there was only one true saga (as myth) for the Black Man, or the Original Man to follow, Elijah's miracle drug medicine. There were three books that contained all you needed to know for the understanding of that magical serum: the Koran, the Bible, and Elijah's own tome, *The Message to the Black Man.* Not only were snails, shrimps, and lobsters barred from the proscribed menu of one meal a day, of course all slabs of the hog were damned. Also, all immodest Afro hairstyles; and funk of all kinds must be driven out. So that in order to redeem this so-called Negro, Elijah believed that the lost/found souls must repudiate nearly all forms of the old Negro culture, which celebrated the life of the body.

I have heard from a very good source that Elijah often referred to the Blues as Nigger music. The Malcolm X believers who were so devoted to the idea of his wily intelligence have recently unearthed new evidence of his knowledge of Shakespeare. If this is so, one must wonder aloud about just how reflective Malcolm was concerning the meaning of the Bard's lines. Was it just rote memory? He might have analytically applied Lorenzo's lines in *The Merchant of Venice* to Elijah's avoidance of music in general, as an index into the psychology of the Messenger. "The man that hath no music in himself, / Nor is not moved with concord of sweet sounds, / Is fit for treasons, stratagems and spoils." Or, he might have applied the wisdom of the power intrigues in the tragedies and the historical plays to his own situation with Elijah, long before he became too outrageous to live with.

The intra-group gospel according to Elijah was this: All dimensions of Negro life, born out of emotion, rhythm, funk, must be rebuked, because, in the Messenger's imagination, these attributes or aspects of the Negro's inner face were part and parcel of the savagery inculcated within the blacks by the white man's teachings from slavery down to the contemporary world. I am not saying that "the Lamb of God," as his intimates called Elijah, really believed that you probably needed to throw the baby out with the bath water, for he alone amongst the contemporary cult creators (in keeping with one of his intellectual fathers, Marcus Garvey) did attempt to lift the thousands of Negroes nobody cared about out of the polluted waters of their suffering with a fullscale mythos and a detailed plan of action. "Soul," as the definitive yeast of black ethos, was pollution in the light of Elijah's eyes.

The idea of Christian mission in the Negro Church of the North was often not one of real outreach, when it came to welcoming in, or helping up the least of these my brethren from the slum and the slime of their bottomed-out condition. I am reminded of a scene in Richard Wright's short story, "The Man Who Lived Underground," when a black man—falsely accused on murder—surfaces in filth and confusion from his sewer dwelling before a Negro congregation, in a storefront church. This man, Fred Daniels, hears the choir singing:

> The Lamb, the Lamb, the Lamb,
> Tell me again your story.

The Lamb, the Lamb, the Lamb.
Flood my soul with your glory.

When Wright's unvarnished "lamb," as Underground Man, elevates himself to the church entryway, he is spurned by his own as so much slime and filth. No doubt these spiritually hollow black church-goers only want to hear an upwardly mobile spiritual story-as-performance—cleaned up, defunked, shouted-out; a mindless joyous jam unto Jesus and nothing about the existential story from the lips of the lower depths, where a man, stripped of all spark from divine afflatus dwells. (Fortunately, the Founder of their faith was much more compassionate.) The Negro church-goers in Wright's story want to hear the "glory" of Christ's story, but not the agony of the Cross. "Flood my soul with your glory" will keep them from having to confront the dire conditions of the race, or for that matter the relationship of lynching in black mythos to the Crucifixion in Christian mythos. At this level, a man like Fred Daniels (Wright's anti-hero in the tale) would be just the kind of man Elijah would have welcomed in with a valiant "Asalam Alaikum" rendered up in his squeaky-clean voice. If only Elijah would have appreciated fiction—other than his own!

Amid Elijah's celebratory idea that the blacks must walk this earth in a kingly and queenly manner (as the expression of their true, superior nature), there was a counter-disdain on the Messenger's part for what they were and who they had become, across the board, culturally. On an individual basis, Elijah intellectually admired those so-called Negroes who had fought the good fight and laid an assault line of verbal torpedoes against the evils of white supremacy. But even these Negroes ultimately fell short of X marks the spot in Elijah's imaginative economy, because few of these elect soldiers against racism had completely broken the yoke of their connection within the white establishment, even as they had drawn their lines in the sand, in certain public ways, or through their writings (as in the case of Baldwin) about what they would not take off of the white man. Elijah also admired certain tyrants, too, like Stalin, for example.

Elijah's self-stylized vision of Islam amongst the Lost/Found Negroes here in North America absolutely shunned moments of ecstatic seizures, which are so basic to the fundamentalist Protestant Christian's electrifying spiritual heritage, which really goes back to a combination of whatever was left over from the African religious expression with the impact the Great Awakening had on the slaves. This highly emotional regeneration was replaced by a studied coming into awareness concerning the true blue nature of the "demonic" white man, and the ultimate destiny of the black man.

"*And I looked, and behold a pale horse: and his name that sat upon him was Death.*"

How did the whites get all of this power? Well, first of all the Caucasian was a "made-man" fashioned by a black scientist, by the name of Yacub, some 6,000 years ago. *Fashioned?* Well, according to the "teachings," the whites were created by a gı ıfting process. They were a diluted race, might be another (most unfortunate) way of putting it. This engineering of the genes resulted in the creation of the whites. Yacub apparently got the idea of grafting away or pulling away from the genes of the black man, by an incident that occurred when he was a precocious lad of six. Elijah explained the revelation of how Yacub got the idea for the creation of the white man, which in the Black Muslim's view was the equivalent of Original Sin.

> The Bible symbolizes the white man Rev. 6:8, as being a rider on a red horse and power was given to him to take peace from the earth. In order to prepare the white man to do this work, he has to be armed. So the Father of the white man, Mr. Yacub, at the age of six (6) was found by his uncle, PLAYING WITH STEEL. He learned how a steel magnet attracted steel. Mr. Yacub, then said to his uncle that when he got to be an old man he was "going to make a people who shall rule you, uncle." Mr. Yacub and his uncle were both Black; not white.

What made Yacub such a mean-hearted, sinister little side-wynder, only Elijah, Fard, and I guess, Allah knew the answer.

According to Elijah's teachings, the white man was given authority to rule over the Original People (or the Asiatic Blackman) for 6,000 years. His time of reign was nearing its end. Elijah, of course, like any creative innovator would purloin anything he could get his hands on in order to work his artifice. I have mentioned the obvious connection to the Garvey Movement: the idea of demanding that the U.S. give the so-called Negroes some several states in the South in order to separate from the white man's presence. The founding of all kinds of self-help businesses appeared to be a combination of Garvey and Booker T. Washington. Although Garvey called for a back to Africa movement, he actually started several enterprises of a nation-building sort, right in the U.S.; as examples, the Black Star Shipping line, and a nurses corp.

Elijah enunciated just the proper lines to keep him aligned with the racist spiel of the white supermacists and the segregationists: "We believe that intermarriage or race mixing should be prohibited." Appealing to segregationist and chauvinistic ideas of the day, he declared in print: "We want equal education—but separate schools up to 16 for boys and 18 for girls on the condition that girls be sent to women's colleges and universities. We want all black children educated, taught, and trained by their own teachers."

In predicting the imminent fall of the made-man (white race) in our life time, Elijah revealed the influence, it seems to me, of the Jehovah Witnesses, who put the world on notice that the coming apocalyptic doom of the world was just at hand. Elijah simply transferred apocalyptic doom of the world to the downfall and destruction of the white man's rule. Also, the very persistent method of the Watch Tower faithful, pushing their magazine Awake! as they went door to door "fishing" for souls, seems to have influenced Elijah's directive to his foot soldiers. And the method of Jehovah Witnesses standing in doorways with their magazines held aloft to get the attention of the outsiders seems to have had some impact on the hawkers of *Muhammad Speaks*. But the enterprising, hard-driving newspaper salesmen, were often former street-corner hustlers who knew that you really had to do a hard sell in peddling your wares, your drugs, your hot goods, or, now the papers of your faith, in these hard, lean, and merciless streets. These hawkers of *Muhammad Speaks* would indeed get all up in your face, with the good news, concerning their new-found faith; they were a blast, with the zeal of the old-time religion pitched to a tune loud enough to awaken the dead—or to chase the Negro out of any Blackman, as the saying goes.

On the surface it seems as if Elijah had left out the largest population in the world today, with his white over black/black over white obsession: the peoples of Asia. Yet he really hadn't, for Elijah (who looked like an aged Vietnamese warrior, a not-too-distant cousin of Uncle Ho Chi Minh himself) had conjured up this strategy of the Asiatic Blackman, which given the Negroid or African cast to the features of many Asian people is fascinating in terms of the genesis of blood lines, or lines of stock in the emergence of the human family, perhaps. But it doesn't reveal a damn thing to our cultural lineage. Still, it worked for Elijah's purposes of finding a missing link to forge ties between peoples of color. During World War II there was much propaganda about the "yellow peril," and Elijah went to jail for not following the draft laws. In one passage in Elijah's blueprint on Blackness, in "Muhammad's Message to the Blackman," we are told this about the whites and their sinister mayhem toward the Asiatic Blackman:

> Their history shows trouble-making murder and death to all darker people from far-off islands and mainlands of Asia as well as the South Seas and the Pacific and Atlantic Oceans. All have been touched by their destructive hand and evil way of civilization and finally the bringing of my people to make their destruction sure.

All of this and much more was a part of "The Teachings." These teachings were bulletins from the credo of faith (not that dissimilar from the Catholic's catechism), carefully honed and set forth by a minister before a blackboard, chalking away the cold facts, in black and white, in a logical, scholarly, zealous yet un-emotional voice. He was dressed in a most "un-emotional," neat, but cheap dark suit and a bow-tie, as if grafted from the attire of the Lamb of God himself. Intellectually excited, as it were, the ministers appeared to assume the mask of a professor caught up in the spirit of revealing the findings from the latest research in his field. So that some of the old-time fire turned into the zeal of euphoria was there, but it was pitched toward the perceived intelligence of the mythos, not the riffing ecstasy of the spiel—at least this was the intention. Now, there might be a cold fury somewhat muted in the minister's voice, but the general theme was to turn rage, anger, furor, contempt, and loathing for the white man into something they could use and that was a logical explanation of the racial madness in this Republic, by dint of the Black Muslims illogical mythos.

Emotional utterance of the facts should be drained off as so many tears of anger and what you were hearing and perceiving was cast forth through the life of the mind, as you were now informed about the swampland of an infested world created by the monstrous, totally illogical value-system devised by the white man (Devil). Also, the emotional spiel gave you a kind of high, or cooled-out succor, that was extremely dangerous, yet electrifying.

The "yes, sirs," or, "that's right, Brother Minister, make it plain," were not part of an echo chamber of ecstatic emotional regeneration of the spirit alone; but rather a furor of mathematical truth and logic, concerning not only the meaning behind the white man's dastardly deeds, but also an explanation of his illogical behavior that went beyond the ideas spewed forth by the black nationalists and progressive integrationist—that the cause of the white witchery was racism, racism, racism. You were brought ashore (or fished out) by someone who was mapping out not only your own experience of being virtually drowned by the evils of white society and white power, but you were being presented with a revelation concerning why you and millions of blacks and third world peoples had been so savagely dominated by the white man. And why you were about to assume your rightful status as rulers of planet earth, once you *deloused* yourselves of Negro cultural impurities.

Processing of souls from the stage of mental enslavement to white supremacy, to the idea "We believe we are the people of God's choice, as it has been written, that God would choose the rejected and the despised," to an enunciated faith in the superiority of blacks was captured in Robert Hayden's poem, about Malcolm X, and entitled "El Hajj Malik El-Shabazz:"

> . . . yet how could he, "Satan" in the Hole,
> guess what the waking dream foretold?
> Then false dawn of vision came;
> he fell upon his face before
> a racist Allah pledged to wrest him from
> the hellward-thrusting hands of Calvin's Christ
> to free him and his kind
> from Yacub's white-faced treachery.
> He rose redeemed from all but prideful anger,
> through adulterate attars could not cleanse
> him of the odors of the pit.

It should also be pointed out that another religion, the Bahai faith, had saved Hayden's life spiritually, and so his mind-set was shaped here by the universalist's vision of the Bahais.

As James Baldwin said in *The Fire Next Time*, in the section dealing with Elijah and the Muslims:

> The brutality with which Negroes are treated in this country simply cannot be overstated, however unwilling white men may be to hear it. In the beginning—and neither can this be overstated—a Negro just cannot *believe* that white people are treating him as they do; he does not know what he has done to merit it. And when he realizes that the treatment accorded him has nothing to do with anything he has done, that the attempt of white people to destroy him—for that is

what it is—is utterly gratuitous, it is not hard for him to think of white people as devils.

Encouraging Americans to occupy the Philippines, even as the issue was under heated argument, Rudyard Kipling wrote: "To wait in heavy harness, / On fluttered folk and wild— /Your new-caught, sullen peoples, /Half devil and half child." So that the idea of the peoples of the third world as pagan, savage, and heathen and part human, part devil was very much a part of the psychology of white supremacy long before Elijah loaded his hypodermic with this potentially lethal loathing.

* * *

"The interests of a Black man in a cellar
Mark tardy judgment on the world's closed door."

—Hart Crane, *Black Tambourine*

Much of Elijah's power within the "personality" of the white power structure's value system was brought home to me in many ways during my work experience with *Muhammad Speaks.* Yet few experiences were more symbolically meaningful than the following event which occurred in the Fall of 1971. At the time I was associate editor of *Muhammad Speaks.* I was still driving my off-white, 1962 Lincoln Continental (with its battered and torn convertible white canvas top), which my fiancé and later wife, Marianne, and I came to call "The White Whale."

On this particular afternoon, I was coming home from the newspaper office, driving on a ticket, and the rear back-up lights of "The White Whale" were not working. Still, I was in a good mood, the manuscript for my first novel had recently been accepted for publication by Random House, under the editorship of a woman who had just been promoted to senior editor, who seemed to be on the way up and was building a stable of writers. Her name was Toni Morrison, and she and I had hit it off swimmingly during a recent trip to the Big Apple, when we met to discuss the manuscript in some detail. My fiancée and

I were contemplating marriage; I enjoyed my job as editor with *Muhammad Speaks*, and generally I was in an up-beat mood, because enough of the care-free bachelor was mixed up with the sense that my life was *finally* taking on a serious-minded state, and my career as a writer was shaping up. I was sailing high but still a little too reckless and irresponsible concerning that damn ticket for a moving violation.

All of a sudden, from out of nowhere, a police car was on my trail, siren sounding off, as I crossed over into the general Hyde Park area. Soon the cop car was curbing me over. Oh, those damn back-up lights. Why hadn't I? Then two white cops, one beefy and one burly, emerged from the police car and curtly interrogated me about my back-up lights. The burly cop wanted to know where I worked. The beefy cop demanded why hadn't I fixed those back-up lights. Then he said: "Let's see that license, fellow." As I dug into my wallet, the warm-up one-liner from the barbershop of tall-tale-telling experts came to my lips: *and now gentlemens, you going to hear lies beyond suspicion.* But this was no stage joke and these cops were deadly serious. So, I bit my lip and told the partial truth, so help me God (or Allah). "Officers even though I am driving on a ticket, I had planned to get those back-up lights fixed tomorrow." Then I handed over the wrinkled ticket I was driving on, and remarked, rather quietly and even piously, that I was an associate editor for the newspaper *Muhammad Speaks*. I knew then that I was in big trouble, once those words got out of my mouth; I certainly was "beyond suspicion," but I gave them my press credentials, too. What the hell, I might as well appear forthcoming.

I knew what was about to happen; I'd have to go to the police station and post bond. The burly cop told me to follow their car to the station. He got back into the squad car; and the beefy policeman returned to the passenger's side. I turned over the ignition and gripped the wheel nervously, waiting for them to start off. I felt like that flying fool of Negro folklore, allowed into Heaven on the condition that he fly on the left side of the road, with one wing behind his back, and maintain certain, very restrictive rules concerning speed. Damn, if he doesn't fly all over Heaven fast as he can wing it only to get racked up in the Tree of Knowledge; what a mess he looked with his battered wings, and smashed up feathers, too. I heard the cops cranking up their chariot coming for to carry me home.

When all of a sudden I saw with my own eyes, the cop car was not speeding forward, but hurling in toward me an angry reverse. Now the cop on the passenger side was parallel to me. Angrily, he motioned for me to roll down my window. Soon he was handing me back my old ticket and my press credentials, tucked away inside, with the following warning rendered up in a voice that was full of piss and vinegar: "Look here, fellow, you're lucky as hell you're with *Muhammad.* Get your shit straightened out." And with that the cops in the squad car sped off, burning rubber in a blaze, as if called off to a designated spot for the hottest tip on the latest available goods resulting from a busted fence's operation, leaving me trembling with a renewed sense of the mysterious power of this little man Elijah Muhammad, within the personnel and the personality of the white power structure. Perhaps the rumor was true that the cops who worked in the area near the Lamb's house were well remembered at Christmas time and during the rest of the year as well.

A deeper truth, however, was brought home to me when I told a policeman friend of mine this story in a bar some months later (and long after I had got my "shit straightened out") as he laughed to a point of almost cracking up. Finally, my cop friend, dressed in street clothes, offered up a bit of philosophical overview, as was his wont:

". . . Forrest, you were a high-flying fool, and you deserve to have your wing clipped. Actually you got off light, my man. But your interpretation of *why* you got off *so* light as a feather is too narrow. After all, look at it from the cops' perspective, other than regular payments in the pocket. The Muslims don't cause the cops any trouble. When do you ever see any Black Muslims shooting up the projects, shooting up their veins, raping women, dealing in hard drugs? Now no doubt many of them did in their former lives. But now, my man, they are a Number One model American citizens, who just happen to be black . . ." Then he whispered to me confidentially: "Look, Forrest, I don't particularly dig a whole peck of their shit, but I respect them, and their clean-up program. Because when I go up into the projects—and hell breaks out—and I'm confronted with a pregnant black bitch, I immediately find myself hating whatever she's got in her mutha-fucking belly *twice*. Because I steady know that if it's a bouncing baby boy, I'm going to have be ready to shoot down his black ass in a very few years because he's going to be giving me and some other cops a whole shit load of trouble with those gang bangers. If the bitch's carrying a gal in her belly, I know that girl's going to get knocked-up soon as she gets her first period, with some little trouble-making bastard teeming in her belly. It's an evil cycle, dig it!

"Now when I see one of those Muslim sisters pregnant and coming out of one of those Your Supermarts, I don't feel that way—because I don't foresee no trouble for me or society stirring up in her belly. Can you dig it? And I find myself respecting her; maybe almost tipping my hat to her as a lady, the way I was brought up to respect a woman who carried herself like a lady. They are polite, distant, and cooperative. Also, a lot of the spooks who once were big-time trouble-makers are cleaned up in ways nobody else has been able to do. If they preach hate of the Honkies, so mutha-fucking what? That's sure no problem to the white cops, 'cause most of them hate Negroes deep down to their final nerve. Yeah, and don't I see it each and every day at the station. . . . So Forrest, when those white Cops were giving your ass a break and telling you to "get your shit straightened out," they were giving praise to Muhammad, to whom praises in terms of keeping the peace and cleaning up these niggers is due forever. Fool, you know how white folks think we all look alike. Hell, they thought you were a Muslim. You were wearing a tie, weren't you?" Then he proceeded to crackup again, gales of laughter almost cavorting him off of his barstool. Then, my cop friend and I ordered up a plate of rib-tips to go along with our drinks.

* * *

Getting down and funky were viewed as attributes grafted onto the true personality of the Original Man, and he must strip this obesity away from his body and soul in order to assume the stature of the Blackman's highest calling, which is to rule planet earth. Given the extensive honor roll of the Honorable Elijah Muhammad's children fathered out of wedlock, one could surely not see Elijah as a Messenger, devoid of pleasure-seeking pursuits, as he went about Allah's mission amongst the uncleansed here in North America. Within the male-dominated infrastructure of the Nation of Islam, one might speculate that these routines, these liaisons were set-up arrangements, probably not affairs of the heart, or couplings scored in hot pursuit, in much the same way that certain quite lively and eager bodies were supplied to a beloved young chief executive by his best and brightest, as energizers to the power hungry lion, the blazingly "gorgeous" leader of the Nation.

Amid the chauvinistic hypocrisy of Elijah's rejoinder to the unbelievably gullible Malcom X, concerning his affairs, there is a certain amount of highly revealing psychological honesty. With his outrageous, Napoleonic ego, Elijah saw himself in the pantheon of the legendary patriarchs and prophets of the Old Testament, probably much more than he envisioned himself as an heir of Mohammed. "I'm David. When you read about how David took another man's wife, I'm that David. You read about Noah, who got drunk—that's me. You read about Lot, who went and laid up with his own daughters. I have to fulfill all of those things," he reportedly told Malcolm X. In Alex Haley's book, some of this is humorless in terms of Elijah's ego, and Malcolm's innocence, too. Since Haley has a penchant for the dramatic scene, it is presented as a confrontation—in dialogue. However, on stage the scene would be nothing short of a scream. Suddenly Malcolm X found himself in the situation of the contemporary spin-doctors of the political arena; the stories about his intellectual father's adulteries were sweeping through the grapevine. Elijah's reputation had to be cleaned up. He had been acting like a brother in the dead world.

Elijah Muhammad's mythos revealed that whites would be brought low soon and the black brought into power. This, too, was an example of Elijah incorporating the idea of a Chosen People, out of the Old Testament, into his own mission map. Instead of the Jews, this time the Chosen People were the blacks. Actually Elijah's faith in retribution and racial revenge (against the whites) was very much in keeping with the Old Testament idea of "an eye for an eye." A sense of some form of punishment for the past, some collection of dues payment for the auction block, yes, and God's venegeance against the whites, was very much akin to what many deeply religious, Old Testament Negroes held to in the secret chambers of their unwritten epistles. The Southern Negro ethos, forged as it was out of slavery, made a profound imaginative connection with their own struggles and the literature of the Jews' struggles with the oppressive Egyptians. I don't mean simply the obvious linkage—so manifest in the recombining of tormented soul struggles in the Negro spirituals—but rather, a loathing and an apocalytic vision for the destruction of the demonically powerful whites. If Yahweh had promised to avenge the wrongs against His Hebrew children, then why not me, Lord? (The opposite of this coin, of course, was the idea of the Promised Land.)

One of the most powerful passages in all of modern American literature evokes this vision. We are relocated to the remembering mind of Florence, concerning her mother's vision of blacks, whites, and the imminent doom of the oppressors in James Baldwin's novel, *Go Tell It on the Mountain.*

> For it had been the will of God that they should hear, and pass thereafter, one to another, the story of the Hebrew children who had been held in bondage in the land of Egypt; and how He bid them wait but a little season till He should send deliverance. Florence's mother had know this story, so it seemed, from the day that she was born . . . She had only to endure and trust in God. She knew that the big house, the house of pride where the white folks lived, would come down: it was written in the Word of God. They, who walked so proudly now, had not fashioned for themselves or their children so sure a foundation as was

hers. They walked on the edge of a steep place and their eyes were sightless—God would cause them to rush down, as the herd of swine had once rushed down, into the sea. For all that they were so beautiful, and took their ease, she knew them, and she pitied them, who would have no covering in the great day of His wrath.

It is probable that Elijah Poole—born in Sandersville, Georgia, 1897—had heard similar stories as sagas of secretly held dreams of retribution and racial revenge. His father was a Baptist preacher. Certainly Negro secular folklore seethes with stories of retribution on the part of the powerless (Brer Rabbit) brought down upon the powerful animals of the terrain.

Elijah cunningly gave the blacks a certain mansion within the Kingdom of one of the major religions of the world, which had as its birthplace Africa. (The idea of Christianity being founded in North Africa, therefore, providing a racial stake, or connection with it, seemed distant, strained, and eccentric to most blacks, even for those who might take the time to map out the sojourn of Jesus.) In one of Elijah's myths, twelve gods (like representatives of the twelve lost tribes?) met and decided that of all of the people in the most ruinous predicament it was the American blacks whose condition needed the most urgent attention (in the form of a miraculous, but invisible showing forth of Allah) in order to awaken and redeem them from their abominable hell-hole condition. So, Allah appeared in the person of one W. A. D. Fard, with the idea of awakening enough of the blacks. Then he split the scene. How he got here, in the form of a black man, who looked like a white man (and, to my eyes, from the picture I saw of him, at the Messenger's house, he looked like a light-skinned Creole Negro, who was fair enough to be taken as a white man, in certain quarters, not French) is an interesting story in itself.

ORIGINS OF THE ALMIGHTY
MYTH

Did Elijah believe in the secret chambers of his mind, yes, all right, Allah is a black; but the so-called Negro in his condition in these hells of North America will never accept a black God; so what we must do is prepare him for this next stage. He may say he is ready to accept God as black, but he really isn't. So we will summon up a white man, as God, who has the nature of a Blackman. Since the so-called Negro has worshipped only a white God for so long, it would be too much of a psychological shock for him to actually accept a black-skinned or dark-skinned Negro as his God. But if we say this man (who looks white) is really passing for white to get information back to us on how the white man runs his institutions, then they'll accept this. Then, too, the blacks have a long-remembered history of so-called Negroes passing for white.

It was at a Savior's Day when Elijah revealed the core of the Fard birth-myth, a passing for white myth, too.

It was not quite like in Greek folklore the meeting of the gods on Mount Olympus and their decision to send Athene into the world in order to awaken Telemachus into a manly striking-out to find the father, Ulysses. Telemachus went out, attended by Athene in the guise of Mentor. Ultimately, he found his father, and the two returned to Ithaca and killed the suitors of Penelope, Ulysses's wife. Like the Greek gods, these Arab gods would deal sexually with female earthlings, too.

According to Elijah, there was a decision, amongst a similar counsel of gods, made to bring Allah to the world in human form to save the so-called Negroes. For this head god to transform all of the necessary knowledge developed by the white man, he would have to come in the form of a white man and learn the ways of his world. So, the head god went up into the mountain and cleaned up a Caucasian woman and fathered a child by her. (Apparently, this was a quickie and not a relationship.) But the babe who resulted from this union, most unfortunately, as Elijah explained it, turned out to be a girl. Obviously a woman could not come into the world and save the Negro. The convention of Muslims were all giving their steady assertions of "Yes, sir," the beautifully clad in white, "protected," Muslim women included.

Well, the god went back a second time. This time the babe turned out "to be too dark." Then the god said: "I missed that time, again." Cries of "Yes sir . . . that's right . . ." and . . . "make it plain, dear Apostle," rang through the hall. *Too dark*, I exclaimed to myself? And what do we have here? This man can tell them anything and get away with it.

Finally, according to Elijah, the God got it right, the third time. And a child was born to this cleaned-up white woman, and he was fair skinned and male. Allelluia chorus. Lots of amens.

Not missing a beat, Elijah went on to explain how Fard secreted his true identity and went about learning the white man's information. He went to their schools to find out what they knew and gave the blacks this knowledge, too.

Finally Allah, in the person of Master Fard Muhammad, appeared in Detroit as a silk salesman, about 1930, in order to awaken the sleeping giant of the Blackman, where among others, he became a close friend of Elijah's. I got into my White Whale and drove home, slowly, mulling over what I had heard.

From all reports, this intriguing chap, this Founder of the Faith, had revealed an increasingly militant posture on race, and the nature of the white man, as he gained the confidence of the Negroes. But of all his top lieutenants, it was Elijah who was his brightest pupil. The mentor, Master Fard Muhammad, so dubbed by Elijah, was finally revealed to Elijah as God, himself . . . Allah, God, who came in the person of Master Fard Muhammad. Thusly Elijah soaked up what he needed of the Christ myth, or how Jesus came into the world in order to save floundering man, and find out what he had to put up with, as human, and to save him from Original Sin. So, we had a white man, who came into this world to save the black man, from the results of what a mad black scientist had created.

NOTEBOOK: Elijah may be as strung out on the whiteness as Captain Ahab was strung up and strung over that abominable White Whale. At home now, I reread not the Bible, but Herman Melville's chapter entitled: "The Whiteness of the Whale," in *Moby Dick*. Turning to my reading upon my nightstand, I found a well-worn copy of Ellison's *Invisible Man*. I was rereading the novel in preparation for an interview with the author, in his New York apartment. There was something that happens early on in the work that reminded me of today's happenings at the Savior Day's Convention. Where was it? What was it? (All those amens to anything Elijah said). Something about the Founder. A sculpture piece on the campus. Ah yes, here.

> Then in my mind's eye I see the bronze statue of the college Founder, the cold Father symbol, his hands outstretched in the breathtaking gesture of lifting a veil that flutters in hard, metallic folds above the face of a kneeling slave; and I am standing puzzled, unable to decide whether the veil is really being lifted, or lowered more firmly in place; whether I am witnessing a revelation or a more efficient blinding.

EDITOR AND PUBLISHER:
DURHAM SPEAKS

I was down, but not out when Richard Durham, the managing editor of *Muhammad Speaks*, took me early in 1969 to meet The Honorable Elijah Muhammad for a job interview, as a reporter for the Nation of Islam's paper.

Richard Durham really built *Muhammad Speaks*. He was a tremendously interesting and complex man. Sly and subtle, well-educated and very much a race-man in the old-fashioned tradition, Durham was definitely a Marxist in his private faith concerning the ultimate need for a socialistic state. He wanted to be invisible to the public; but he also hungered to influence important issues of race and class, media, the arts, power and government, but strictly from behind the scenes. He was well-read and creative in his ability to apply his learning to actual situations in the world around us. And whether I agreed with him, or disagreed, I always found his thinking imaginative, cunning, thought-provoking. He was a clever student of human nature.

For example, I always found fascinating the ways in which Durham linked up the outlook and mental picture of Elijah and King Lear. I was intrigued by the fact that although he was most definitely a Marxist, Durham enjoyed Negro culture and didn't see it as a tool to the worldwide revolution (although he was capable of giving this notice rhetorical obedience in certain quarters), but rather as a rich resource upon which blacks could and had based a thriving culture; and as a certain evidence of how a people maintained their humanity amid an attempt to destroy the souls of these black folk. Still, like any good Marxist, Durham stressed the political, or ideological, possibilities within the cultural component much more than I might.

A first-rate journalist and a winner of a Peabody Award for his radio scripts, Durham was without question the best writer on the newspaper; and I think we all learned from him: I know I certainly did. Because he had assembled such a good staff of reporters, the managing editor had the freedom to be just that—a creative editor who came up with story ideas for his reporters; and who oversaw the make-up and the general production of the newspaper each week.

Richard Durham dreamed of evolving a certain separation of church and state of reportage between *Muhammad Speaks* and the Nation of Islam, which would be similar to the apparent relationship of *The Christian Science Monitor* and the Christian Science hierarchy within the religion. This took subtlety, time, and ingenuity on Dick Durham's part. It meant that he had to develop a very close and highly respected range of confidentialities within Elijah Muhammad's priorities. It meant that he had to court the often wayward and complex mood shifts (here we might reflect on Lear) of the Messenger. In order to get his priorities over for the newspaper, Durham had to spend many evenings at the Messenger's dining table to influence his publisher.

When I started working for *Muhammad Speaks*, there weren't any Black Muslims on our regular editorial staff. You may immediately wonder out loud about this situation. First of all Elijah knew that about 75 percent to 90 percent of the blacks who purchased the newspaper were non-Muslims and that to attract the so-called Lost-Found you first and foremost must have a newspaper that covered traditional news, and second of all report the stories not covered in the white or the Negro press. He also wanted a paper that appealed to the Asiatic blackman, or people of color in the world outside of America.

In all of these areas it was necessary to have an editorial staff that was non-Muslim to court this majority world of blacks who were generally discontented with all the news that was fit to print according to the white and Negro press. Durham, with his race-pride and Marxist agenda, seized upon this possibility. He knew that so much of the crisis in black life was absolutely not being addressed in any hard-hitting manner by the national Negro press; the white media could care less, of course. His problem always was to keep the Muslim news buried, or subordinated as much as possible. Priority was given to stories concerning the crisis of black America, the economic tragedies facing the Third World, and then the ways of dealing with the vestiges of colonialism around the globe. None of this did violence to Elijah's general view of the world, but you needed to court him to make sure he didn't think you were trying to reshape his view of the globe, with a contradictory vision of a new world order in his paper. Thusly, the analogy of the *Muhammad Speaks* and *The Christian Science Monitor*—that is, religious news be kept in a certain section of the paper. That Durham was able to convince the Messenger time and time and time again that the Muslim's best interests were served by keeping the Nation of Islam's "progress" sectionalized, nay segregated, from the rest of the general news was an act of the highest journalistic valor, in terms of the relationship of the managing editor to the publisher. It was also one of the reasons why the paper had such currency and respect within the black community. This relationship between Durham and Elijah, carried out over nearly a decade of living, forms an infinitely more complex match-up than the one between Elijah and

Malcolm; in a duel of this sort, Malcolm was hopelessly outclassed, and out-boxed.

Elijah found Durham's vision for the paper useful. First and foremost it was not dissimlar from his own. *Muhammad Speaks* under Durham's direction was constant in its assault upon all manner of white imperialism, corruption of the neo-colonial fat-cats, and the exploitation of the black masses within the United States. Secondly, by having the newspaper proper in the hands of Durham and his able cadre of non-Muslims, Elijah was able to keep the power of the pen away from ambitious members of his flock who would use the paper in the name of Allah, as a way of building up their own small fiefdoms within the Lamb's Kingdom.

All of this had to be handled with kid gloves. Articles, other than strictly religious ones, were included within the paper, by fledgling Black Muslim writers, on a regular basis. However, this gradually changed as the Durham-Elijah duo began to fade, or when Durham retired from the paper. By the time I became managing editor, in 1972, over half of my staff was Muslim. I, in turn, was the last of the non-Muslim editors. But my point is this: For nearly a decade, from 1963–1973, very little of the central editorial policy, and the story ideas, the intellectual shaping of *Muhammad Speaks*, was crafted by the Black Muslims.

To say that Durham was very adept at dealing with Elijah would be a gross understatement; he was masterful. It is my interpretation that he saw this wrangling with his boss (done with great respect, of course) about what should go in or the emphasis on certain stories as part of the antagonistic cooperation an editor often has with his publisher. Obviously, when Elijah didn't want something in the paper, period, that was that. For example, we were not to write anything about the Black Panthers. The Messenger saw them as a dangerous element in the black community. Also, Durham had several run-ins with certain Muslims who were on the way up who saw Durham's handwriting on too much of the newspaper's philosophical bent. (Engagingly enough, Durham never wrote any stories under his own byline); therefore, they tried to bring this non-Muslim editor down.

One story has it that a group of Black Muslim ministers dedicated to Durham's immediate demise went to Elijah and told him that they had evidence that "Editor Durham is a Communist." Ever the Georgia Fox, Elijah reportedly told the ring leader of the planned coup: "Well brother, at least Editor Durham isn't with the Devil." And that was that. Having a non-Muslim staff that he could count on, led by a crack-shot managing editor, allowed Elijah to keep ambitious Muslims, who would have cornered their own market in columns of X's, made the paper unbearable to read, unless you were reading for a conversion experience, and turned the paper into a feverish "fishing" format, at bay. It also gave *Muhammad Speaks*, a journalistic credibility, during a time when the Black Muslims, and Elijah, himself, were fighting for "respect" all across the board, despite what they said about the need for separation.

Then there was the old point about Elijah, psychologically: He really thought the faithful were children. Now they could grow up to be great as a Nation; but for just now they were still underdeveloped, and it was best that the non-Muslims hold the power over the pen. Just as they might believe Allah to be black—as it was revealed to them, through him—but to be on the safe side, it was best to present the idea of God as coming in the person of a white man, or a white-looking man, W. A. D. Fard. And when you reflected upon it, the idea of Yacub being a black scientist loaded the equation against the ideal of black perfection and introduced treason on the part of one's own kind, in Elijah's version of Paradise Lost. And just who was the specific snake in the garden, who caused the downfall of the black race, and Original Sin.

I did not make the connection at the time of my hiring, of course, but I did think it more than just passing strange that before we went to the house of Elijah for my job interview Durham had repeatedly stated that I should emphasize my contacts with the *white media* and my educational experience at the University of Chicago, and that mentioning the black news-gathering organizations that I had worked with would garner little respect in the eyes of Elijah. I had, for example, been, at the time, the editor of The Woodlawn Organization's news-paper. Well, as it turned out, Elijah didn't think very much of that crowd, nor the Alinksy-spun philosophy. After my interview with the Honorable, I came to bear a most affirmative witness to the *teachings* of Mr. Durham, concerning the vicissitudes of the Messenger of Allah.

I started working for *Muhammad Speaks*, as a reporter, in February, 1969.

During my first months with the paper, we were under a strict gag order not to say anything against the new administration of President Richard M. Nixon, because he had expressed an interest in creating Enterprise Zones for business development within the black commu-nity. He had pulled this balloon out of his bag of tricks from contacts his staff had made with some of the "more respectable elements inside the Black Power Movement." Self-help programs would deride the failed programs of the Kennedy–Johnson years, Nixon let it be known. Elijah "self-help" Muhammad was certain that President Nixon would be calling on the leader of the Nation of Islam for counsel (and maybe with resources or seed-money) to advance these Enterprise Zones. Perhaps in Elijah's imagination, these Enterprise Zones sounded like some of those separate areas Elijah had been carping to obtain for years. That they might have been bantustans was not reflected upon by the Messenger.

Of course, Tricky-Dick Nixon wasn't going to do anything about this Enterprise Zone project; it was merely a political trial balloon blown up just in time for the election in order to make blacks think that he was actually troubled over their plight and that he had a plan to relieve their suffering. In the imagination of Nixon's white conservative silent majority, it spelled relief from Negroes on relief. On the other hand, with King dead and the Civil Rights Movement floundering and dying and Black Power on the rise, Nixon felt he did not have to deal with the old-line Civil Rights leadership any longer; and that perhaps he could develop a small but useful voting energy within the militant, yet conservative mood within the Black Consciousness movement. You'd have to select certain of their numbers and make them respectable in order to pull the thing off, for during the course of his 1968 campaign for the White House against Hubert H. Humphrey, Nixon and his staff realized that they were in for a very close election and that a high tide of emotion amongst the blacks for HHH might throw the election to the Democrats. Humphrey, of course, was popular with blacks, and he had a very fine voting record on Civil Rights. Indeed, no other Democrat in this country had Humphrey's impressive credentials on this issue, going back to the 1948 convention when he challenged the Dixiecrat movement within the party over a Civil Rights plank he was trying to get installed as part of the platform. Nixon figured that if he could shave off a few points from the lock HHH had on the black vote he might win the election. Or, his inner staff believed, short of that, if you could get enough blacks who were extremely disillusioned with the voting process anyway not to vote, this would help the Nixon cause as well. To that end, money was spread and promises made to gang-leaders in Chicago—and perhaps other places as well—to discourage blacks from voting. This is all the more heart-breaking when one considers how long blacks fought to get the vote in the South. The Voting Rights Act wasn't passed until 1965. Also, in his initial challenge for the White House, Nixon remembered that it was the Negro vote that tipped the election to Kennedy.

Once Dick Nixon was elected, Elijah thought that a conservative president of the Nation would call upon the most successful, self-help promoter amongst blacks, the leader of the Nation of Islam. (After all, certain leaders of the Chicago gang, the Blackstone Rangers, had been invited to the Inaugural Ball as payment for discouraging blacks not to vote in this election, a sub-text, no doubt, of Nixon's Southern Strategy.) But here, again, Elijah's idea of separation went too far. He completely discouraged blacks from voting. And his followers were instructed not to vote. Black Muslims not voting might have helped Dick Nixon slightly; but since they were a conservative bloc, who didn't vote at all, Nixon couldn't see how he could develop their potentiality in the new small core of black conservatives he was tempted to develop. The Silent Majority Dick Nixon courted voted. The Black Muslims were a silent minority amongst the blacks (once you got past their rhetoric), but they didn't vote.

At *Muhammad Speaks* we, of course, refrained from saying anything about the Nixon Administration (until we heard differently). But at the same time, we continued to blast away at the institutional racism within every major structure of the American way of life, government included. *Government, not Nixon, was the word,* Durham told his staff. We also knew that Durham could smooth this over with the Messenger, if things got too raw or delicate, and some clever chap within the hierarchy of the Nation tipped Elijah off, or awakened him to the fact that Government was synonymous with Nixon.

That Richard Durham saw the importance of history and culture in the story of the Negro in America is richly acknowledged in the major role he played as the creator of the most important radio series about the African-American story ever developed and presented in this country. It was called *Destination Freedom.* This program, which presented the saga of the black experience in the Americas through memorable biographical sketches in a highly dramatic form—started in 1948 and ran through much of 1950. Not surprisingly, given Durham's vision, the programs not only featured stories of black Americans but also stories of Toussaint L'Ouverture, the Haitian revolutionary leader and the man who defeated Napoleon. These programs were presented on WMAQ radio "in cooperation with the *Chicago Defender,*" and the spectrum of these biographical dramas was impressive—from Denmark Vesey, Harriet Tubman, and Frederick Douglass to James Weldon Johnson and Gwendolyn Brooks. During the 1950s, Durham worked as the national program director for the meat cutters trade union. He was managing editor of *Muhammad Speaks* through the 1960s.

When Durham left the paper, he wrote the first black soap opera "Bird of the Iron Feather," a title from a line out of a speech by Frederick Douglass. He also wrote the life story of Muhammad Ali. But Durham's role was essentially as-told-to-writer as stenographer. From everything he indicated to me, it must have been a very frustrating event. This book was called *The Greatest,* and it suffered from certain restrictions placed upon Ali and Durham by the Muslim leadership. He was a good friend of Studs Terkel's for over half a century. Durham was a speech-writer and consultant to Harold Washington. He was no doubt responsible for Washington's famous reference to Jean Baptiste du Sable, the Haitian founder of Chicago, as "my fellow tribesman."

* * *

"I saw Jesus in the Projects."—Richard Pryor

Comedy, of course, allows for pratfalls and a constant stripping away from personality all newly aligned obesity, pomposity, self-inflation, superiority of vision, and puffed-up idealogy. We humans are ever in need of a cleansing of the portraits we paint of ourselves. Because Elijah had created a religion of his own invention, there weren't any forms within his Nation of Islam, for healthy release to mock the institutional fallacies within the new man and woman the Messenger was recreating. He must have said within himself: *Look the American nation has failed blacks; but the American ideals, or Puritanical ideals of hard work, genuine effort, thrift, family, respect for women, tidiness, group nationalism (even racism), good homes, small business entreprises, deferred gratification, respect for authority, vigilante groups (as seen in the Fruit of Islam), good health care, and good schools, all of this works quite well in this country for other groups. I'll reapply those virtues, as edicts and commandments, along with the teachings, as I try to restructure this so-called Negro into his proper mental health. As he stands right now, he's almost dead. And for my metaphorical purposes, he is dead. Just as Yacub made the white man, I'm going to remake the blackman into his rightful condition.*

With his Southern Negro ethos of hard work and doing for one's own, Elijah was able to get thousands of African-Americans thinking in terms of a kind of immigrants drive toward making their own way. And when you got away from the racism in his philosophy (which probably wasn't any different from some species of white racism most white ethnics were brought up on) he often sounded like a modern day Booker T. Washington: "We must learn how to train our Children into the Knowledge of Self and into higher education from the kindergarten to the universities. We must get away from that old kindergarten of letting our Black children lay around and play and stay there for months studying the alphabet. We must use the faster method of advanced education in order to begin our Black children's qualification and keep them busy studying while in the classroom instead of playing."

In Elijah's own classroom of student ministers, Malcolm was probably the brightest and, Lawd today, the best. Yet, he remained in their relationship an errand boy for the Messenger—school boy to master teacher—emerging out of the shadow of his intellectual father, to be sure, in terms of the world, particularly younger blacks, but probably never totally evolving out on his own in terms of the Malcolm Little, or the Elijah-created Malcolm X. He was never really Icarus, not inwardly, when the word was given—not until the last nine months of his new birth and maybe not then, probably, despite all that fair-skinned lambs business he proclaimed seeing at Mecca.

Looking over some of Ras's speeches in Ellison's *Invisible Man*, 1952, I must say Malcolm never spieled forth a rhetorical flourish of such range, wrath, and rage as the Exhorter, and without religion, nor a white-looking "master" to praise. If U.S. blacks had been students of the book, they would have been primed for Malcolm and his dislocations, before he emerged in the mid to late 1950s, through Ras, and what in turn Ras came out of. Notice all the black hate amid the rage against the whites, too.

> "And you, Mahn," the Exhorter said, "a reg'lar little black devil! A godahm sly mongoose! Where you think *you* from, going with the white folks? I know, goddahm; don't I know it! You from down South! You from Trinidad! You from Barbados! Jamaica, South Africa, and the white mahn's foot in your ass all the way to the hip. What you trying to deny by betraying the black people? Why *you* fight against us? You *young* fellows. You young black men with plenty education; I been hearing your rabble rousing. Why you go over to the enslaver? What kind of education is that? What kind of black mahn is that who betray his own Mama?"

Or, put another way, too bad for Malcolm that he didn't know how to read literature as cathecism, because that would have allowed him to read about all the tricksters in *Invisible Man* and it would have prepared him for this Elijah, and his teachings. Elijah didn't need to read literature, on a certain level though he was well read enough for his own purposes in the Bible and the holy Koran; those texts possess some of the best literature available. Elijah was too busy creating the mythos of his own literature. Reading about the tricksters might have allowed Malcolm to think back upon all the tricksters and players he knew once upon a time. *And* the main-line trickster con-man he was in the old-skin, in the so-called dead world, might have prepared him for the coat-hanger thematic riff throughout the novel, "To Whom It May Concern, Keep This Nigger-Boy Running," and how this riff comes again and again in the novel from people the narrator trusts the most. Part of Malcolm's problem—and most other Muslims as well was this: They believed that once you were "saved" by Elijah's Islam, you left the dead world consciousness in the polluted waters forevermore and entered into the land of the living; and that there was nothing of use from that old way, in the soul of that old skin, for you to reapply in this New World. Meantime, Elijah was busy as a bee spinning out those oldspar parts—with his penchant for reverse psychology—from the dead world into sleek new models for his auto show. Also, Elijah played all roles in the creation of this nation. He was a trickster both in the sense of the magician, and in the spirit of the trickster, as demon. He took on the role of playwright of his own play, "The Recreation of The Blackman," raiding the Bible and the Koran, like Shakespeare raiding Ovid, and Joyce soaking up the *Odyssey*; he was actor *cum laude*, always looking for a straight man; stage manager, telling all where they stand; and director, always giving the ultimate interpretation to his self-created script. Oh, how it must haunt Elijah even unto the grave to know that it is Malcolm, not himself, who has been canonized saint (picaresque saint?) by the thousands of young blacks, so hungry for an ideal of rowdy underworld life, reborn into a state of blissful brotherly perfection, when it comes to dealing with The Man. The fact is Malcolm never had to really deal with The Man, other than to tell them off. The

Man he needed to deal with was Elijah. But that would have been like stepping into the ring to duke it out with Muhammad Ali—The Man of boxing. In order to compensate for the neglect of his true intellectual father, Louie Farrakhan has sought to canonize Elijah.

GOING TO MEET THE MAN

He was diminutive. I remember on one occasion when I was called over to the house for special praise (after I had written a eulogy for the Messenger's wife, Mrs. Clara Muhammad) telling my wife, Marianne, how I had looked Elijah right dead in the eyes and discovered that I was a few inches taller than the Lamb of God. "Well, Leon," she started up, "Napoleon met Napoleon." NOTEBOOK: If Elijah and Malcolm were actors upon a stage, Elijah would have played his spokesman off of the stage. He was a very complicated man. Had Malcolm read Shakespeare's *Othello*, with more of an analytical mind and stored the lessons of the play in his memory bank, he might have been aware of how Iago is playwright, director, stage manager, manipulator in the Elizabethan comedy routines, and stage actor, as well as soldier and "ancient" to the Moor. And if could have recombined this knowledge with the teachings he had learned from the jungle-like streets and never abandoned this wisdom for Elijah's teachings, but employed that savvy from the pits, as an instrument for judging all people, he might have been saved from the ultimate havoc. But in his process of becoming, he could call upon that street knowledge to awaken the Lost/Found, and thereby expand upon his Master's biding, while out "fishing" for Lost/Found and dead souls. "Sometimes the dark that gave his life/its cold satanic sheen would shift/ a little, and he saw himself/ floodlit and eloquent," writes the poet Hayden, speaking of this process. Malcolm's soul was a perfectly blank page to write the new intelligence upon, because Elijah's student was able to completely erase the horrible saga out of his advancing, forward trooping soul.*

---

*An apt student, Malcolm had total recall of everything Elijah taught him to say and repeat out loud.

He was perfect conversion material. And so Elijah was able to grow and groom a tree within ventriloquist Malcolm that went beyond even the Messenger's imagination, and beyond Malcolm's brightest dreams. It's an old story, too. The good teacher becomes known as excellent when his former student becomes a famous CEO, goes back to the high school, and tells all of the students (as he does before hundreds of gatherings each year) that were it not for Elijah X, I would not be standing where I am standing today. But when he says this at the high-school reunion, with Elijah in the crowd, instead of the old man being proud of his contribution to the success of the student, he rises up to say: "Yes, and I taught you everything you know." In studies of the transformation of the self, the good teacher gets known because of the famous former students. But the individual teacher is but one of the many influences along the way; and it was something remarkable in the individual that will out.

Without Elijah's teachings Malcolm might well have become a famous hood for the Mafia upon release from jail and thus been assassinated at the age of 39; or a hard-working cop in Harlem, who rises to the top, say as lieutenant, or captain, after a ten-year career of pursuing drug addicts and is killed by the syndicate because he knows too much and is too dangerous as captain over a district in Harlem at the age of 39.

In the old days, Elijah was capable of speaking for hours on end. He probably got away with it because his audiences perceived rightly or wrongly that he was revealing a completely new way of dealing with racism, religion, and reform amongst blacks in this society. They also probably felt that he was a divine man, divinely blessed with such important intelligence for the Negro, so practical on the one hand, and mythical on the other. So what if his voice was small and rather raspy and his looks less than grandly. What is it that Dilsey says when her daughter criticizes the undersized preacher from St. Louis in town to give the Easter Service sermon in Faulkner's *The Sound and the Fury*: "I've knowed de Lawd to use cruiser tools dan dat."

Elijah saw himself as the curious tool of God, or Allah being put to special use. On this level, he was genuinely humble, if not modest. That God would pick him up—this least of these—for a special charge of lifting the Blackman up to his proper stature was still baffling to Elijah, because he had absolutely no preparation for the task.

As a black writer I can appreciate something of what must have been working within his mind on this score. You start off from scratch as a writer (no pun intended). You never think that you have enough education, formal and informal; nor are you ever confident about the range of your experiences; and the richness of your inner life. You might read a lot, of course; in fact, it is quite by accident that you discover that you have the stirring yeast of talent. Usually the whole process is an out-growth from something that happens to you, in connection with your reading. It's the reading that inspires you to try your hand at a certain kind of story, using a set of experiences that you are familiar with. You rarely get any encouragement. Finally one day you sell a story; then you can win a local contest. All of the hundreds of people who said you were wasting your time are proven grossly wrong. You are redeemed twice. And you really do come to believe that you are especially blessed, endowed, or even gifted, when 10,000 or more people buy your books, and you win the praise of the critics. You have a source, and an inner glow, that is talent or genius and that was given to you by some higher power (or perhaps some accident of the gene pool). But you come to think of yourself as a writer. You are also talking about an enormous ego that must work alone without any recompense for years, before he or she gets any recognition.

Multiply this kind of saga a thousand fold in the case of a truly great writer, like Faulkner . . . or in this case under scrutiny: Elijah Poole Muhammad. So that by the time his nation-building program finally began to take off, Elijah had hundreds of small victories to show for his efforts; and by the mid-1950s and the 1960s (just as the movement that threatened most of his philosophical positions on race and democracy in America was reaching its zenith), the Nation of Islam was really soaring with influential force. If you were to have probed him as to whether he truly believed that he was the Messenger of Allah, or some especially blessed, chosen figure, at this time, doubtlessly he would have spat in your face: *Look at the evidence. See the empire for yourself, that Allah has blessed us. He raised me up from nothing in order that I might give the Blackman His Message.* Then he would point out the manifestations of that empire: the hundreds of mom-and-pop stories, the success of *Muhammad Speaks* with its readership reaching nearly 700,000 per week; the list of the mosques around the country numbering over 100; scores of farms, clothing stores, educational centers, and heath facilities. In praising what Allah (in the person of Master Fard Muhammad) blessed him to do, Elijah might recall Homer Barbee praising the Founder (and Bledsoe) for the evolvement of the college, in his Founders Day speech, in *Invisible Man.*

A personal memory: You certainly did not open your life up to most Muslims, nor did they seek this kind of friendship, which was fine with me. But on occasion every iron-clad code breaks down under the weight of the day in and day out social intercourse. I was talking with a PR man for the Nation one afternoon about the impending publication of my first novel, *There Is a Tree More Ancient Than Eden.* There had been some mention of the novel being accepted by Random House in Irv Kupcinet's column. The PR man wanted to know how long I had been working on the novel. I responsed about six years. He was silent for a moment. I guess I was hoping for a literary question. Then he turned to me and said: "In all things like this and the patience it takes to achieve a given goal, I think back to the Messenger, Brother editor, and how he worked on building this nation for over 35 years." And he went on and on. There was no way that you could not bring up a subject, or get involved in something as distant as literary pursuit, without the Messenger's achievement getting into the act. Yet in a calmer mood, later on, I came to think aloud that there is a connection between the patience needed to build a novel, and the time, and the patience needed, to build an enterprise of this magnitude. Maybe there is some linkage, too, in the kind of egocentric personalities needed to accomplish in either of these spheres.

* * *

The central quality of Elijah's face is pain, and his smile is a witness to it—pain so old deep and black that it becomes personal and particular only when he smiles.

—From *The Fire Next Time*, by
James Baldwin

Elijah could be quite grandfatherly and gentle. There was also something of the evil eye too, in the shifty glance he could spin out amid the weave of this smile he unfolded before your very eyes. If "sleep knits up the ravelled sleeve of care," as the nightmarish Macbeth tells us, then Elijah never knew a night of splendid slumber. His countenance always wore a mask shaped from the troubles he'd witnessed, or the trouble he had wrecked out upon the disbelievers amongst the faithful. The Honorable Elijah Muhammad was capable of working long hours, at a stretch—fourteen to sixteen hours—day after day, so that his obsessiveness for work met his magnificent obsession of building a nation within a nation, even though many held that we were all already in that condition, as a people. He was at the height of his powers when working thoughtfully and methodically with small groups of the faithful and, in turn, transforming them into leadership roles of ministers within the nation. In this kind of setting Elijah was most effective, domineering, and even powerful. I've seen this happen with certain professors. You'll meet them outside of the classroom and they appear to be nobodies. Probably are nobodies, too. But once you put them before that blackboard, or in a classroom, at the lectern, a different man is summoned forth.

Working, developing, and curating these small groups of ministers over the years, on an individual basis, Elijah Muhammad probably knew each one of them personally and their psychological profile intimately (enough to lift the fellow up and bring him back down). This personal knowledge and existential wisdom of penetrating the individual's weaknesses, particularly, and his strengths was the silent thunder of Elijah's many attributes for character building and character assessment. This intimate index into why an individual would need to surrender to the Nation of Islam placed the individual in the shaping hands of Muhammad, and he belonged to Elijah forevermore. The Honorable might be freeing the individual from the clutches of white racism, but he was dropping his yoke of discipline and servitude upon the neck of the wretch. And even though he probably did believe that the blackman was greatly benefited by becoming a Muslim, he also believed that no matter how successful the individual member of the faith might become (as, for example, Malcolm X who had carved a very considerable life on his own in the mind-set of thousands of young blacks), Elijah felt, I do believe, in his bones: *Fool, you could not have made it without me. And as long as you stand with me, nothing can harm you. Nor help you when and if the day comes, when I decided to drop you.* Indeed I'm paraphrasing something Elijah said about Malcolm, in this context.

These small groups were apparently an outgrowth of Fard's method of developing his ministery. Like Brother Tarrypin and the old inch worm that keeps inching along in African-American folklore, Elijah kept developing his small cadres slowly and meticulously. His patience was almost furious. He worked like combined precinct captain, on the one hand—learning all of your needs and developing a life within your life, for the life of the party—and a tutor on a one-on-one basis, going over and over a set of details, or lessons, or *teachings*, by the old Southern Negro method or rote memory. Because many of the blacks were still Southern Negroes in their ethos, in the early days of the movement, Elijah's Southern-based instincts were on the mark. But as blacks became more and more Yankee born and bred in the slums, unto the second generations, you needed someone who was closer to the bottomed-out havoc of that wayward experience—a person like Malcolm, who had actually died, gone through a period in the hole underground in the hell of his nightmarish soul, and been reborn in Islam. Elijah had a tough life. The leanness of it, the years in jail, the many personal maladies of health he faced were but a portion of his many trials on earth; but he was never self-destructive the way Malcolm had been. He was never violence prone, and a criminal against his people the way Malcolm was once upon a time. He had never been a pimp, a body and soul hustler, and dope pusher the way Malcolm had lived. Elijah was too much of a family man and too much of a Southern gentleman to go this route. His personal hang-ups were of a different kind.

Elijah was also a "master" of reverse psychology in terms of penetrating the individual's weaknesses. But he had in his direct arsenal the old Southern Negro's verities of thrift, commonsense, patience, story-telling, a long memory of racial hurts, a way of keeping everything in and resolving all things within the muscles of inner strength. Learn to out-think your enemy have a basic mistrust for the ultimate intentions of white men, even those few who might do you what seems to be a good turn. Maintain a basic mistrust on a private and individual basis for all people until proven different and then retest them again and again. His was a deeply held index into all that has gone wrong with the Negro in this country and how to counteract it, on the one hand, and how to manipulate it, on the other.

Because he was a man always building character out of the profound failures about him, Elijah was also keenly aware of how close his followers were to the precipice of destruction. One false step on this slippery slab for even the best of our Nation, and they will go tumbling down, right back into the slimey pits of the dead world. Therefore, you had to always be on guard, against your neighbor and yourself. Ultimately you didn't trust anybody, and particularly your own mind, unless it reflected the latest word from Elijah. For Elijah had given lift to the people nobody else cared about. Why wouldn't they trust their new-found lives to their Savior?

Like many leaders, Elijah ultimately believed that his flock of grown-ups were really children. They could be trusted to take very, very little into their own hands. And if they did, they would go cart-wheeling off into peril. He was a man fitfully obsessed with what he was doing, all of those years, awaiting his time, in Allah's time, to come and for the white man to fall (the white power structure, at least, doing everything wrong, or wronging the Negro, in every way imaginable and playing right into the hands of the master-builder, Elijah). Like a driven artist, Elijah used only what he needed; and, of course, he had his blind sides. For some of the materials he discarded all around him had to do with his narrowness of vision and his ill-focused lens on the changing life of American society, amongst blacks. Yet frankly, given what Elijah had built up, he couldn't use these "counter-revolutionary" occurrences. For example, the whole of the Civil Rights Freedom Movement just swept by Elijah, but there was absolutely no way he could accommodate to it, given the hellishness he envisioned about midstream American life and the evil nature of the whites. *He who rides the tiger, may not dismount* Chinese folklore instructs.

And as for the hard-working black integrationists who had labored so long to pull down the racial barriers to a free and open society for African-Americans? Well, frankly, it was difficult to give Elijah more than a passing nod of respect for what he had accomplished for a segment of the black underclass. If you had worked hard all of your life for Civil Rights and against the racism so epitomized by the Ku Klux Klan and the Nazi party, how could you not spurn Elijah, when he invited leaders of the White Supremacy group to the 1964 Savior's Day Convention in Chicago and praised them as forthright white men just as the Freedom Train was climbing to the top of the mountain and not to a perilous, slippery precipice. For Movement people of this ilk, Elijah had slept through the Freedom Struggle.

Many dimensions of the Black Power Movement, which his organization in certain ways helped to ignite, vaulted over Elijah's head.

The growing power of black women, as dominant forces, in all phases of black life found Elijah numb to the news. Given the fixed chauvinism of Elijah's Nation, he couldn't awaken to the Feminist Movement. Probably he would have said that it was the devil white woman's movement. Best place for the black woman was back in the house and behind her man.

The leadership potential of the African-American woman—remained totally excluded from the power structure and the decision-making process of Elijah's Nation. Elijah recalls those Southern white men, who placed a wreath of protection and a yoke of enslavement about their wives as a form of a necklace, amid the illusion of freedom they cast over the claustrophobia of the females' existence. To all of this Elijah would have probably said: *Well, Brother Forrest, I see you are still brainwashed. Aren't you aware of the way in which the white man (devil) has always lifted the black woman over the black man to keep the black man down, and at war with her. He has used her as his hand maiden and his whore to keep our black brothers down. She must be cleaned up and lifted up, but in the proper way, by the black man, not the Devil, Brother.*

I am referring to Elijah's way of way of playing off the leaders within his flock, as a loving but manipulative father plays off his children, one against another . . . *I have done everything for you; if it had not been for me, you might be dead. How can you ever forget that time when I saved you from certain death? What have you done for me, lately? How could you do what you are currently doing behind my back, to undermine me, and not only me, but the family, and the race?* Elijah saw his experience as metaphor and his role as symbolic father over his wayward flock. For even after they were reborn in Islam, they were still wayward and in need of constant chastisement. I am the father, you are all my children (Malcolm types as well), and you never get too old for the rod of my wrath. You are advancing finally under my direction and tutelage, but you are still children. For not only had he given them life, he had returned them from the dead!

Doris Kearns, one of the biographers who had direct access to Lyndon Baines Johnson, tells a memorable story of wandering about the ranch one day with the former President. They spotted a Negro woman and a young boy, probably her son, standing near a fence, looking at some monument. The former President goes over and explains what it all means and what he had done to help uplift the Negro's cause, when suddenly he turned on the boy and told him that he might have become President, himself, one day, "if you hadn't of rioted." The child, of course, didn't know what in the world the President was talking about in terms of the guilt trip this old white man was trying to lay upon his shoulders; nor what he (the lad) had to do with rioting.

The President, who had every reason to be proud of his work in getting major Civil Rights legislation passed, was guilty of blaming the victim. Lyndon Johnson saw his work as central to preparing the blacks for real freedom, even leadership, but in the final analysis, they were still children, spoiling things for themselves, and not following the road Daddy had opened up for them, by rioting, looting, and burning. Elijah, too, believed in this kind of larger-than-life metaphorical idea of his symbolic action in "freeing" the so-called Negro into a higher state of consciousness and into an awareness of his destiny and the "tricknology" of the white man. But he felt unappreciated by people like his "son" Malcolm (and Negroes who still didn't listen to his clarion call to "do something for self," but would listen to Malcolm's improvisation on those very same words, borrowed from his master).

At another level—with regard to Malcolm—Elijah was in a position not dissimilar to that of Johnson and J.F.K. People praised the glamorous sparkling President; younger blacks (whites, too) knew only of Malcolm's rhetorical rage, which they really could dig. Yet, it was Johnson who had worked for Civil Rights legislation, as a majority leader, and it was L.B.J. who had labored to get the major Civil Rights legislation passed from 1964–1967—and not "that young hero," as Johnson liked satirically to call the late President. Elijah labored in the vineyard for thirty years, bringing the many strands of his philosophy for Nation-building into fruition. But it was that upstart Malcolm who was regarded as the leader.

If the former prisoner Malcom Little had crawled back he could have been redeemed or reborn into Elijah's care and keeping. This would have been a great victory for Elijah's campaign for humbling the undisciplined; and it would have had a great impact upon the followers. For, if Malcolm, who had become so big in the eyes of the world, is thusly disciplined and then comes back crawling after his suspension, the Messenger's power is greater in the eyes of Allah than we believers ever dreamed. But Malcolm had outgrown the father. Few fathers can deal with this situation (even when they claim differently). If Elijah needed him, then it would appear that Malcolm needed Elijah and the organization and the Messenger's organizational skills even more. Malcolm couldn't organize anything. The excitement of his particular form of charisma was his genius to draw people out to hear him tell the story and indict white America, and to get blacks excited about the Nation of Islam, as an alternative route for the liberation. But what to do about the audience of Lost/Found have left the stadium or the rally in the park? There you needed the organizational apparatus to regiment all of that yeasty energy so ready for change, who have been stirred by the word.

Even when Malcolm started his own organization there was none of this kind of skilled instrumentality, in the day in and day out, from the bottom up building going on that Malcolm had left behind with the Nation of Islam. Most of the people in the new organization represented the discontented bourgeois nationalists. There were few foot soldiers in Malcolm's Organization of African Unity; the kind of people who will go out and "fish" for souls day in and day out. And these were not the skills of Malcolm X, either.

A sentence from that all-time great phrase-minting-maker, Jesse Jackson, throws some light—for me at least—on the essential attributes of Malcolm's *condition*, as a leader.

Speaking of himself—*naturally*—Jesse has said: "I am a tree shaker, not a jelly-maker." How aptly this description, in shorthand of course, applied to Malcolm. But the jelly-makers are what we need; we seem to have a national penchant for, and an abundance of tree-shakers (and rhetorical rattlers). This was what Elijah saw, preached, and lived by—build, build, build. Ultimately, of course, in a more harmonious mood, you need both; and you need a balance.

Elijah needed another form of Malcolm's charisma and his linkage to the newly doomed urban black males whose numbers were growing by leaps and bounds. Just as they didn't have a *feel* for Dr. King's nonviolence and were more attracted to the Black Panther Party and other eye-for-an-eye black movements, they also felt somewhat uncomfortable, to say the least, with Elijah's self-sacrifice program and his commandments to self-discipline, which actually were supposed to bring on a state of inner peace within the individual. If they were to accept discipline, it must be the soldier's discipline, in preparation for war. They also felt that the Muslims were too mythic and separate from the America they wanted to shake violently up now; they did not wait on Allah to bring the power structure down. Still others wanted to exploit and hold America directly accountable. For certain facets of the wayward young, the Black Muslims seemed too far removed from the vital juices of the soul of the race.

In the Muslim mythos, the white man was created by a black scientist. That idea seemed too off the wall and was a form of blaming the victim, too. The answer was simple. Blacks didn't need yet another religion; they needed some guns!

But Malcolm could speak the rhetoric of the new frontier of African-American alienation, on the one hand, and the rhetoric of the disposed, Bigger Thomas-types brewing in our ghettoes on the other. *And then, along the way, show them the way to Islam.* Obviously, this was a role Elijah could not play. He had become mythical and dead in the imagination of the young long before his actual death. Yet, it also must be said that things move so fast in America and that Malcolm was not on the block day in and day out. But because he could reflect light upon their story, by telling the outrages of his own saga Malcom was the living saint of their imaginations; he had turned their story into his story, and his story into their story, thereby transforming it all into a kind of mythos. Malcolm, as Elijah saw it, was out there high flying on his own, developing his own mythos. He didn't mean to do this, of course, at least not on a conscious level. For he was always giving praise to the Honorable, Fard, and Allah—the holy trinity.

A character at a banquet in James Alan McPherson's short story "Widows and Orphans," picks up the kind of impact a Malcolm would have upon the unusual within the lost down in the hood. "I say to you that out of twenty junkies on the corner of 243 and Cypress, there is likely to be one with a little backbone, and a little imagination. If he can free himself, that is the man for the other junkies to watch. What he chooses to reify—and what he selects to value—remains implanted in the imaginations of the others. They will not forget him, no matter how forcefully they dismiss what he does. But achieving this image is a matter of discipline, and also a matter of love. . . ."

A DIVIDED NATION

I do not pretend to know all of the intricacies of why Elijah split the scene in Detroit shortly after Master Fard—his intellectual father—"vanished," but enough intriguing information is known about an impending civil war amongst the chosen for us to form a reflective intelligence report concerning the state of today's Nation (or should I say the divided Nation).

Apparently there were two camps of interpretation over *Master (I wonder where Elijah got that from?)* Fard's meaning and the direction he wanted the Black Muslims to take. It seems clear that Fard did appoint or anoint one Elijah Poole as head of the study group he formed in the slums of Detroit, when he wasn't selling his silks. Also, at this time (1934) Master Fard told Elijah to return to his former slave master, the white man, the slave man, Poole. In place of that slave name, Master Fard gave Elijah the Islamic name of "Karriem." Still later (specifically how all of this was made manifest I certainly don't know, but Muslim lore holds that some divine visitation occurred), Elijah was renamed once again, this time he was proclaimed, Muhammad.

We do know that two factions had evolved in Detroit. The one Elijah led had a definite racial agenda for its program of up-lift and an ideological interpretation of Islam. (The Devil business, for example.) The other faction declined any emphasis on a racial agenda in its interpretation of Islam and opted for a much more aggressive spiritual revelation of Islam and the holy Koran. A leader with Elijah's drive, intelligence, and vision did not emerge from their ranks. This was the Depression and blacks needed something with more of a substantial program of up-lift than simply another religious cult. Elijah realized this.

Many of the Fard devotees who interpreted him as a religious Savior and not an ideologue ultimately became peace-loving Sunni Muslims. At this time, from all that I have been able to cull out of the oral bulletins of the past, Black Muslim life got so hot in Detroit that Elijah finally came to Chicago (a city not known for its solitude) in order to evolve the solidarity he sought for the rigorous birth of his nation.

I am intrigued by how all of this recalls the phases of factionalism that resulted shortly after Elijah Muhammad's death in 1975 on the eve of Savior's Day, February 25th (the birthdate of W. A. D. Fard); and the interpretations that finally put the Nation where it is today: *divided.* Wallace Deen Muhammad—the next to the youngest son of Elijah—took the reins after Muhammad's death. Muslim mythos holds that just before he vanished, Fard himself proclaimed that one day the infant Wallace, whom "the Savior" had named (and even wrote his name on Elijah's door), would lead the Nation. For years, Wallace carried himself as something of a Prince in Exile, coming in and going out of the Nation, according to his Father's will and whim.

One of Wallace's first acts after his father's death was an attempt to mend fences with Louie Farrakhan, the Iman of the New York Mosque. Farrakhan moved to Chicago in order to show forth his good faith in the new leadership—the Muslims brothers could work together in the name of Allah and in service to the up-lift of the Blackman. But this brotherly embrace didn't work out.

The incandescent, super-star ego of Farrakhan's was too explosive to hold still for the peaceful manner of the lackluster, programless Wallace. More importantly, Minister Farrakhan (whose name means "Minister of Fire") wanted to return to the Devil-watch interpretation of Islam, partially in order to fire the Black Muslims up. He wanted to relive the fiery agenda set forth by Elijah. He soon proved that he was Elijah's true intellectual son. And he cunningly exploited this idea to the hilt so that the perceived line of authority went: Fard, as Allah: Muhammad as the Son (now deceased, therefore, canonized in the Muslim mythos and given legendary powers, now because his word, as sacred script, could be called upon as The Word from the Old Man of the Mountain no longer amongst is in bodily form, but alive in the words and deeds he left behind for us to follow). Farrakhan himself was now the fiery-tongued Holy Spirit, or interpretator, of Elijah's words in our day, especially since his biological son had virtually abandoned the teachings and letter of the Messenger's word.

Toward this end, Farrakhan started up a newspaper—after he split with Wallace's Nation of Islam—and commenced his own cult, called The Final Call, which took his name from the over-line heading Elijah employed when he first started publishing his column in Negro newspapers around the country, long before there was a *Muhammad Speaks*. Farrakhan even purchased the mansion Elijah built and lived in before his death.

He has tried to revive many of the self-help enterprises Elijah started. He also reinstituted the elite corps of the Fruit of Islam, that tough, honor guard of disciplined male "soldiers" of the Nation. With Elijah's vision brimming inside of him, Farrakhan also believed that the African-Americans needed that crackle of divine spark mixed in with the furor of nationalism in order to truly awaken the most defeated of men on the black bottom. Meantime, the meek and goodly Wallace seemed eager to put a wrecking ball to the racialism in Elijah's philosophical projection of Islam. He sought a fundamentally religious interpretation of Islam, emphasizing that Islam means "Peace." The drive to build and the appetite to develop an economic base seemed lost in the new order of spiritual space. Wallace had none of Farrakhan's rhetorical glamor; nor the trickster's snake-oil sophistry. Wallace seemed bent on winning respectability among other ethnic groups and he instituted a Unity Day March, in which many faiths trooped through downtown Chicago, celebrating a kind of ecumenical spirit, which could have awakened his father from the grave, as the saying goes.

Just as Elijah's fiery group flourished (because they had a program and a hard-driving leader) and the Detroit faction became virtually invisible, the Farrakhan movement seemed to be prospering, and

Wallace's faction appeared to be fading or splintered off into a mild, politically ineffectual order.

Once you split the tongue of Louie Farrakhan from the rhetorical rantings, he is mouthing a strict constructionist message to the letter of the conservative program. He believes in those ideas that his father-figure Elijah hailed: self-help; dress in a stylish but modest attire; live an abstemious life, shun alcohol and tobacco. Avoid the pig at all price. Promote family values; build within your own community. Black women must be protected, but they must play a much more muted role—as maintainers of the home and mothers of the Nation—than they do in the larger society. But here, too, Farrakhan has opened up more than Elijah, realizing that one of the failures of Elijah in the long run was his inability to attract the sprawling middle class and the cadres of women, who have impressive jobs, good incomes, and a potential for leadership. Women have been "allowed" an expanded role.

Before he came under the spell of Malcolm and then Elijah, Farrakhan was a Calypso singer. Later Louis X recorded a song called "The White Man's Heaven is the Black Man's Hell," which was quite popular in certain circles. Verbally, Farrakhan's the spitting image of Malcolm X (if anything he's a lot smoother than Elijah's spokesman) and the Messenger encouraged his career the way he did Malcolm's. For if both Louie Farrakhan and Malcolm Little were looking for father-figures, Elijah was surely looking for charismatic sons to take forth the baton of his mission-obsessed vision and fly with it: *but don't try to fly too high, as Daedalus warned Icarus.*

In the early 1970s Farrakhan took over where Malcolm had once stood in the eyes of the Muslim watchers; for from 1964 to 1975 Malcolm's name was equated with a form of dirt and not to be mentioned within the walls of the Nation. He was generally referred to when it was necessary to mention his name at all, as "the double XX." It wasn't until Wallace's reign that the good name of Malcolm was rehabilitated. Outsiders could see what insiders saw but would not admit, that Farrakhan was Malcolm all over again. By 1972, Farrakhan was high riding and riding high for a fall. He was almost tripped up by the gossip-mongers and the jealousy peddlers who had brought the loyal, faithful Malcolm down, who had loved his master not wisely, but too well. The well-read and self-educated Malcolm might have reflected upon his worshipful homage to Elijah, as overpowering his service to Allah. What is it that Wolsey says in Shakespeare's *Henry the Eighth*: "Had I but served my God with half the zeal/I served my king, He would not in mine age/ Have left me naked to my enemies."

Although Farrakhan doesn't have Malcolm's high IQ, he has a lot more commonsense and savvy than Malcolm did, and was able on several occasions to flank those who sought his downfall in the early 1970s. He knew first hand the terrible price his "big-brother" Malcolm had paid losing face with the Lamb of God.

By the late 1960s Elijah wasn't able to check on his ministers the way he had once upon a time. Farrakhan started making anti-Semitic remarks about the Jews controlling the media. It is known that around 1972 *The Protocols of Elders of Zion* could be purchased at the bookstore in the Harlem Mosque.

ELIJAH'S LEGACY: A GESTALT

Recently a reporter for the *Miami Herald* questioned me about the successes Farrakhan's cult of the Nation is having in the war on drugs in Washington, actually reclaiming a neighborhood under drug dealers' control.

I tried to explain to the reporter how the group Elijah founded believed that the black man had a special relationship to Allah.

A local leader of Farrakhan's group now called Lost-Found Nation of Islam in the West, Dr. Abdul Alim Muhammad said: "We say we are successful because we represent a moral force that's commanding and compelling."

The removal of dealers of crack and cocaine in the murder capital by the patrolling Muslims and members of the elite cadre of the Fruit of Islam recalls to mind how powerful were the Muslims in New York City, when the confrontation was between the Fruit of Islam and the New York police. Yet in both cases the Muslims never fired a shot. Now the battleground is more internal. For it is very difficult for the drug dealers to ply their trade, or to recruit, when the Black Muslims are patrolling (and recruiting), mainly because many of the Muslims were defeated by cocaine dealers once upon a time and are able to handle these new drug dealers with a kind of moral superiority and to stand as powerful role models for the young who are tempted to take on the life of drugs. There is this muscular, cleaned-up, karate-chopping, no nonsense, highly disciplined black man, who came from the turf, and is determined to reclaim the turf. I am the wretch, I was there, I suffered. This is but a fragment of the moral authority and weight of their presence in the reality and in the imagination of the young; and why they are so convincing—and least in these initial steps—and why Malcolm X had such an immediate impact in his day in dealing with those who have been so dislocated by the drug culture. Equally important is the kind of apparatus that Elijah developed, and it is apparently operating in Washington. For example, the Muslims opened a clinic and started up a drug rehabilitation program. R. A. Zaldivar, the journalist who interviewed me reports that "several Muslim families have moved into apartments once used by the dopers." Not surprisingly, attendance at the local mosque has gone up.

I tried to explain to the reporter that their appeal has to do with the Black Muslims being able to create a sense of manhood in a group of men who have been completely destroyed. This resurrection is something of a gestalt, in which the total man (and woman, too) is addressed, spiritually and intellectually. The emotional part (which ecstatic furor of redemption plays in many Black Protestant churches) is muted and reshapen into a euphoria that is part black nationalism, part black superiority, and part self-help, as this example in Washington reveals.

Reclaiming of the "dead" by shock treatment is the supernatural part of the movement, and unfortunately is the racist aspect of the Black Muslims rehabilitation program. Like all forms of racism it is based upon the idea that my group is superior to your inferior group. But the Black Muslims have never moved on any white folks violently in this country. They may practice civil defense, but they have never practiced racial offense. The particulars of their militancy and their military posture is never addressed, in terms of what they don't do. Dr. Abdul Alim Muhammad told reporters Zaldivar: "What we have is mostly ordinary people going about their business (now) . . . I'm trying to deemphasize the militaristic aspect."

Ultimately, in studying the rise of different ethnic groups—and nationalism within sectionalism—we need to look at the portion of nationalism to racism within these groups that drove them to achieve and to overcome prejudice. Certainly nationalism is deeply rooted in other groups—Irish, Polish, Italian—and often times the racism in these individual groups came out only when a Negro moved into the neighborhood and then suddenly the battlelines between the white ethnics fell back and they all came together around the central theme of "get the nigger." But some species of nationalism is absolutely essential to the political rise of any ethnic group in this country.

There was, of course, the nationalism of the frontier, in which a whole ethos evolved. The movement westward—54–40-or fight—had a very real racialism in its bottom line and so did Manifest Destiny. The confederation out of the secessionist South was founded in a kind of nationalism and racism, based on specialness of the Southern experience, and rage to maintain the economic bounty carved from the bodies of the slaves. The South was determined to become a separate nation, in fact. The right-wing factions that arose during the 1960s, the Birchites, for example, were evidences of this meshing of white nationalism and racism, once you cracked their doctrine.

As long as we view Elijah's movement against this backdrop and the relationship of nationalism to racism in America, then he will get a fair hearing historically, not better, not worse. But that's not enough; he must also be judged by the lives he saved by dint of the obsessive faith he conjured, and the self-help programs he developed. All of this must be placed into the equation; because after all America didn't extend its noble hand of up-lift and opportunity to this peculair branch of the defeated black American, but rather cast them below the demarkation of humanity, where they could not be seen. Elijah came along and extended to them a life-raft. From everything we've seen with the contemporary crack-cocaine scene, for all of the holes in that life-raft, it still beats nothing at all; and it still has its uses, long after Elijah himself, has split the scene.

LUMINOSITY

A CONVERSATION WITH
RALPH ELLISON

"In a city of a million and a half blacks, I'll bet there aren't 100 who know or care about the Art of writing, in the way you insist on using that term, Forrest. It's not relevant, nor is Ellison, I am afraid," the Chicago street corner friend declared.

Yet I had just spun my friend down with the joyous news that we had a pending interview with Ralph Ellison, the man generally considered the greatest living black writer in the Western World. My friend's dual reaction to the Ellison news expresses a not uncommon ambivalence, for he was actually very proud that we had obtained an interview with the man who wrote, according to 200 top critics in 1965, the most important novel published in this country, since World War II, *Invisible Man* (1952).

* * *

It is because we have had such great writers in the past, that a writer is driven far out, past where he can go, out to where no one can help him.

—Ernest Hemingway

FORREST: Could you explain what you believe to be the role of literature, the contribution of literary art to a people over the long haul?
ELLISON: Literature is a form of art wherein Time can be reduced to

manageable proportions; and the diversity of experience can be assembled to show an immediate pattern: to conserve memory, focus energies, ideals and to give us some idea of the cost and glories of those ideals. Art unites the people, and extracts that which is meaningful, rendering through its attention to details, which unite the members of a group, into a concord of sensibilities . . . Literature is a form through which a group recognizes its values—values from without and values from within . . .

Ellison feels that because so much of the fiction by black and white authors is written in terms of clichés, not the humanity of the Afro-American, it often goes "from Sambo to Nat Turner, which of course means, you've left out most of us." His faith in the ranging possibilities of the novel form have to do with its "resonance, because through that form you can deal with complexities, but it exacts a price; it demands that the writer refuse the easy opportunity to publize or make public power out of his perspectives of the world." Much of the psyche the writer brings to his desk has to do with the "tendency to deny the humanity and the diversity of slaves—that a slave was a man and possessed complexities . . . And what of the slaves who were skilled? That always gets left out."

FORREST: "What constitutes the universal literary shaping and terrain of the writer's kind of mind"?

ELLISON: I suspect it is the type of mind, while not losing sight of the factual nature of reality, is obsessed with extracting those characters, nuances, and rhetoric, which as he recombines them in terms of literary forms, he conveys what he considers most important in life . . . The life of the imagination leads him to combine those images he has extracted from reality. The writer trains the imagination by reading imaginative writers, reading biography and autobiography of certain writer's lives and what they have to say about their own work.

We talked of the meaning of Hemingway for a time, and he said that Hemingway was a writer who employed the organizing principal of how the many task-memories of his life fitted into the vocation of his life, fiction . . . journalism for instance.

FORREST: What is the role of reading in the shaping of the writer's mind?

ELLISON: The sense of form comes from a great deal of reading, so that a variety of structures are constantly informing the intelligence centers or nourishing the imagination.

FORREST: It is a highly associative mind, is it not?

ELLISON: Yes. And the writer develops a sense of the literary possibility and a special alertness, in many areas, for the seasons and their changes to a football game, and of course the drama inherent in both.

Ellison sees the processes of the novel, at its best, as an "attempt to make an eloquent form, so that the sections are true." He is constantly elaborating on the many themes that came up in the course of our conversation. He places a high value on good, meaningful conversation, and as he shapes and hones his thinking, he often makes a statement so noble and memorable, that the statement itself, is literature. "Art has to do with the process of reaching down into repressed values and giving it some luminosity," he says.

FORREST: Would you discuss the role of rewriting in the craft? Perhaps it would be meaningful for the very young writer, if you would?

ELLISON: For me writing is a rewriting. I sketch out an idea and it tends to grow. The image of blowing on a flame comes to mind here. The process of the novel has to do with the attempt to make an eloquent form, so that the sections are true.

He warns the immediately successful young writers "to be careful lest you are praised for the wrong things."

Underneath all of the conversation is the quest for the mastery of craft, discipline and the continuity of memory within diverse history . . . And underneath that, is something very old, timeless and absolutely Black and it has to do with the way a Black drop-out uncle, who has become very successful in his own business, might say to a young Nephew, home from college for the summer (taking the map away from the student) and declaring: 'Now Nephew let me show you how to properly scrub that floor. There is a right way and a wrong way to do everything. And I'm not about to allow you to run the family (race) business until you've mastered all phases of it—lest you give me the business and yourself the shaft.'

* * *

. . . And another kind of relative, underneath that: "Son, after I'm gone I want you to keep up the good fight, I never told, but our life is a war and I have been a traitor all my born days, a spy in the enemy's country ever since I give up my gun back in the Reconstruction. Live with your head in the lion's mouth. I want you to overcome 'em with yeses, undermine 'em with grins, agree 'em to death and destruction, let 'em swoller you till they vomit or bust wide open." They thought the old man had gone out of his mind. He had been the meekest of men. The younger children were rushed from the room, . . . "Learn it to the younguns," he whispered fiercely; then he died.

—From *Invisible Man*

He is profoundly concerned with the escalating crisis in our schools. Part of the problem he believes, has to do with the "teacher's capacity to maintain a sense of hope in his vocation." The teacher must believe in the miracle of education, Ellison said. "The intelligence of our young people is there. But the teachers must orient and motivate the young and present them with viable models to follow. But when you glamourize the pimp and the prostitute on the one hand and make the man who works hard for a living and the craftsmen seem insignificant to the life of the community, you are building a terrible situation."

FORREST: I have been personally shocked and dismayed about the way a man like Gordon Parks was taken in by the hustling joke rhetoric of Eldrige Cleaver, who represents a terrible image for young people to follow. And the general waywardness of Parks, who is a great photographer, in his current movie-making fiascos.

ELLISON: But you must understand Mr. Forrest that because a person has standards in one area of culture, doesn't mean that it is going to be carried over in other areas, at all.

But in Ellison there is continuity of standards across the board. He ranges in first-rate lecturing from the impact of the U.S. Civil War upon literature to the heavy terrain of the mighty Russian novels: he has written the best study of the top black painter, Romare Bearden, and the finest panoramic view of the musician Charlie Parker; he has supported himself by building whole hi-fi systems; Ellison is one of the very real experts on U.S. jazz living today, he was a first rate trumpeter. Virtuosity of craft is a hallmark in his life.

Ellison is very sensitive to the forms merchandising of social crisis takes, and how this is all reflected within the larger reviberations of society and those who play on society's hunger for that which is novel, or the novelities syndrome. He comes down hard on certain sociologists of the last decades, "who have become the power brokers and experts on our dilemma: they spell it out, how it is, and where it is." Moynihan, for instance, with his 'benign neglect theories,' which of course were preceded by his notion of the destroyed, ruptured black family and the black matriarchy.

The very narrow and small-minded black press comes in for a wholesome analysis from Ellison. He stated: "There is every reason why the black newspapers should be cracking the great stories. We should be the people to affirm the people's right to know." For instance, Ellison explained, "It was Adam Clayton Powell, not the reform Democrats—Mrs. Roosevelt's group—who broke the power of Carmine De Sapio, in Tammy Hall in New York. You don't need the white newspapers to do this."

Ellison was referring to a slant on the news that the Black news media might have used when De Sapio was released from prison. He was referring to much more of course; he was talking about a whole way of approaching the news, a whole shape of the reporter-writer's mind.

FORREST: You have spoken of the possible uses of folkart in the sermon. But what is the process, the metamorphosis that goes into remaking a speech or sermon into Art?

ELLISON: It is a blending of forms: church, congregation, and drama. It is involved with re-birth and transcendence . . . It is involved with themes of consciousness of characters; theology and any other literary consideration.

Ralph Ellison is actually a very easy man to interview. I do not use a tape recorder. We are sitting in the front room of his large apartment. There are many fine pieces of African sculpture and Romare Bearden paintings across from where we are sitting. There are thousands of books in his Riverside Drive apartment. But it is not the lavish pad many have described; rather it is the well-lived-in apartment of a writer who is a cultured man. Different from many other black writers, Ellison lives in a building that is basically black.

Even his rambling is controlled, and part of his search for the right word, or phrase, just as he says the life of the imagination of the writer must be, whereas fantasy is more "life-dreaming." There is that kind of precision. And although he has been asked all of these questions hundreds of times before, in the hundreds of lectures he has given, Ellison re-creates each question, as he once again tests and re-examines his thinking about the world.

A hard-headed and enormously proud man, Ellison surprisingly is always in search of clarity. It is related, one suspects, to his obsession with hitting the highest mark in literature, in his private work, and to make reality (which is constantly shifting, yet ever constant for him) clean and true and just. And in this sense he is also a very humble man, before the great ranges of "felt-life" experiences that he has touched, and for those things that are awesome, or that he doesn't know about. Ralph Ellison is one of the most river-deep militant race men I have ever met. His very soul is anchored to black pride and excellence. He is likely to use the word Negro, as he does black . . . Yet his pride-filled pronounciation for the Afro-American is Nee-GROW. The performance of Alvin Ailey Dancers makes him weep, because of the baptizing, compelling, memories it evokes and affirms. He has developed an epic file of memories, and he always relates questions posed to those memories. The public memories are recalled with much of the same zeal, humor, or fury that he brings to many of his own personal memories. But when he speaks of his mother—whom he apotheosized—the ringing tragedy that he feels over her death, at the hands of an incompetent Negro medic is telling, with regard to his fury about excellence. "Because you see, Mr. Forrest, this was a man who did not do his homework, and the consequence of all of this incompetence at every level, is indeed life destroying."

Peripheral, perhaps to this segment of the conversation was the joy he expressed over the celebration of the black woman as depicted by Miss Judith Jamison, and her tribute to the all-black women in her dance-solo rendering of "Cry," in the Alvin Ailey troupe program.

Ellison is married to a black woman, who is highly devoted to him and his work.

Literature and the humanities have disciplined and ordered that fundamental fires and passion of his days. But in his call for an understanding of the continuity of history he understands that life is based in tragic rhythms, and movements.

He is a man bent on artistic deliverance, who accepts the fundamental role of literature as an agent that renders harmony and lucidity out of the ever-constant fires of chaos in man, and in the ever erupting world about him.

LUMINOSITY FROM
THE LOWER FREQUENCIES

I should like to discuss certain intellectual, cultural, and historical influences upon Ralph Ellison's sense of the hero's character-in-process and the structure of the major chapters throughout his monumental novel, *Invisible Man*. Several influences come to mind: Kenneth Burke, Lord Raglan, Dostoevski, and Faulkner, as well as the artistic and jazz-like rendering of folkloric sources.

From the literary critic Burke, Ellison came to see the possibility of using a formula to structure a chapter. Burke held that a pattern could be employed to achieve character-in-process progression through the formula of *purpose, passion,* and *perception:* Each chapter begins with a *purpose* for the hero, but then much of the action of the middle section involves a struggle, or *passion,* over this *purpose,* or quest. Out of this mix or confrontation with others and the self, the hero comes away with a heightened *perception,* a keener awareness about his life, so that a metamorphosis, or rebirth, is implied. But these moments are stages of his processing into life, and the cycle, once completed, unleashed new problems and struggles.

Another literary influence on *Invisible Man* came from Lord Raglan, whose seminal book *The Hero* argues that a constant pattern of biographical data defines the lives of the heroes of tradition. The heroes Raglan calls forth run a gamut from Oedipus Rex to Elijah, Zeus, Orpheus, and Robin Hood. The pattern traces some twenty-two steps from birth to death. But the central constant in Raglan's pattern of heroic dimension is this: that the hero dies, goes through a life underground, and is reborn. Raglan's concept meshes neatly with Burke's formula of *purpose, passion,* and *perception.* For instance, the passion, or conflict, is quite similar to the turmoil in the mental underground and all of the attendant agonies. The idea of a heightened *perception* can be linked to Raglan's concept of rebirth, or even redemption in the Christian sense, and to discovery and self-recognition in the Aristotelian sense.

In the major chapters of his novel, Ellison—a jazz trumpeter who studied musical composition—orchestrates and improvises upon an introductory theme raised through a character at the beginning of a chapter. And he ends the chapter on an upbeat thematic moment (sometimes with an enriching, elusive literary statement, that speaks for the chapter and the intelligence of the novel as a whole "at the lower frequencies") which stands in opposition to the opening thematic idea. Our sense of luminosity is heightened with the hero's, because of the sweeping poles or polar distances traversed from the beginning to the end. These are mini-odysseys of purpose, passion, and perception.

Ellison's arrangement of characters and themes standing in during confrontational moments forms a constant source of instruction, as we see the hero's character-in-process evolve and the novel evolve; and it helps the reader to see how these apparently oppositional forces are really quite closely connected. This device recalls anthropologist Levi-Strauss's concept of *thesis, counterthesis, synthesis.* And it is related to Dostoevski's uses of *doubling* and of character. One way of looking at doubling is to see it as a blending of opposites—characters who stand in sharp opposition to each other and yet have much in common.

The novel abounds with instances of this Dostoevskian doubling. There is for example the Norton/Trueblood pairing—a one-to-one confrontation, with the Oedipal desire/act forging a linkage between the rich, white, blue-blood philanthropist, Norton, and the poor, black, uneducated peasant farmer, Jim Trueblood. In Trueblood's dream, we discover an abundance of underground images indicating that Trueblood lusts for power in the real world as much as the powerful Norton lusts for the body of his own daughter—behind the monument of money he has donated in her honor to the school. Another form of Dostoevskian doubling occurs in the reverberating manner in which characters in apparent oppositional quest, status, or station are paired by a theme at completely different stages and times.

For instance, the theme of *eloquence*, its manipulation, uses, and misuses, links the tall, Lincoln-like Hambro, mouthpiece for the Communist-like Brotherhood, with the spokesman-versifier for the Negro college and the American white way, the blind, Founder-celebrating minister. Homer Barbee. Short and ugly like Homer, Barbee gives a high-priest choral arrangement and tribal eulogy for the Founder that sounds like Whitman praising Abe Lincoln (note Ellison's parody on the great Whitman's grand blindness to Abe's angularity, his blemishes, his body-and-soul torment over slavery, his complexity of motives. Now these two high-powered word-artists-cum-magicians, in turn, represent two power-mad, master tricksters. For Hambro illuminates the enslaving dogma espoused by the one-eyed Cyclops. Brother Jack, *Head White Man in Charge* (HWMC) of the Brotherhood. And as Hambro attempts to drop the illuminating (but really enshrouding, and blinding) veil of "understanding" over the student-hero's eyes, he also blinds himself to pranks of public policy that enslave the individual for the public good of this most private, elite of American parties. Thus he is veiled by his own public pronouncements.

And that high priest of bamboozlement, Odyssey-echoing Homer Barbee, eloquently drops the enslaving veil of intellectual blindness across the students' eyes, to please that manipulator of polished slave chains, the college president Hebert Bledsoe and his captive audience of white trustees, that is, overseers. For in this situation, at least, Bledsoe is not only the Head Nigger in Charge (HNIC), but he has actually reversed the plantation system so that he is slave-master on this plantation, with Barbee as slave-driver of history. And Barbee, in turn, is blinded like the statue of the Founder, as he drops the veil honoring institutional power, which is manifested in the body and soul of the Founder's epic story (not in the students' learning and intellectual development). Barbee participates in his own self-impaling ceremony: he dims the light of his own intellectual and moral vision of history, preferring the luxurious delusion of "sweet harmonies" over the reality of the chaos of African-American life. And as he extinguishes his vision with his words, Barbee recalls Oedipus, who, having seen too much, tears out his eyes with the clasps of Jocasta's gown. Barbee's physical blindness seems a fitful banishment from the lost North Star light of daring freedom and progress, or as he himself says at one point, as he recalls the declining luminosity in the Founder's life on the train:

> I remember how I looked out of the frosted pane and saw the looming great North Star and lost it, as though the sky had shut its eye.

In this sense, too, the phrase-polishing Barbee becomes a kind of scapegoat for Bledsoe, as minister Homer leads the lamb-innocent Negro students to a slaughtered rendering of their history. Yet their only hope for escape is the Underground Railroad, as it were, and that too on an individual basis. For each must read his or her own way through Barbee's fabulous spiel, and the only hope for escape from reenslavement is to hold fast to the undersides of their history, beneath Barbee's words and memories, and hope that probing questions will ignite a liberating response from their fellow blacks. Indeed they must be ready to commit a kind of "treason" like that "snowy-headed man" at one of the Founder's ceremonial lectures who demands that the Founder cut the accommodationist spiel and

> "Tell us what is to be done, sir! For God's sake, tell us! Tell us in the name of the son they snatched from me last week!" And all through the room the voices arising, imploring, "Tell us, tell us!" And the Founder is suddenly mute with tears.

Like Ulysses escaping the Cyclops in the cave, the students must approach Barbee's story with cunning to match the blinding light of his language and, like Ulysses, must catch hold of the sacred and the profane aspects of their history under-the-belly, and hold on for dear life—as Ulysses says, "so I caught hold of the ram by the back, ensconced myself in the thick wool under his belly and hung on patiently to his fleece, face upwards keeping a firm hold on it all the time." For the students would need to reverse so much of Barbee's speech and to reveal the truths from oral history handed along by the great storytellers, truths that he constantly subordinates and countermands. This is a central problem for a young Negro confronted by all of the distortions of that peasant, underground history—a fact that the Klan-beset snowy-headed man in Homer Barbee's saga-spiel knows only too well.

Ellison is concerned there in the Barbee-Founder-Bledsoe trinity, as it were, with the unquestioned reverence for leadership that still seems to haunt certain groups within the race vulnerable to the cult of the personality, especially when touched by the fires of political-religious enterprise. But there is a yeasty truth in Barbee's saga. Barbee knows the language of power, and he manipulates it as it manipulates him—and in that sense he's masking the wisdom of his peasant tongue. Similarly, it is not so much what Brother Jack says about the Party but the fact that he lost his eye which keeps him from facing his underground history. When his false eye drops out into the glass of water in a moment of confrontation with the hero late in the novel (over the Invisible Man's unauthorized speech for Tod Clifton), he must drop the Party line that covers his vision and babble back into his peasant tongue or into the obscuring language of power. The dropping out of Jack's eye recalls the revelation of Barbee's blindness at the end of his spiel, as he trips in his darkness after having maintained his verbal high-wire act with such deftness, symmetry of line, and balance of power. It recalls chaos-loving Rinehart's manipulative spiel of eloquence that extracts handouts from the blinded, lamb-innocent church ladies. Rinehart's spiel is tied to the profane eloquence of chaos-destroyed, hypersensitive Tod Clifton, whose streetcorner spiel about the Sambo doll—that it will be whatever you want it to be—reflects the gist of what the streetcorner hustler tells all slum dwellers hungry to be recognized or loved.

Even in small segments of the novel we see how these clusters, formulas, and influences operate with Ellison's materials. Chapter 9 starts off soon after the hero gets to Harlem on his way to Mr. Emerson to check out the job reference letter give in to him by the powerful black president. The hero was booted out, you will recall, because quite by accident he showed the white trustee, Norton, the underground of Negro life and the black madness manifested at the riotous Golden Day, and showed him, as well, the base human passions (and by indirection Norton's own purposeful passion) revealed by Jim Trueblood's eloquent saga of incest.

Now our hero starts off with the purpose of finding a job, but early on he runs into a bluesman whose song celebrates the powerful, sexually fulfilling catharsis he achieves from his love-making lady, whose praises he sings, as follows:

> She's got feet like a monkey
> Legs like a frog—Lawd, Lawd!
> But when she starts to loving me
> I holler Whoooo, God-dog!
> Cause I loves my baabay,
> Better than I do myself. . . .

Now this blues song celebrates the fulfilling sex life of a poor bluesman at the bottom, whose woman's beauty is questionable according to standards of beauty in the upper world. Yet their sex life is an affirming glory of life at the bottom, and it leads him to swear that he loves her better than he does himself. The second point is this: the blues singer is certain about his identity, about who he is sexually; and as it turns out, he is a fierce individualist who tries to tell the hero to be what he is, not to masquerade himself, not to deny the bluesman.

Now toward the end of the chapter the hero comes to discover and recognize his new fate, when he finds out that the masquerading trickster, Dr. Bledsoe, indeed has written the hero out of history and driven him toward the unattainable horizon, not with a job reference letter, as the hero assumed, but rather with a prank piece of paper that says, in effect—"To Whom It May Concern. Keep This Nigger-Boy Running." At this agony-filled, perception-sharpening junction, another kind of song comes bubbling up to the surface of the hero's consciousness, rescuing him from self-pity—a mock dirge, played traditionally in the Oklahoma area. After a burial, Negro jazz musicians would light up into this dirge once they hit the Negro business section of town. It expresses the attitudes central to the black man's memory of his history, that if he is to survive he must not allow himself to wallow in self-pity over death, or over the constant dream-shattering, death-dealing experience that is his fate, his mocked fate. The dirge goes:

> O well they picked poor Robin clean
> O well they picked poor Robin clean
> Well they tied poor Robin to a stump
> Lawd, they picked all the feathers round
>   from Robin's rump
> Well they picked poor Robin clean.

The bluesman's song is filled with life, possibly, affirmation of love and identity through fundamental sexual confrontation and confirmation. The dirge stands in apparent opposition, since it comes at the time of a death; yet it is life giving and intelligence heightening, even as it is innocence destroying—mocking our hero's false pride and his naive hero worship of Bledsoe. The song mocks and thereby instructs him that each person must constantly die, or shed the skin of his innocence, in order to grow. The mock dirge comes after a moment of the hero's mock murder, through the pen of bloody Bledsoe. Finally, the song says that savage experience picks us clean of the plumage-like illusions round our baby-soft rounded rumps and leaves us picked clean to the bone of our innocence—but then, perhaps that is indeed the necessary price of eating of the forbidden fruit of experience and knowledge. Unlike the blues, "which allows no scapegoat but the self," the dirge allows us to "lighten our load by becoming one with the bird, as he symbolically takes over our bone-picked sorrow."

This pattern of death, agony, and mocking affirmation or momentary rebirth informs the entire novel, but is pointedly suggested in that marvelous skeleton of a call-and-response sermon by the black minister in the Prologue. There, in the cellar of the hero's racial consciousness where Ellison's version of Underground Man is dwelling, the preacher says, "I said black is . . . an' black ain't . . . Black will git you . . . an' black won't . . . It do, Lawd . . . and' it don't—Black will make you . . . or black will unmake you." Bledsoe, the black president of the college, has undone the hero. And minister Barbee looks through a glass darkly, never face to face. But it is a black dirge that sourly surges forth from the underground racial past and it helps rescue, school, and repair the hero at the junction in chapter 9. Here again the movement from affirmation through denial to affirmation, or from thesis to counterthesis to synthesis, is treated dialectically as it was by the man at the bottom, the bluesman, Peter Wheatstraw.

The bluesman is "doubled" with the hero in the Dostoevskian sense. The streetwise bluesman knows everything about northern idiom and what it takes to get along in this here man's town and on the lower frequencies; and yet Peter Wheatstraw is lost and homeless in the world of power, unable at the higher frequencies to manipulate its symbols or to manifest his vision, and he's uneducated in the school sense. At the other end, the Invisible Man is lost in the streets of Harlem and is also homeless in the world of power: indeed, the most powerful man in his world has just kicked him out of this world (upstairs, you might say, to the North) to Harlem, which is, of course, *nowhere*. And the Invisible Man is undereducated in the street sense. Still, there is synthesis possible for the hero if he but trusts his underground peasant intelligence and memory. For as the hero reflects upon one riff in Peter Wheatstraw's spiel he thinks:

> I liked his words though I didn't know the answer. I'd
> known the stuff from childhood, but had forgotten it: had
> learned it back of school . . . [Ellipsis in original].

But at this junction, too, the hero and the bluesman are tied
together again because it is very important to him that this "new boy"
in town not deny him. Peter Wheatstraw's concern is almost prophetic
because, at the end of the chapter, the hero is to be denied by his *Peter*,
Hebert Bledsoe. Bledsoe is glad to see him at first and then denies
him privately. The fear of being denied by race brother, by public
power, and by father figures sets the stage for the hero's next
confrontation.

In the middle of chapter 9, the hero undergoes the *passion* phase of
Burke's law via a confrontation with young Emerson, a man of
shattered dreams, denied personal fulfillment, at the top of the economic
spectrum. His sexuality is confused and so is his identity about a host of
subjects, ranging from the way he really feels about blacks to the
ambivalence about his powerful father, who has figuratively devoured his
son, as Cronus did unto Zeus. Young Emerson, a homosexual undergoing
a form of psychoanalysis which apparently brings him no affirmation,
stands, then, in direct opposition to the solidly based, blues-singing,
dirt-poor, black man of the streets at the beginning of the chapter, who
knows who he is. Yet this pairing also recalls the Norton-Trueblood
pairing and doubling.

And this pairing also recalls the old American story of the man who
has everything and nothing: young Emerson is rich, white, free and
twenty-one, yet he really has nothing but a world of confusion; and the
bluesman has nothing but a batch of blueprints showing his dreams of
powerful towns and country clubs that he will never erect. He has
everything, though, in a real woman who loves him with a great sexual
power, even though her beauty, at the lower frequencies, is invisible to
all but the naked eye. It is young Emerson, the homosexual, who
unfolds the truth of the letter to the hero, just as it is the remarkable-
looking lady of the bluesman who gives him the sexual, naked truth

and renders him a celebrant of her naked powers, body and soul. One recalls how it is the blind hermaphrodite, Tiresias, who bears to Oedipus the truth below the king's self-righteous existence. But the homosexual at the top and the bluesman at the bottom are also linked; for both are existential outlaws in our society, yet at the same time both are high priests from the peripheral underground, warning the hero of hidden reality. (Tangentially, we might reflect here that so many of our current musical dance patterns have their genesis in black bars, on the one hand, and gay bars, on the other, long before we all began to dance, dance to the music.) Indeed, one recalls that young Emerson tells the hero about a kind of peripheral bar, the Club Calamus:

> "You haven't? It's very well known. Many of my Harlem friends go there. It's a rendezvous for writers, artists and all kinds of celebrities. There's nothing like it in the city, and by some strange twist it has a truly continental flavor."

At this point the hero has undergone a mini-motif of Lord Raglan's pattern in this chapter—he has figuratively died, undergone an underground agony, and been reborn tougher and more perceptive and able to laugh at himself. Finally the wonderful spiel delivered by the bluesman as he is advising our hero has provided the first confrontation the southern-born hero has with a northern black, and it is significant that, although they are speaking the same language, he hardly understands the bluesman's transformed tongue, at first. Migrate from one part of America to another and you are often lost in terms of idiomatic meaning. Yet in the case of the black man the genesis of language has an ancestral underground root in the old country of the Southland. To show Ellison's many dimensioned use of idiom, let me now attempt to unravel one of his bluesman's riffs:

> "All it takes to get along in this here man's town is a little shit, grit and mother-wit. And man, I was bawn with all three. In

fact I'maseventhsonofaseventhsonbawnwithacauloverbotheye-
sandraisedonblackcatboneshighjohntheconquerorandgreasy-
greens—" he spieled with twinkling eyes, his lips working
rapidly. "You dig me daddy?"

Let me suggest that here Ellison is rendering up the fusion of myth
and lore which is the genesis of Negro/Black/White/Afro-American
idiomatic versification. "The seventh son of a seventh son" comes from
the Scottish-English influence upon the former slaves and suggest how
myth-bound and haunted the slaveholders were and refers to one who
is born lucky. "Bawn with a caul over both eyes" suggests one who is
born with a grit of clairvoyance; and has an Ashanti linkage from the
African aspect of the heritage. "Raised on black cat bones" is from the
Afro-*American* version of voodoo and the context is this: in voodoo,
which always reverses meaning (as does so much of Negro idiom): you
throw a live black cat into a boiling pot of hot water; after the flesh has
fallen away you pick out its bones and gnaw away, and if you are lucky,
and gnaw down upon the right bone, you will become *invisible.* "High
John the Conqueror" is a mythical hero from slavery, an invisible hero
who sided with the slaves, during bad times, with good advice. And
"greasygreens," of course, refers to African-American cuisine, in the
old country Southland.

The hero's presence in the North at this time in the novel recalls the
migration from the South to the North of blacks who came, often on
the run, pursuing the dream of a peaceful kingdom, jobs, and personal
fulfillment. But the hero's dream becomes a nightmare through a
mocking note that, unknown to him, reads: "To Whom It May
Concern: Keep This Nigger-Boy Running." It is significant, and one of
the ironies of the meshing of race and class, that (while looking for
employment) the hero discovers this dimension of his representative
fate in the North from a rich white entrepreneur's son whose mock
employment has brought him no fulfillment.

But it is even more significant that the hero first recalls the
"Nigger-Boy Running" joke via a recalled dream that he has of his

grandfather, at the end of chapter 1, just after he wins his scholarship to the Negro college. For in the dream, through his grandfather, the hero is ritually warned and instructed:

> He told me to open my brief case and read what was inside—and I did, finding an official envelope stamped with the state seal; and inside the envelope I found another and another, endlessly, and I thought I would fall of weariness. "Them's years," he said. "Now open that one." And I did and in it I found an engraved document containing a short message in letters of gold. "Read it," my grandfather said. "Out loud!"
>
> "To Whom It May Concern," I intoned, "Keep This Nigger-Boy Running."

And there is an underground story beneath this memory. For in the old South, a form of black-baiting which had its genesis in slavery would proceed as follows: A Negro newcomer would arrive upon the scene, looking for gainful employment; he would go to a prospective white employer. This ordinary small-town white businessman would immediately spot the fact that this was not one of the local blacks and would tell the black outsider that he did not have work at this time but that he did know of someone who might have jobs available down the road, perhaps.

The white businessman would then give the horizon-seeking black a sealed letter to take to the next prospective employer. Upon reaching the next white man, the letter would be presented, opened by the white man, read and mused over, and then the Negro would hear the same old story—"No jobs" here but perhaps "Up the road," and then the white merchant would scribble something on the note, reseal the communiqué (like the Negro's fate), and hand the letter back to the outreaching dark hand. This would happen again and again, until the black finally opened the letter and read the message, or got the message, and read out his symbolic fate (or some variation upon the theme): "To Whom It May Concern, Keep This Nigger-Boy Running." This brutal joke of course had its antecedents in slavery, when many or most slaves couldn't read or write, and could only go from plantation to plantation with a note signed by the Master, or his *earthly* representative. The slave didn't in fact know what might or might not be written down on that note. And although this tortuous ritual or bad-faith convenant came from the pastoral scenes of the gallant South, actually the "jobs" search and its attendant mocking ceremony were often played out in the industrial North. Or more to the point, the duplicity operative at the Paint Factory in *Invisible Man*, which in fact did hire our nameless hero, but only as a scab (union strike buster), signified the way industrial bosses pitted the racial and ethnic groupings of the underclasses against each other. And when the Invisible Man's day labor was used up, he was discarded and put on tentative welfare after signing some papers which freed him from work—new slave papers meant to quiet his aggressive appetite for employment.

It is structurally salient that Ellison establishes early the ancestral tie with the grandfather's folk voice, via the underground avenue of the dream. For the grandfather's appearance and intelligence in the dream is the deeper Underground Railroad reality beneath the American Dream for the Negro. And the grandfather is the oldest ancestor within the hero's family memory. And who is the *grandfather's* authority? No doubt the oldest member of the tribe in his memory, perhaps *his* grandfather—and then we are back into slavery; so that in a highly oral culture the grandfather is the proper high priest to pass on mythical reality and survival wisdom from the battle zone. Throughout the novel, a warning or extolling voice issues forth from underground (often coming to the hero's aid, like Tarp's voice at the bottom of the Brotherhood) during moments of agony, conflict, trial, public and private passion. *And* (like the rescuing dirge, or High John the Conqueror) this intelligence informs his hard-won experience, thereby constantly presenting the reader with a hero's awareness or perception that is heightened. Not all of the underground warning voices confer benefits upon the hero as they warn him, however, as Lucius Brockway, in the underground of the paint factory, demonstrates. Brockway becomes a most trying combination of Tar Baby and Proteus for the Invisible Man.

Now in some cases the ancestral voice comes directly out of the remembering hero's own past, as did the rescuing dirge. The second kind of ancestral voice issues from the hero's consciousness when he recalls moments from his own personal history, which then leads to racial memory, as did the dream of the grandfather. The third kind of historical-ancestral linkage comes from symbols or specific items which don't touch the hero's own past but which form a lucid part of his racial memory and the consciousness of the race, in the Joycean sense, suggesting then a duty and a task and a covenant or responsibility to the ancestral community.

Now these symbolic objects surge forth at moments of passion or trial. For instance, when the hero, late in the novel, discovers another kind of "Keep This Nigger-Boy Running" note on his desk at the Brotherhood's office. Brother Tarp, the man at the bottom of the organization, gives the hero a picture of Frederick Douglass, our man at the top of Negro leadership in the nineteenth century. Later Tarp gives the hero his own leg irons, retained from a chain gang. The hero must learn to trust those symbolic ancestral tokens, voices, or manifestations—yet he must sort out the consulting surge of past and present counselors. Indeed one of the hero's many agonies is to learn not to accept the advice from authority figures without question and to wrestle with advice until he's made it his own and understood it, or spurned it, or accepted it and by accepting it, made certain he's reshaped the advice to fit his own experience. For the other side of the most profane or the healthiest advice is that it renders the hero somebody's "running boy" and does not allow him to be his own man.

So, motifs involving power, sex, women, images of light and dark, broken taboos, Afro-American folklore, papers of importance, quests for identity and responsibility, individualism, music, violence, uses of eloquence, all come in clusters and order the improvisions of Ellison's orchestrated novel. Here we can see the influence of William

Faulkner's *Light in August*, in which the major scenes are ordered by the presence of sex, women, food, and money, and are in turn connected with images of light and dark, religion and slavery, as integrating forces which undergird the associative patterns of each narrative section. In terms of power Ellison's improvising upon the whole plantation system as a metaphor for understanding American institutions. This improvisation on the plantation like hierarchy can be seen in the "descent" section of the Prologue, in the pecking order at the paint factory scene, in life at Mary Rambo's room house, in the Brotherhood, at the college, at the battle-royal smoker, and at the Golden Day.

Connected with this imagery of the plantation is another, deeper dimension of Ellison's metaphoric patterning in which he projects a symbolic model of American history—thereby joining the very select company of Melville, Hawthorne, and especially Faulkner in this recombing of metaphorical vision with history. All of Faulkner's major works involving the black presence, it seems to me, possess this epic design. For instance, in *Absalom, Absalom!* the "design" of metaphor can be read in the following manner: Let the French architect stand for America's "borrowed" French principles of refinement, creativity, artistry, ideals of culture, freedom, and liberty (indeed our fitful intellectual indebtedness to the French Revolution); and let Sutpen stand for American know-how, cunning, outlandish daring, bigotry, savage frontiersmanship-hustle, furious energy and industry, and white-ethnic class hatred; and let the Negro slaves of Sutpen's Hundreds stand as the enslaved basis of the American economic order.

Sutpen must reduce all others to "niggers" (blacks, women, his family, outside family, poor whites, his son) as he hacks his insanely ambitious way to the top. The new American Adam must reduce the French architect, at the other end of the social spectrum, to a subhuman, to a nigger, once he has used up the architect's expertise. And he then attempts to free his body from Sutpen's clutches. Sutpen, in turn, reenacts a mock French Revolution by bringing down the French aristocrat-artist. But the French architect only flees when he discovers that he too is enslaved—thus the synthesis between slave and aristocrat is forged by *slavery's* chains. And the French architect's flight and Sutpen's pursuit of him with hound dogs recalls that of a runaway slave and the ritual pursuit by hound dogs.

Dostoevsky's hero in *Notes from Underground,* and the illumined Invisible Man of the Ellison Prologue and Epilogue are manifestations of hyper-awareness and terror concerning the inner meanness of the outer world: they observe it as a treacherous terrain. Structurally, the Prologue contains within it all of the materials needed for Ellison's invention; and the core of the work then goes on to illustrate and orchestrate these materials. In Underground Man's world, Part 1 is a presentation of the arguments, and in Part 2 we have the illustrations. *Notes from Underground* can be seen as a monologue rich with personal and political commentary. The grand sweep of the many monologues in *Invisible Man* carries a similar personal, political "doubleness." But Ellison's monologues have a kind of epic grandness that goes beyond Dostoevski. Witness, for example, Trueblood's saga and Barbee's sermon.

At every turn in *Notes,* Underground Man is out to shock the reader, to *shock* reason itself. The Invisible Man is out to shake the reader into an awareness that is streaked with a soured humor and a great gift for hyperbole. Both novels are within the tradition of the memoir, and, like *Notes, Invisible Man* is seasoned in the tradition of confessional literature of the seductive underground diary.

The Russia of Underground Man's day was highly repressive, and so for Ellison's hyperaware man there is ever the feeling of alienation and dispossession. (And you will recall that the Invisible Man's second public address treats the theme of dispossession, and he uses it in his third address at the stadium.) In Dostoevski's Russia you either accepted your socioeconomic status as your fate or you dropped out. No mobility. Faced with the fitful combination of power, race and wrenching leadership, the Invisible Man faces a comparable terrain, cut off in the cellar from upward movement. Perhaps even more in keeping with the vaulting, scorning attitude of Underground Man are the men in the Golden Day, who remain as Afro-American examples of broken men, though madness has consumed their soured brilliance.

Both narrators appear to be onto something concerning the way the normal world of power operates in a system of deceit—especially if you are highly aware, you are apt to be driven to treason. For example, after seeing too much, in an ancestral dream of the shattering past in the Prologue, the Invisible Man recalls:

> *And at that point a voice of trombone timbre screamed at me, "Git out of here, you fool! Is you ready to commit treason?"*

Both narrators suggest that the mind of highly aware man contains much spite and even vengeance. Underground Man seeks revenge, not justice. But the Invisible Man would seek both. There is a sense in both works—particularly in *Notes*—that hyperconsciousness leads to paralysis. Therefore the only action issues out of a sense of willfulness and spitefulness. The Invisible Man, though, is obsessed with responsibility, and cultural enterprise, and the rage for freedom that remains a viable ancestral imperative. The Invisible Man, however, frets about overstaying his time of contemplation in the underground and knows he is bound to come up; he seeks love, and spite can only lead to disintegration of personality, as in those memorable figures in the Golden Day. Ultimately, of course, going underground is a kind of psychological going within oneself for both narrators.

Ralph Ellison starts out wanting to reverse the idea, current at the time he conceived *Invisible Man*, that the Negro was invisible. The narrator says, "I am invisible simply because you refuse to see me." But having committed himself to assaulting the current sociological metaphor of the day, Ellison turns the metaphor into a dialective vision of modern America as a briar patch. The metaphor of invisibility is "doubly" enriched by his constant allusions to the plantation system. The logic is as follows: *Thesis:* You (society) say I'm a slave. *Counterthesis:* but I'm not a slave in my soul, or in my mind. *Synthesis:* I'll admit that slavery is the system in which I dwell, but I see myself as slave in that system only if you'll accept the metaphor of how the system enslaves us all, Master . . . And because I've lived with this knowledge longer, I've learned how to make the plantation my briar patch; though it enslaves my body I have learned how to keep my mind and spirit free from its damnation of the spirit. And Master, economically your survival depends upon my body's productivity in the slave system that obsesses your mind and spirit. Alternatively, the Invisible Man asks himself, and us, as he weaves through the possible meanings of the grandfather's advice in the Epilogue,

> Was it that we of all, we, most of all, had to affirm the principle, the plan in whose name we had been brutalized and sacrificed—not because we would always be weak nor because we were afraid or opportunistic, but because we were older than they, in the sense of what it took to live in the world with others and because they had exhausted in us, some—of the human greed and smallness, yes, and the fear and superstition that had kept them running.

Like Dostoevski's Underground Man, the Invisible Man puts down the idea of racial invisibility; he embraces the metaphor, assaults it, then reverses it. He discovers at the height of the race riots in Harlem that he cannot return to Mary's, either, that he is invisible to Mrs. Rambo as he is to Jack, Ras, and Bledsoe. For like Underground Man, he discovers that statistical computations for the collective good, or institutional asylums for the individual's good, or visions of the individual's good by powerful figures and forces constantly leave out one important impulse: man's urge and capacity to conceptualize his humanity beyond statistics and regimentation; his willfulness to do what he wants, in the underground economy of his imagination, to turn a plantation into an underground briar patch or a hostile terrain into the sources and resource points of escape via the mind's Underground Railroad.

For finally the Invisible Man is underground indeed; but he has decided that it is time to end his hibernation and come up to meet a new level of experience. It is plain to me that at the end of the novel, our hero, reborn, is about to emerge from his womb of safety in the underground; yet it is also clear that he is trapped in a personal way between two voices. For as he acknowledges:

> Thus, having tried to give pattern to the chaos which lives within a pattern of your certainties, I must come out. I must emerge. And there's still a conflict within me: With Louis Armstrong one half of me says, "Open the window and let the foul air out," while the other says, "It was good green corn before the harvest."

Now the "green corn" motif comes from a Leadbelly song and refers to a state of innocence before the harvest of experience. Innocence is beautiful but it carries dangerous naiveté with it—a naive skin that our hero sheds.

But first of all the hero hears a lyrical line from the man who makes poetry out of invisibility, Louis Armstrong, a song which suggests the sophisticated, toughened shape the hero's perception of reality has taken on out of the furnace-like bad air of passion and conflict which has been his experience throughout the life of the novel. The line refers to a song by Buddy Bolden which Louis Armstrong—also known as Dipper-Mouth and Bad Air—used to sing:

> I thought I heard Buddy Bolden say,
> Funky-Butt, Funky-Butt, take it away,
> I thought I heard somebody shout,
> Open up the window and let the foul air out.

The Funky-Butt was a powerhouse jazz nightclub in New Orleans, where the solos on the horns were as furious and glorious as the sex act itself, filled with bad air and ecstatic charges, savage thrusts and stellar flourishes. Armstrong, as a kid of ten, used to stand outside the door of the Funky-Butt and listen to Bolden, the great jazz trumpeter who ended up in a madhouse, blowing and singing and wailing. Bolden would sing the song in tribute to the funkiness and the foul air in the dance hall, caused by the jelly-tight dancing.

Without the liberating bad air that riffs through the chamber of the good-bad horn of plenty (which also resembles the chamber from whence all life emerges), you can't have the real music of life, or the dance. For as the hero comments,

> Of course Louie was kidding, *he* wouldn't have thrown old Bad Air out, because it would have broken up the music and the dance, when it was the good music that came from the bell of old Bad Air's horn that counted.

$$\boxed{\text{GOING TO THE TERRITORY}}$$

Two of the major works in Ralph Ellison's collection of 16 essays entitled *Going to the Territory* are ground-breaking in terms of structural form, as they brilliantly explore a range of themes: the uses of individual memoir as a meditation on Afro-American cultural history and its linkage to the national life; the reshaping of our collective consciousness, as seen through the impact of the minority member, who acts as both a carrier and a reshaper of that culture, even as he is segregated and often appears as an outsider, or an invisible man to the majority population; the keening relationship between American values of refinement and baseness; the pursuit of literary and artistic excellence as an issue of national honor and morality; anecdote, folklore, tall-tale, and vernacular, as prime fulcrums, when measuring the influence of geography upon identity; and the layered, angularity of the American Character—often times, many American selves, rolled into one.

Starting off his volume with the essay "The Little Man at Chehaw Station" is similar to a bold manager sending up Willie Mays (who was himself, several great ballplayers "*roled*" into one) as the lead-off hitter. What else is left? How do you top this? But this all-purpose gestalt of an essay orchestrates the thematic territory ahead for the whole collection. Here Ellison trumpets his vision of American life as one of cultural wholeness amid diversity, pluralistic, political deals, and the identity agonies of our separate states. He is alive to these "states" through the uses of vignettes; a highly associative memory; a felt-knowledge of inwardness that must always lead to projections of outwardness to, and linkages with, the larger American scene and back again. And what is the memory-as-message behind this essay?

Ellison—who was a trumpeter, majoring in music at Tuskegee Institute, with aspirations of becoming a classical composer—had just made a poor performance before faculty members at the monthly student's recital. "I had sought solace in the basement studio of Hazel Harrison, a highly respected concert pianist and teacher." Miss Harrison had known Prokofiev, in Europe, and she immediately informed the student: "You must always play your best even if it's only in the waiting room at Chehaw Station, because in this country there'll always be a little man hidden behind the stove. . . . There'll always be a little man whom you don't expect, and he'll know the *music*, and the *tradition*, and the standards of *musicianship* required for whatever you set out to perform!" This memory became a motherlode and a springboard for a series of attributes Ellison came to see incorporated in and flowering out of this mysterious, chorus-like figure (and tied to the American Character); free floating, and reappearing through the writer's own consciousness over the years, in various forms of sophistication. "Connoisseur, critic, trickster, the little man is also a day-coach, cabin-class traveler. Being quintessentially American, he enjoys the joke, the confounding of hierarchal expectations, fostered by his mask: that cultural incongruity through which he, like Brer Rabbit, is able to convert even the most decorous of audiences into his own briar patch and temper the chilliest of classics to his own vernacular taste."

In both his magnificent fiction and his essays, Ellison has often employed this underground figure, who appears powerless and almost invisible on the surface (and hidden). But he is revealed as a knowing figure with many salient clues to his identity: he lives a paradoxical life; knows the nation's hidden history; and is a troubled and troubling witness to our riddled Democracy. Indeed the essay ends with Ellison now in process of transforming himself from musician to writer, picking his way through the basement of a New York tenement, hoping to gain enough signatures for some forgotten cause, when suddenly he comes upon a group of black workmen violently arguing behind a closed door "over which of two celebrated Metropolitan Opera divas were the superior soprano!" These base workingmen are really witnessing Chorus "cousins" to our man behind the stove at Chehaw Station (and the refined Miss Harrison). Where do they get their first-hand knowledge of opera? "At the Metropolitan Opera . . . strip us fellows down and give us some costumes and we make about the finest damn bunch of Egyptians you ever seen. Hell, we been down there wearing leopard skins and carrying spears or waving things like palm leafs and ostrich-tail fans for *years!*"

Ellison expresses this sense of the complex cultural interplay of American Culture best:

> . . . but perhaps the phenomenon is simply a product of our neglect of serious cultural introspection, our failure to conceive of our fractured, vernacular-weighted culture as an intricate whole. And since there is no reliable sociology of the dispersal of ideas, styles, or tastes in this turbulent American society, it is possible that, personal origins aside, the cultural circumstances here described offer the intellectually adventurous individual what might be termed a broad "social mobility of intellect and taste"—plus an incalculable scale of possibilities for self-creation.

Recreating the essay in "An Extravagance of Laughter," Ellison produces a work that structurally suggests the essay-as-novella; spiralling the reader upon cycles of fabulous humor and stunning insights, this piece, will in time, I believe, stand with Virginia Woolf's path-breaking essay, *A Room of One's Own*, as one of the major essays in the language.

The musical imprint of Ellison's openness to innovative structure appears in these essays (and in many others) wherein he writes with the virtuosity of a jazz trumpet player in solo flight, extending riffs of improvisation upon the basic themes, in a score of directions. But these master essays are also deeply influenced by the tradition of the monologist, the stand-up comedian, the frontier orator, the folk preacher, even as they recall the concerns of Twain, Melville, and Whitman, with American Democracy and its failures as the central questions for an American author to meditate over and write about; in turn each of these major American authors was profoundly touched by the presence of the black American upon the stage of our history and as a gauge of our collective freedom. In "What America Would Be Like Without Blacks," originally published in a special issue of *Time*, Ellison reveals his artistic ability at synthesizing many ideas into a powerful vision:

> Whitman viewed the spoken idiom of Negro Americans as a source for a native grand opera. Its flexibility, its musicality, its rhythms, freewheeling diction, and metaphors, as projected in Negro American folklore, were absorbed by the creators or our great nineteenth-century literature even when the majority of blacks were still enslaved. Mark Twain celebrated it in the prose of *Huckleberry Finn*; without the presence of blacks, the book could not have been written . . . For not only is the black man a co-creator of the language that Mark Twain raised to the level of literary eloquence, but Jim's condition as American and Huck's commitment to freedom are at the moral center of the novel.

Two essays—"The Novel as a Function of American Democracy" and "Perspective of Literature"—round out the cluster of literary exploration forged by *Society, Morality and The Novel*, which is an important contribution to the critical canon. For although Ellison has revealed himself in this volume and in the 1964 collection of essays, *Shadow and Act*, as a superior critic, he is primarily known as the author of one of the half-dozen great American novels of this century, *Invisible Man*. Any reflective statements he gives us about the working novelist have added weight and illumination, that we came to expect from that consummate critic and novelist Henry James.

. . . For, as with all the fictive arts, the novel's medium of communication consists in a "familiar" experience occurring among a particular people, within a particular society or nation (and the novel is bound up with the notion of nationhood), and it achieves its universality, if at all, through accumulating images of reality and arranging them in patterns of universal significance. It is not, like poetry, concerned primarily with words, but with action depicted in words; and it operates by amplifying and giving resonance to a specific complex of experience until, through the eloquence of its statement, that specific part of life speaks metaphorically for the whole.

Norman Mailer and James Baldwin have made important breakthroughs in the form of the essay; exploiting the private life to speculate upon the meaning of larger American issues, sometimes to good effect, but often amid much wound-licking. But Ellison's essays are never narcissistic; he's always bent on enriching his reader's intelligence, orchestrating the form, using his profound imaginative powers, which are rooted in chapters of reality, ever rich with symbolic action, as a way toward illumination not speculation.

The minor essays and reminiscenses affirm Ellison's anchoring and his analysis on important Afro-American cultural heroes. Essays on his fellow novelist and friend, the late Richard Wright ("In him we had for the first time a Negro American writer as randy, as courageous, and as irrepressible as Jack Johnson"); and the artist Romare Bearden, whose works Ellison has been following closely for over 40 years, expand upon the earlier themes and advance the importance of individual excellence and fortitude against the odds. And in a "Homage to Duke Ellington on His Birthday," Ellison reflects the large, celebratory spirit which so engages this whole volume:

> It is to marvel: the ageless and irresponsible Duke Ellington is seventy, and another piano player of note, President Richard M. Nixon, has ordered in his honor a state dinner to be served in the house where, years ago, Duke's father,

then a butler, once instructed white guests from the provinces in the gentle art and manners proper to such places of elegance and power.

Several of these essays, like the Ellington piece, were written for an occasion of celebration. But two of the essays grew out of speeches Ellison gave at the beginning and the end of a conference devoted to the study of his own works at Brown University in 1979. "Going to the Territory," the title for the conference, and taken from a line in a Bessie Smith song, is also touched to Ellison's own Oklahoma history, of heading out westward for new frontiers. Ever the careful craftsman and bold frontiersman, in his experiments with form Ellison also revealed himself at the conference—and throughout the terrain of these essays—as an important American statesman, when he declared:

American democracy is a most dramatic form of social organization, and in that drama each of us enacts his role by asserting his own and his group's values and traditions against those of his fellow citizens. Indeed, a battle-royal conflict of interests appears to be basic to our conception of freedom, and the drama of democracy proceeds through a warfare of words and symbolic actions by which we seek to advance our private interests while resolving our political differences. Since the Civil War this form of symbolic action has served as a moral substitute for armed warfare, and we have managed to restrain ourselves to a debate which we carry on in the not always justified faith that the outcome will serve the larger interests of democracy.

MORRISON'S MAGIC LANTERN

> The wantonness described in much urban Black literature is really the wantonness of a character out of touch with the ancestor.
> —Toni Morrison from
> *City Limits, Village Values:*
> *Concepts of the Neighborhood in*
> *Black Fiction*

Early in Toni Morrison's novel, *Sula*, we find Shadrack in jail, falsely charged with vagrancy and intoxication, after his recent release from military confinement in an Army hospital overseas. Now imprisoned in his native land, *this* Shadrack had initially lost his identity through the fiery furnace extremes of wartime experiences; he saw a buddy's face blown away during combat. Morrison projects the following description with the photographer's art of a close-up shot.

> Wincing at the pain in his foot, he turned his head a little to the right and saw the face of a soldier near him fly off. Before he could register shock, the rest of the soldier's head disappeared under the inverted soup bowl of his helmet. But stubbornly, taking no direction from the brain, the body of the headless soldier ran on, with energy and grace, ignoring altogether the drip and slide of brain tissue down its back.

It should not be missed here how Morrison is reapplying the Hemingway definition of courage, as "grace under pressure," when she captures in slow-motion print Shadrack's memory of the horrors of war, and concretely the soldier's will to go on.

Shadrack is psychologically blown away by this ultimate male experience of combat, particularly as he focuses upon "the face of a soldier near him fly off," and as he observes "the headless soldier ran on . . . ignoring altogether the drip and slide of brain tissue down its back." Shadrack is made aware of the fact that the soldier has lost his physical identity; he also bears witness to the invisible but real life force drive; or that man is never defeated, only destroyed; yet another bulletin from the Hemingway canon.

Because of this experience at war, Shadrack flips out and is placed in a military hospital, where we vividly see just how much he has lost control of himself. His lost identity is revealed by his inability to control his hands. Now Shadrack is estranged from who he *was* when he gets back to the combat zone of "home," experiencing what any black man, whether he be tramp, lawyer, mercenary, hero, minister, servant (or historically a slave captured without his free papers on the streets in the North) might face because of his race.

For Morrison—as we shall see—Shadrack must come to transform his blackness back to an earlier state of consciousness, and wash out the negative, bottomed-out, stereotyped-riddled side of blackness, which formed the prejudicial "reason" why he was summarily arrested when he returned. For this is not only Shadrack's ultimate combat zone of experience, but it also is the highest form of experience: to use the imagination as an instrument to awaken from the racist image of blackness so deeply and profoundly engraved upon the psychological landscape of the American imagination. In order to accomplish this, he must rediscover himself by getting in "touch with the ancestor," or the ancestral spirit.

Now we see Shadrack in another fiery furnace, as it were, a prison cell, and as the inmate of his own outraged condition, stripped of who he is; and attempting to rediscover his identity now through reinvention out of anguish—wherein the essentials of his life are reduced to the bottom. Shadrack must come from the bottom up—or up from the slavery of his lost identity—by resubmitting himself, transforming himself back to the slave memory, at the very bottom of African-American ancestral consciousness. And he must embrace the other side of the self via the mask, or the get-up or the outfit slaves once donned, in order to see his visage upon the waters of time. Shadrack must come face to face with what it was to look like a slave, in order to save his face, and in order to face his modern day reality . . . and get his face back. Actually his condition isn't totally different from that of the combat soldier, whose face was blown away in war, at this point.

In the prison cell Shadrack must come from the bottom up—in this specific case, the toilet bowl that is—in order to see himself clearly. The reinventing Shadrack uses the toilet water to capture the visage of his lost identity—like a set-up shot for a photographer, he must make a self-portrait. Shadrack can only rediscover his washed-out humanity by submitting his face to the toilet bowl water, in the first instance, and then reinvent himself.

Morrison conducts us dramatically through the steps of this film-making process of awakening Shadrack to face his soul. Her technique might remind the reader of viewing the stages of discovery in a slide show. Morrison handles this ritualistically too, I believe, because actually Shadrack must also make this rediscovery of the soul-redeeming instrumentality of reinvention, and relocation, step by step.

> Like moonlight stealing under a window shade an idea insinuated itself; his earlier desire to see his own face. He looked for a mirror; there was none. Finally, keeping his hands carefully behind his back he made his way to the toilet bowl and peeped in. The water was un-evenly lit by the sun so he could make nothing out.

What Shadrack does now is to complete the transformation cycle by relocating his spirit back into time, and in so doing he is able to put together the chaos of his physical identity. He must surrender to his people's history in order to achieve this physical and spiritual whole-ness. When Shadrack's individuality and his blackness become visible to him his visage recalls those photographs of nineteenth-century slaves. This ancestral photograph comes to his rescue, as it were. And Shadrack is on the way toward remembering who he is by recollecting the way we were. Or, as Morrison might say, rememory. Also, Morrison now appears as novelist-turned photographer, when she writes:

> Returning to his cot he took the blanket and covered his head, rendering the water dark enough to see his reflection. There in the toilet water he saw a grave black face. A black so definite, so unequivocal, it astonished him. He had been harboring a skittish apprehension that he was not real—that he didn't exist at all. But when the blackness greeted him with its indisputable presence, he wanted nothing more. In his joy he took the risk of letting one edge of the blanket drop and glanced at his hands. They were still. Courteously still.

Self-discovery then leads to the other dimension of reinvention—*style*, or that attribute of black consciousness that celebrates life through fashion embossing elegance upon symbolic agencies of affirmation. "In his joy he took the risk of letting one edge of the blanket drop." Finally there is the reward or the confirmation; for not only has Shadrack discovered his face, he now discovers his hands (an important discovery, too, for the coming into consciousness of a babe). "They were still. Courteously still."

Here indeed is an example of the black relocating himself, at the bottom through mythic time, space, and consciousness. The agencies of redemption and reconstitution, and perhaps I should even say reconstruction are the toilet water and the blanket reinvented, and reshaped by Shadrack, in order to save his face, so that his black existence can surface upon the face of the toilet water as visible. It's as if Shadrack suddenly becomes a photographer by submitting the negative of his face into the water and now the solution of his history reproduces a positive print; a blackness according to Morrison's lens that transcends slavery, even as it is born and bathed out of the toilet bowl-bottomed-out condition that slavery was. Ironically enough, donning the blanket renders "the water dark enough to see his reflection." Too much exposure to light would kill the negative before it becomes a photograph, rendering it a washed-out "still"-life.

But to discover all of this in the bathroom, in the toilet bowl, to boot? Well, I would remind you that many inventive amateur photographers (hard pressed for space and time) have used the bathroom as their labs, or darkrooms, for film-making processing—placing their negatives in large jars filled with solution in the face bowl. We are reminded, too, of the manner in which photo-journalism has taken over the modern imagination, starting back with the "stills" of the Civil War up to the cinematography of the Viet Nam War. Our national memory of combat has become affixed to the flicks of the camera's magic lantern.

So many of the pictures taken of blacks in the South during slavery are very similar to the mug shot the prisoner Shadrack sets up here. Read from this prospectus we can see the photographer's art operating—within Morrison's magic lantern motif of reinvention—as Shadrack sees his face not through a negative visage of blackness, nor through a glass darkly, but now face to face. Different from the soldier whose face has been blown away earlier, Shadrack can now live again by relocating his reconstructed face, projected up from the bottom of nightmarish historical memory.

Those of us who have read *Sula* will recall how Morrison uses the metaphor of The Bottom as her most ironical associative touchstone throughout the work. The black section of Medallion is referred to as The Bottom. The great American dance, the Black Bottom, surfaced upon white American's consciousness, from the bottom up, out of the black bottom of the ghettos, to become an "in" dance amongst bohemian, swinging social white whirls of the 1920s. Morrison has said in a most illuminating article, "*City Limits, Village Values*," that:

> When the Black American writer experiences the country or the village, he does so not to experience nature as a balm for his separate self, but to touch the ancestor. When he cannot (because the ancestor is not there, or because he

cannot communicate with him), then and only then is he frustrated, defeated, devastated, and unregenerated. When he is able to, he is regenerated, balanced, and capable of operating on a purely moral axis.

Although Morrison was not talking about her own work in this article, the intelligence of this statement surely speaks for the scene in *Sula*, and the general vision of life she projects throughout her fiction. I should also point out in connection with this scene, and Morrison's statement in the article, that by accepting the newly emerging face of blackness, Shadrack must go back into history, and accept slavery as fact of his ancestral condition in order to move forward. For Morrison this relocation of the spirit is essentially didactic concerning the contemporary African-American quest for identity: that you must accept the past and participate in its re-creation, before you can talk about "being black," and all the other slogans toward affirmation that the black spin-doctors of the late 1960s and early 1970s, plucked out of the air and hawked, without surrendering to the trial and agony of history, and concretely participating in its re-creation.

Now, in accepting the newly discovered face, it seems to me, that this is also not absolutely Shadrack's face in toto, but rather a memory mask culled up from slavery, which appears before him, out of the waters of another time; even as he participates in its creation. Obviously, I am talking here about the ways in which a mask is created. It is your creativity weaved or shaped out of an historical presence. I am reminded here of a Romare Bearden collage character, in which a face out of the past is superimposed upon the neck of a contemporary figure, in this superb African-American painter's gallery of Northern/ Southern characters. Often times Bearden stripped these pictures from faces in newspapers, or magazine photos from the past of peasant farmers, and placed them upon the bodies of his black Yankee citizens, in an attempt to reveal the manner in which the past is ever instructive and alive in the present; and to show something of the metamorphosis of group consciousness. Or, in other cases, the way in which he used the train as a symbol of linkage between Southern and Northern spiritual and cultural memories, and in the quest for freedom.

After he is awakened by this historical anointing, Shadrack's relocated spirit projects an image of one who has just received some form of spiritual communion:

> Shadrack rose and returned to the cot where he fell into the first sleep of his new life. A sleep deeper than the hospital drugs; deeper than the pits of plums, steadier than the condor's wing; more tranquil than the curve of eggs.
>
> The sheriff looked through the bars at the young man with the matted hair. He had read through his prisoner's papers and hailed a farmer. When Shadrack awoke, the sheriff handed him back his papers and escorted him to the back of the wagon.

This last paragraph refers to Shadrack's free papers of severance from the Army, which would also contain his record in combat during his time of military conscription. Still, Shadrack must be sent to the back of the wagon, of course, I don't care how much woe and trouble he's witnessed in combat, defending the country. And it is a tribute to Morrison's thinking that no matter how affirmative this scene may appear to be in terms of Shadrack finding an identity, he also remains slightly shell-shocked from the general combat out of the experience with war, and racism. Black men returning from the service, after all the wars this nation has fought, have had to face the immediacy of discrimination and racism.

Shadrack's situation recalls somewhat that of a slave who has been given his freedom by his master from the institution of slavery and then goes North and is seen going along the streets, where he might be picked up as a fugitive from the law. He'd better remember that he was once a slave and still a slave in the eyes of many of his fellow countrymen, when his black face surfaces on the streets. So, this historical slave had better keep his free papers on him at all times—lest he end up in a prison cell, as a vagrant in the North, where he thought he would be free. *Or,* he might be picked up as a vagrant even if he does have his free papers on him, because this ex-slave may be free, but he is still black, and his people are still in bondage, so he is not free. (And as we remember from the fugitive slave law, if a slave gets to a free state in the North, he is still the property of his master.)

Shadrack comes to life twice; or he awakened twice in this scene. First when he reinvents his life, and discovers his blackness, as a force for freedom and harmonizing; secondly when he awakens from his sleep, he is given his papers of freedom by the sheriff, so that he may leave the second institution of his confinement.

Ultimately all of this leads Shadrack to extend the idea of reinvention into the not so peaceable kingdom of The Bottom in Medallion, with the idea of National Suicide Day. This reinvention through taboo-breaking ritual—in which Shadrack comes up with an apparently new ritual, actually goes back in time too; and recalls earlier forms of purifying through the embracing of excess, or danger and death, as well as dealing with the psychological fear of death. The perversely creative idea of setting aside a particular day, or set of days, as a way of getting rid of the fear of death, or finding a place for it, and then dealing with it, comes to Shadrack first through the experience at war, and secondly through his rediscovery of his blackness. In her article "City Limits, Village Values," Morrison has written: "For the true ancestor is frequently a social or secret outlaw like Ellison's Grandfather on his death bed saying, 'I never told you but our life is a war and I have been a traitor all of my born days, a spy in the enemy's country.'" Shadrack does recall to mind those shell-shocked vets in the Golden Day in Ellison's novel *Invisible Man.* Like those vets, Shadrack has been shell-shocked not only by war, but the experiences with racism in peace-time America. Shadrack also reflects some of their perverse intelligence bulletins, hurled up through their hypersensitive, frightfully keening projections concerning the African-American condition.

In her article, Morrison goes on to say, that the "ancestor must defy the system . . . provide alternate wisdom . . ."

Concerning Shadrack's own alternative wisdom we now learn that he has gone through a time of reflection and evolvement of an idea, in the back of the wagon (segregated section?).

> . . . Shadrack began a struggle that was to last twelve days, a struggle to order and focus experience. It had to do with making a place for fear as a way of controlling it. He knew the smell of death and was terrified of it, for he could not anticipate it. It was not death or dying that frightened him, but the unexpectedness of both . . . he hit on the notion that if one day a year were devoted to it, everyday could get it out of the way and the rest of the year would be safe and free. In this manner he instituted National Suicide Day.

National Suicide Day reminds me of the uses of Mardi Gras in New Orleans. A period of time is set aside in which the citizens live dangerously, as they embrace their appetites totally. No wonder the peak of the time frame is also called Fat Tuesday. This period of time, which is allowed for pleasure, or letting it all hang out, sets the stage for the forty-day time-span of spartan sacrifice of the Lenten season, wherein the believers are to give up their most fondly held pleasures as a tribute to the Redeemer, who "gave up his life for us all," in the ultimate sacrifice of death, that "we might live again in eternal life." That culminating time of sacrifice and glorification forms the passion of the weekend of the Crucifixion and the Resurrection, Easter Morning. It is through letting it all hang out, on the one hand, and stripping down to a lean, sacrifice on the other, that we may come to know who we are and what we might become; our potential for wanton abandon and our possibilities for ultimate spiritual toughness.

This is also a time when the revellers in the Crescent City allow themselves to embrace the other self through wish fulfillment in which participants masquerade, or mask up to embrace, or become another, or the other side of one's most fantasied dreams. The parade and the pageantry give form to the chaos of Mardi Gras, even as it reveals the relationship between nightmare and dream consciousness that we all are possessed by. Donning a mask allows for both. It is one of the few times when the individual is allowed to let his imagination dominate human chaos. By taking on the outer form of an animal, or that of outlandish citizen, or fabulous character stripped from the pages of history, or legend, the reveller also reveals his dearest fantasies, or his most wanton lusts.

Shadrack who has seen the excesses of war, and the extremes of societal injustice at home, in peace time, and then rediscovered himself in the spartan world of the prison cell has not only found a symbolic bridge recreating his own image and his own racial identity of blackness, by creating a face that he could not initially see upon the water, he has now given us a metaphor for dealing with our deepest fears. Shadrack has faced the two greatest fears, the actual experience of war's horrors, that the immediate theater of ground combat can engender; and he has dealt with what the dread of the total loss of who I am can mean. The self-created ancestral mask aids him in bringing his identity back into focus. Now Shadrock offers up the idea of National Suicide Day. A day to deal with the first great fear of death, and as a way to get it out of the way; to let it all hang out, as it were. Because death is also our greatest truth; or our most fitful reality, that can haunt our conscious mind forevermore. But here it is presented as a ceremonial act; as a ritual of triumph over death. You make a place for death in your imaginative economy; you can get on with the process of living.

And in her next novel, *Song of Solomon*, Morrison starts the book with a ceremonial ritual of affirmation through suicide, in which Robert Smith, the insurance man, leaves this world in harmony with himself, donning mock wings, as if he could fly. He's going to fly off the top of Mercy Hospital. Here, too, Morrison embraces the theme so deeply engrained and engraved in American literature of regeneration through violence. Smith's suicide note is not a bitter message. Later we are made aware that as a member of the group called the Seven Days,

Smith was no doubt aware of the excesses of violence and racism visited against his people by whites. He has also known the excesses of racial revenge attempted by the Seven Days. The novel ends with the ritual suicide of Milkman. He has a life time of experience packed into the last year of his life. He has figured out the riddled history of his family (and to some degree that of his people) and now that he is in harmony with himself and his people's history, he is ready to give his life for the revolutionary needs of his buddy Guitar (a life for a life) if it takes that to both satisfy and awaken Guitar to the uselessness of wanton violence. After all Guitar has just accidentally assassinated the motherlode of the race, in the form of Pilate, when he was actually aiming his rifle for Guitar. So instead of avenging the whites for the crimes against blacks, Guitar turns on his own. Here Morrison criticizes the excesses of black on black crime, as practiced in the name of revolutionary purification. Guitar has become obsessed with a strike for gold; and he has turned on his "brother" Milkman. It is one of the supreme ironies of the novel that it was Guitar who first led Milkman to Pilate, who symbolizes the motherlode of the ancestral connection in the work. She is also Milkman's aunt.

By coming face to face with the meaning of the ancestor's faith that at one time the Africans believed they could fly, Milkman is affirmed: "For now he knew what Shalimar knew: if you surrendered to the air, you could ride it." Shalimar and now Milkman may believe in the idea of the Africans, that at one time they could fly . . . And the family myth is that Shalimar flew back to his ancestral home, and thereby escaped slavery. In his very fine study of contemporary African-American literature entitled *Fingering the Jagged Grain*, Keith Byerman has written of this ending: "This act of identification is simultaneously an act of differentiation, for unlike Solomon, Milkman flies into history and responsibility rather than out of it."

For me this flying out of history, or into history and responsibility, is doubtlessly based upon an earlier form of ritual, or ceremonial suicide. And so is Shadrack's National Suicide Day.

But awakening to the nightmare of the contemporary/historical reality, by going back to the ancestral nightmare of group ethos, and using those slave materialities, or symbols, born of mayhem in the furnace of group affliction, implies for me an example of Reinvention, and surely an inverted parody upon Stephen's refrain in Joyce's *Ulysses*, that history is the nightmare from which I must awaken. There are many patterns in *Song of Solomon* that recall *Ulysses*; but Morrison starts her own patterns, with the Yeatsian idea of nightmare leading to responsibility, with this crucial sense in *Sula*, and with Shadrack's emergence.

BROWN'S BODY AND SOUL

> O de ole sheep dey knows de road,
> Young lambs gotta find de way.
> —Negro Spiritual used by Sterling
> Brown as the epigram for his
> collection of poems, *Southern Road*

Among the many artistic attributes of Sterling Brown's poetry is this great story-teller's ability to wed spiritual and blues resources. So often in the art of African-Americans, this uneasy marriage was thought to be nothing more than a common-law arrangement, not to be sanctioned by those climbers up the rickety ladder of respectability, who could not countenance the fact that the same angular voice that brooded over "rocks in my bed" on Saturday night could possibly, *also*, sing out the spiritual lines: "Went down to the rocks to hide my face, the rocks cried out no hiding place" (on Sunday morning). Yet even this line is seasoned out of a humorous base of one hiding one's face, mask-like; and rocks that can cry out; a species of the comedy of faith is achieved. This is meant not in a blasphemous sense, but rather to point out that a folkloric base of human experience always undergirds the miracle of the spiritual experience. And that humor is streaked in this folklore at every artery and vein.

Sterling Brown has said: "I love Negro folk speech and I think it is rich and wonderful. It is not dis an dat with a split verb. But it is 'Been down so long that down don't worry me,' or it is what spirituals had in one of the finest couplets in American literature: 'I don't know what my mother wants to stay here for. This old world ain't been no friend to her.' "

If we are to trust the spoken word by the late Mahalia Jackson, the greatest of Gospel singers, or the verbal ideas expressed by that wonderful blues singer Big Bill Bronzy, these body and soul artistic rejuvenators of Negro folk culture were "kept separate." Yet you cannot sit still without rocking and even rolling while listening to a recording of Mahalia singing "Elijah Rocks." The sincerely seasoned secular lyricism, coupled with street savvy, are all attributes of the blues. Mahalia always reminded us that she grew up listening to Bessie Smith and Louis Armstrong. How can we forget the manner in which Mahalia turned the secular world on fire—if not around—at Newport, in a wind storm, when she seemed to make a musical miracle appear with the rowdy power of her spiritual rendition of *Didn't It Rain* at a gathering of unwashed Jazz buffs, in 1958. The specific on-stage artistic performance of Mahalia was also undergirded by the hard-driving, often blues-based Lyricism of Mildred Falls, who could play a wicked piano, as the saying goes. As Mahalia's accompanist, she approached boogie-woogie splendor, as she jammed on "Didn't It Rain." Underneath this, Mahalia was deeply influenced by the blues pianist Thomas A. Dorsey, the man who went in and out of the church. When he finally found faith, the founding father and composer of the new music (which brought the Blues and Spirituals together) actually cradled the whole world of Gospel, in his hands.

I do not mean to imply that Brown is a religious poet, nor that he is driven as an artist over the issue of the spiritual agony of the embattled Negro soul. When it comes to the African-American ethos, Sterling Brown sees that the marriage of the spiritual source is bedded down in the blues chamber: the wedded state of Afro-American discordant harmony, working together in a wonderful kind of "antagonistic cooperation," like any successful marriage. There is much spiritual seriousness and religious folk tradition in his background. The Reverend Sterling Nelson Brown, the poet's father, was minister of Lincoln Temple Congregational Church. He was also professor of religion at

Howard. A relative on his mother's side had been one of the earliest members of the Fisk Jubilee singers during Reconstruction. And who can forget that it was Sterling Brown who authored the excellent study of the spirituals of *The Negro Book of Folklore*, edited by Langston Hughes and Arna Bontemps.

The symbolic properties of a secular blues often informs, then, the fitful materialities of linkage for Brown's engagement of the other self of the spirit. But Brown's art always wants to bring this spiritual zest and soaring power back to the world of its wondrous base, its earthly delight, and its origins. It's as if Brown were playing off a call and response ritual between the blues and the spirituals, as he forms, or forges, the new music of much of his poetry.

Bear witness with me—if you please—to old-time secular fundamentals of African-American life, undergirding the spiritual, in a poem entitled, *Sister Lou*, and here transformed:

> Honey
> When de man
> Calls out de las' train
> You're gonna ride,
> Tell him howdy.
>
> Gather up yo'basket
> An' yo' knittin' an' yo' things
> An' go on up an' visit
> Wid frien' Jesus fo' a spell.
>
> Show Marfa
> How to make yo' greengrape jellies,
> An' give po' Lazarus
> A passle of them Golden Biscuits
>
> Scald some meal
> Fo' some rightdown good spoonbread
> Fo' li'l box-plunkin' David.

Here we see some old-time symbolic-secular instruments of the transforming Bluesman's art, "married-up" with the good news of gospel . . . *trains, golden biscuits, meal, spoonbread, box-pluckin'*. And, of course, some of Brown's bold, wonderful, comic, and celebrating pride, spun from the getting place and often reminding the contemporary reader, white and black, of how much one misses (just possibly) by not being a *Negro*. Even Lazarus, an early model of Jesus's resurrection, needs and can use folk food for life itself, transformed into "a passel of them biscuits," or Soul Food. What a holy (secular) communion! And David, himself, the singer of Psalms, is transformed into a "li'l box-plunkin" bluesman; and the transforming meal of his redemption into the folk is made all the more wondrously homespun by an offering of "some rightdown good spoonbread." The transformation of green-grape jellies (the real preservation of the spirit, *canned*); and then Golden Biscuits echoing golden slippers or golden tambourines of the old-time Negro spirituals. Even the harp of David is changed, into a fundamental, original jazz instrument, homemade, 'box-plunkin.' All of this of course suggests Brown's interest in the reinvention of life forms based in the Basin Street of the blues. Yet it must also be pointed out that several prominent spirituals are known for their wit, cunning, and secular humor (among them, "Scandalize My Name" is the most famous), but here I think of certain lines from "Over My Head/Lil' David." "Done told you once, done told you twice, You'll never get to Heaven a-shootin' dice. Lil' David play on your harp, hallelu . . . Lil' David done play'd on that harp, hallelu." For me it is not so much that these materialities are changed into spiritual agencies of the Good News—in the poetry of Sterling Brown—but rather the good news is seeded, saved and bedded down in the folk attributes of the blues. For in this poem it would appear as if the folk are sitting around telling those free Heavenly children all of their stories and what it truly means to be cultured, as spun from the voices of those who were slaves, once upon a time; and segregated all of the time. "An' sit aroun'/An' tell them Hebrew Chillen/All yo' stories . . ." That is blacks were schooled secularly and spiritually from the stories of the

Hebrew children, and African-Americans mixed these sagas with the epic of their own immediate and historical agonies. All of this forged a large portion of the spiritual canon; but *now* we are going to tell them our stories. We'll do the schooling this time.

This poem—like Old Lem, and Strong Men, in the Brown canon—is a good example of the poet's power with the epic sweep of oral tradition. Notice how he sings against the outrages of racism—even as he reconvenes the Heavenly League of Biblical super-stars—up there.

> Honey
> Don't be feared of them pearly gates,
> Don't go 'round to de back,
> No mo' dataway
> Not evah no mo'.
>
> Let Michael tote yo' burden
> An' yo' pocketbook an' evahthing
> 'Cept you' Bible,
> While Gabriel blows somp 'n
> Solemn but loudsome
> On dat horn of his'n.
>
> Honey
> Go straight on to de Big House,
> An' speak to yo' God
> Widout no fear an' tremblin'.

And not only is Sis Lou to do some instructing of the Hebrew children—our former tutors—she is to do some psychological counselling to certain complex New Testament figures; and then enjoy a joke with Jonah, who like the blacks was caught up in the belly of the whale of bad times, once upon a time.

> Give a good talkin' to
> To yo' favorite 'postle Peter,

An' rub the po' head
Of mixed-up Judas,
An' joke awhile wid Jonah.

Sterling Brown, the humorist, knows that much of the story-teller's tragic art is based in the early folk humor of pratfalls and mocking of the serious for purposes of a higher, earthly salvation and delight, that of the questioning mind and vulnerability of the individual initiant to the trickster. His excellent parody in *Seeking Religion* is a satire on the vulnerability of all who seek armfuls of salvation without thinking about it. Brown knows the fitful marriage of the blues and the spiritual, the spiritual and the sexual. That the spiritual weep is based in the sexual cry: body and soul. In *Seeking Religion*, Sterling Brown introduces other spirit-driven forms and influences, such as superstition, folklore; the myth of the girl seduced in the woods, as she seeks out the divine; ghost-haunting; all attributes of the spiritual otherness. Lula goes into the woods seeking her spiritual self, but the terms are placed in ghostly language and what Brown's Hester finds or discovers is that her body has been discovered by man not God; though by a godly man, acting most ungodly, Lawd-Gawd.

Waiting for her visions, but not so very eager,
Lulu sat still with a crescent moon above,
Lulu dreamt dreams a creaky-jointed parson
Hadn't so much as warned her of.

Jim found Lulu sitting in the shadow,
Lulu was sobbing, her head upon her knees;
Jim spoke to Lulu, and realized her visions,
And scared off the strange things lurking in the trees.

Jim sought Lulu when harrowing was over,
The slim moon up; and with a convert's joy
Lulu sought religion in thick deep-shadowed pinewoods,
Lulu found religion in a chubby baby boy.

This poem is one of the many biographical sketches in the Sterling Brown canon. Lula—in *Seeking Religion*—is projected here from the superb collection of the poet's gallery of portraits; and she also recalls, somewhat, the tragic vulnerability of certain women, who were portrayed in the special canvasses of Jean Toomer's female characters, in his hypersensitive, yet classic novel, *Cane*, published in 1923. Sterling Brown did in fact read *Cane* and other works by black writers, including Langston Hughes and James Weldon Johnson. At Williams College, Brown had been fundamentally influenced by poets who projected a rich, elusive simplicity, especially Robert Frost and E. A. Robinson, and Whitman. Around the time of the publication of *Cane*, Brown took his master's degree at Harvard, and he has said:

> I went into careful study of American poetry. I learned from Edwin Arlington Robinson's *Tilbury Town*, where he took up the undistinguished, the failures, and showed the extraordinary in ordinary lives. I learned from Robert Frost. I learned from my own; the man I was brought up on was Dunbar. I learned from Claude McKay.

These were also poets who were often engaged intellectually by the idea of projecting character portraits (and the development of character-in-process) in their narrative poems, as one way of entering into the grain of the reader's appetite for story-telling. Obviously we were talking here about an important linkage from oral tradition to literary tradition.

Before Sterling Brown started teaching at Howard University, in his native Washington, D.C., he taught at colleges in Lynchburg, Virginia, St. Louis, Missouri, and Nashville, Tennessee. He was the kind of rare professor who learned—willfully so—much from his students. He was absolutely enthralled by their talk, their songs, their zestfully loaded vernacular. The beguiled Brown paid one of his students a quarter for every song the professor would pen to paper. Probably the first blues Brown ever heard was a recording a student brought him. So that the third most important linkage of his artistic evolvement of oral tradition was developed in a conscious manner through a thoughtful and painstaking gathering-in by this poet of ballads, blues, spirituals, and work-songs of his people. Brown saw this gathering-up and gathering-in of these materialities as the basis for expressing the ethos of African-Americans in the poetry he wanted to write and was attempting to write at the time. Brown's own words here best express this evolvement.

> I taught at Virginia Seminary, where I learned a great deal that I could not learn at Williams. I learned the strength of my people, I learned the fortitude. I learned the humor. I learned the tragedy. I learned from a wandering guitar player about John Henry, about Stagolee, about "The Ballad of the Bollweevil." I learned folktales. I learned folkstuff.

In the famous poems, *Strong Men* and *Old Lem*, poet Brown appears in the guise of a folk secular high priest, virtually forcing the reader to bear witness, and read aloud. He also uses the chorus voice of the Negro church in a call and response variation, coupled with the actual role of the chorus in Greek tragedy, as the *suffering* voice and agency revealing group ethos, in a most troubling, beguiling litany. And out of this agony, and suffering, Brown adds a dimension to the Greek chorus role of suffering—that of affirmation in terms of the people's progress, which is naturally slower than the leader's call to memory.

Notice, for example, the spiritual nurturing—as *the* Gospel—in the "you sang" sections of the chorus, throughout *Strong Men*, as *the* chanted response of these earthly saints, which underpins the leader's or the preacher's powerful blues-based litany.

> You sang:
> Keep a-inchin' along'
> La' a po' inch worm . . .
> You sang:

171

Bye and by
I'm gonna lay down dis heaby load,
You sang:
Walk together, chillen,
Dontcha git weary . . .
You sang:
Me an' muh baby gonna shine, shine
Me an' muh baby gonna shine . . .

The ethos-bearing *you* here gives the chorus's role added intimacy *and* universality. Brown is doing some engaging improvisations on the call and response format here, too, between the *You sang* voice and the out-chorus, lining out structural voice of the larger Chorus role, which is so much a part of church liturgical dialogue. And each one of those voices plays off a different psychic energy, spirit, and layer of the nerve endings of the group's ethos. For example, the first one: "Keep a-inchin' along/Lak' a po' inch worm . . ." is a directive stripped from everyday proverbial instruction. This commonplace oracle promotes the idea of getting ahead by advancing one slow step at a time, while living out the grain in the sand, petty pace of day-to-day living, all of which appears on the surface to be getting nowhere slow. By the way, like the turtle joke in the Brer Rabbit Tales (all of us turtles look alike), the inch worm's progress might go unobserved, because, after all, they all look alike. Everyman's fate and primary existential travail are dealt within these lines. Finding a way out of noway; not only enduring, but the lines also hint at prevailing through eel-like progress of gradualism; an important overview in the long haul struggle of an oppressed people, in the early stages of their epic journey. The second voice of the Chorus suggests the second stage of the African-American saga and reveals a new energy born of this day in and day out "a-inchin' along" of the group's enduring racial memory, that ultimately, or in the long march forward, we poor inch worms will be able to lay down the burden, the "heavy load," that is the psychological burden of racism, which is the black man's burden, as well as the physical labors forced upon the Negro throughout slavery and segregation. The third oracle-like cluster ("Walk togedder, chillen, Dontcha git weary") informs us of the imperative of any rising race, or ethnic group that you must learn to hang together, or you will hang separately—the importance of group unity . . . "Walk togedder chillen, Dontcha git weary" is a line out of a spiritual and presented in the poem as a line out of what might be seen as the protest layer of a spiritual, or Gospel song.

The final Chorus riff suggests the freedom of the individual or the group to express itself, once unshackled from this heavy load.

> You sang:
> Me an' muh baby gonna shine, shine
> Me an' muh baby gonna shine . . .

Group criticism too is presented by the use of the lead voice as the folk preacher's voice. Brown suggests the rightful posture of recollecting the actuality of historical memory in the grand sweep and manner. Here is the Negro's real religious mythology; not the Negro preacher remaking his group experience through the agony of the Hebrew children, as we see in the deeply moving Negro spirituals. His memory is the group's lived out experience, his words are stripped of adornment, and muted as "Taps." The preacher's voice is an epic enunciation, as it catalogues the victims of the war of destruction against the new world Africans, and the Negro slaves.

> They dragged you from homeland,
> They chained you in coffles,
> They huddled you spoon-fashion in filthy hatches
> They sold you to vie a few gentlemen ease.
>
> They broke you in like oxen,
> They scourged you,
> They branded you,
> They made your women breeders
> They swelled your numbers with bastards . . .
> They taught you the religion they disgraced.

Leon Forrest

OLD LEM

by Sterling Brown

I talked to old Lem
and old Lem said:
   "They weigh the cotton
   They store the corn
     We only good enough
     To work the rows;
   They run the commissary
   They keep the books
     We gotta be grateful
     For being cheated;
   Whippersnapper clerks
   Call us out for our name
     We got to say mister
     To spindling boys
   They make our figgers
   Turn somersets
   We buck in the middle
     Say, "Thankyuh, sah."
     They don't come by ones
     They don't come by twos
     But they come by tens.

   "They got the judges
   They got the lawyers
   They got the jury-rolls
   They got the law
     They don't come by ones
   They got the sheriffs
   They got the deputies
       They don't come by twos
   They got the shotguns
   They got the rope
     We git the justice

In the end
And they come by tens.
"Their fists stay closed
Their eyes look straight
Our hands stay open
Our eyes must fall
They don't come by ones
They got the manhood
They got the courage
They don't come by twos
We got to slink around
Hangtailed hounds.
They burn us when we dogs
They burn us when we men
They come by tens . . .

"I had a buddy
Six foot of man
Muscled up perfect
Game to the heart
They don't come by ones
Outworked and outfought
Any man or two men
They don't come by twos
He spoke out of turn
At the commissary
They gave him a day
To git out the county
He didn't take it.
He said 'Come and get me.'
They came and got him
And they came by tens.
He stayed in the country—
He lays there dead.
They don't come by ones

They don't come by twos
But they come by tens."

The secular litany of the body and soul of the blacks is seen
wrenchingly enough in the poem *Ole Lem*. Here again we have the
leader as a kind of masked folk preacher with the Chorus's powerful
spell-binding refrain throughout the poem, in reference to the way in
which the white powers within the law or on the outside of the law
would come down on the individual black, with the weight of their
numbers, as a collective force that came to be known as the white
power structure.

Brown artfully presents the catalogue of historical suffering in the
form of a call and response litany, in which we hear the voice of Old
Lem reciting the agony as a secular credo about the racial crisis. Yet
within Old Lem's singular voice, we hear the echoes of several voices
that imply the borrowed stories of various forms of oppression, as well,
as an immediate call and response. Again, recalling *Strong Men*, this
poem is presented as a kind of study in performance, so inherent in
African-American oral and literary tradition.

> Whippersnapper clerks
> Call us out of our name
> We got to say mister
> To spindling boys
> They make our figgers
> Turn somersets
> We buck in the middle
> Say, "Thankyuh, sah."

In keeping with the standards of oral tradition, the poem moves in
layers, or blocks, or cycles. In other words, each stanza gives not only a
sense of starting all over again, each conveys a feel of new material
handed along to the poet as story-teller, so that the process of telling is
ever improvisational, like the preacher's sermon, in the orchestrated, folk
tradition. Brown—who was a noted raconteur at Howard University—
ends the poem by introducing a new character for the gallery, as a way of

existentially undergirding everything that's gone before in the public tribunal of the poem. Brown's concern and method here are typical of the unsettlement over authenticity that any story-teller within the oral tradition, might feel. Although I've tried to convince you by presenting the agonies we've faced, I know as a story-teller there is only one way to ultimately take over your imagination . . . to win the confidence of your imagination . . . So, I'll call to the stage, or the witness stand of this courtroom, a heroic figure, who lived the experience, and let me show how he, too, was cut down . . . Brought low by the forces that control our group and attempt to destroy our people. Let me show you. I can show you better than I can tell you. Or, if you don't believe what I've been saying, I'll show you better than I can tell you. This is the process that went through the poet's mind, and story-teller Old Lem's thinking, it seems to me.

Then Brown falls back on his faith in characters' voices, telling their own story. So we have Old Lem telling his saga of the group's agonies to the interviewer throughout most of the poem, who like his general listener might need more processing into believability. Finally he tells the story through the last days and life of a buddy, who is larger than life, on the one hand, and an everyday, common man, on the other, who defies the god-like/demigod powers of the white power structure, by performing, acting out; not only speaking out of turn, but also telling the whites "come and get me," after they've given "him a day/To git out of the country."

Early in the poem we have noted Old Lem's representation of two levels of African-American consciousness, when the black folk came in for the weighing up of their cotton, or corn crops, and the duplicity of the sharecropping overlords that follows. Then the call: "They keep the books" and then the echo of observed intelligence of the group, fashioned here as the response to the call . . . "We gotta be grateful/For being cheated;/ Whippersnapper clerks/ Call us out of our name/ We got to say mister/ To spindling boys/ They make our figgers/ Turn somersets/ We buck in the middle/ Say, "Thankyuh, sah." This last line is the old traditional response of subservience; but the real observed intelligence is located in the "They make our figgers . . . Turn somersets" (or somersaults). The observant share-cropper may not know exactly what the figgers ought to read, but he does know that the figures are turned on their heads and bowed against him. And he must bow to them. So that it may be said that the white man has got his figgers and niggers bowing to him. Or, as the old Southern proverb used to go—"An oughts an ought and five's a figger . . . All for the white man and none for the nigger." Also, what the whites attempt to do is make their niggers turn somersaults, which when you think about it starts off with a bow in the middle (or a buck in the middle) and then a tumble, in which you lose sight of your head.

> "I had a buddy
> Six foot of man
> Muscled up perfect
> Game to the heart
> They don't come by ones

By the time we get to the "They don't come by ones," in this stanza, we commence to shudder and tremble with both terror and pity (the great emotional and intellectual conditions of Greek tragedy and catharsis) because we know already the inevitability of Old Lem's buddy's fate. The wasting way of the power idea gives way to the idea that his power will be wasted away in any confrontation with the god-like power of the *They* (white power structure). Recalling the hero of tragedy, Lem's buddy will challenge the powers, the fates, the gods, or in this case the powerful authority of the whites (who play by unfair, racist rules) as an ultimate expression of his manhood. Like gods, or rank punks, they don't fight a fair fight—"they came by tens." Indeed Lem's buddy seeks no hiding place down here. "They gave him a day/ To git out the county/ He didn't take it. He said, 'Come and get me.'" His gallant gall before the cruel gods recalled a mythical hero of Sterling Brown's, John Henry. His presence in the poet's source material is very real at this stage in the poem. He is an ancestral link to Lem's buddy.

John Henry said to his captain,
"A man ain't nothin' but a man.
But before I'll let dat steam drill beat me down,
I'll die wid my hammer in my hand,
Die wid my hammer in my hand."

To a white Southern male chauvinist, the worst thing that could happen would be for a black man to assert his manhood, all up in the white man's face. This was perhaps second only to catching a black man sleeping with a white woman; or catch the rumor of a black man looking at a white woman.

* * *

For me a wonderful example of the sexual and the spiritual can be observed in the poem *Glory, Glory*. Here Brown celebrates the curvaceous form of Annie Mae Johnson, as something of the Divine, recalling the beauty of the face that launched a thousand ships, Helen of Troy. When Helen, the wife of Menelaus, King of Sparta, eloped with Paris, the siege and chaotic destruction of Troy was brought on. This event, of course, is at the body and soul of the great narrative tragic poem, *The Iliad*. But in *Glory, Glory* it is the fabulous form of Annie Mae—not the face—that becomes the call to chaos and comic farce. Why even the street lights lose sight of their manmade ordered changes, when setting sight on Annie Mae Johnson:

The last time I saw Annie on the avenue,
She held up traffic for an hour or two.
The green light refused, absolutely, to go off at all;
And the red light and the amber nearly popped the glass,
When Annie walked by, they came on so fast,
Then stayed on together twenty minutes after she went past;
And it took three days for to get them duly timed again.
Even so, they palpitated every now and then.

Brown continues his wonderful sweep of hyperbole about this traffic-stopper, whose walk across the street upon this occasion not only stops traffic, but leads to an apocalyptic wreck, or so it seems, even as it brings all manner of folk out onto the street to celebrate the divine figure-in-motion of Annie-Mae. Brown knows the difficulty of getting groups of the many strands of the remnant and the African-American diaspora together, at one time for any event; so as the poet celebrates Annie-Mae's great gait, he satirizes this issue of unity amid diversity. At the same time Brown knows how blacks are often amongst the numbered, but rarely amongst the counted, and so he ends his poem.

> Aaaah, Lord, when Annie Mae lays it down . . .
> If you want to take the census proper better
> come around.

So deep is this secular-spiritual base that in the poem *The Last Ride of Wild Bill*, we find that when a famous and powerful urban numbers runner is tricked by the law and finally brought low and killed, our outlaw-hero wakes up in a Hell that looks something like a policy king's inferno-paradiso. Brown appears to suggest how crime continues to pay. Wild Bill appears to be still consulted in a prison of death. At first his old world numbers players seem to be his comforters in the inferno, seeking to get the word on what number fell for the day. Actually they are his tormentors in the new world of Hell, which the old world of the living was for them.

> The devils rushed at him
> In a swarm,
> And the cool
> Wild Bill
> Grew awful warm.
> It looked like he'd
> Broke up a meeting;
> But this was the Convocation's
> Greeting:
> They climbed all over
> His running board
> "Wild Bill, Wild Bill!"

Their shouting roared
And rang through all the streets of Hell:
"Give us the number,
Wild Bill,
Tell us
What fell!"

In this marriage and satire of the secular and the spiritual in the narrative poem's denouement Brown mocks the group's obsession—even unto Death, and in the land of the dead—with the old world numbers game. For in their felled condition, the fallen ask the same question, but now in the form of a declarative, celebrating greeting to Wild Bill—still demanding to know what fell. They in turn mock their old world tormentor and Wild Bill's fall—with the fitful query turned declaration—"What Fell!" not in a question mark of interrogation, but rather as a rib to their old world tormentor, whose own number's not only up but rather *down*. (*Well, Death got you too*.) In typical African-American understatement of signifying that suggests the imprecision of Wild Bill's knowledge: he's finally reduced to their state and condition. Or, what a number has fallen. Or how have the mighty fallen. Not the grave as an equalizer, nor even Death, the old religious answer; but rather a mocked welcoming home of the reduced numbers king—finally one with their numbered fell—body and soul.

FAULKNER/REFORESTATION

Reinvention is a primary attribute of intelligence, identity, and endurance in the character make-up of many memorable black figures in William Faulkner's *The Sound and the Fury*: Dilsey, Deacon, Louis Hatcher, and Reverend Shegog. I believe that this major Afro-American cultural attribute—reinvention—was also used by Faulkner as a salient and ironic instrument of structural linkage to reveal the discontinuities and the failures of Quentin Compson, Jason Compson, IV, and the decline of the South.

The idea of reinvention suggests a broad spectrum of personal invention, when we turn to such divergent characters as the artful Dilsey, or the highly adaptable, ever-reappropriating Deacon. They appear to stand in sharp opposition to each other on the character spectrum, yet they are connected around this thematic pattern of reinvention out of chaos, or disorder, as *the* condition of this old world.

Let me simply point out here the idea of Deacon as trickster, who reinvents his situation and his identity out of an array of materials and clothing. Reinventing himself out of chaos, Deacon's identity, ironically enough is of a cloth; although his attire remains chaotic in appearance; and Faulkner weaves a cunning suit of social satire through Deacon's inventive apparel, concerning our American rage for upward mobility. For the white audience of incoming students he plays up to, Deacon must ever appear to be the butt of jokes played on him by society and history, not the captain of the chaos he so masterfully manipulates.

Recalling those Negro stage performers of the nineteenth and early twentieth centuries who had to blacken up to get on the stage, play the "darkie-role," and somehow through it all place their stamp of individualism upon their art, to transcend the greasepaint, Deacon blackens up enough to save his act (and endure at Harvard); but he also satirizes his assigned task, by becoming an individual and even a power in the consciousness of the white students, precisely by mocking several American institutions and identities, while appearing to honor them so much on the surface. Quentin also observes this about Deacon: "They said he hadn't missed a train at the beginning of school in forty years, and that he could pick out a Southerner with one glance. He never missed and once he had heard you speak, he could name your state."

One of the central problems for Quentin—the white Southerner, whom we see confronting Deacon in essentially comic stage scenes—is that of identity. The hypersensitive, highly intellectual Quentin is mastered by the smear of fantasy and reality about his inner and outer worlds. Deacon is at home with chaos, fantasy, reality, and he manipulates identities for his advantage at Harvard. Ultimately Deacon's presence in the novel forces us to reflect upon another trickster, Jason. But Jason is an example of the trickster-as-demon, as we view the cruel intentions of his staged, evil designs and deeds. The cruel pranks Jason plays almost always backfire on him. We are intrigued by his perverse angle of comic vision; but his failures at reinvention make him again and again the butt of his own racial and chauvinistic jokes.

From all appearances, jokes seem to be played on Deacon all of the time, and he courts some of these jokes, to appear as simply the traditional minstrel-show "darkie" buffoon. Deacon can be seen as constantly dressing up or reinventing the properties of his act into a comic wholeness. As presented to us through the eyes of Quentin, Deacon is a combination of trickster, wise fool, confidence man, confidante, shape-changing proteus, psychologist, "darkie" buffoon, and old plantation master.

Deacon has set up his own school of parody on the white South's imposed role of servitude for the Negro (at the railroad station, in Harvard's very backyard, as it were) by pressing into constant service a white boy to *caddy* the bags for newly arriving students. We can see and hear Deacon manipulate the masks of his act (while he instructs the white boy, as *red cap*) and shape-change from "darkie" buffoon, then trickster parodist, now commanding ole master, himself, through the listening and observant Quentin:

> "Yes, suh Right dis way, young marster, hyer we is," taking your bags. "Hyer, boy, come hyer and git dese grips." Whereupon a moving mountain of luggage would edge up, revealing a white boy of about fifteen, and the Deacon would hang another bag on him somewhere and drive him off.

I do not want to make too much of Deacon's powers for reinvention here, by extracting him from the sociology of his condition. He can't transcend the racist terrain of current thinking, nor the roles assigned his people; but he can and does artfully manipulate a slew of stereotypes, and, as we see elsewhere, patterns of Americana. Deacon is willing to demean himself—play the "darkie"—because he knows that's the final word the whites want to hear, South or North. For as he drives the white boy—as lackey—off, with the luggage, we hear Deacon embrace the "darkie"-lackey role, when he says: "Now, den, dont you drap hit. Yes, suh, young marster, jes give de old nigger yo room number, and hit'll be done got cold dar when you arrives."

Yet Quentin must leave his clothing to Deacon as an overshadowing legacy of master-servant relations. Using the scenes between Quentin and Deacon as a kind of metaphor for the overarching power and shadow of the Negro upon Quentin's soul and the soul of the South, Faulkner deploys a wonderful kind of parody on the "Me and My Shadow" routine of the American dance theatre, in which a white dancer did a soft-shoe dance upon a semi-darkened stage, with only a spotlight upon him, while in the background, a Negro dancer, danced in the white man's shadow, imitating the Caucasian's footfall. But in point of fact, as often as not, the actual steps the white dancer was performing were culled from patterns and routines he had either stolen or simply incorporated from black dancers he had observed or learned from—his *masters* in other words.

Something similar is happening here in the novel as Quentin is shadowed by the presence of the Negro, along with his other obsessions. In leaving these clothes to Deacon, as *the* Negro—who reminds him of Roskus—Quentin attempts to order chaos, personal and private, back to the order of the Old South, in which the blacks were given the handed-down effects of historical interpretation, and clothing, by the white man, playing out the role of the Great White Father, Patriarch, and The Man. This joke of history is now on Quentin; his fantasy or re-creating the old order, or reinventing it, is as dead as flat-irons attached to a drowning man's shoes.

Dilsey, of course, was Faulkner's most beloved character personally. We are intrigued by her innovative qualities and her ultimate needs for spiritual transformation and renewal, even as she successfully manipulates, through reinvention, the virtual chaos of the Compson household, and its dying light condition.

We mainly see her in the famous Dilsey/Faulkner section; her quest at this point is to put the household together and coordinate the morning breakfast. Soon we come to see that spiritual transformation is Dilsey's deeper quest (beneath the many layers of clothing apparel, as she dresses and redresses); and that her soul motive is quite similar to what her preacher sees as his flock's need, when a minister from St. Louis, the Reverend Shegog, is called to resurrect the spirit of the congregation by reinventing the Easter story through the resurrection sermon. Faulkner was wrong when he said that Reverend Shegog at first sounded like a white man. What Faulkner meant, or was trying to get at here, I believe, was the manner in which a black folk preacher will start off his sermon in a very serious, proper diction, even stately intonation and pronunciation, before he goes into the idiomatic-folk voice.

From her Negro perspective, the secular side of Dilsey accepts the idea of trouble and chaos as the condition of constant initiation and, perhaps I should say, constant reinitiation into the world as the perpetual agony of humankind. Trouble and confusion is the state of this world, and of existence, but out of this you recreate life around you. Experience is your talisman, reinvention your discipline. This means that personality is ever in process, nothing is ever static, in this secular truth of existence; therefore reinvention is the order of everyday. (The furor and excitement over this secular perception of the world was best revealed, I think, when Southern blacks often sang—"Hurry Sun Down, see what tomorrow brings.")

Although much of Dilsey's life could provide seasoning for a blues lyric, she is not a blues woman; she needs spiritual renewal. She may be able to bring a semblance of order to Compson-chaos, through reinvention, but she cannot reinvent herself spiritually; and this is what she needs on that fateful Sunday; and she needs a revelation of meaning that her life with the white folks surely cannot provide. Dilsey Gibson needs spiritual nourishment for her considerable intelligence about the meaning of the Fall of the house of Compson, the South, and the imminence of death in life, reinvention of the Resurrection for her, and in her own time, before her spiritual identity can be rested. Quentin thinks he can reinvent himself through suicide. His fantasy is that of cleaning out Hell for himself and Caddy, as a final dwelling place-kingdom-come. His *reality?* Handing down his clothing to the Negro, Deacon, who as it turns out, has found his heaven at Harvard. (But it's important here to remember that Deacon is not an-enslaved-to-tradition Southern black, in another way; he may be tied to Brer Rabbit; but he's a new kind of reinventive, black Yankee stage trickster that Quentin's static notion of the Negro has not prepared him for.)

Reverend Shegog and Dilsey may be bound for the kingdom on the character spectrum around the theme of spiritual reinvention; but the practical Dilsey was always aware of the dialectical relationship between the need for reinvention and private chaos; and how private chaos connected up to social disrepair and imminent familial doom. And as she ushers Benjy into the carriage, at one point, we hear:

> "Git in, now, and sit still until your maw come." Dilsey said. She shoved me into the carriage. T.P. held the reins. " 'Clare I don't see how come Jason won't get a new surrey." Dilsey said. "This thing going to fall to pieces under you all some day. Look at them wheels."

And from my earliest reading of the best in William Faulkner, I have continually been impressed with, and deeply influenced by, his respect for the significance of black folklore; his willingness to explore some of the ranges of racism, as this poison circulated within the tormented souls of his characters of mix-blood; his willingness to confront the racial agony of the South, and eloquently to lift this travail to stage center, as the ever-constant moral issue at the very heart and soul of this Republic; by the brilliant way he, on occasion, seized upon the genius of the race in terms of reinvention and celebrated it. And I am thinking not only here of the great Dilsey/Faulkner section in *The Sound and the Fury*, but the jazz-like motifs in the passages in the Quentin section with Uncle Louis and the lamp. And there are many others; but for me as a black novelist, Faulkner reached his greatest heights in celebrating and exploring this attribute of reinvention with the character of Rider in "Pantaloon in Black." His descriptions of Rider handling the loggers tasks, with fabulous rhythms, grace, and élan, might serve as a primer for any writer, black or white, attempting to describe, say, Michael Jordan's reinvention of the game of basketball, as he does some of his unbelievable moves on the court each night. Faulkner's experimental approach to the very form of the novel certainly has influenced my sense of artistic possibility. Conversely, I believe that the powerful presence of the black agony, in his vaulting imagination, provided Faulkner with the *essential* materiality for his greatest novels, and the towering and tragic vision, so central to the Faulknerian canon: *The Sound and the Fury; Light in August; Absalom, Absalom!; Go Down, Moses* (and sections of *Intruder in the Dust*). To strip these works from Yoknapatawpha would be like excluding the black presence from the body and soul of this, *our* American culture.

THE TRANSFORMATION
OF GRIEF

In memory of Perrin Holmes Lowrey

> One of the most interesting socio-
> logical studies I can imagine, if it
> hasn't been done, is the study of
> Faulkner's awareness of the true
> race problem that existed and how
> it's depicted in his work, chrono-
> logically.
> —Shelby Foote, at The South
> and Faulkner and
> Yoknapatawpha   Conference,
> 1976

Of the title, "Pantaloon in Black," William Faulkner is aware of the visual impact of pantaloon trousers hanging up, which creates a kind of eerie portrait of the dangling lower human form, suggesting not only the lynching that threatened black men in the South, but is also an illusion to Rider's ultimate fate. At the beginning there is the grief in black of Rider at the funeral for his beloved, deceased wife, Mannie.

In this folk opera of the South, Faulkner can only suggest the savagery of lynching by commingling the tragic with the macabre; thus the peculiarly powerful use and meaning of the title, which implies a grisly comedy that could be enacted upon the black male's body, if he asserted his spirit or will or acted willfully against injustice.

A pantaloon might originally be a staged joke played on a weak buffoon in an Italian comedy, but in the American reality, this was no

189

stage joke. Savage comedy is set against not a buffoon but a most assertive, heroic Rider figure; and it is the sheriff's deputy, as buffoon, who provides gallows comedy, in his monologue at the end of the story. Mannie's death has ironically released Rider's repressed rage at being dealt out of the game by the white man's loaded dice, even as fate has swindled him out of his beloved. When Rider returns to their house, his soul is momentarily awakened from its mourning by the illusion of her spiritual presence.

The sheriff's deputy is rendering up his grisly monologue to his wife against Rider and the blacks, who are looked upon as buffoons in black face by this lawman. This white husband and wife have lost each other spiritually in life. Now in order to enliven their marriage the deputy deploys deadly racism for her entertainment. His monologue recalls the fostering voice of frontier comedy—the stand-up monologist.

This staged set piece in "Pantaloon" implies the corruption of a primitive art form of our national humor and reveals the way racist material was passed on the white oral tradition through profane story-tellers. Many of the monologists were close to the frontier revivalist, thusly the most religious fervor with which the sheriff's deputy damns, and suspends his epithet upon the hanging form of Rider's memory. Dominating the last pages of the story, the deputy's tale reveals the Southern reality and the police state power over life, no matter how much we identify with the mythical powers of Rider.

The symmetry of the story takes on the actual structure of the segregated world of the South. One section is all about the black grieving soul within segregation. Then there is the spirit of movement, which manifests confrontation with the forces of white oppression, and finally a revelation of the myriad white racist voices locked within the deputy's monologue.

When Rider returns home, after Mammie's funeral, he thinks he sees the shape of his beloved's presence in the kitchen doorway. Immediately his beloved starts to fade from the presence of her Rider. Now the reality of her momentary presence sets in, and he says: "Den lemme go wid you, honey." For it is her spirit that he has lost to death, more than her body. If I can't go with you physically, then let me go with you spiritually, his grieving heart seems to be saying. He had himself participated in the burial of her body, earlier, had even attempted to shovel up a mound in her honor. But when Mannie's spirit fades, the very spirit in Rider descends into the land of the dead, and he is plunged into his deepest grief, beyond pedestrian and into the supernatural.

Before he was suddenly awakened to her in the shape of woman, and Mannie brought a nonconfrontational orderliness into his existence, Rider had lived life to the brim. (He had the world in a jug, but it was a bachelor's world, free, but reckless.) Soon we hear him speaking to those spirits, just as if he were talking to a natural man. Here Faulkner reads what Rider's unconscious voice would have said to the white supremacists, who have such a dreadful yoke upon his world. "Come on now. You always claim you a better man den me. Come on now prove it."

Rider seems to be saying if Death can steal my beloved off into the underworld, and the land of the dead, and rob my very soul; and alcohol, as an agent of death, can challenge and take my body, then the only way I can claim back my manhood is to embrace those forces by confronting and combatting the deadly arms of swindling power over my life that I have mentally deadened myself to and have avoided facing: the crooked white dice keeper, who symbolizes this burdensome, grievance weight in the real world.

To assert his manhood, the grief-stricken Rider must come off of his knees before the god-like forces of the crooked white man's powers. (Just as earlier he would not fall on his knees to the Christain God—in order to placate his aunt—who put his beloved Mannie to sleep forevermore.) The dice of fate is loaded against Rider, just as the white man-trickster-as-demon plays by another set of rules and with another pair of loaded dice; so, too, the cruel powers of the gods of nature who take our breath away when we are by love possessed; or, take the breath out of our beloved, with a similarly capricious flick of the wand or roll of the dice.

This story has an almost Hemingway-like turn to it; in confronting the dice keeper, Rider calls out his own encounter with death, as a further test of his manhood, at the precipice of existence, in the land of the spiritually dead, in a game for men only. Rider can no longer deal with a loaded force that evades manly confrontation. Like Othello, Rider cannot live with doubt.

Rider displays an African-American style of reinvention as he dispatches the dice keeper, turning violence itself into an art form, using not the knife ultimately but his natural hand, as a shield over the razor. The dice keeper and capricious nature can act unnaturally, but Rider is driven by a higher code of manliness. Earlier in the story Faulkner's description of Rider turning the loggers' labors into lyrical flips of artistic rhythm. Here Faulkner's 1940s description celebrates the gift of rhythm that so often graces the basketball courts of our day through the magical movement of black athletes ever reinventing the fluid game, with last second flights of imagination, which are filled with power, beauty, élan, and daring. Once again, we have a confrontation between white man and black man, with the gun and the razor:

> The razor hung between his shoulders-blades from a loop of cotton string round his neck inside his shirt. The same motion of the hand which brought the razor forward over his shoulder flipped the blade opening on until the back edge of it lay across the knuckles of his fist, his thumb pressing the handle into his closing fingers, so that in the second before the half-drawn pistol exploded he actually struck at the white man's throat not with the blade but with a sweeping blow of his fist, following through in the same motion so that not even the first jet of blood touched his hand or arm.

It is significant that this story comes after WAS; and "The Fire and The Hearth," two stories devoted to the lot of Negroes of highly mixed ancestry and blood-ties with the white McCaslin family. But here we have a black whose make-up implies no mixture of white stock, nor any blood-tie to the McCaslins. For Faulkner, Rider represents the epitome of black manhood physically. The whites might be fascinated by a quadroon, or mulatto; he or she was held as being superior to the dark-skinned Negro, because of a white drop of red blood. Indeed many blacks themselves were not untouched by this illusion of better "blue-blood." The stories that make up the novel *Go Down, Moses* are mainly about highly mixed Negroes, who are quite remarkable, but in Rider we have Faulkner's most memorable black male character.

Faulkner wanted to reveal the potential for grief in the soul of this kind of man, most strongly. White readers would be far more willing to accept a mulatto's embattled, bereaved, enlightened humanity; or that of a grieving black woman. In an almost didactic spirit Faulkner seems to be saying you think you know grief, well you haven't seen grief—this most human of tragic feelings—until you've seen it and read the implications of it in the soul of a dolorous black male; Rider's going to show you dimensions that will transform the bounds of your sense of the human possibility for grief.

Often in folk operas the hero or heroine (who never loved before and were quite chaste) finally falls madly in love, only to have that love suddenly snatched away. Rider joins other great lovers in literature—Orpheus, for example, who erupts after his beloved Eury-dice's death—with a grief beyond transformation. When the vision of Mannie fades to the land of the dead, Rider returns to the world of the physical to recreate his soul in a land of danger and death. In the myth Orpheus turns his grief into the art form of a sorrow song, so compel-lingly rendered up that it transforms the gods into a species of solace. He is allowed to enter the land of the dead and bring his beloved Eurydice out, if he will not turn back to look upon her physical form. But physical temptation is so overwhelming that he must turn to see, to look upon the beautiful Eurydice, and she is immediately swooped back into the land of the dead, forevermore, as the price of his disobedience.

The swift snatching away of the beloved often creates in both lover and audience a sense of fatalism and the sheer absurdity of the beloved's passage. Remember, too, that Rider had known Mannie before he saw her and saw her before he knew her when the bloom of her womanhood was upon her. Here again the title is used ironically, even sardonically, you can stage a tragic love story on the stage in black, but you can't stage or really conceive of a love like theirs. Indeed, this great love story brilliantly prepares us for the section, "Delta Autumn," in which Roth Edmonds abandons his black lover for the safety of the hunt, and the woods, and leaves her an envelop of cash, as the seal to his heart, for their baby's care and keeping. The light-skinned black woman tells Uncle Ike that she could have made a man of Edmonds. We are reminded that Rider's encounter with Mannie has made a man out of him, within the structure of marriage. In abandoning his heart for the hunt, the bachelor Roth Edmonds has cut off the potential for growth into manhood, through a commitment to an extended relationship, and not a fleeting affair of the heart. He has also forced his former lady to become the huntress.

Faulkner was aware of the many legends of larger than life black heroes, and vagabond outlaws, who were quite romantic. They often led powerful sex lives; some were highly competent artisans, or blues musicians, jazz-men, cowboys, or loggers; but one day they suddenly ran into what is known as a stopper—and were completely subdued into the throes of love—some times these figures also died for love, yet for all of their savvy about women, these heroes of black myth were completely unable to know the genesis from whence came this power over body and soul; particularly since they were so inviting to the opposite sex, so lucky at the dice throw of careless love. ("C. C. Rider, just see what you have done, you made me love you now your woman's come.") When this sudden lightning-like power over them is swiftly vanished from the scene, they can only read it as the savage, eternal loss of luck in all areas of their existence. Rider says it best, at the door of the crap game. "Open hit. Hits me Ah'm snake-bit and bound to die." Faulkner throughout the story beautifully captures the tragic rhythms of life and death. Remember at the beginning of the story Rider is seen at Mannie's funeral suddenly not only intruding himself into the ongoing burial ritual, but:

moving shovel, flinging the dirt with that effortless fury so that the mound seemed to be rising of its own volition, not built up from above but thrusting visibly upward out of the earth itself, until at last the grave, save for its rawness, resembled any other marked off without order about the barren plot by shards of pottery and broken bottles and old brick and other objects insignificant to sight but actually of a profound meaning and fatal to touch, which no white could have read.

Here Rider is seen creating through personal reinvention a monument to Mannie. The immediate landscape of her burial place is described in mythical references to ancestral group ethos through Ashanti holdovers of scattered ornamentation about the gravesite, which appear as chaos on the surface. "No white man could have read" is helpful too, for at the end the sheriff's deputy is unwilling to read the humanity into the grief of Rider's cross. And at the end of the novel, in the title story "Go Down, Moses," old, black Aunt Mollie, who can't read, insists that the editor of the town newspaper place the story of her grandson's death by violence in the paper, so that all can read about it (and presumably *read* out their own guilt about not opening up the South for him to find a place where he could grow and expand.)

For the patience-riddled Mollie Beauchamp feels that Roth Edmonds and the other powerful whites have made it too difficult for her grandson to live in the modern South, have sold his opportunity to achieve his life to Pharoah. Forced him to live in a condition that was. Sold his birthright, as it were. Drove him out of the land of his ancestors, by closing a viable life off from him. Gavin Stevens ("Phi Beta Kappa, Harvard, Ph.D., Heidelberg, and whose serious vocation was a twenty-two-year-old unfinished translation of the Old Testament back into the classic Greek,") is the moderate lawyer-intellectual who turns out to be the white man who can't read Mollie's protest lament, in which she and her black friends reinvent the old Negro spiritual, *Go Down, Moses,* suggesting the cracking of the Negro's patience, and forebearance, but not his will, as she weeps in her wilderness over her youngest grandson, Samuel Worsham Beauchamp, who himself has gone wild in the Northern Kingdom, in the land of Pharoah, repudiated the old handkerchief-headed way, processed his head, in an attempt to establish a new identity, to escape the agony of his racial past, and attain a new birth of freedom from grieving. His fate ultimately is most grievous.

We learn initially how he was damned by the corrupt lights of Northern exposure. Imprisoned for killing a white policeman, Samuel Worsham Beauchamp is stripped of his new false identity by his Yankee jailers who "came and slit the expensive trousers and shaved the expensive coiffure." Much of Gavin Stevens' life is devoted to scholarly transformation, at the shrines and oracles of the intellectual gods of Western thought—Harvard, Heidelberg, the Old Testament, the Greeks. Yet *his* Northern exposure and polished litany of learning, outside the South, never helps him to forge a new, more enlightened consciousness, nor to desegregate his heart, nor to transcend the entrapment of dedication to segregation. Rather his sophistication is deployed to intellectually supporting the racial status quo.

We know, of course, that the character of Faulkner's mentor, Phil Stone, supplied some of the stock for Stevens' personality, but perhaps the novelist was also thinking of certain Southern intellectuals in the Senate, like Richard Russell, Sam Irvin, John Sparkman, and James Eastland, who used their keen training, and their eloquence to defend segregation, and to read the Negro out of his birthright of freedom, by Jim Crowing his opportunities. Mollie's runaway grandson has stripped himself of his black Southern heritage, only to become enslaved to the slippery material *fronts* of Yankee freedom. His ancient Southern white kin—the offspring of the old slaver Carothers McCaslin—sold their half-brother into a form of slavery, like Joseph's brothers. And here Mollie bemoans a similar fate for yet another generation (her Benjamin, as it were), still unrecognized unless he's returned in a coffin. Samuel Worsham Beauchamp is tied in blood to Edmonds, therefore a sense of the South, for Faulkner, as one extended, but tortured family.

Mollie here becomes the motherlode of memory and the outraged conscious of not only the blacks, but of the South. We can't forget that she nursed both her black baby and the white man's baby, into life at the same time, after the death of the white baby's mother. Therefore she is the *old mother of the soul of the South*. It has gone beyond bloodlines and patriarchial power, too, for the reader, who on his initial reading is hard pressed to remember the grandson's specific ties to the old McCaslin line, made so immediately vivid by the presence of Tomey's Turl in WAS and memorable by dint of Lucas's litany of male-tie lineage in "The Fire and the Hearth." It is now a matter of profoundly reinventing the old flagship standards of the South—honor, heritage, responsibility, history, redemption—that drives Gavin Stevens from the room.

Stevens, the intellectual, can't deal intellectually with the moral implications of the oracle-like ranting litany of Aunt Mollie, as she and the other blacks update in a kind of jagged spiritual long-song, *Go Down, Moses*, at Miss Worsham's house. He flees from the agony of her presence, into the land of deadly status quo, based in taking care of the Negro, keeping him in his place, but not opening up a space of equality for them. Stevens is bent on doing the obligations of the white man's burden, helping to bring an orderliness to a chaos his apathy engendered. Mollie and her black friends go through a litany based in song and the slave experience, recombined with the Old Testament. This grief in black lamentation turns now into a jeremiad and a song of protestation. Spirituals were often known for their distilling of Negro suffering, and their control; many didn't read the protest for earthly change in their lyrics. Just as many didn't read the anguish, and anger in the Negro's celebrated forebearance.

Twenty years after this novel was written young blacks in the South were taking the old spirituals and remaking them into protest songs of the church-born Civil Rights Movement. If the indolent white fathers read Mollie's grandson out of the South, by closing him off from a chance of developing his manhood, then her song hunts down and chases the status quo out of the house of the liberal spirited Miss Worsham. Stevens can't deal with the guilt-hounding moral implications of Mollie's litany. Her suspended grief in black, transformed into a protest song, and the outraged humanity that the WAS of a closed society is still operative in the now of the mid-1940s. Although he has a more complex fate, Gavin Stevens recalls Uncle Buck and Uncle Buddy who moved the slaves into the Big House, and moved out of the quarters, but chased down their part-Negro half-brother slave seventy-five years earlier and played cards over the fate of his soul, and his marriage bed, in the mock fare of Slavery's "WAS." Buddy, Buck, Edmonds, Ike, Zack, Roth, Gavin Stevens fit into the myth of the flawed white Southerner, who if he was presented with the opportunity into manhood on race, might do the right thing. Might not, too. But it is the challenge of their history that Mollie and her kinsmen lay before the conscious of the region that most stirs us here.

For Mollie and I believe Faulkner, it was grievously important—as a form of a remembrance mandate—that the South 'move on this thing'; and *read* out its own history through the memory of the Negro, and change not so much by depending upon some change in the law, but to transform its grief internally, and change its mind, and its soul, by opening up its heart. The circumcised heart, as it were. But the white males in authority can't seem to act, in time, in order to transform contemporary history, because moral evasion is the unfortunate jewelled timepiece of the status quo for powerful men, if they can get away with it. Old, withered-up Aunt Mollie—who can't read—is offering up to the sophisticated Gavin Stevens a chance to reconsider the callous and brutalizing exclusiveness of his manhood. Intriguingly, for our day, it is two women who must offer up the agony; one black and the other white, Mollie and Miss Worsham.

> Then he could hear her behind him—the crisp, light, brisk yet unhurried feet as he had heard from descending the stairs from his office, and beyond them the voices:

"Sold my Benjamin. Sold him in Egypt."

"Sold him in Egypt. Oh yes, Lord."

He descended the stairs, almost running. It was not now; now he could smell and feel it: the breathing and simple dark,

and now he could manner himself to pause and wait, turning at the door—the high, white, erect, old-time head approaching through the old-time lamplight. Now he could hear the third voice, which would be that of Hamp's wife—a true constant soprano which ran without words beneath the strophe and anti-strophe of the brother and the sister:

"Sold him Egypt and now he dead."

"Oh yes, Lord. Sold him in Egypt."

"And now he dead."

"Sold him to Pharaoh."

"And now he dead."

"I'm sorry," Stevens said. "I ask you to forgive me. I should have known. I shouldn't have come."

Obviously Stevens is asking the wrong person for forgiveness. The lady of the house's answer is *still* compelling:

"It's all right," Miss Worsham said. "It's our grief."

"It's our grief," indeed. Now the deep moral implications for the sensitive white Southerner is not moving out of the Big House and giving it over to the Negro in a symbolic gesture; nor helping to defray costs for funeral flowers. But actually identifying with their grief, as our grief; and feeling our way into the grain of their grief, and then going beyond empathy, by seeing their suffering as the source bed of our collective guilt, our collective collusion with injustice.

Mollie and her friends have called attention to the strain on the spirit of the oppressed, through reinvention out of the collective sources of her literature, the Old Testament and the Negro Spiritual. Where once upon a time she was driven to the brink of divorce, when her husband, Lucas, started acting like a money-crazed white man, and profaned the God-given divine land for a fool's gold with a divining rod, *now* Mollie has opened up her soul to the civic virtue and moral-social implications of her grief by calling the white powers to a higher moral code of recognition—even if she (and Faulkner) were not clear on the specific route to transformation.

Mollie is so agonized over the metamorphosis occurring from within that she can only render it up in a form similar to an oracle-like riddle. Yet when we reflect upon the implied criticism earlier of even Lucas (whose going through a species of male menopause in his gold-seeking midnight rambling), we can't help but meditate upon the lack of opportunity, in the closed-off world of segregation, for creative enterprise and expression, which also drove the normally solid Lucas to distraction, and now Mollie's grandson out of the South. [A potential for creativity expressed so openly in the vaulting life of Rider, as a logger, as artisan, and lover, in "Pantaloon in Black."]

Mollie's character seems forged out of attributes of the prophetic tradition and the smitty of its antecedents. The prophetic tradition appears to have been a merging of two traits in Israel's religious development, which may help us to understand what Faulkner was getting at, in part, with Mollie, as symbolic of the evolvement of the Negro ethos. Before this period in the prophetic tradition, most of those who were called "prophets" were recognized by their ecstatic behavior—dancing, singing, trances, and, yes, divination—like that of the dervishes. They were often maintained in royal households to discover the Divine will on important issues and then to *read* them out. Is it too much to speculate that Miss Worsham—who is pictured as something of a white eccentric radical-liberal—has brought Mollie into her household not only because of her love for her colored childhood playmate, but also to get the tribulation-riddled read out from Mollie on the meaning of God's will for the South? [Yea though it be rendered up in a agitated and grief-strickened manner.] After all, Mollie's Negro existence in the Southern household always WAS. ("Mollie's and Hamp's parents belonged to my grandfather. Mollie and I were born the same month. We grew up together as sisters would.")

As Mollie and her "mad fellows" cry out at the feverish edge of tongues, in Miss Worsham's upper room, as it were, they recall these earliest folk prophets, who were known to get caught up in their violent excitement, but were also interpreted as God-possessed. That's how Miss Worsham probably views Mollie, whereas Stevens no doubt views Mollie's carrying out as self-abandonment, and typical of Negroes' lack of control under stress. They haven't been transformed into civility yet. This is what he means when he says, "I should have known," how they would act out. But Miss Worsham's been listening to this Southern-Negress-turned-prophetess. Typical of African-American reinvention, Mollie and her followers have turned Miss Worsham's house into a temple, a praise shack, a storefront church, but *now* one of agitated protest, even as they gather in a kind of wake for not only her grandson, but the impending doom of the closed society that is the South and its ultimate downfall for self-imposed claustrophobia of the spirit. Less than two decades later, blacks were turning the church into an agency for the Freedom Movement, throughout the household of the Old South, singing out similar litanies heard this day at Miss Worsham's.

The second attribute in the prophetic core of Mollie's being is that the messages of the early revivalists were filled with such religious insights, political significance, and poetic expression as to bring prophecy to another dimension. When I read Mollie here I can't help but think of these ancient figures, who were so much like the leaders of early Hebraic history. Spiritual leaders who waged warfare against paganism and religious hypocrisy and spoke out for justice and freedom in crucial situations. Some of the leaders proclaiming, often against the very priests or princess of their time, what they regarded as the will of God, and became the conscience of their nation. Among these forerunners was Moses himself. Thus, here is another dimension to the title story; and the novel, and the role the blacks play throughout the work.

We are not unprepared for Mollie's *radical* behavior. How can we forget when Lucas goes half-mad over a dream of plundering gold from the land, sacrifices his work, and abandons the hearth he so honored that Mollie almost kills herself carrying away his foolish divining machine to bring him to his senses. How she after forty-five years of marriage refuses to live with Lucas until he ditches his crush on gold and his phallic divining rod. In revealing to Roth why she must have a divorce, she sounds like a high priestess evoking and ringing down an oracle: "'Because God say, 'What rendered to My earth, it belong to Me unto I resurrect it. And let him or her touch it, and beware.' And I'm afraid. I got to go. I got to be free of him.'" Her wisdom is forged from the link of God in Nature, too, and a reverence for the land from which she and her kind have culled their existence. Faulkner believed that in general the Negro was closer to the land, in his *natural state* in the South. What Lucas is doing is unnatural.

Mollie's wisdom is closer to what the South has inherited from the Indian, yet different, more complicated, for their belief is that the earth is no man's but for all men. Man can turn over God's earth for crops to replenish himself; and to bury his kind (which links us back to the Indian mound, defiled for a whiskey still, earlier) but not to profane the earth, the way Lucas is doing and in a manner that's no longer just for sport, or gold, but belief: and "What's rendered to My earth" by Nature, that is, "belong to Me unto I resurrect it," which, of course, suggests the Judgment, or the divining Time of humankind's days upon this earth, when God will overturn the earth and do the divining, and the judging, and the reading out from the book of recollection concerning one's days upon this earth.

Now the divining rod is an unnatural manmade tool to defile the earth for the hunting of gold and suggests the modern machines that take men like Lucas out of their natural state of mind for the pursuit of gold. The divining machine would divide man from woman—just as divorce too would also divide what God has put together. The divining machine and divorce are false *machineries* that would take man from his natural enterprises—waste away his powers—and they are carefully united here by Faulkner. Mollie can hardly articulate the word "divorce" but it is her way of calling Lucas back to his natural self-through the shock treatment such a declaration would infuriate within him; she is afraid for Lucas's moral soul—indeed for what lies before him upon the day of the resurrection of all life, when all graves will be opened and the final reading will be given; and not only her marriage.

Mollie must take on this extreme form of behavior because Lucas is trying to resurrect out of the Lord's earth by the sweat of his brow, not bread, nor crops, but gold, in order to bring him back to his senses about the land, the fire and the hearth. Roth Edmonds only thinks she's talking about the gold and the marriage.

Roth's advice would initially be that Mollie go out and take the divining machine.

> Wait till he comes in with that thing tomorrow morning, then take it yourself and go down to the creek and hunt buried money. Do it the next morning, and the one after that. Let him find out that's what you are doing—using his machine while he is asleep, all the time he is asleep and can't watch it, can't hunt himself. Let him come in and find there's no breakfast ready for him, wake up and find there's no supper ready because you're still down in the creek bottom, hunting buried money with his machine. That'll cure him.

Here Roth is promoting the deployment of the very devices of subterfuge the Negro might apply on the white man to gain advantage, since he, the Negro, is powerless—like the female Mollie—to take on the white man, or, in her case, her husband Lucas, who is something of a chauvinist. These are also the rules of deceit and trickery that the white man has applied against the Negro and the Indian. And as we read Roth it all recalls, terribly enough, what happened when Mollie came under his father's roof, and in the manhood search, and the heartbreak of Lucas. When Lucas came into his own house evening after evening and found that "there's no breakfast ready for him, wake up and find there's no supper ready . . ."

Roth's advice, like his father's action, would take Lucas's woman from him; and take her from his hearth. This is what Lucas is referring to when he says: "I'm a man. I'm the man here. I'm the one to say in my house, like you and your paw and his paw were the ones to say in his. You ain't got any complaints about the way I farm my land make my crop, have you?" He's talking about his work, in relationship to his manhood; and how all of that must not be viewed any differently in his house than it is in the white man's house—particularly the house of Edmonds, *with their history, and my business.*

Now the prophets were known primarily for the ringing power of their declarations, known as oracles. There is for example in Jeremiah, the idea of "the circumcised heart."

In many cases the original oracles represented those brief two-line statements uttered by a prophet, in an ecstatic seizure, usually pregnant with meaning and polished in form. The prophets would repeat them again and again; improve them so that they would be memorable in rhythm and sound. These ancient oracles, collected decades after they were uttered, were supplemented with later material and finally arranged without recognizable change, but were written by at least five different sources. No, the prophets were speakers, not witnesses alone. Don't forget Mollie has not witnessed the agony of her grandson's Northern experience; but she certainly witnessed the troubles of the black experience in the South, and its failures.

And it's the failures of the white South to open up a closed society, for their native son(s), which have driven Mollie up a wall into a dervish. The prophets were not writers; they were prophets. A few of Isaiah's lines were written down; Jeremiah dictated some of his materials to Baruch. Each prophet had his storehouse of oracles; and in death, oracles were expanded upon to include what the writers thought the prophets might say. This perhaps recalls an analogue with Plato's *Dialogues.* Or were they Socrates? Most of the preexile prophets were prophets of doom. Their message is that you are doomed. You ought to correct yourself, but you won't. Their message is obsessed with piety for God and ethical or societal criticism under pressure of impending doom. Mollie's oracle at Miss Worsham's surely sounds like a doom dirge to me.

We have come to call the last section of *The Sound and the Fury*, The Dilsey/Faulkner section. I would like to carry this view over somewhat to the writer's relationship to Mollie. Aware as he is of her evolvement at this point in the novel, wherein she had gone to the white man, Carothers Edmonds (in the old traditional way of seeking help from a "decent" white man) seeking a divorce from her wayward husband of forty-five years, Lucas Beauchamp, who had abandoned the marriage bed and the hearth in order to defile God's earth in the hunt for gold, with a crazy divining machine (and the erection of a whiskey still within the land). But before that, earlier in her life, Mollie had abandoned her hearth and bed to go under Zack Edmonds roof to nurse this very same Roth Edmonds for the first six months of his life, because of at least three factors, which all somewhat converge: maternal instinct and love for the abandoned child of her husband's kinsman; the Negro Mammy tradition, and the directive power from the white man's singular authority over the life of a black woman in the South—all of which brought out Lucas's understandable masculine anger. For not only is she nursing the white man's child, under his roof, she is nursing Lucas's son there, too. No doubt he couldn't think something to the effect: *If you are sleeping and nursing under that white man's roof, you've already defiled my manhood and my bed. I don't need to know whether you are sleeping with the white man. In his house he can do as he pleases . . . I know males . . . and I know the white male, who in this land can do as he pleases. But no more, at least not as far as Lucas Beauchamp is concerned . . . All of that kind of relationship was in the WAS . . . but not in my mind-set.* So, in order to reclaim his manhood, Lucas faces down Zachary Edmonds, the infant's father, almost kills him, and demands the return of his wife. At this point, too, we are reminded of the power of men over the lives of women, so memorably played out over a deck of cards, in the first story, "WAS."

But *now* Mollie is in the process of laying down a mandate to the white male authorities, as the oracle-like voice of a wrathful God.

Faulkner's "rewrite" of Mollie's oracle symbolizes for the illustrious Southern novelist the movement of the Negro character's evolvement from internationalization of religion to an active societal criticism, in which *this* specific Negro character, Mollie, no longer simply recalls scripture, but she improvises upon written scriptural tradition recombined with the most famous of the Negro protest spirituals out of oral tradition. No longer quite under the overarching power of the white man, she has found some elbow room within the structure, as she comes into her blackness and into her womanhood. From this perceptive, we can look upon Faulkner—as he writes out her lines—as Mollie's Baruch. One who has "read" her phrases of grief and transformed them into a lyrical art, worthy of the agony of Mollie's people. Here she becomes something of a female Moses . . . Go Down, Moses and Let My People go . . . Not quite a Harriet "Moses" Tubman, to be sure; but in the sisterhood. I am also talking here about the novelist's relationship to the "super-subtle fry" of his characters who come out of the batter of a yeasty dough of oral tradition, and that connection and relationship to literary lyricism. As a black Yankee novelist, this is surely one of my deeper connections to Brer Faulkner.

But I would also like to point out how beautifully the novelist Faulkner associates this biblical tradition with secular updating, written tradition, with the reading out loud of history, the relationship of written literary tradition to oral tradition, and the discovery of moral duty to other sections of the novel, in general and specifically, the discovery scene in Part Four of *The Bear*, on the part of Isaac McCaslin. When Ike's cousin Cass Edmonds—his mentor of woodsmanship—says that there are places in the Bible that rationalize slavery as the proper situation of blacks, Ike tells him: "There are some things (God) said in the Book, and some things reported of Him that He did not say." He goes on to argue that the Holy Scriptures were written to be "*read* . . . by the heart, not by the wise of the earth because maybe they don't need it or maybe the wise no longer have any heart." For Ike these men who really wrote the Scriptures "were writing about truth and there is only one truth and it covers all things that touch the heart." (This is how Faulkner saw his writer's relationship to Mollie, it seems to me.) And there is also the shock of recognition of terror, similar to what happens in Greek drama, when Ike discovers while leafing through the modern text of transaction of the commissary ledgers and reads out in the handwriting of his father and uncle the business transactions of the old plantation and the journals kept on the slaves—births and deaths, included. It is in the course of reading these journals that he comes upon the shocking story of incest by his grandfather, the founder of the dynasty, Old Carothers, whose saga sounds very much like an ancient biblical patriarch. For the journals reveal, indirectly, but obviously, that Old Carothers sired a child by his slave daughter. Because the deed of his inheritance of the land is based in the deed of not only slavery, but incest, Ike attempts to expiate his grandfather's sin by repudiating the bequest of the land. Perhaps as honorable as this rejection is intended to be on Ike's part, Mollie's commandment of not repudiation but redemption through the responsibility out of the nightmare of history, in the title story, seems to me even more honorable. More reading out of history and reality? Mollie must still go to the white man for help, for the WAS is still Now, but changing. Gavin Stevens, the white attorney in Jefferson to whom she turns, to get her grandson's body returned home, discovers from the wire service (our modern-day secular scripture, linking oral to written tradition), with the help of the local editor, how, in fact, the young man died. He arranges for the paper not to print how and why the young man died. Also, Mollie will be told that he died up in Chicago and that he will be buried there. But Mollie wants the truth recorded in the paper, so that it can be read, and for her grandson to be brought back home and given a real burial on this his native land, which has been so often defiled.

* * *

The prophetic tradition stressed an internalization of religion and rendered an assault on external form, where there was ritual without meaning. For example, Jeremiah's idea of the covenant of the heart, or the circumcision of the heart, which argues that the true meaning of religious ritual is inward, of the heart, and the condition of the heart is the true relationship of God to man. In the secular-spiritual sense, this is the young woman's meaning in "Delta Autumn," when she tells Uncle Ike, about love: "Old man, have you lived so long and forgotten so much that you don't remember anything you ever knew or felt or even heard about love." Here she is bringing together all forms of love, eros, agape, and filia. This issue of the heart and form is at the bottom of the conflict between Jesus and the Pharisees, the need for an activated personal witness.

The drive to make religion real was also at the center of the social struggle of the Freedom Movement, for oftentimes the religiously ecstatic experience had become so ritualized and grief so stylized within the black church, as to numb its followers from societal confrontation with the sin of segregation, as a moral evil of the Southern kingdom, and a moral blight upon the national body politic.

The tradition that Mollie comes out of was also nourished by the idea of the covenant, which can be traced through the whole history of the Bible from the preprophetic view of responsibility, duty, obligation, interpersonal relationship with God and Man (you do this for me, I'll do that for you) to finally a burden and even an agony. That is, for all of the power of a messianic role in the history that the Jews found in the Old Testament, the Civil Rights devotees of the Fifties and Sixties believed that these forces were operating in their history. In both cases each group might be heard to exclaim that *it isn't easy being a chosen people.*

Mollie's agony symbolizes the shifting of her vision and her energies inward and then projecting them outward from her grieving, in this act of transformation, and it provides us with a metaphor of the coming consciousness of the Negro people, for Faulkner. Indeed the spirit of movement in the work leads us to the very capitol steps of the Civil Rights Movement in terms of the condition of Mollie's heart. But her agony (and that of her fellow blacks, with Miss Worsham) is *presented by Faulkner behind closed doors.* And yet as Ralph Ellison said in an interview, in 1965: "If you would find the imaginative equivalents of certain civil rights figures in American writing, Rosa Parks and James Meredith, say, you don't go to most fiction by Negroes, but to Faulkner."

Dramatizing the message was yet another tradition of the prophets, so alive in the symbolic acts of the Freedom Movement. For example, one story has it how Jeremiah was ousted from the temple, because he preached an unpopular gospel that Israel would be overrun by opposing neighbors. His message of doom was unpopular. But upon the next occasion he showed up with a wooden yoke about his neck in order to reveal their attempt to hinder him from telling them the truth, and what God wanted them to know. Again, he was seized and barred from the temple, and the next time he turned up preaching with an iron yoke about his neck. How close the Civil Rights Movement was to this? Confrontation over and over again forged out of creative ways of encountering evil publically, born out of Mollie-like private utterances and wrenchings and litanies, but public, on the courthouse steps, the restaurants and on to the temples of power.

Now let me pause here for a moment to suggest where Faulkner stops in terms of symbolic action juxtaposed with symbolic gesture by calling your attention to a story written by Richard Wright, in his collection of stories, *Uncle Tom's Children,* published shortly before Faulkner's novel, *Go Down, Moses.* In the instructive, but contrived story of Wright, "Fire and Cloud," the role of leadership of the blacks in a movement flames out of the cloud of the religious fog of fear. Blacks ultimately march out of their sufferings in a protest for food, and change; their minister as civic and political leader comes into his manhood at the height of the march even unto a point of having the mayor of the town come to him. This was a rare kind of story for Wright to create: a story in which a black man came into some semblance of his manhood by dramatizing his people's agony and by transforming the grief of his private abuse into a public act of defiant declaration of independence.

For me, the Freedom Movement recalled the prophetic tradition of dramatizing the message in a most public way. What needed to happen was an evolvement of Mollie's private energies recombined, reinvested into public confrontation—in the form of the seamstress Rosa Parks—with peaceful resistance as the philosophical overview. It is perhaps one of the supreme ironies of our culture that the one major American writer, who could see the potentiality of black character in terms of its capacity for suffering, forbearance, humor, sturdiness of spirit, quest for honor, capacity for deepest memory, did not see that the blacks would have to take the leadership role in order to heighten this patience and forebearance into a movement of marching bodies and a physical confrontation with evil, if not only the blacks but the South was ever to free itself, and heal its history; and that to some degree the Federal Government would have to help in this effort; even if it came to the introduction of military force (which it did in point of fact, at Ole Miss, a month after Faulkner's death).

Shelby Foote, the Mississippi novelist and Southern historian, who knew Faulkner, expressed his own interpretation of Faulkner's view of the Civil Rights struggle at the 1976 Faulkner and Yoknapatawpha Conference, at The University of Mississippi:

> His sympathies were largely with the Negroes in the thing. And he was ready to stand up for them. But he moved into that position gradually. He began with the belief somewhat similar to Booker T. Washington's, that a man ought to attain his dignity, and then the world would be obliged to recognize it. Let down your buckets where you are, and all that. He didn't stay with that too long. That was the first tenuous turning loose of the old thing that he was born and raised to believe. He began to believe that the Negro's true hope was Lucas Beauchamp's way: personal dignity to confront the yahoos with. Later he realized that it was not enough—that you can't ask a man to be dignified when you haven't given him a place to take a bath and you pay him four dollars a week to shine your shoes—and he moved considerably.

Yet closed off as he was from the growing world of the black middle-class leadership in the South, Faulkner didn't see the intellectual fervor with which the black middle-class church and its allies was ready to combine its efforts with that of the furor of Mollie's old-time religion. He probably didn't realize that the laws had to be changed; that the blacks were ready to go down dead in order to charge Mollie's riddled agony into perils of dangers through a confrontation with evil in the form of civil disobedience and to face it en masse (without alcoholic spirits too, born out of the troubles they'd seen, the perils Rider encountered with the crooked white dice keeper, without razor, or avenging fist). Probably Faulkner didn't realize that the sheer economic potential of desegregation would help to open the eyes of many white industrialists, and civic leaders. Yes, and that there would have to be some blood shed. And that perhaps a fraction of the South was closer in spirit and memory at least to the relationship of Mollie and Miss Worsham (and Faulkner and Dilsey) than it was to Orval Faubus and Miss Daisy Bates.

Stevens flees from Mollie's presence to the easy task of white folks' required duties of setting up the funeral arrangements pro forma and later to the safety of his scholar-lawyer's desk, where he can *read* his papers in peace; just as Roth Edmonds in "Delta Autumn" fled earlier from his responsibility (into the woods and the easy prey of the hunt for the female deer) rather than face the duty of the desegerated heart he had incurred in the bed: the Negro woman he impregnated. (Faulkner knew something about runaway fathers.) This light-skinned Negro woman—whose complexion might have been described as Delta Autumn—has a bundle of life for Roth and he has a bundle of cash for her. Money is not central to her—she wants to know about the condition of the heart. "I could have made a man of him" she says of Roth to the old bachelor, Uncle Ike, that is, I could have transformed him. "He's not a man yet. You spoiled him. You, and Uncle Lucas and Aunt Mollie. But mostly you."

Uncle Ike now discovers three things: he learns that she knows his family legend and that she is related to the white lineage through both miscegenation and incest. But first of all he knows that she is a Negro. Now he moves on a completely different level of feeling when he thinks of the relationship of Roth to the attractive huntress of the heart. "Maybe in a thousand or two thousand years in America. But not now!" He cried, not loud, in a voice of amazement, pity, and outrage: "You're a nigger!" (In all of the sections that make up *Go Down, Moses*, a species of social schizophrenia is implied. The white reaction to the abundance of life is that you must repress the elemental feelings, or the natural passions, for if you don't that means you are acting like a "nigger." For the Negro you must repress the elemental and act similar to the white form of behavior the whites claimed to live by and seal over human passion and the heart and sexual conduct by the light of day. But as this story of the young woman in "Delta Autumn" suggests, these rules were not strictly enforced, not lived by in the South, when that evening sun went down; still and all for the blacks you must repress the elemental and act similar to the white manner . . . and at a certain level the refined Miss Delta Autumn has done just that, with her good education and her fine English; but she has not repressed the feelings of her heart, and because of this and because she has acted upon those feelings, she is acting like a "nigger," in the eyes of her lover, who can't own up to his responsibility of bed, or babe, and the fact of their love.

If Mollie's heightened consciousness—as voiced through wrenching protests—has taken us up to the frontier of the Freedom Movement, and dropped us too, then Roth's lady speaks out her demands about her former beau's shiftlessness, with a clearly stated eloquence, which takes us to the borderline of the Woman's Movement, even as she stalks out her dear runaway in the woods, in the vanishing ecological frontier to civilization. Actually she wanted to civilize Roth.

There are several puns and humors behind all of this, of course, recalling the story "WAS." The freest people in the South were the Southern white man and the black woman; and the older story, that a man chases a woman until she catches him. The action of Roth's unnamed lady—every woman, I take it to read now—marks the turning point, symbolically, of a kind of relationship between black women and white men, at least in this case, as the bargain over freedom, and responsibility through the bed posts of segregation. In her attempt to civilize Roth she has brought her protest to the very heart, if not the soul of the hunting grounds of male preserves, the woods. She reads Uncle Ike off in the most encompassing, unriddled, uncompromising language—that all runaway fathers, white and black, might well learn to read and to transform themselves by. She also speaks of the covenant of the heart that might well be rendered up to Roth. She speaks artistically for Faulkner's highly associative novel which is also addressed to the sheriff's deputy in "Pantaloon in Black" who was dead to the heart: "Old man have you lived so long and forgotten so much that you don't remember anything you ever knew or felt or even heard about love?"

MOLLIE'S GRANDSON:
EXECUTED IN ILLINOIS FOR KILLING
A CHICAGO POLICEMAN

We were standing before the bar. Not the bar of justice, but a bar in Chicago, and I found myself somewhat enjoying the company of this Southern white acquaintance. The conversation had drifted into the difficulty of teaching young American blacks and whites in today's environment about culture, history, and particularly literature, mainly because they haven't read anything, or don't know how to read life in literature. This encounter occurred in the late 1970s.

I could also tell that my acquaintance apparently felt he needed to get something off his chest and was feeling enough Southern comfort in this Yankee exposure to use me as a sounding board. We had initially struck up a conversation about a panel on Southern Literature, in which the presence of Faulkner's work dominated the discussions. And we had both felt a certain absence of renewal in the interpretations of the papers on Faulkner at this MLA (Modern Library Association) session. As it turned out, we both drank the same kind of bourbon and already found that we were firm believers in the instructiveness of tall tales, argumentation, civility, and the significance of Faulkner on American letters. But what of the lines of demarcation.

Sounding very much like Shelby Foote—in both voice and historical vision—my acquaintance said to me: "Look we were ready . . . all right we, the white remnant of the South who grieved over our land and its cultural history . . . in the matter of race . . . and wanted to see it move forward, enough of us, anyway, to make a difference. Were ready to move, with the blacks. There was a historical sense. But we did not have the energy nor the will. Hell, the guts, the will to lay it on the line, the fortitude. The courage. And that's what I guess you were criticizing about the panel of papers this afternoon. So, that's why I did what I had to do. I mean I had to kick this black kid out of my——"

"You did what?" I said, thinking, oh brother, here we go. Who did he think he was—Quentin at Caddy's wedding? What black kid? Who was this scant acquaintance talking about? I had certainly wanted to kick any number of kids, black and white, into tomorrow, for not showing a proper respect for history. Yet, if they were ignorant, who was to blame but my generation and myself. If they lacked civility and respect of literature, then blame it on us.

Now in the true spirit of Oral Tradition, my acquaintance started up all over again:

"I kicked his butt out of my class. Oh, we had quite a confrontation all right."

"You did what?" I repeated, immediately assuming the look of Ali and the energy of Frazier, as if called to arms in a civil discourse.

But where my retort would have been enough to bruise the hearts of many liberal Yankee friends into a state of *nevermore,* my acquaintance was too serious about history, hardy over his culture to go down dead. And so I thought we may be in for a night of it. For if he was bent on playing Zack Edmonds I had neither the will, nor the razor to play either Lucas, or Lawd today, Rider. Maybe we might just simply end up hand-wrestling, in the name of Brotherhood, and even manliness. But I must hasten to tell you that I didn't like the way his red neck moved as he spoke of this black kid he had kicked out of his class. What Southern gods had this young African-American despoiled to prick the Southern soul of this white Southerner? Robert E. Lee? Or Jefferson

Davis? Was my acquaintance a real-life, true-blood relation of Gavin Stevens? After all, he too had attended Harvard. But now my acquaintance was reading it off, royally:

"This kid just didn't understand who he was up against, nor more importantly what he was up against when he talked about Martin Luther King, Jr. He was the saviour of the South. He saved the soul of the South. So when this black kid, couldn't or *wouldn't* pay proper respect to the memory of Dr. King, I kicked his royal ass out of my class." Now I was turning red. Then I said:

"You mean instead of reading him off, you kicked him out?" . . . This was getting to be some contemporary version of "WAS."

"I'm telling you, Mr. Forrest, I had tried all of that. But he simply would not listen to reason—nor history."

"What did he call Dr. King? De Lawd?"

"Well, at first, but then it got worse. Called him an Uncle Tom, and honkies like me his master. Said he sold the Negroes out. Now nobody calls Doc King an Uncle Tom in my time to my face! I can take the a-buse. Look, we were ready to move, enough of us; but we couldn't because we didn't have the guts. We were in a mark-time-mark situation. But we needed somebody to come out of our guts with the guts to march us into tomorrow. But none of us, or very few of we moderates could, or would take the leadership. So if the country calls Lincoln its Redeemer, then I say, Dr. King was our Southern Saviour."

And so he went on and on. Agitated. And we went back and forth. I was still pissed at the idea of a white man kicking a black kid out of his class over a disagreement about a black man's role in history. As it turned out, the ill-mannered, protesting student had been as uncompromisingly worshipful of Malcolm X as my acquaintance was of Dr. King's role as saviour. At one point I even speculated what Mollie would have thought about him kicking one of her own grandsons out of his classrooms. *But I also thought: Well now, I can see how Dr. King had the impact upon this man's psyche that Lucas Beauchamp had on Chick Mallison. Chick was as haunted by Lucas, as the South was and is haunted by the Black Presence.*

"Well, she would have given me a fairer reading than you are giving me," he said. "She would have understood what Dr. King did with our grief." And suddenly I was remembering one of the great passages in Faulkner's *Intruder in the Dust.* From Chick and about Miss Habersham and, of course, Mollie:

> and now he knew what it was that had nudged at his attention back in his uncle's office when he had recognized her and then in the next second flashed away: old Mollie, Lucas' wife, who had been the daughter of one of old Doctor's Habersham's, Miss Habersham's grandfather's slaves, she and Miss Habersham the same age, born in the same week and both suckled at Mollie's mother's breast and grown up together almost inextricably like sisters, like twins, sleeping in the same room, the white girl in the bed, the Negro girl on a cot at the foot of it almost until Mollie and Lucas married, and Miss Habersham had stood up in the Negro church as godmother to Mollie's first child.

I had not been willing to share Dr. King with my acquaintance, even though when all was said and done, Martin Luther King belonged to us all, but most particularly the South that he helped save economically and politically—and helped redeem spiritually, morally, and histori-cally for my new-found friend.

And we both ended up wondering why was it that the literary always drives us back to the verbal, and the oral, for a deeper intellectual slugfest, and, of course, not satisfied there we must have panels to gain leverage and restore order, honor, and civility of tongue, to read and remember, reflect and hopefully not to forget—to be truly free.

In memory of Allison Davis

P articular poetics of Herman Melville's *Benito Cereno* illuminate the story-telling power of this novella and undergird the endless linkage of oppositional forces that abound through a synthesis of intelligence, bearing surprises of instruction via violation of the expected, concerning a contemplation and an interrogation with historical process, role-playing masquerades, life as an imitation of art, the complex nature of evil, innocence, and power; the coming of the American character in the nineteenth century; Shakespeare, Christianity; slavery; minstrel shows, race relations, national types, racism, and finally the existential nature of man's experience, and the apocalyptic revelation of life as a process of constant upheaval.[1]

The narrative, action, and plot of the novella can be easily summed up, but it is this complexity of language that engages the reader's contemplation of "shadows present, foreshadowing deeper shadows to come."

The year is 1799, the setting the waters off a small uninhabited island near the southern tip of South America. Captain Amasa Delano, whose ship, *The Bachelor's Delight* (a combination of sealer and general trader) has anchored at the island for water; he sees a strange sail, showing "no colors."

---

[1] *Benito Cereno, Billy Budd and Other Tales*, a Signet Classic. Subsequent references are to this edition and are placed in the text.

Observing that the ship is in distress, the New Englander, Delano, lowers his whaleboat so that he may board the vessel and help to bring it in. As he comes closer it looks like a "white-washed monastery." Finally Delano sees the ship as a Spanish merchantman carrying slaves, amongst "other valuable freight," from one colonial port to another. Captain Delano notices the "oval of the shield-like stern piece intricately carved with the arms of Castile and Leon, medallioned about by groups of mythological or symbolical devices, uppermost and central of which was a dark satyr in a mask holding his foot on the prostrate neck of a writhing figure, likewise masked."

Whether the ship has a figurehead is not clear to Delano, as he nears the *San Dominick*, for a canvas masks the bow, below which has been painted ("follow your leader"). The name of the ship appears in corroded letters, once gilt. Recalling for the reader many slave quarters in the South, the blacks outnumber the whites on board; and more than is usual Delano notes on a slave transportaion.

Turning to see who is in command, Delano sees Don Benito Cereno, the Spanish captain, and Babo, the small African slave and the Spaniard's's apparent body servant. Observing without knowing or understanding typifies Delano's imperception throughout the work, and Melville writes: "As master and man stood before him, the black upholding the white, Captain Delano could not but bethink him of the beauty of that relationship which could present such a spectacle of fidelity on the one hand and confidence on the other. The scene was heightened by the contrast in dress, denoting their relative positions."

Delano and the reader do not know that, in fact, Babo and his crew of slaves have overtaken the ship, murdered many of the Spaniards, and suffered Benito Cereno and a few whites to survive only so that the *former masters* (italics mine) can navigate the ship back to Africa. But the artistic point made here is typical of the kind in which Delano's observation will fail to bring him insight. "The black upholding the white," on the other hand is instructive to us on reflection, as it suggests the reverse relationship of slave to master. The slave upholding the institution through his bodily presence. Master dependent on slave.

Delano's second kind of imperception is unleashed by the role-playing masquerades that Cereno and Babo create throughout much of the first part—with Babo bodily conducting Cereno's spirit, as he carries off his staged charade. Recalling the Shakespearean stage manager's role, played by Hamlet, or more to my point, Iago, in *Othello*, Babo has set up his own play, within a play, as a way of masking his real role as revolutionary-mutineer.

In one of the more famous staged scenes, Delano witnesses Babo shaving and barbering his master, with great dexterity, and the Yankee captain can't help but think of the way in which Cereno's propped up head reminds him of one being prepared for the beheading guillotine. But he quickly dismisses this observation. Babo nicks Cereno in the shaving process. Later, Babo nicks himself, in sacrifice it appears, and Delano's unsettlement concerning Babo's fleeting breach of the Negro body-servant's craft, is assuage.

But while Delano is preparing to return to his own ship, he is shocked by the action of Cereno, who without warning, jumps off the *San Dominick* into the departing boat, *The Rover*. Cereno explains that he is trying to escape from the Negroes, who have mutinied weeks earlier—guided by their leader, Babo. Babo is subdued and captured when he leaps after Cereno and tries to kill the Spaniard in Delano's boat. The African is held as the head of the mutiny. After Delano is taken aboard *The Bachelor's Delight*, he directs his own men to arm themselves, board the runaway slave ship, and subdue the mutineers. A parody on an impending civil war ensues. The mutiny is put down. The two ships proceed in company to Lima, where court action is taken against the slaves; they are punished for the rebellion. Babo is executed and beheaded. And the embattled Cereno eventually enters a monastery near Lima and soon dies.

The second part of the work is the Deposition of the trial itself. Melville found the genesis for the story in Chapter XVIII of Amasa Delano's *A Narrative of Voyages and Travels in the Northern and Southern Hemisphere (1817)*. But he edited and rewrote the deposition for his own artistic purposes. The final section is a yeasty epilogue-denouement, between Cereno and Delano, after the mutineers are brought to trial and before Cereno enters the monastery.

But it is this remarkable poetry of violation, deviance, and synthesis that I want to concentrate on now. Early on, from the vision of Captain Delano we are told:

> Upon gaining a less remote view, the ship, when made signally visible on the verge of the leaden-hued swells with shreds of fog here and there raggedly furring her, appeared like a white-washed monastery after a thunder-storm, seen perched upon some dun cliff among the Pyrenees. But it was no purely fanciful resemblance which now, for a moment almost led Captain Delano to think that nothing less than a ship-load of monks was before him. Peering over the bulwarks were what really seemed, in the hazy distance, throngs of dark cowls; while fitfully revealed through the open port-holes, other dark moving figures were dimly described as of Black Friars pacing the cloisters.
>
> Upon a still nigher approach, this appearance was modified, and the true character of the vessel was plain—a Spanish merchantman, of the first class, carrying negro slaves, amongst other valuable freight, from one colonial port to another.

Delano's mental processes of movement from innocence to flickering awareness here is instructive, for the whole layered unfolding of the work. At first we have the "leaden-hued swells," the vapours, "the fog," the stormy existence before he discovers man and man, as slave . . . A kind of first-day strangeness of Creation exists, before the Fall of many virtues of terrible experience of knowledge. "The leaden-hued swells" are suggestive of primary industrial evolvement [or discovery], of lead in the smelters' mold; the Christian image of the appearance of Western Man (Delano) and Christian mission. Once Delano moves from seeing the boat through a glass darkly, he sees the *San Dominick* as a "white-washed monastery" and only for what it is—a slave ship. The last thing Americans wanted to see was our nation as a slave state; rather it be a "white-washed monastery." Melville unites these oppositional forces which were primary to Western Man's experience—Christianity and the industry made out of slavery.

At another level Delano's appearance out of the vapours and fog symbolizes the coming of the white man, out of the foggy Middle Ages, with Christianity and gun powder, exploring and exploiting the Word and the world as he Christianized it—the world cut off from techno-logical advances and the Renaissance. Civilizing, Christianizing and enslaving—the Word made flesh, indeed. We have a parody on Christian symbolism "white-washed monastery" as seen through a kind of pun, the humor is sardonic—not monks at peace with God, at meditation, in this meditation upon history, but rather slaves, without peace, though they are as we are to discover with Delano ostensibly free. Both the institution of slavery and the monastery (as well as the life on a ship) are ordered by a complete domination over the individual's life in the name of a higher master for the good, profit and purgation of the soul, through Christianity. The theme of the angularity of free will haunts the novel. The rationalization of the slave masters was that enslavement would bring Christianity to the heathens. Whereas in fact, the slaves, like those on the *San Dominick*, were being brought to the New World to serve the white masters, as Gods, body and soul, for financial profit. The mask of Christianity was employed to make the slaves as devoted to the profit of the so-called Master race as uniformed monks were supposedly devoted to their Almighty Master's Word.

The linkage between God, Christianity, and theories of white supremacy were deeply enshrined in the nineteenth-century vision concerning the very nature of man; and in this sense, too, the ship—and our ship of state—was a "white-washed monastery." Darkly robed monks unleashed a host of pictures of piety, humility, and devotion—peaceful souls slavishly devoted to their Master in the public mind that, of course, had nothing to do with individuals, who streaked to Christian vows and the monastery in order to avoid the troubling world from within, as Cereno does just before his end, when he enters a monastery. We hear echoes of Paul's Epistles in the New Testament throughout, which are loaded with these inverted plays upon enslavement, duty and freedom in slavement for a higher good. For example in Romans 6:19–23 verses, we are instructed:

> Just as formerly you presented your bodily organs to uncleanness and lawlessness as slaves for the doing of lawless deeds, present them now as slaves to justice so that you may become holy. When you were slaves of sin, you were free from Justice. But what fruit did you reap? Now you are ashamed of those things. And their goal is death. But now that you have been freed from sin and have become slaves of God. . . .

In the genesis of the New World American imagination, black slaves conjured up a host of images of piety and devotion to master—the masquerade of peaceful, devoted darkies—not plotting slaves, and nothing to do with the inner self. In both cases the public mind would not think the monk or slave would have much of an inner life short of meditations upon Master, and incapable of self-mastery. Actually the triad of African leadership (Babo, Ataful, and the mulatto Francesco), masked before the eyes of Delano as obedient, or noble savage, or mulatto aristocrat, were united in one thing below the mask: their desire for freedom and fierce revenge.

We come to know Cereno as monk, who has become corrupted and instructed, riddled and resurrected by too much knowledge, monk to his imminent doom. The trinity of mission-obsessed monks—Delano, Cereno, and Babo—recall other religious themes in inversion throughout and remind us of another triad at the end of the novella, all meeting in Death, following the leader, Christ in Death (Babo, Aranda, and Cereno). Each has been a "slave master" at one time or another on the *San Dominick*. With the head of Babo in the public plaza placed upon a pole to remind our national conscious of the Christian potential for peril of this Cinque-like Babo, but also for Melville's purposes to reflect upon the black-face side of our shadowed American evil of slavery that Americans dared not look upon but must not escape from seeing; the fear and guilt Babo and his revolt recall and, of course, the image of the church and the monastery . . . presented here as a parody on the Transfiguration:

> The body [Babo's] was burned to ashes; but for many days, the head, that hive of subtlety, fixed on a pole in the Plaza met, unabashed, the gaze of the whites; and across the Plaza looked towards St. Bartholomew's church, in whose vaults slept then, as now, the recovered bones of Aranda: and across the Rimac bridge looked towards the monastery, on Mount Agnoia without; where, three months after being dismissed by the court, Benito Cereno, borne on the bier did, indeed, follow his leader.

Monk-like Delano is obsessed with the uplifting concept of goodness, service, industry, civility, hard work, and working one's way up. Monk-like Cereno is doomed with the martyrdom of reversals of fate, fortune and God, as he must serve the purposes of his God-like Satan, Babo. But that high-priest of mutiny, Babo, must serve his old master-god, Satanic Cereno. Each must enslave the other in order to be free.

Captain Delano comes as a Christ figure of generosity and trusting, with a will for an orderly, peaceable kingdom; each of the three main characters becomes a kind of variation on Christ. Babo as the daring revolutionary side of Christ; crucified for his beliefs (lynched, I should say); canonized in our American imagination, in the plaza; and Cereno comes to represent Christ in the Garden, suffering over the American agony of slavery. But the innocence of Christ in Delano, concering man's nature, must be crucified upon the cross of the existential experience with slavery for him to be redeemed from the slavery of his imperception; his tendency to record everything and yet to understand so little of the complex, knot-like angularity of life before his eyes.

Melville is doing parodies on the Christ story throughout. One interesting parallel-as-burlesque springs from the mocking interrogation scene when Jesus is brought before Pilate (shortly before his crucifixion) on charges of blasphemy and not giving sufficient tribute to the state. In the mock interrogation scene in the novella, Atufal is summoned before Don Benito—with Babo as witness and Delano as spectator—for the ostensible purpose of humbling the African. What we have is an example of Melville doing a parody on the mock trial of Christ before Pilate. Christ and Atufal refused to back down concerning their pride and who they were. Both continued to blaspheme by mute refusal to perform worship of the alien masters before them; both declined to ask forgiveness. We learn that this royal man, Atufal, was once a king in his own land; his kingdom (like that of Christ's) is surely not of this New World. Each man stubbornly sought his own vision of the ultimate redemption of man. In league, of course, with Babo, in this burlesque-within-a-parody, straight-man Atufal's mute refusal to give tribute foreshadows Babo's refusal to be interrogated at the end, before he is "crucified," and before we enter upon the courtroom deposition.

The symbolic emblem of dependence—role-playing duplicity in the larger sense of race relations as a kind of relic from the past—can be seen in the Cereno-Babo relationship and in the following observation of a physical art form on the boat, the oval stern piece . . .

> But the principal relic of faded grandeur was the ample oval of the shield-like stern piece, intricately carved with the arms of Castile and Leon, medallioned about by groups of mythological, or symbolical devices; upper-most and central of which was a dark satyr in a mask, holding his foot on he prostrate neck of a writhing figure, likewise masked.

Here we have slave-master relations turned into an art form, as symbolic of the boat's dreadful misadventure and life-imitating art, but now with Babo, masked as master and Cereno as slave. Yet Cereno is still master because the slaves can't get the boat back to Senegal without the Spaniards' services; Cereno must don the masks of hopefulness, then "good darkie" in order to maintain his quasi-freedom. Babo may seek repatriation himself, but according to his own words, he lived something of a slavish existence in Senegal.

Both "slaves" are playing larger and more dreadful roles than their individual personal identities; roles bound up in national identity, slavery, and freedom, and the ever-popular minstrel blackface shows of the day; each is "masked," setting in motion the "blackening-up" routines they perform when Delano as middle-American audience attends the staged show on deck. Cereno must "blacken-up" to save his white hide; Babo must blacken-up for the American audience de-manded that Negro minstrels, no matter their hue, blacken-up with cork, distort their features with white lip paint and play the "darkie" role. A black entertainer could not get the freedom to appear upon the American stage unless he performed and presented a distortion of the Negro. Thus even revolutionary Babo is not free from outlandish minstrel performance.

> As Ralph Ellison has said in *Shadow and Act*:
> This mask, this willful stylization and modification of the natural face and hands, was imperative for the evocation of that atmosphere in which the fascination of blackness could be enjoyed, the comic catharsis achieved. The racial identity of the performer was unimportant; the mask was the thing (the "thing" in more ways than one), and its function was to veil the humanity of Negroes thus reduced to a sign, and to repress the white audience's awareness of its moral identification with its own acts and with the human ambiguities pushed behind the mask.

The "darkie" minstrel act continues. We learn that Babo instructed Cereno to seek out information about the material composition of Delano's vessel. But the Spaniard also can use this minstrel mask of body-servant, as go-between intermediary, and as a way of finding a wedge of useful information for his own freedom, not Babo's even as he represents the Negro slaves' chain to freedom; but by ruse and burlesque, because, of course, the Spaniards have no intention of navigating the *San Dominick* (which means friendship in Spanish) back to Africa.

The memorable shaving scene raises the question of how long have they been conducting this charade even when Delano is not aboard. Cereno's deposition would hint it was only for the Yankee's bamboozle-ment—can we believe this is all to the performance?—especially when we consider the artistry, even virtuosity of Babo's performance, and other moments, obviously based in an older, patterned relationship of master/body servant in the New World. Melville's contemplation upon cultural history allows an immense yield as he recombines master/body-servant relations in the New World South and black-face ministrel shows, Northern style into the Babo-Cereno act (with whatever he knew of New World slavery rituals in the Western hemisphere) and the previous conditions on board before Babo took over, with the Shakespearan idea of a character acting as a stage manager, i.e., Iago throughout *Othello.*

The artfulness of Melville's fitful stern piece makes us contemplate the complexity of master/body servant in the New World and man to man; who is master when the body servant could hold so much freedom of possession over his master's body—body and soul, which was exactly what enslavement meant to the slavers. The satyr mask is suggestive of a complex vision of both master and slave, and alluding to animal and man of mythology. It alludes to the bestiality, shame, dishonor, and inferiority cast forth from slavery, which made all wear masks of embarrassment or deceit before public scrutiny, implying also the bestial image imposed upon our national identity of the black slave, as part man, part animal, and of the blacks as the ground-down victims of Western history.

This relic oval stern piece foreshadows a climatic moment when the gentle Captain Delano becomes fitfully embattled with the experience of slavery. Freedom-seeking, "runaway slave" Cereno jumps ship into Delano's boat that has arrived to return the Yankee to his home vessel. Babo jumps after his master into *The Rover* not to save him but to slay

him. It is only then that the gullible Delano realizes who is also slave
and who is also master.

> At this juncture, the left hand of Captain Delano, on one
> side, again clutched the half reclined Don Benito, heedless
> that he was in speechless faint, while his right foot, on the
> other side, ground the prostrate Negro; and his right arm
> pressed for added speed on the after oar, his eye bent
> forward, encouraging his men to their utmost.

All of this takes place symbolically, across the Mason-Dixon line, as it
were, in Delano's (*border-state?*) boat—for the racial chaos of the other
America could hardly be contained then to the ghetto of the *San
Dominick*'s decks; this reality mocks Delano's earlier statement to
Benito Cereno when he invites the Spaniard to enjoy an evening of
tranquility upon his ship and Cereno spurns the offer. Of course he
can't leave—I realize that—but more is operating here. Delano tells
Cereno:

> The ships will lie together as near they can, without
> swinging foul. It will be little more than stepping from deck
> to deck; which is but as from room to room. Come, come,
> you must not refuse me.

Written in the 1850s when the clouds of an apocalyptic civil war
hung over the nation, Melville realized that neither could the country
remain half slave and half free anymore than could slavery be ever
maintained in one territory without flooding over, or "swinging foul,"
into each new state. This was the culminating political issue—whether
each new state would come in free or slave . . . and the compromises
made. (Let Maine come in as a free state and Missouri as a slave state.)

As the "enslaved" Captain Benito Cereno leaped over into the
Northern "free" territory, it was the black body servant, the masked
slaver, Babo, who is bent on the recapture of his freedom-seeking,
runaway slave, the Spaniard who fled the territory. In turn he, Babo,
needs Don Benito to get him out of slavery. So Babo must reenslave

Don Benito, or kill him. Babo tries to kill Don Benito, brandishing the knife, thus recalling those slave masters who caught runaway slaves and punished them even unto death. But Babo must try to kill Cereno because the Spaniard (like many runaway body servants, or house slaves from Southern plantations) had too much information about the inner workings of the Big House or, in this case, the big boat, to report to Yankees like Delano.

The sudden fitfulness unmasked in the gentleman-Captain Delano of this scene suggests how deeply one could get enmeshed in the other self of slavery's madness by masking other values of normal order over the fact of this peculiar chaotic institution. The picture of the three hurled together becomes the possible religious relic of our nineteenth-century embattled spiritual condition.

Babo represents the way men really are beneath the mask: a seething world that Delano either by nature does not know or is cut away from, as symbolic of one level of Americans' lack of awareness, rooted in their stubborn will to remain ignorant or distanced from harsh realities.

Babo represents the other-self, which starts off for Melville as a kind of racial pun, the darker side of man's nature and that is part of what is meant in the denouement, after the rebellion is put down, the deposition recorded, and saviour Delano says to Benito Cereno:

> "You are saved . . . You are saved . . . But what has cast such a shadow upon you?"
> "The Negro."

A pun on "shadow" that still belies Delano—knowing and not knowing throughout and a satire on Christian salvation, "You are saved," which is also what the slavers, in effect, told the Africans, like Babo, when they enslaved them in a mangled chain of Christianity. You are saved Nigger, we have cast you out of the bondage of enslavement to your heathen gods. Delano's statement suggests that he has not understood Cereno's existential experience, as slaver and as slave: the full range, metaphorically speaking of the experience with slavery. The joke is on Delano, too, because he doesn't see the shadow of death upon Cereno's melancholy soul; nor how the malignancy of slavery has enveloped Cereno in its evil shadow, body and soul; nor how slavery has cast its "shadow" as a menacing metaphor, over the consciousness of Western Man—an awesome presence, as that of the myth of the Fall of Christian "memory." ("Shadows present, foreshadowing deeper shadows to come," indeed.) Delano is lost within the shadow of his own inperception.

Cereno's famous muted and tormented reply: "The Negro." The underside of the unconscious, of guilt, of blackness, or evil, but also the aware side, the perceptive, cunning, perverse side of man's intelligence (that the Negro, too, is indeed capable of); that comes out not only because Babo was a slave, but becaue Babo was Babo . . . That this side of man's nature dominates life . . . That the American ship of state—like Ezekiel's vision of the Dry Bones in the valley— could not be saved, nor resurrected outside of slavery's overshadowing experience without violence; and that "enslaved" Cereno has had to live as a slave—play roles and seek out stealthly strategems for survival and had to be a black man's slave—all have heightened, informed, and finally exhausted him. (He is like a shell-shocked veteran.)

What Delano fails to recognize about the human condition is revealed when Cereno tries to make him see the duplicity and the masquerade of capitulation that with Babo were central links to their common survival while Delano was on board. Or as Cereno says:

> "Do but think how you walked this deck, how you sat in this cabin, every inch of ground mined into honeycombs under you. Had I dropped the least hint, made the least advance towards an understanding between us, death explosive death—yours and mine—would have ended the scene."

And Delano's reply indicates how out of focus he remains:

> "True, true," cried Captain Delano, starting, "you have saved my life, Don Benito, more than I yours; saved it too, against my knowledge and will."

But actually it is not a question of *knowledge* (a body of facts codified in an orderly fashion) nor sheer *will* (an instinct to muster strength of purposeful resolve into action), but rather the undergoing of the mysterious passage and agonizing process of the existential slave-forging experience, in which all previous knowledge is of little help; and *will* is tested wtihin a completely new set of crucibles. Delano seems not to recognize that life is process—noncodified. Not logged. Not a *Bachelor's Delight.* Life is rebellious change and metamorphosis. This is the problem of the character of this personality, at base, even without the radical experience of slavery. This side of paradise, man's nature, is chaotic, an inferno, but also here is unleashed the citadel of man's perverse creativity as manifested by Babo's rebellion and his performance—or Melville's parody upon Milton's *Paradise Lost*—and again our trinity.

For let Babo stand for Lucifer, the perversely brilliant fallen angel, whose bodily presence here introduced the original sin of slavery and the experience of blackness into the Western laboratory and imagination; and Cereno stand as Western Man, who must undergo this agonizing experience, but through imitation, as a masked actor-monk doing the Stations of the Cross in black face; and Delano stand as representative of Michael, who comes to right it all, but who must fall from "the paradise" of his gullibility. Or again, let Cereno stand for the beautiful Lucifer who introduced the sin of slavery, as the Fall of Man, into the Western experience, but who must die overwhelmed by too much experience from his creation and Babo stand as that recreated, inverted Christ figure of the New World man, whose life must be sacrificed in order that America might be redeemed, but in a bloody, apocalyptic manner. And let Delano stand for Michael (the Noble Savage of Rousseau's making) who must now come face to face with the brazen brilliance of a black man's brain—Babo's head, "that hive of subtlety."

Babo takes stock from Shakespeare's Iago, and it is Captain Delano, the white man, who recalls Commander Othello, the black Moor of gullibility, nobility, imagination, and imperception concerning the inherent evil within the nature of man. Like Shakespeare's Othello, Delano suffers not from a lack of imagination, or experience through the world of his captainship, or precise observation, but from a lack of an analytical intelligence and a deeply etched sense of the labyrinth of human nature. At the end of the play *Othello*, once Iago's plot has brought the Moor low but to a higher awareness concerning the maladies of personality, and Iago's knot-like plots are unravelled, the monster Iago says in Act V, Scene II: "Demand me nothing; what you know you know: from this time forth I never will speak word." At the end of the novella *Benito Cereno*, Babo refuses to speak.

There is a profound relationship of Othello to Benito Cereno in terms of emotional and experiential turmoil from within, over the coming prevalence of evil not only over their soul, but as a statement about the human predicament. Iago has enslaved Othello's soul with the poison of malignant jealousy; Babo has made Cereno profoundly aware of the malignancy of slavery and the slave's countermanding humanity and willfulness to be free. Both characters are linked in terms of old world refinement and baseness . . . Christianity and baseness. Cereno must cut out the malignancy placed there by the institution of slavery via Babo's presence.

Of this latter motif I want to now concentrate through a particular passage late in the work. For in a manner that unveils yet another duality, Melville employs both the techniques of public rhetorical declaration *and* private self-wrenching confession in order to unmask several sides of Don Benito's soul, as the Spaniard declares "sadly" to intermediary Delano:

> ". . . you were with me all day; stood with me, sat with, talked with me, looked at me, ate with me, drank with me; and yet, your last act was to clutch for a monster, not only an innocent man, but the most pitiable of all men."

For me it is not enough to reveal this statement as simply a speech directed by Benito Cereno to Amasa Delano, or captain to captain. On the surface he is saying having "stood with me, sat with me, talked with me, looked at me," eaten and drunk with me, you still completely misread my nature. The Don is saying that not only did you fail to see in me "an innocent man," he extends his litany of his silence, his despair . . . That "you were in time underceived" provides no comfort.

Behind the mask of this statement to Delano, I believe that the Don is reflecting his own self-tormented state, superimposed over Delano's presence. Unleash the marrow of the statement to a deeper hue, and Cereno, the Catholic, is confessing not simply to his innocent priest, but to himself, the embattled state of his own soul, slavery, and the impact of Babo, and evil, and the complex body-servant relationship of plantation life. We do recall earlier how the other confession that Melville ascribes to the Spanish captain—in the desposition—revealed the Don as attempting to justify the status quo his slaves have disrupted and to canonize himself at their expense as a martyr whose kindliness and trust they have cruelly betrayed. Here the Southern Hamlet, as the Don, has been often called, reveals a deeper inner agony and ultimately not so much to Delano, but about his own soul condition. From this private confession, the character-in-process of the Don can be seen evolving somewhat over the duplicity of his public trial statement. Yet still revealed in masquerade . . .

". . . You were with me all day; stood with me, sat with, looked at me, ate with me, drank with me." A virtual litany of body-servant intimacies with master . . . Or, even though I (maybe we) were with the Negro all day; stood with him, sat with him, looked at him, ate with him, drank with him." I/we still viewed the Negro as less than human . . . "and yet, your last act was to clutch for a monster, not only an innocent man, but the most pitiable of all men." Remember what I said of him at the trial. Remember the image of the monster I clutched for and projected even though he was innocent . . . "not only an innocent man, but the most pitiable of all men," which, of course, would be the Negro slave in the New World and the Babo-cast shadow within the soul of Cereno, and the malignancy of slavery grown within the Don's soul, as slaver, and as slave. (At this point we remember that it was the tormented runaway slave Cereno who Delano reached for, who was indeed both monster and innocent—recalling perhaps the significance of the "dark satyr in a mask, holding his foot on the prostrate neck of a writhing figure, likewise masked.")

We also hear strains of the Southern slave holder, as mock Hamlet echoing through the Don's moralizing, filled with self-pitying and self-righteous admonitions to Yankee outsiders, often as not picked up by white historians, and projected in white-wash print as *prima-facie* examples of the desolate white plantation owners, who were the most tragic victims of slavery, not the Negro. We cannot fail to hear that out of the Southern Hamlet's mouth *words, words, words* remain masquerades, hiding, even as they reveal meaning: "To such degree may malign machinations and deceptions impose. So far may even the best man err, in judging the conduct of one with the recesses of whose condition he is not acquainted. But you were forced to it; and you were in time undeceived. Would that, in both respects, it was so ever, and with all men." Which, of course, it cannot ever be since only I can know the experience truly. You have no memory. On a certain level, in order to find themselves, all three men must lose memory to find the meaning of the new memory, which is slavery.

I do not mean to diminish the depths of the Don, as Hamlet's self-confession, in these final pages of this New Testament of the American agony. At this point the kindly and trusting New Englander tells the Spaniard:

> "You generalize, Don Benito; and mournfully enough. But the past is passed; why moralize upon it? Forget it. See, yon bright sun has forgotten it all, and the blue sea, and the blue sky; these have turned over new leaves."
> "Because they have no memory," he dejectedly replied; "Because they are not human."
> "But these mild trades that now fan your cheek, do they not come with a human-like healing to you? Warm friends, steadfast friends are the trades."
> "With their steadfastness they but waft me to my tomb, Senor" was the foreboding response.

"You are saved," cried Captain Delano, more and more astonished and pained, "You are saved: what has cast such a shadow upon you?"

"The Negro."

Recalling the Babo of his soul here, too, the Don falls to utter silence and enters a monastery where silence is held in respect because it is the preamble to righteous reverence. Babo's innovative plotting and his "voiceless end" have encouraged critics to connect him too closely with Shakespeare's Iago. Both surely are stage managers, yet Iago acts without any overwhelming or compelling motive in plotting the Moor's doom. Babo seeks out his enemy's destruction as the necessary means to his freedom and his peoples' salvation. As Jean Fagan Yellin has pointed out in "Black Masks: Melville's *Benito Cereno*." "Babo's silence expresses not only the intransigence of Negro rebels and voiceless black experience, but the status of black slaves in America, legally deprived of the right to make themselves heard, even in the courtroom."

Writing against the tide of racist and so-called scientific documents which projected the Negro as intellectually inferior to the whites, Melville's characterization of Babo generally flies in the face of white supremacist teachings. Babo is not a brainless beast, but we are reminded that "the black—whose brain, not body, had schemed and led the revolt." He is definitely the most intelligent figure in this novella. There are several examples of Babo's subtlety of mind that Melville links to the superb sculpture of African art.

Babo, it seems to me, also represents how men really feel below the mask of false harmony that works against their true self-interest; that men are murders, cut throats (his own throat is cut at the end by men of law and order), and will do anything for freedom or to introduce their own power order over reality—this is what Delano must come to know about the nature of man. But in this special sense, Babo and Delano are based upon two sides of pastoral man: one embracing the forces of violence and knowing in his nature through experience and the other embracing innocence and knowing/unknowing ritualized codified living; Babo at one end and Delano at the other come to represent the extremes in the makings of the New World man, and the American character. Delano ostensibily has all the tools for knowing, observation and history, culture without the conceptualizing mediation upon the meaning of history's remembered experience.

In connection with the idea of the self and the other-self, in this novella of war-in-peace let the *Bachelor's Delight* then stand for the surface qualities of the Puritan ethnic, order and peace, true-blue industry, as exemplified by Delano; and the *San Dominick* stand as the other-self of the New World American sensibility, where from beneath the mask of harmony, we have ritualized white supremacy, war, racial duplicity, slavery, class upheaval, into a nightmare; where we are at war with the self. The idea of a two-faced America works well, I believe, in fostering our understanding of the mask-wearing Babo and the masquerading Cereno. For on the *San Dominick* we have a good analogy to plantation life, who had power and who didn't; the burlesque by blacks of white manners down in the quarters and the mask of subservience in the Big House; the imitation and exploitation of the black ethos in the Big House and upon the American stage: body and soul. At the same time we have a parody on the assigned slave tasks on a plantation from the meaningless oakum pickers right on up to the body servant.

One is struck by the contemporary aspect of the work. For example, the following instruction from Delano to Cereno on how to keep the young black male slaves occupied at the meaningless busy work, as a safeguard against riot and rebellion, sounds very much like a modern-day politician's advice to his colleagues concerning unemployed young slum-dwelling males:

> "I should think, Don Benito, that you would find it advantageous to keep all your blacks employed, especially the younger ones, no matter at what useless task, and no matter what happens to the ship."

Babo represents the proximity of the house Negro to the master—shaving and actually dominating his body. You don't slit the master's throat, you draw his blood little by little, or nick by nick, or theft by theft—if a cook, a bit of poison here and there. Francesco, the mulatto cook, had wanted to do just this to Delano's food. Babo nicks Cereno in the barbering scene in order for Cereno to know his place; as a slave master might whip his favorite slave who rustles about too much in order to keep order and for his favorite slaves and the others to know their place. Babo must also nick himself to show a false bloody face of "darkie" subservience to Delano; thus the extremes of Babo's situation are frozen and captured in these acts that indicate how he is entrapped in the state of master and slave; how to be free he must never master the body-slave mentality—for it too might be useful for his ultimate freedom.

Like many revolutionary spirits, Babo is obsessed with an attraction for the power and beauty of his old master Cereno. Here, ironically enough, Babo and Delano are doubled; both are fascinated by Cereno's presence. Delano has a fascination for the family name of Benito Cereno (Was this one an imposter to title?—More of the mask-wearing theme, too.) even as he shuns Don Benito's apparent easy rise to power and the slackness of his command. Thus, our American fascination with the beauty of the Old World—our love-hate, as well. Babo is fascinated by Cereno as he shaves Don Benito. Babo, no doubt, carried off the revolt because of Aranda's slackness of command, or his inability to be a loathsome slave master—unaware that a black could try anything a white man was capable of. Loathing for and fascination with the power of evil have come to dominate Babo's soul—obviously if he must keep this charade alive of order each day he gains a kind of perverse pleasure in dominating his former master by virtual threat of the knife that also barbers Cereno's head into beauty.

Nicking of the master is perhaps a disciplining to suggest to Cereno he had better maintain the mask of his words, and his face. Babo, in turn, nicks himsel as a way of not revealing himself, or his other face, even as he shows Delano the blood he has shed upon the mask of his face, as it were, for his master in sacrifice for the slippage of his sharpest razor. Babo may also be disciplining himself for the slippage, a harsh enough punishment, to be sure, but the discipline of the rebellion beneath the apparent chaos on the ship is a tribute to Babo and the others strictness of purpose where mutiny depends on a highly immediate, existential transformation of power, violence, and cunning, where shipshape order is improvised on the spot and where there is no daily log to consult on activities, as Delano has on the *Bachelor's Delight.* In making up the new order of the rebellion, Babo has existentially re-created himself into a highly ordered instrumentality of cold white steel (foreshadowing, perhaps, the improvisational quality of Afro-American life in this country, in which one makes up as one goes along, in order to survive.) He would nick himself for discipline for what other master, or biblical log could he turn to for self-discipline?

Even the pathology of it all. From the deposition we learn this intriguing story of Babo's trafficking with Evil and his all-consuming passion for racial revenge, consumed in his own shadow, as it were. For when Cereno asked about the whereabouts of his slain partner in the crime of slavery (Aranda's body), Babo finally

> . . . showed him a skeleton which had been substituted for the ship's proper figure-head the image of Christopher Colon, the discoverer of the New World; that the negro Babo asked him whose skeleton that was, and whether from its whiteness, he should not think it a white's; that, upon (his covering) his face, the negro Babo, coming close, said words to this effect: "Keep faith with the blacks from here to Senegal, or you shall in spirit, as now in body, follow your leader . . ." that the same morning negro Babo took by succession each Spaniard forward and asked him whose skeleton that was, and whether, for its whiteness, he should not think it a white's . . .

This apocalyptic vision is suggestive too of how the black might become obsessed with whiteness and also whiteness as a color symbol of evil and death ("pale horse, pale rider," the slaves were later to sing); just as in the white man's imagination, black was linked to evilness and in Spanish "el Negro" may mean "the darkness" or "the blackness" as well as "The Negro." Melville sees Babo as high priest of a kind of pagan ritual in one way but as a New World black bent on racial revenge not on the books. That Babo finds no spiritual harmony in even rebellion and the slaying of the whites is a kind of assault on their total mythology, as the Western white man's cultural religion that Babo seems horrified by. Babo seems to be saying if your language and your enslaving actions say blackness is evil and a curse and that death is black, evil is black, then whiteness is the color of your death. The reader may recall Chapter XLII, "The Whiteness of the Whale," in Melville's *Moby Dick*, in which he attempts to deal with the awesomeness, horror, wonder, and terror of *Whiteness* buried in Western Man's psychology, and his mythology:

> This elusive quality it is, which causes the thought of whiteness, when divorced from more kindly associations, and coupled with any object terrible in itself, to heighten that terror to the furthest bounds. Witness the white bear of the poles, and the white shark of the tropics; what but their smooth, flaky whiteness makes them the transcendent horrors they are? That ghastly whiteness it is which imparts such an abhorrent mildness, even more loathsome than terrific, to the dumb gloating of their aspect.

At a less extreme dimension, Babo's action implies that in death we are equal; but it takes a violent death to equalize us—look at our bones! They are white. Can you indeed tell from their whiteness were they those of a white? Just as in life, all men cast a dark shadow. Babo's actions—in carrying out the revolt and his ritual conducting of the whites forward to look upon the bones—also reflect upon a dimension of the American Character, regeneration through violence: a theme that is not only part of our frontier experience as a nation, but a staple of our American Literature.

Babo and Benito Cereno are tied to other characters in Melville's works; men who are obsessed by the overwhelming experience that a particularly brutalizing encounter unleashes. Although he lacks Ahab's vindictiveness, certain attritubes of the psychological profile of the melancholy Spaniard (who, like the Dane, knows that there is something rotten in this Western Hemisphere) also recalls to mind the tormented inner life of the raging Captain of the *Pequod.* Both Ahab and Cereno have been charged and terrorized by the larger-than-life implications of the White Whale, on the one hand, and Slavery, on the other. Melancholy Cereno ultimately cracks up, it would appear, finding no peace in the monastery. For each man, the encounter with the unknown brings on a catastrophic vision, that both regenerates them and destroys them. This also can be said of the fate of Babo, as well.

Ahab is maddened by his "bodily woes and the intellectual and spiritual exasperations" and finally by the mutilation of the White Whale. Ahab has seized upon a single "truth" and in a "monomaniacal" way is acting upon it. He shapes the revelation of his motivation into a philosophical overview, when Starbuck cries that "Vengeance on a dumb brute that smote thee from blindest instinct" is not only madness but blasphemous . . . Ahab bellows forth:

> "Hark yet yet again,—the little lower layer. All visible objects, man, are but pasteboard masks. But in each event—in the living act, the undoubted deed—there, some unknown but still reasoning thing puts forth the mouldings of its features from behind the unreasoning mask. How can the prisoner reach outside except by thrusting through the wall? To me, the white whale is that wall, shoved near me. Sometimes I think there's naught beyond. But 'tis enough . . . He tasks me; he heaps me; I see in him outrageous strength, with an instrutable malice winewing it. That inscrutable thing is chiefly what I hate; be the white whale agent, or be the white whale principal, I will wrought that hate upon him. Talk not to me of blasphemy, man; strike the sun if it insulted me . . ."

In *Benito Cereno*, we are also presented with the cunning relationship of the author himself, as Melville evolves out of his materials, transcending the stereotypical view of the blacks, as natural-born servants—which was the view of many whites and specifically Delano—to a powerful indictment and a satirical one-butt shuffle in the face of this view of harmless and sweet-spirited, harmonious darkies. Melville savages any hope that such minds can ever be illuminated, even in the face of mayhem.

Melville suggests that Art (the first part and the last) renders a far greater yield than the so-called straight facts appearance extracted from Cereno's deposition. Thus, the theme of appearances and reality is refined. Refined again because Melville rewrote the extract. Just as moments of dullness or nonperception on Delano's part are joined and followed up structurally with lucid examples that belie Delano's bigotry, or his imperception. For example, at one point Delano's racial chauvinism—or his imperception—reflects in a manner that casts him in the shadow of a joke, not on the Negro but himself:

> The whites, too, by nature, were the shrewder race. A man with some evil design, would he not be likely to speak well of that stupidity which was blind to his depravity, and malign that intelligence from which it might not be hidden? Not unlikely, perhaps. But if the whites had dark secrets concerning Don Benito, could then Don Benito be any way in complicity with the blacks? But they were too stupid. Besides, who ever heard of a white so far a renegade as to apostasize from his very species almost, by leaguing in against it with Negroes?

Just then Delano is confronted with the deeper reality of the blacks, in the form of the old man who looked like an Egyptian priest, who is later described as being quite simple with his knot. Yet for intricacy, Delano had never seen such a knot on an American ship, nor indeed anywhere else. This becomes quite an involved symbol. The complicated fashioning of the knot by the African, of course, shows the shrillness of Delano's initial remarks that shrewdness or complexity would alone be the designing gift of the white man's imagination. The joke, too, is on Delano, who is rather incapable of shrewdness, or a perceiver of complex evil design. He apparently is capable of only limited powers of associative conceptualizing—one of the hallmarks of intelligence.

The highly associative knot suggests the complexity of culture at a fundamental level that Africans and all cultures possess. And, lest Delano catch onto the knot's symbolic value, i.e., if one of them can design this what can't their minds conceive of, the elaborately artful knot is thrown overboard by the African—lest the knot, like the elaborate ruse of reenslavement on board, be undone. For Melville the knot has more in its capturing weave than simply the old man and Delano. It is an allusion to the fact that the complex, knotted-up, we might say, Cereno will also go overboard later, when the complexity of Babo's knotty scheme is too difficult to maintain and the moment of freedom presents itself. Also, the knot is tied to the New World Negroes, like Babo, who will also go overboard. There is a sense in which the slaves here—mutinous, becoming more complex, speaking Spanish, encountering new cultures, power situations—are moving from their edenic past, or relatively ritualized existence in Africa, and are already on the way to becoming complicated, New World Africans. Similar is Delano's existence as it moves through the work, from an innocence to a first-day edenic strangeness, to the exposure of too much knowledge of what he though he summarily understood.

From the perspective of specific history we note that the novella was also influenced by the *Amistad* case, one in which a group of Africans were brought to trial at the insistence of Spain because they had revolted against the Spaniards who had sought to enslave them; the slaves killed several of the officers and in attempting to sail the ship back to their homeland found themselves off the coast of New England. The incident occurred in 1839 in an act that culminated in an historic Supreme Court argument in the slaves' behalf by former President John Quincy Adams. The incident was central to the origins of three great social sea changes for blacks—civil rights, public education, and the missionary movement.

The fifty-three Africans spared only two of the Spanish crew to help them navigate to Africa. The Africans ordered the pair to steer the ship into the sun, but by night the Spaniards pointed toward North American in hopes of landing in the southern United States. The zig-zag pattern finally led them to Long Island, where the slaves were taken prisoners by a United States cutter, jailed in New Haven, and charged with murder and piracy.

The group of abolitionists known as Friends of the *Amistad* fought the case through the federal courts and retained for the Supreme Court test in 1841 Adams, who was considered the most eloquent lawyer of his day. His plea in the first civil rights case ever to reach the High Court prevailed and the thirty-nine blacks who survived the *Amistad* takeover were freed, later to be repatriated to Sierra Leone.

Friends of the *Amistad* devoted themselves to missionary work, then in 1846 merged with other such groups to form the American Missionary Association. At the close of the Civil War, the association turned its attention to the education of freedmen, creating more than 500 primary and secondary schools and founding colleges, including Howard, Dillard, Fisk, Talladega and Tougaloo.

Finally, if I might be allowed a depositional post script: that Cereno cannot come to know the humanity of Babo and by implication the blacks' total humanity and transcend the stereotype of the Negro until the slaves revolt with both cunning and violence. Delano is unable to grasp the human complexity of the Africans who believed, like himself, so much in freedom that they were willing to kill for it. Babo cannot be a man at one with himself until he has re-created himself, albeit through violence. The slaves' violent rage for freedom and the cunning to obtain it cracks the stereotype of the meek mask and thereby links them and particularly Babo with all men who would revolt to be free. That they must traffic with evil in order to be free cast the shadow upon Cereno's face, for nothing in the lexicon of remembered history had prepared him for this revelation about human nature caught in the horrible web of this most peculiar institution; just as nothing in the lexicon of all their ancestral warnings nor the masked gods of their forebears' religious tribal mythology had prepared the Africans for the tribulation of this peculiar, horrific experience.

```
┌                                              ┐

        FORGED IN INJUSTICE

└                                              ┘
```

There are several intriguing levels to Allison Davis's superior psycho-
biography of four black leaders, Frederick Douglass, W.E.B. Du Bois,
Richard Wright, and Martin Luther King, Jr. In *Leadership, Love and
Aggression*, Davis combines a Freudian approach with his own penetrating insights as both an eminent social anthropologist and a keen
student of Afro-American life. He enriches his study with a novelist's
angularity of vision and appetite for character motivation and a
story-teller's drive for narrative power.

Each portrait reveals what Hemingway said of the true writer: that he
is forged in injustice, the way a sword is forged. Each man was a writer
or orator of eloquence; each suffered outrageous personal or public
misfortune, and all appeared as antiheroes to many of their fellow
countrymen. Davis's Freudian analysis goes a long way in overcoming
the dearth of intelligence about black leaders and the highly diverse
Afro-American familial experience. This work is essential to an understanding of the historical complexity of the black family.

Davis's work is beautifully written. He has a tough-minded, ennobling sense of these men and a willingness to go where the conflicts in
their lives lead him. All four started off with a fundamentally Negro
base of concern and agony; but in the long run each in his own way
sought to anchor the Afro-American experience to the causes of the
larger community. Throughout these essays, there is the impression of

hearing Leontyne Price sing "Deep River" in the shadow of the Lincoln Memorial.

The author's interest in the phenomenon of caste as a salient factor in the study of race is central to this work. Written in the seventh and eighth decades of his life, Davis's study is often as bitter as his four heroes were about the dreadful impasse of America's race problem. But reflecting the experiences of Douglass and King, Davis emerges with a largeness of vision and love that can deal with the terrors of racism, with a vision that sharpens our perceptions of inner battles with the drives of self-destruction.

Aggression as an instrument of striking out for the noble cause of freedom of the oppressed is seen in the life of Frederick Douglass (1817–1895), an abolitionist, orator, and journalist who was born a slave in Maryland. His mother was a slave; his father, a white slave owner. Douglass was a furiously angry man who once fought off a slave breaker with his fists and left him lying in a pile of manure; and yet Douglass expressed his aggression as a philosophical tool for freedom, not vengeance:

> Those who profess to favor freedom and yet deprecate agitation . . . want crops without plowing . . . rain without . . . lightning . . . the ocean without the awful roar of its many waters . . . This struggle may be a moral one, or it may be a physical one, but it must be a struggle. Power concedes nothing without a demand.

But Douglass was also a complex man who came to see the perils of aggression unleashed.

While certain 1960s militants soured on Frederick Douglass because intellectually they could not live with his rejection of John Brown's Harper's Ferry plan for armed insurrection against the U.S. government, Davis finds Douglass's conduct not only correct but also an example of how the rugged runaway mulatto slave transformed "suicidal hate into constructive energy." Yet Davis also writes of the impact that Brown had on Douglass's thinking. For initially, after his escape from slavery, Douglass spent six years traveling with William Lloyd Garrison and other abolitionists.

Although Douglass viewed Garrison as something of a father-figure, he had already "begun to perceive that several basic tenets—insistence that slaveholders could be converted by moral suasion, that the free states should secede from the Union, and that abolitionists should in no way recognize the legal, economic, and political realities of the slave system—were naïve and foolish." But of Brown's influence on Douglass, Davis writes:

> Douglass had moved completely away form Garrison's nonpolitical, nonviolent program. Not only did he use his home as a hideout for runaway slaves—at one time he hid twelve slaves until he could arrange their escape to Canada—but also he was an active conspirator with Brown: advising him, raising money, and making contacts for him with wealthy Radical Abolitionists. In Douglass's home, Brown drew up a constitution for the free state that he planned to form out of conquered areas.

Douglass was willing to join Brown in carrying out the original plan of running the slaves through the Alleghenies, but the raid on Harper's Ferry was an attack on the national government and was doomed to failure. Pursuing the point, Davis writes:

> True, [Douglass] wanted war against the slave power, but he wanted a war waged by the United States Government. It was clear he would not join Brown in a war against that very government. As he said years afterward. "It is gallant to go forth single-handed, but is it wise?"

In turn, this complex set of relationships is connected, in Davis's view, to Douglass's agonized relationship with his own white father and with Garrison. Garrison could control him, but he could not deal with him as an equal or as an intellectual superior. Both Brown and Garrison were purists to the point of megalomania about "their" cause, slavery.

As Douglass, who was still a slave, came to be an international spokesman for freedom, Garrison grew to loathe him; and when a group of Englishwomen put up enough money to buy Douglass out of bondage, Garrison felt wounded and betrayed. Garrison wrote of Douglass: "He reveals himself more and more to me as destitute and malevolent in spirit. He is not worthy of respect, confidence, or countenance." Davis writes:

> It was clear by this time that Garrison had fallen into a paranoid hatred of Douglass. His insane antagonism to Douglass smacked of that same cancer he found in Southern slaveholders, racial hatred. The maniacal excess to which Garrison's contempt and hatred drove him was demonstrated in his claim that Douglass and [his white benefactress] were sexually intimate. That claim was typical of the age-old American image of the Negro as always and everywhere innately sexual . . . To Garrison, Douglass suddenly became black, primitive, bestial, and, most of all, sexually degenerate (in fact, he had led an exemplary married life for forty-three years).

Yet through all of this Douglass never had a bad word to say about Garrison; he recognized the central role that Garrison had played in the antislavery movement and remembered that it was his newspaper, the *Liberator*, that had first inspired him with the words of freedom. This father-figure had gone wrong, and so had his own white slave-master father, who had shown him some kindnesses but who had fiercely beaten Douglass's kin.

Davis's exploration of Douglass's family tree—black and white—and of the profound impact that it had on him, on his confidence, savvy, and daring, is stunning:

> At the center of his early personality were two intense needs: the first was to win acceptance and recognition from his white father and master, the second was to secure, and enjoy, the trust and love of a woman, since he had lost his

247

mother and grandmother [both blacks] before the age of seven. . . . [Yet] Douglass learned his basic social identities from his black grandmother. . . . His grandmother also taught him ambition: the kind she herself had, for by hard work, skill, and determination, she had become the most influential slave on the Tuckahoe plantation. She instilled Fred with a strict conscience, too, and it endured throughout his life.

Out of his heritage Douglas evolved a complex vision that drew him into the public world early on:

During his adolescence, free Baltimore Negroes taught him the skills of public speaking and organizing. This they accomplished through civic and self-improvement associations, in which he was the only slave accepted. From them he learned new goals; and among them he met his future wife, Anna Murray. In New Bedford, too, free Negroes taught him their Yankee values, especially thrift. They also introduced him to the Massachusetts Anti-Slavery Society, and provided him with a discussion group as well as a platform.

The most tragic story in *Leadership, Love and Aggression* is that of W.E.B. Du Bois, the most brilliant black intellectual of this century. Even the briefest biographical outline suggests a profound achievement against the odds. Du Bois was born in Great Barrington, Massachusetts, in 1863, and he died a Communist in Ghana on August 28, 1963, the day that Martin Luther King, Jr., led the march on Washington. Du Bois was the first Negro to earn a Ph.D. from Harvard. (His thesis was entitled "The Suppression of the African Slave Trade to the U.S.A. 1638–1870.")

In his autobiographical writings, Du Bois attempted to cover up a poverty-stricken youth with an embellished version of a happy early life. He did not mention the rented rooms in a slum near the railroad tracks in which he and his beloved mother were forced to live, or the racial rejection that he encountered in school. According to Davis, he created a myth about himself:

> His fantasies provided an escape from Great Barrington, where he was regarded as a poor "darky," and probably an illegitimate one. In the deepest sense, his brilliant career was a reaction to and compensation for the disgrace of his mother.

Yet, as Davis notes, Du Bois's mother instilled in him the idea that educational excellence would in time overcome all barriers of discrimination. She represented the genteel strivings of the lower middle class, and the fantasies of the middle class, leading Davis to the following sharp-eyed perception:

> The black middle-class code actually was in some ways even more stringent than the value system of the white middle class. It taught Du Bois to work harder and renounce more than a white boy of his low economics status would; and it encouraged him to commit himself to academic achievement as the highest goal, whereas most working-class whites—among older Americans as among German, Swedish, and Irish immigrants—put education last, and money or politics first.

For a long time, Du Bois tried to live up to his mother's stern educational edict. He won high academic honors at Harvard and at the University of Berlin. For a time he taught and did research in the South. On the one hand his experiences were rewarding and led to one of his profoundest works, *The Souls of Black Folk*. This sheaf of essays was culled from his experiences of living and teaching in the backwoods near Fisk University, where "he helped poor rural blacks organize a school, taught it for them, lived with them, and came to enjoy the incomparable vitality of their children and their songs." Yet Du Bois could not avoid seeing the limitations upon his people and the brutality that they faced:

. . . He came to realize that the black middle-class belief that education would overcome white prejudice and white oppression had led him into a blind alley. As had most educated blacks, he found that whenever he sought to compete with whites professionally, he met the impasse of color . . . Du Bois had to live with the brutal fact that 200 to 300 blacks in the South were lynched each year—over 2,700 had been lynched during his years teaching there. His defense had been to withdraw from all contact with Southern whites. . . . But by 1910, after twenty-three years of research, and after witnessing the Atlanta race-riot murders, he realized that his intellectual work and his morality were powerless to stop lynching, peonage, or terrorization. Furthermore, he saw that, unlike Booker T. Washington, he had no actual *power*, either political, social, or economic; and finally he realized that he had withdrawn from social and economic reality. By limiting himself to research, he had—in his own works—"tried to isolate myself in the ivory tower of race."

But in 1905, when Du Bois, attempting to move out of isolation, called for a meeting of Negro leaders from seventeen states, Booker T. Washington persuaded white foundations to cut off financial support for Du Bois and for Atlanta University. In the long run, however, Du Bois's efforts led to the founding of the National Association for the Advancement of Colored Peoples; and Du Bois became the editor of the organization's powerful magazine, *Crisis*. Driven out of Negro education by Washington, Du Bois soon became the best-known leader of the civil rights movement:

He attacked lynching, disfranchisement, segregated schools, and a hundred forms of racial discrimination. Over the following two decades, his independence of judgment, his fearlessness, and his powerful intellectual grasp of the Negro's problems served to educate both the Negro middle class and the liberal white world.

Financially, Du Bois's days as the editor of *Crisis* were far from pleasant. For eighteen years he received a salary of $5,000—there were no raises. At the age of 60 he lost all his savings due to the deterioration of a building he owned in Harlem. Nor did he have any insurance—the Negro company that had handled his policy had gone bankrupt. He was forced out of the NAACP in a power play by Walter White, on the grounds that he was too far to the political Left. From 1934 to 1944 he taught at Atlanta University, but at the age of seventy-six he was retired without notice at the "instigation of a powerful white treasurer of the school." Although Du Bois returned to the NAACP for a time in the 1940s, he was again forced out. During the McCarthy period, the U.S. government would not allow him to travel. In the last years of his life, an embittered Du Bois embraced Communism and, at the invitation of the government of Ghana, moved to Africa in 1960. He died in Accra in 1963.

Davis's critique of the Mississippi-born Richard Wright offers more insight into the hounded life of the author of *Native Son* than can be found in any literary study.

> It is true that Wright learned to hate white people in Mississippi, but it is accurate to say that he did not hate them any more than he hated the Negro high-status group, or , in fact, any more than he hated blacks in general. His hostility to the Negro bourgeoisie was deep and bitter. Later, in Chicago, he found a tremendously complex Negro class system, whose top rungs were occupied by physicians, officials of black insurance companies, lawyers, and a few businessmen.

Chicago blacks will find much of interest in what Davis has to say about Wright's view of the black middle class (and lower class, as well). Apparently, little has changed about their reading habits since 1940, when *Native Son* was published:

> I [Davis] attended a house party given for Wright on Fifty-first Street in Chicago . . . The guests were white-

collar workers and professional people. Except for one or two white book reviewers. . . . everyone was Negro. Wright seemed completely out of place in this Negro middle-class group; I have never seen a man more unhappy at the celebration of his own triumph. Actually, of course, he had little in common with the group, since few of them read serious books or bought them. They were not interested in the world of literature where Wright's future lay, but in the world of insurance companies, business, and school-teaching.

Wright's black male and female characters were often empty of substance and humanity and, like the author, were dominated by self-hatred and by a vicious, racist caste system. Chicagoans who are offended by his nonthinking beast of a man from the South Side (Bigger Thomas, in *Native Son*) should look into the wounded psyche of the young Richard Wright, who grew up in racist Mississippi in a family of sadistic women; a man abandoned by a well-meaning but worthless father.

> Wright's hostile "death wishes" toward his mother and grandmother were very powerful and lasted throughout his life . . . His deepest conflict, then, was that between his conscience and his resentment against his mother. Wright was tortured by guilt for his own hatred because he, like his mother and grandmother, had a puritanical conscience. This deep-seated and unconscious guilt led him to the self-loathing and self-contempt that are manifest in the male characters of his novels.

Apparently Wright wanted to be dependent and yet fiercely sought the independence that his father had never achieved. But by turning his self-destructive forces outward, by becoming aggressively intellectual and creative, Wright probably saved his literary life, and his own life, literally.

Yet, as Davis points out, Bigger Thomas was a powerful metaphor for the destructive terrain of the slum-dwelling young black male of the late 1930s and '40s.

Wright took the all-important first step in dealing with repressed conflict: he articulated the anger. He spoke with such force as to startle the nation into attention. "Bigger" was unreal, larger than life, but a dread symbol of what our society was producing.

Of the four leaders presented here, only Martin Luther King, Jr., came from a solid middle-class setting where a balance of love and discipline was established by his family.

King's image in the public mind was nonviolent. Yet, as Davis reveals, King was anything but passive. Davis argues forcefully that, unlike the essentially masochistic Gandhi, King was an aggressive man of large appetite and passion who resisted his own powerful but loving father's attempts to dominate his life. He learned to implement his drive for racial freedom with love and ideas of Christian redemption, and he forged programs that Frederick Douglass would have appreciated, if not always followed.

Many have argued that King was discredited in his last days, that the movement was in ruins. Davis finds that King's critics were the ones who were bankrupt. And he keenly points to the ways in which King's ideas have transcended his death, while his venomous detractors have already become a fleeting footnote to history.

```
┌─                              ─┐
         EULOGY TO
        ALLISON DAVIS
       DECEMBER 4, 1983

└─                              ─┘
```

For me Allison Davis's legacy was three-fold.

First, there was the man's courageous intellectual toughness, and his angularity of vision; secondly, his capacity to continually expand his powerful analytical and interpretative gifts; and thirdly, there was his creative ability to transform those ever renewing ideas, in writing so that even as his scholarly contributions set the highest standard on the theoretical level, his angle of vision also provided a viable and dimensional scale model of society—enriched by his aptitude for sifting, ordering, and revealing the riddled labyrinth of racial, ethnic, caste, and class differences, into cohesive patterns. So that the practitioners and social engineers for dynamic change could incorporate his creative contributions for progress into their own works either as criticism of their specific fields, or as new routes to educational progress. Thus the reinspection, the deemphasizing, and dropping of the importance attached to culturally biased IQ testing, and the emergence of the positive Operation Head Start. These are but two examples of direct improvements—all anchored in Allison Davis's pioneering scholarship.

Allison Davis was a scholar who recombined his superior training with what he had observed in a long life of research, *and* with what he was observing in the immediate social upheaval. Beneath this foundation Allison brought to his scholarship three sources of illumination: a vast library of knowledge in several disciplines; a willingness to enrich his intellectual renderings with what his own common sense and nonsentimentalizing, but ennobling heart informed him to be true about the forces at work in society concerning the honorable versus the hypocritical, within the performances of the powerful; and the specific troubles of the neglected and the despised. And thirdly, against the flux and flow of events, Allison always kept a firm scale-model of history in view, shaped by his personal memories of the unadmitted saga of our Afro-American past.

Allison had a wonderful, sinewy ability to sum up the character of a man, a scene, or a situation without diminishing the humanity of the observed. Many times those penetrating observations turned out to be epiphanies of eloquent insight. Even when I disagreed with him, I often found myself, months, or years later, hearing the echo of Allison's voice, and seeing the truth of his wisdom; reflecting an especially clear-eyed focus, an oracle-like rendering of a dreaded truth, or a delicately renewing perception.

He looked like a handsome aristocrat—an elegant envoy on a mission—with his regal bearing, ramrod posture, and majestic profile. But he had the gift of feeling his way into the grain and texture of the human predicament with the withering wit of a wise and sorrowing peasant. He was forever discerning and clear about the baseness in all levels of refinement, filtering out the artificiality in societal mores, and governmental morality, behind the visage people wear before the world.

Allison knew instinctively what the slaves' wisdom warned us of, that "tomorrow may be the carriage driver's day for ploughing." With his keen awareness of history, Allison saw that the new economic gains blacks were making were to be viewed in the light of this slave peasant wisdom. For economic reversals are the wont of our economic system and the last hired often are the first fired if you are black and things get back to Depression-time scratch and crunch.

There was no segregation in the man's mind about the possible gold beneath the mire at the base of society—for here might dwell the backbone for greatness; or a high intelligence beneath the untapped mentality of an essentially nonverbal rural, or city-dweller.

He always took the high ground as a thinker—not as an escape route—but rather as a position from which he might gain perspective of the bottoms, the low lands, the least of these, the whole view, the total lay of the land.

The hallmarks of his consuming interests? The plight of the underclasses; the attributes and the education of the gifted, whether they were from the lower class, or from the upper middle class; the nature of heroic action; the sources of the drives of leaders who turned their aggression and their existential experiences to the elevation of the base of society . . . who brought up the rear—how these exceptional achievers refined their vision and society by intellect, spirit, pen and action.

In reading those keening essays in *Leadership, Love and Aggression*, there is the impression of hearing Leontyne Price singing "Deep River," in the shadow of the Lincoln Memorial. *Leadership* is a zealous oracle amid the chaos over the thrust for public power versus private anguish; the turmoil over caste, and class; the hero-as-outlaw; the nightmare of slavery; the wrenching plague of racism at the heart and soul of our American form of democracy; the impact of family and the search for transcendent love. In this his last work, Allison Davis enlarged our socio-political quest for a truly democratic republic. He opened up new paths, I believe, for future study and understanding concerning the complexity of the Negro family; and he offered us new patterns for looking at the foundations of contemporary black leaders.

Allison knew with the folklore of the past that it makes no difference how far a turtle extends his two front feet, he cannot move his body until he does something about his hind legs. Thus Allison sought to uplift thinkers, teachers, and administrators with his findings and his knowledge so that we might find ways to bring up the economic rear of the race, and the underprivileged—the economically deprived black underclasses now unto the third generation. How to heed the ancient ancestral commandment—pull up as you lift up, in our time.

He made no form of segregation between the levels of possibility and background and he found beauty and refinement in what many saw as abject baseness. From this persceptive Allison's vision was whole and solid. Any catalogue of his heroes will indicate this solidity and the creative tension beneath the solidity. Heroes who refined eloquence into an active, oracle-like statement out of the base materials of the human predicament. Louis Armstrong; Allison's contemporary from Washington, "Duke" Ellington; Adlai Stevenson, whose warnings about the horrors unleashed by the growing threat of the bomb, and Adlai's thrust for peace, deeply engaged Allison Davis's vision of our imperiled species . . . Frederick Douglass, whose complexity (slave and saviour, abolitionist and journalist) was best captured by Allison in the new book; and the uplifting, claoco-low-elegance within the poetry of his classmate, Sterling Brown. And finally, Martin Luther King, whom Allison came to see as the greatest man of our age, because he was able to recombine love and aggression into meaningful action for the least of these, as Allison wrote in summation of King.

> He believed that men can save themselves from their own mutual hatreds, for they have the capacity to turn hatred into its opposite—mercy and love of mankind . . . He was always willing to try again with people; he wholeheartedly asserted his faith in the human animal, who—however blinded, vindictive, and embittered—is capable of learning to love.

> It follows that the cure for the world's repetitive hatred and revenge lies in seeking leaders who first can convert their own hatred into constructive initiative, and then can direct their full efforts toward saving mankind from its hatred into compassion, a "brave new world" of love does seem possible.

When a dear friend—who so companioned our days with his gifts, as did Allison—is suddenly swept from our presence, we are, of course, heavy with the immediacy of that loss. A vital member from the body politic is severed from our needful existence. After the initial shock to the spirit there will always be for us, the felt knowledge of his presence and the grain and texture of his voice and the depth of his deeds. These renewing memories will act as the healing agent with instruction and enrichment, just as these memories will soon become Allison's permanent *memoir of remembrance* to his living friends and family. And the brilliance of his achievements, his books, his scholarly contributions are now his radiance to share with the ages. So that in death Allison's spirit will not diminish though the life of the body is no more. This is the especial sense in which Allison's gifts can and will facilitate all of our unfolding days with good humor, rekindled spirit, and warning wit to contribute but not to take ourselves too seriously.

So we gather not for a catalogue of mourning obsequies but in celebration of the life of a profound citizen-scholar, who sought to stir our spirits—with the powerhouse of his illuminating intellect.

The inextinguishable poetry of the man was ever alive as Promethean fire even in the winter withering of his autumnal days. There was a magnificence and a loneliness about him; a sternness, and the hope of a dreamer; a harpooning humor; a deep well of loyalty for close friends; a fierce argument about ideas and life and a controlled meditation; an anger tempered by a finely wrought balance of civility; with his superb logic, Allison understood the outlaw within the nature of the special achiever; and he had an acute spirit for the underdog. And, for me, touched to that majestic profile, there was a tissue as sensitive and as refined as a bouquet of roses.

```
┌─────────────────────────────┐
│  AN INDICTMENT OF           │
│  THE SOVIET SYSTEM          │
│  VIA RABELAISIAN SATIRE     │
└─────────────────────────────┘
```

In order to lift the great curtain of secrecy concerning, "oppression in totalitarian, soul-stripping" Russia since Stalin, scholar-philosopher Alexander Zinoviev has turned not to research, nor to philosophical-sociological tracts, but rather to "the great book of life"—the novel.

Comfortable in the novel, *The Yawning Heights*, as his outraged, fellow countrymen—Dostoevsky and Solzhenitsyn—Zinoviev leads us to the "heights" of indictment of the Soviet system through the genre of massive Rabelaisian satire, in order to unfold the dimensions of the death of the Soul Struggle in contemporary Soviet Russia. Indeed Dostoevsky's idea of the uniqueness of the Russian Soul, and the concept of the embattled Soul at War with itself—spiritually, politically, intellectually—has all turned to waste in Zinoviev's world as seen in the mythical society that is Ibansk (or Russia). The name of the society, Ibansk is forged upon a wild pun (typifying the rich, bawdy humor throughout the work); Ivan, the most pedestrian of Russian names and the verb, *yebat*—an expletive meaning to fornicate. . . . And Zinoviev proceeds to show how fouled up the Russians are.

Zinoviev employs the literary device of telling us that the novel was pulled together from scraps of a manuscript discarded in an Ibansk dump pile. Early in *The Yawning Heights* we learn that this was the same plebian rubble where the city manager served up a legendary decla-ration of independence; "The age old dream of mankind will soon come true, for already visible on the horizon are the yawning of heights of sotsim" (or socialist realism). But from Zinoviev's indictment and the scientific analysis found in the garbage, we come to see that the daily spillage of propaganda concerning "the gleaming heights of socialism" or even the "shining peaks of communism" are a sham and that the real truth is buried in the discarded manuscript, which records in one section. . . . "the mysterious Ibanskian soul is nothing but the Ibanskian whorehouse, carried to the nth degree and transposed to the Ibanskian mind, but not transformed thereby."

Dostoevsky's seminal "Notes from the Underground" obviously influenced this novel; in the mid-nineteenth century Russian man projected in that brief novel, the individual either accepted his social/economic status or became a dropout; in Tsarist Russia there was no mobility. In the post-Stalin era of Zinoviev's encyclopedic analysis, the individual can move up all right, but only if he strips away his individualism and then to a soulless "height," for the society is no longer politically, intellectually, spiritually engaged; all is group-think, and the party line. The great warring Russian Soul is reduced to a statistic (a warning Dostoevsky sounded in "Notes") in the name of material security, even secular salvation of the whole, and a heightened humanity. For the chief criteria for mobility in Ibanskian man is inaction or to "be like everyone else." Dostoevsky's Underground Man said that the man of action is necessarily stupid; and in *Heights* we learn: "A remarkable mind is seen as an abnormality, and remarkable ignorance—as a remarkable mind. Here highly moral people are perceived as immoral scoundrels, and highly base nonentities—as models of virtue."

Indeed one of the yeasty attributes of the civilized man's intellect—as we have come to observe the intellectual—is that it often possesses the qualities of spite and ridicule, *always* alive and engaged concerning the possible withering away of individual freedom by the state. In this sense the intellectual is often always radical, no matter the change or shift in governments, or even ideologies—thereby protecting the rights of the average citizen. Little of this hypersensitive attribute lives in Ibansk/Russia according to Zinoviev. Instead, cunning and personal conniving become the *raison d'etre* and the key to movement to the false heights of power; and as one leader in Ibansk is heard to say: "The leader is to present his personal interests as those of the group he leads, and to make use of the group for his own personal interests . . . Success in his career comes to a leader as the result of apparent, but never real, improvements and refinements." And we learn that the higher the post, the lower the leader's intellectual capacities, his culture, and his professional ability.

Movement and individual progress are neatly tied to rank and caste system. (The spirit of the 1917 revolution has turned into a whore, as it were.) The novel is *peopled* with bureaucratic types and allegorical figures, some of whom recall famous Soviet leaders. Among the cast we meet: The Boss (Stalin), Leader (Brezhnev), Hog (Krushchev); as well as recognizable types and figures behind such names as "Shizofrenic," "Member," "Thinker," "Pretender," or "Babbler." None of these figures appears to be a person, with a real life of his own; they are voices rather than people, which is of course Zinoviev's point about the farcical fantasies of their lives.

Of the average citizen in the post-Stalin era, started by the "Master-Owner" (another nickname for Stalin)—Shizofrenic says: "A new type of social individual and system of social relations appropriate to its nature was being born. An individual was produced who stood a head taller than Homo Sapiens, but his head was very small, and the heart was empty (or made of stone)." Ranks of leadership lead to a bevy of higher perks and the "better life." Better quality of food is available at lower prices, roomy government apartments at cheap rents, free vacation homes and health spas, all go with rank.

The brilliance of Zinoviev's satire in this monumental novel ranks him with Orwell, Swift, and especially Voltaire.

Zinoviev agrees with Solzhenitsyn concerning the perils of detente and that the United States is being manipulated by the current leadership in Russia. In order to satirize this situation in his novel, Zinoviev evolves a scene in which the government of Ibansk allows a monument to be placed at the grave of Khriak (probably Khrushchev) and then allows a low-ranking artist to show his wares at the public dump. Then liberals in the West extol, "The Ibanskians have reformed! They've improved!" Also in exchange for a few dissident thinkers the Ibanskians import large amounts of *shchi*, a Russian national dish of cabbage soup.

With his larger than life satire, Zinoviev has won the praise of critics throughout the world wherever the novel has been translated: But like Dostoevsky and Solzhenitsyn before him, this great author has also garnered the condemnation of his government. This prophet without honor was a professor of philosophy at Moscow University and at the Institute of Philosophy of the Soviet Academy of Sciences until he was ousted for writing *The Yawning Heights*. Finally he was allowed to leave the Soviet Union, after much harrassment from the KGB. Currently Zinoviev is a professor of philosophy at the University of Munich. By decree of the Praesidim of the Supreme Soviet, he was stripped of his Soviet citizenship in September, 1978.

*"Then said he unto me, Son of Man,
hast thou seen what the ancients of the
house of Israel do in the dark, every man
in the chambers of his imagery?"*
—Ezekiel 8:12

Much of James Baldwin's artistic vision of life in the novel, *Just Above My Head* projects an old obsession with sexual exploration as the sole instrument toward uncovering the deeper self, identity-wholeness, spiritual togetherness, and love. Not only is sex the body but the soul of his toppling, structurally open-ended, uneven book. Thus one of the central failures in the work occurs in conjunction with its minor success: the achievement of memorable minor characters, who not only strip the insubstantially drawn, love-seeking initiates bare but seduce the reader's attention and care away from Baldwin's heroes and heroine. Rather than profundity of character development in his main figures, Baldwin gives us the graphic details of their sexual flings, which are by and large poorly, even amateurishly rendered.

The first of three central characters is Hall Montana, the novel's uncommanding, seeing-eye narrator who eventually becomes the business-manager for his younger brother, the hero of the work, Arthur Montana. Arthur is a gifted Harlem gospel singer; his thinly portrayed odyssey moves from Harlem to the Freedom Movement to Paris: he lives a varied sex life, or so we are told, and dies of a heart attack, as the novel opens, in a London bar . . . recalling Rufus Scott's early suicide and the structural problems that his death unleashed in Baldwin's 1962 novel, *Another Country*. Like Rufus, much is held out for Arthur, but once again little of the inner man is revealed.

Hall Montana's story is consumed in the witness-bearing, running notes he delivers about the rise and fall of his brother's fortunes. Sometimes this is a complicated device for Baldwin, who uses the weak technique of having Hall hear about his brothers love life via letters. But we are presented scant evidence of these letters. The letters come Hall's way when Baldwin swoops big-brother off to the Korean war, as he does Arthur's first lover, and piano accompanist, Crunch, a well-drawn minor character, who overpowers our interest in Arthur. But since we know next to nothing concerning the impact of the Asian experience upon these characters when they return, we feel manipulated. Writing the novel in the first person through Arthur's viewpoint might have forced Baldwin to forge the character of his gospel singer into a real witness. Nor do we know why Baldwin decided to make him a gospel singer, since we never feel the spirit moving in him.

Baldwin often writes well about the impending terror of mass crowds upon the sensitive, modern individual, and some of the scenes at Civil Rights rallies in the South, where Arthur sings to raise money for freedom groups at black churches—with vigilantes in the foreground—are memorable. The tenderness, wiliness, and courage evidenced by Southern blacks, as both participants and culturally astute witnesses in the struggle, suggest new avenues of growth and perception in Baldwin's fictive enterprises and powers.

The third central character—another witness—is Sister Julia Miller, the precocious child evangelist. She gives one excellently rendered sermon in an early scene, and the reader is briefly reminded of Baldwin's "felt-knowledge" in evoking the litany of the Negro sermon, in his brilliant first novel, *Go Tell It On The Mountain*. Sister Julia leaves the church ostensibly because of her mother's death. More importantly, Baldwin suggests that the super-star status accorded Julia and the harness of performance demanded by her parents placed the child upon a kind of psychological leash, which resembled a straitjacket. Finally, her faith is driven asunder in one of the more compelling sections, when her father—the epitome of modern, though ancient evil—takes his saint-innocent child to bed, and becomes the continual lover of her body, as his sated soul disintegrates in the fires of incest. This minor character, Joel Miller, a kind of minister of corruption, seizes the reader's attention, and some of Baldwin's best character probing and evolvement occur as he traces the pimpish, preacher-dandy father's decomposition, with both pity and terror. But what of the impact upon the fourteen-year-old daughter? This is never ex-plored in depth; instead we become faint witnesses to Julia's introduc-tion to the contemporary commerical world of Afro-American possibility—she becomes a swinging model; Julia's physical appearance touches upon a certain faddish quest for an Afro-Egyptian counte-nance, yet we learn little of her psychic scars. The fact that Julia is able to rebound with such American Zeitgeist implies Baldwin's rage to be a *Now* writer and the influence of movie and television script shortcut devices—the early Sister Julia suddenly becomes Diahann Carroll's TV *Julia.* To gainsay this leap in Julia's metamorphosis, we hear rumors that Julia hustled for a time to support her brother, Jimmy, whom she "saved" from the supportive arms of their grandmother, down in New Orleans.

Jimmy Miller turns out to be a wild, pleasure-loving brother, filled with an Adonis adoration for Arthur; he vamps the gospel singer and they become easy riders for a time, in the middle phase of the so-called "Soul Emperor's" sexual odyssey. In another rung up the novel's myriad of invisible odysseys, and the author's attempt to plug into the contemporary black fad of seeking immediate identity fulfillment in Africa, Baldwin swoops Julia off to Abidjan to seek out her symbolic blackness.

Because Baldwin's talent is so seething with the materials of the grand themes of life and literature, and because he sets his literary troupe and drama, stage center, upon these issues, we have every right to demand that he convey the *Weltanschauung* his mind presents to his imagination. Yet here novelist Baldwin replaces his embattlement with a formula of coupling serious themes with easy, slick sex, set pieces.

Baldwin's literary invention has always been better served in the forms he employs in many of those stimulating, prophetic essays. But in *Just Above My Head* a sameness of set pieces, easy lays, redundancy of language, repetition of nuance creep through these scenes. This slackness of invention carries over to character: thus Arthur Montana is no more sophisticated and exploring about his inner self when he gets involved with Crunch, who is not to be seen as gay, but male and black, than he is at the other end of the spectrum and near the end of his swinging days, when he becomes involved in a kind of Parisian Eden with a Frenchman, Guy, who is gay.

Baldwin, the romantic, sees certain attributes of the homosexual encounter not as sexual confrontation but as the epitome of idyllic love, and he seems to regard the homosexual act—no matter how brief—as a freeing agency by which men may know the good news of their deeper sexual natures and themselves. Serious readers—straight and gay—will, I believe, find Baldwin's naked bliss unbearable, an embarrassing, sophomoric, phallic fantasy, just above their heads.

One is tempted to say that the freedom a gifted male homosexual writer may now feel as he approaches his materials has divested Baldwin of his literary quest of shunning easy relationships, and for *showing* the heart-breaking embattlement and fought-for beauty of a relationship heightened by a muted lyricism as revealed in "Giovanni's Room." Now he seems bent merely on telling us a sexual twisting was beautiful, therefore the relationship was beautiful. These out-of-the-closet, Doris Day-Rock Hudson romantics turned inside out, "would give the blues the Blues" and mar the reputation of the James Baldwin who has often fought as artist to reveal the dark, tormented inner soul of "every man in the chambers of his imagery"; after all, as some squares and all Blues believers know, it's only through the agony of a relationship that one is allowed the deeper meaning of sexual ecstasy, then and only then, as the Blues instructs, "you mellow down easy."

$$\left[\quad\right]$$

EVIDENCES OF
JIMMY BALDWIN

The last time I saw James Baldwin was late autumn of 1985, when my wife and I attended a sumptuous book party honoring the celebrated writer in the Hyde Park home of an upper middle-class black couple. Earlier in the day, Baldwin had been received by the first black Mayor of Chicago, Harold Washington. The hostess for this party was connected with the Washington administration.

Baldwin was in Chicago, as part of his book tour, promoting what was to be his final publication, *Evidences of Things Not Seen*. This long essay turned into a brief book was an outgrowth of an article Baldwin had written for *Playboy* on his investigation of the Atlanta murders. It will be remembered that in June of 1981, after twenty-two months and some twenty-three corpses, a middle-class young black man, Wayne Williams, was arrested for murder. All of the kids who were slain were male, black, and poor, in a city known for its sprawling middle and upper-middle-class black population. The administration of Atlanta was also black.

Jimmy Baldwin greeted his guests in a small room just off from the spacious dining area, where a fine array of hor d'oeuvres were in abundance and a lavish dinner was spread out over three large tables (including carved ham and beef) awaited the devotees of one of the two or three most stunning African-American literary talents of our age; and one of the most eloquent American essayists of his generation. The caterer's active cadre busily and efficiently waited on the sixty or more gathered guests.

I had met Jimmy Baldwin many years before, and long before I had actually published any fiction. Upon this occasion, I told him quite frankly and from the heart too, that along with Ralph Ellison his eloquence had been a very important influence upon my own writing; and that it had meant a lot to me to have his essays and *Go Tell It on the Mountain*, along with *Invisible Man*, as guiding standards, written by blacks. We also discussed the novelist Toni Morrison, my editor at the time, and Baldwin's good friend. During the course of our conversation Baldwin said to me: "I didn't know Chicago could produce a writer like you."

Finally the gathering was led down to a large basement area, where piles of *Evidences* were stacked upon a table set up in the corner by the owner of one of the best bookstores in Chicago, Richard Bray. Copies were there to be purchased and Baldwin was ready to autograph the book after his official introduction. The man designated to introduce James Baldwin was the noted executive editor of *Ebony* Magazine, Lerone Bennett, Jr.

In addition to Bennett, there were in that room many of the most well-known Chicago blacks in the arts community. Looking around the room, I saw the novelist and short-story writer, Cyrus Colter; the distinguished sculptor, Richard Hunt, with his lovely wife, Lenora Cartright; Gwendolyn Brooks and her husband. Obviously, I am also hinting at (and not so subtly, either) that the stalwarts in the arts community amongst blacks formed and are a very narrow grouping in Chicago. As Bennett started his introduction of James Baldwin, the white waiters and bartender, as if on cue, ceased their work, or virtually froze in space (as black waiters would have acted in another time, perhaps in this very house, under different ownership, when a noted white authority was being introduced). Then Baldwin put down his Scotch and water, held on to his cigarette, and stood up to speak.

Baldwin basically sounded the theme expressed by the late Lorraine Hansberry at Bobby Kennedy's New York apartment, that blacks "didn't want to be integrated into a burning house." Probably three-fourths of the especially invited guests at this party were African-Americans; they all seemed to be doing quite nicely socially not only in this splendid Hyde Park home, but also in the larger house that is America. If the house was burning, the blacks here surely didn't want to see it go down in flames, for they were already integrated inside many of the American halls and chambers of power. Also, they were very much alive to the impact blacks had upon the cultural ethos of this country. Baldwin's general indictment of the Republic was tough and rang true, but not especially for now, and not for this crowd, and not for the specifics of the grievous condition many poor blacks faced in the day-to-day realities of America today.

For those blacks, completely outside the physical and psychological space of this room, any talk about not wanting "to be integrated into a burning house," was as off-the-wall as peddling the same spiel to those of us attending this homage to Jimmy. For the blacks in the underclass, the values of white society and those of the middle and upper-middle-class African-Americans are but a wonderland, seen perhaps on the *Cosby Show*, or if they go downtown, get off at the wrong stop, and see the black and white upscale denizens of the city shopping along the Magnificent Mile. No, upon this occasion, there were no Clytie Sutpens in that basement ready to set this house on fire; nor to set to burn the symbolic American house down either.

On the other hand, Baldwin seemed unaware of the growing species of African-American Bourgeois Nationalism, which doesn't seem interested for the slightest moment in being integrated into a burning house; even as this current is very much caught up in the value system of the house. The book club that Bennett belongs to epitomizes some of this distance of Baldwin's own world, for it is called "The Great Black Books Club." The book Baldwin was promoting suggests evidences of the growing cleaveage between the stratas of African-American life in this country; the *de facto* segregation between poor blacks and middle-class blacks in Atlanta and through a lot of the African-American world.

For me, Baldwin's verbal virtuosity turned into literary fire was one of Jimmy's priceless jewels.

I could not help but think back to what he had said earlier, that he "didn't know Chicago could produce a writer like you." Where I appreciated certain aspects of the compliment, I held to a different notion of the writer's evolvement that Baldwin's rise as an excellent writer best revealed that the writer, to a large degree, shapes up his own talent in connection with certain literary traditions he or she is fiercely attracted to. Anyway a writer is shaped by a library, as Ellison has indicated.

What Baldwin had been saying about America had been true and was an example simply of the writer's vision being frozen in a time in which his own vision of life flourished. In this sense, Baldwin's arguments with Richard Wright and Faulkner, concerning the ways in which the world had changed around them, seemed to especially apply to Jimmy's later work and certainly the vision he uttered at this book party in his honor, attended by so many upscale African-Americans, who were there to celebrate one of their own who had made it big, and against the odds, in this troubled house that is our American home.

The brilliant essayist had said something that many of the blacks at the party would do well to remember, *and* identity-seeking younger middle-class African-Americans (who have read Baldwin out as essentially an obsolete assimilationist) must force themselves to recollect: "The one thing that all Americans have in common is that they have no other identity apart from the identity which is being achieved on this continent." The fact that Baldwin was still attempting to wage war with this Republic—a kind of civic/Civil War—was as much about his lover's quarrel with America as it was concerned with his great despair over this country's countless infidelities with loathsome suitors, who would pluck out the vision of a more perfect union, impale its energies upon a cross of mercurial might, in foreign intrigues, and enslave its soul upon an auction bloc of materialism. In this sense Baldwin was in keeping with the verbal-literary statesmen and women of our Republic: Thomas Paine, Frederick Douglass, Walt Whitman, Adlai Stevenson,

Martin Luther King, and Barbara Jordan, among their number.

Believing as I do in the artistic individualism as the primary key to the evolvement of the writer, I had rejected the notion of the city's impact upon me, as Jimmy Baldwin's comment earlier in the evening had implied. Indeed, as far as I was concerned Baldwin himself epitomized the concept I have always held to, the uniqueness of the individual writer's capacity to shape his vision and to mold his art. On reflection I must say that the idea that the city (in my case, Chicago) produces the writer is true of course. Yet it seemed to me simple-minded at first to accept. Baldwin's statement was, however, consistent with his view of society's power over the individual. He had often said that "You," meaning white America, "created Jimmy Baldwin." What he also meant was that America (white and black, too) must take responsibility for the care and keeping of the individual children of our Republic. That Jimmy Baldwin should have ended his literary career writing about the murdered children of Atlanta, and why this occurred speaks powerfully to his concern for the least of these in the true Christian sense, and as Baldwin reminds us in *Evidence*: "Years ago, after the slaughter of the four little girls in the Birmingham Sunday school, Ruby Dee, Ossie Davis, John O. Killens, Odetta, the late Louis Lomax, and some others, including me, rented New York's Town Hall to demand that Christmas, that year, be declared a day of mourning. We held that a Christian nation had no right to celebrate the birthday of the Prince of Peace before it made an attempt to atone."

This makes us recall that although Baldwin was using the "I" of his experiences in his essays, as a representative of the many sides of the "we" who have suffered, or the collective *we* of the total American experience, he has always tried to inculcate the form of the essay with the many shapes the outraged condition took under the heel of oppression, using his mind, body, and soul as the metaphor and the measurement. The autobiographical vignettes gave shape to many voices that Baldwin heard and paid witness to, which in turn opened the reader up to a brilliant arsenal of well-crafted literary tools, informed by a first-rate library and the skillful imagination to put the tactics into motion, as we are conducted through his tour and a vision of the torment over race, in America, that white Americans declined to deal with.

One sees the novelist's art alive in the complex associative patterns that Baldwin sets in motion in the best essays, as well as the novelist's penchant for eloquently lifting stories or vignettes from life, but taking them to a higher pitch of literary statement; and then allowing these sagas to hang out on their own power within the reader's imagination, and his conscious.

There is the manner in which Baldwin's fiery language, and his larger than life vision of the racial crisis is informed by the Old Testament scripture and the sagas of the great figures of the Bible. There is, of course, the identification with the great struggles of the Old Testament Hebrews, and the linkage that saga forged in Baldwin's imagination with the trials of the African-Americans in this country. The title of his last book comes from the New Testament, and it is from St. Paul: "Faith is the substance of things hoped for, the evidence of things not seen." Baldwin's essays can be read as epistles (recalling Paul's letters and epistles) to the outraged soul of America. The essays often have the intimacy of private letters made public. Or again, there is the feeling that he has taken a few pages from his private diary and inculcated them right into an ongoing essay. One of Baldwin's most famous essays is entitled *"Notes of a Native Son"*. In this essay and others, there is a feel of the journalist collecting his running notes as he sets down his story, with everything on his mind, as he re-creates an important feature story.

Baldwin's art of the essay also belong to the heritage of confessional literature, and these letters from the heart are influenced by writings from prison, as well as the prison of the lonely heart; and on certain occasions the Negro as the imprisoned party in this land of the free; or, for Baldwin, the homosexual as prisoner.

Baldwin's writings are not only influenced by the language of the Bible but the vision of certain characters of the Bible, and the tradition of the prophet who stood outside of the temple, telling the worshippers you ought to improve, but you won't. He also found resonance in the apocalyptic vision of the Old and New Testaments, and particularly the Book of Revelations, as a thematic chord of both imperial power in his essays (and in many passages in his novels, particularly in *Go Tell It on the Mountain*). One can almost always hear the boy-preacher in Baldwin, and the sassy, hypersensitive, bitchy secular-cabaret singer going from table to table and turning the pale-face clientele red face with what must happen for a redemption of the races to occur—that they must cast off their obsession with their whiteness (culturally, political, socially) go through a confession-like agony, similar to the one Baldwin is going through in his essays, engage their secret and private worship of white supremacy, and confront America's racism, actively. He is preaching and singing to them about the difficulty of being whole; you can't be whole and be an American; admitting to the divided self (white side/black side) is where you start. Because to live for Baldwin was always to discover the hidden self within, and how that self was related to what we as Americans were hiding about ourselves as a people. This was true for him, about both race and sexuality. He speaks to his audience at each table, as a wounded lover concerning the way you Americans have treated me.

Baldwin's voice was also a combination of the prophet-as-outlaw. Outlaw because he was a self-educated intellectual; outlaw because he was a hypersensitive black male; and outlaw because he was a homosexual. Behind this was Baldwin's own existential willingness to run the risk of discovering life through the adventure of playing out these three attributes of his identity, no matter where those drives took him. For Jimmy Baldwin it was at those extremities of life that you can really confront the self, since Americans are bound up in a deep set of denials and hypocrisy and hatred linked to race, sexuality, and the life of the intellect.

Structurally many of his essays move very much like the art of the folk preacher. His essays are orchestrated (here I am thinking of "Stranger in the Village"; "Notes of a Native Son"; "Many Thousands Gone"; "The Fire Next Time"; "Uptown, Fifth Avenue") and the structure of these works recall the story-teller's art, in which the tale moves saga-like in sections. At his best, Baldwin was creating symphonies out of the essay form. He didn't know any history to speak of—any more, that is, than the lay person, who has a fairly good working library of historical references undergirded by the heritage of his own group directly in mind. His main sense of history was history as oral memory. He certainly didn't know any economics, and probably not a lot about the ways in which a power structure works internally. Jimmy's was a voice absolutely grieving in the wilderness over the crucible of race, and along the way, he created some unforgettable phrases or "oracles," with his lyrical phraseology. Much of that style that was so much James Baldwin can be traced to the powrful impact Henry James had upon this writer.

Another strategy of Baldwin's, it seems to me, was to take certain pivotal moments from heated verbal arguments he had had over the issue of race, then reshape this material into a text for his essays, particualrly, the moments of confrontation and summation. This is another way of looking at the relationship between oral tradition and literary tradition in James Baldwin's essays.

At one time I read Clarence Darrow's summations from his great trials. They were very literary appeals. In some ways Baldwin's petitions and his arguments in many of the essays are very much like eloquent summations delivered before the court, the judge, and the jury, concerning this victimized Negro, who has been unjustly accused of practically every offense against the state and civility imaginable and unimaginable. As the Negro's friend at court, we hear Baldwin (echoing Whitman): "I am the man, I suffer'd, I was there."

In his summations, Baldwin champions the defendant by accusing the state of inhuman cruelty against the Negro, of blaming the victim for their wrongs. The jury appears in an angry mood, ready to vote to string the defendant up. The judge looks as if he's poised to throw the book at Jimmy's Nigra. Yet Baldwin's appeal is to the conscience of the jury, in that it takes the form of a plea to each juror, face to face, on an individual basis. He speaks to each with a certain confidentiality and his stirring message is to their willingness to apply or extend the principles of Judeo-Christian democracy to the least of these, and to strike down the deeply inbred concepts of racist faith, which excludes African-Americans from all attributes of the human family.

Many of Jimmy Baldwin's essays form a withering scripture in black and blue about the central issue of race in America. The best of the compositions have cracked open the American canon—the highest tribute is the writer's burning stake upon the literary terrain—even though Jimmy Baldwin never won any major writing awards. You simply cannot put together a collection of essays about American life since World War II without including the highly intelligent, raging, tormented works of this furious voice for freedom.

CASTING LIGHT UPON
A WRITER'S WORK

The reader's interest in the heralded interview with a leading author often stems from the desire to make the writer more human, because the body of work, or the individual novel, seem so awesome . . . "Is he down to earth?" "How close is the writer's actual life to his fiction?" In general, interview junkies tend more to hang on the author's public words than on the words of his text, forgetting that the serious writer's creation is in itself an attempt to humanize, civilize, and reveal the meaning of an area of life.

But at another dimension, the serious reader often does seek out an intermediary between himself and the books of a writer, and not so much the personal biography of the writer—which often is quite unremarkable—but some reflection into the work habits that produced a remarkable work; or the specifics of the author's reading library . . . perhaps the author lives under some particularly horrific experiences and we are interested in knowing about this side of his world. Indeed, the best two interviews in Sixth Series of *Paris Review* come from writers who have lived under the gun of dreadful dehumanizing regimes: Nadine Gordimer, a sensitive white woman living under the system of apartheid in South Africa; and Gabriel Garcia Marquez, a great Latin American novelist who has known all forms of power-hungry dictators.

Here the serious reader is interested in finding out whether a renowned author can make articulate the meaning of everyday life across the globe. Can he or she offer clarity about values in a plain-spoken way that does not profane his language and my intelligence, about my world, the reader asks? This kind of intermediary connection, in terms of our needs for illumination, is best expressed in the interview with Gordimer, as she speaks of her constant opposition, not to any sort of abstract idea, but to the actuality of an oppressive state, and that relationship to those who live in the vapid Western countries:

"It amazes me . . . I come to America, I go to England, I go to France . . . nobody's at risk. They're afraid of getting cancer, losing a lover, losing their jobs, being insecure. It's either something you have no control over, like death—the atom bomb—or it's something with which you'll be able to cope anyway, and that is not the end of the world; you'll get another job or you'll go on state relief or something of this nature. It's only in my country that I find people who voluntarily choose to put everything at risk—in their personal life."

Much of the success of the *Paris Review Interviews*, of course, is connected to another salient intermediary, the intelligent interviewer. George Plimpton himself started the tradition and set the standard for these collections with his great dialogue with Ernest Hemingway in the first "Writers at Work" number. For example, the good question often is the one that leaves out everything and implies much about the core of a writer's art and the impact of the book[s] on the audience; what the work[s] opened and revealed to a readership. When this occurs, the result is a dialogue in which the interviewer seems to ask that large question [one that can really get the juices of the writer flowing] and the question that we ourselves would like to ask.

Understanding the relationship of theme to character, vis-à-vis the author's vision of life, is quite important here. In his interview with Garcia Marquez, Peter H. Stone has aroused the Nobel Prize-winning author on the relationship of power and character in "The Autumn of the Patriarch" to dictators in Latin America. . . . But now the interviewer recombines this line of questioning with a theme from Garcia Marquez's masterpiece, *One Hundred Years of Solitude.* "You often use

277

the theme of the solitude of power," he observes, and this is enough to spark a highly articulate definition from Garcia Marquez:

"The more power you have, the harder it is to know who is lying to you and who is not. When you reach the absolute power, there is no contact with reality and that's the worst kind of solitude there can be. A very powerful person, a dictator, is surrounded by interests and people whose final aim is to isolate him from reality; everything is in concert to isolate him."

Interviewer: "What about the solitude of the writer: Is this different?"

"It has a lot to do with the solitude of power. The writer's very attempt to portray reality often leads him to a distorted view of it. In trying to transpose reality he can end up losing contact with it, in an ivory tower, as they say. Journalism is a very good guard against that. That's why I have always tried to keep on doing journalism, because it keeps me in contact with the real world, particularly political journalism and politics."

Many of the writers in the collection *Paris Review Interviews Sixth Series*—Kurt Vonnegut, Rebecca West, Stephen Spender, Elizabeth Bishop, and John Gardner—are not as articulate about their works as Garcia Marquez. Tennessee Williams' interview breaks down into a series of puffy epigrams about famous people that he knew. Some of the writers express themselves, however, with a language and tone that recall their fiction. Bernard Malamud admits what some writers don't admit—he does read the critics:

"I dislike particularly those critics who preach their esthetic or ideological doctrines at you. What's important to them is not what the writer has done but how it fits or doesn't fit the thesis they want to develop. Nobody can tell a writer what can or ought to be done, or not done, in his fiction. A living death if you fall for it."

We are always interested in what a major writer, like a Malamud, has to say about a contemporary issue. The interviewer has just asked Malamud, "Will you predict [relationships] between blacks and Jews in the future?" Malamud says quite candidly:

"How can one? All I know is that American blacks have been badly treated. We, as a society, have to redress the balance. Those who want for others must expect to give up something. What we get in return is the affirmation of what we believe in."

Often in the brilliantly rich short stories collected in *The Book of Sand*, the intellectual artist-as-hero is haunted by fantasy. His moment of enlightenment results from a confrontation with peace-disturbing realism (beautiful feminist, myth of origins, philosophical idea, or Lucifer). The new angle of vision transforms the hero's reality while heightening and challenging the specter of his long-held fantasy.

In "The Other," Jorge Luis Borges creditably uses his own persona as a device for plunging the reader into a confrontation with the self over illusion, reality, and fantasy. The story shows an indebtedness to Dostoevsky's "The Double"; but the old, day-dreaming professor, who thinks he hears a facsimile of himself in the voice of a new arrival, at the other end of a park bench, speaks to our common humanity—"I had the impression of having lived that moment once before." The *two* converse. The stranger, it turns out, is as much another aspect of "Borges" as he is a person. And the *two* sides of Borges duel over the question of precisely remembered family history—employing contending voices within the same body.

The aged narrator of "Ulrike" sees something deeper in the cold feminist Ulrike's facade: "A line in Blake speaks of girls of mild silver or of furious gold, but in Ulrike were both gold and mildness." Ironically, feminist Ulrike possesses an ethos pregnant with romantic male-dominated myths, her imagination must lust upon the bacchus of mythhood before sex can blossom. The lover's conversation becomes a beautiful, slippery fairy tale. Yet spinning us back to reality, our narrator, Javier Otalora, informs us he can't pronounce the damsel's name and she can't pronounce his (love transcends language!) and she says, "I shall call you Signed."/"You will be Brynhild," says he.

Synthesis of fantasy and reality is a cornerstone of Borges' art. Yet even art can be perilous to the poet; for a bard must die and his king be diminished to a mendicant, in "The Mirror and the Mask," when the versifier abandons the elevated, rhapsodic terrain of war homages and echoes God's personal wrath into the tyrant's ear, and "commits the sin of having known Beauty, which is a gift forbidden to men."

The title story shows the impact of Melville's "The Confidence Man." The blond, Lucifer-like Bible salesman-antagonist has a marvelous (but monstrous) Holy Book in his bag, "The Book of Sand." The narrator swaps a traditional Bible for this one—momentarily peddling his soul? —and naturally this illustration-ridden (illusion-riddled?) book becomes a nightmarish source. Since its wisdom and terror issue from the bottom of life, the narrator "loses it" or buries the Bible at the bottom of a library.

In "The Disk," a kindly stranger presents his God's one-sided disk to a wood-cutter, who, once upon a time dreamed of cutting down all the trees in the forest. With that rape-pillage passion unrealized, he sees in the disk, perhaps, a link to God, the primitive's scent at origins, or salvation. But in axing the king to death for the disk, the woodcutter's vision of a flaring disk perishes, eternally. (He who lives by the sword shall perish by the sword!) On reflection the disk was more glitter than gold. . . . Or only a flash-in-the-pan of salvation's eternal light? Or was "The Disk" the primitive's tablet of knowledge?

These yeasty, elegant tales are rendered with astonishing beauty, wisdom, and haunting lucidity by a virtuoso of literature, whose lyrical art sings and insinuates itself into our very being . . . a mixture of gold and silver, indeed.

The eloquence of Borges' poetry picks up where story levels leaves us—at a transcending height. Borges sees the poet's mission, as high-priest, "to restore to the word, at least in a partial way, its primitive and now secret force." Borges' lyrical link between story and poem is clear. He writes: "In the earliest times, there can have existed no division between the poetic and the prosaic. Everything must have been tinged with magic. Thor was not the god of thunder; he was the thunder and the god."

> I shall be all or no one. I shall be the other
> I am without knowing it, he who has looked on
> that other dream, my waking state.

("The Dream" and "Inventory" recall a line from Dylan Thomas: "The centuries throw back their hair.")

Borges often takes on ground trod by the masters. Good fences don't make good neighbors in either poetry or in the life of the writer's imagination. Yet sometimes influences can be overwhelming; fortunately Borges is a master himself, thus in the title poem, a deep debt to Blake is present, but "The Gold of the Tigers" has a truth and a beauty of its own. . . .

> the amorous gold shower disguising Zeus,
> the gold ring which, on every ninth
> night,
> gives light to nine rings more, and
> these, nine more,
> and there is never an end.
> All the other overwhelming colors,
> in company with the years, kept leaving me,
> and now alone remains
> the amorphous light, the inextricable shadow
> and the gold of the beginning.

In Borges' selected later poems, "The Gold of the Tigers," we witness, again, the marriage of myth and reality—giving us a magical synthesis, "Susane Bombal" (recalling Ulrike of the stories) is "tall in the evening, arrogant, aloof." Yet her presence in a garden transforms that garden ('Eden?'), and she also becomes a fantasy angel of mythic form . . . "but simultaneously I also see her haunting ancient, twilit Ur of the Chaldees/ or coming slowly down the shallow steps/ a temple, which was once proud stone but now/ has turned to an infinity of dust."

The world of "The Dream" stirs and provides Borges' vision with that other side of man's experience that must be expressed for us to know ourselves as whole. Yet significantly only in our dreams can we face the truth, Borges seems to be suggesting. (This poem is a good companion piece to the intelligence of the story, "The Other".) But for the poet the great gathering-up memory must contain the splendid peculiarities of the sea's denied unconscious. . . .

> I shall go, farther than the shipmates of Ulysses
> to the territory of dream, beyond the reach
> of human memory. From the underwater world I save
> some fragments
> inexhaustible to my understanding:
> grasses from some primitive botany,
> faces which all the time are masks
> and at times, horror, unlike anything
> the day can offer us.

GARDNER'S FINAL WILL
AND TESTAMENT
TO WRITERS

The notebook, *The Art of Fiction*, represents the final will and testament to bright young writers and zealous coaches of creative writing. Not only is it valuable to apprentice writers, it is a worthy and instructive companion for the constant reader who seeks to understand the process behind the mysteries of artistic power, the relationship of imagination, inspiration, and the flint of experience in a writer's work.

Gardner knew in his artistic bones that any first-rate writer must have a rich library of reading intermingled with his primary materials of experience; thus Gardner advises that the writer must become a highly intelligent, analytical reader, or be doomed to never seeing into the mysterious ironies of life. "No ignoramus—no writer who has kept himself innocent of education—has ever produced great art. One trouble with having read nothing worth reading is that one never fully understands that the argument is an old one [all great arguments are], never understands the dignity and worth of the people one has cast as enemies."

For the distinguished author of *October Light*, literature meant what it signified in the lives of many European intellectuals and artists of the nineteenth and early twentieth centuries—the very meat and potatoes of serious conversation and discourse, against the backdrop of daily events. One almost never encounters this kind of associative intelligence in the literary diet of intellectual circles in this country. That we segregate life and art so blandly but so boldly is perhaps the reason why certain serious American writers—like Gardner himself—turned to the university for intellectual sustenance and artistic dialogue.

Yet, like any true artist, Gardner was constantly reexamining all received opinion when it comes to creative writing technique and approach. For example, we have all been told, as the first command-ment of writing, write only about those subjects you know first-hand. To that edict of Holy Writ, Gardner wisely renders his own rejoinder: "The writer writes well about what he knows because he has read primarily fiction of just this kind—realistic fiction. . . . The writer, in other words, is presenting not so much what he knows about life as what he knows about literary genre. . . . Write the kind of story you know and like best."

As the book instructs the writer about craft, it also engages the mind of the serious reader through Gardner's eloquent expression of what we all seek from literature: moments of magical revelation. "The value of great fiction, we begin to suspect, is not just that it entertains us or distracts us from our troubles, not just that it broadens our knowledge of people and places, but also that it helps us to know what we believe, reinforces those qualities that are noblest in us, leads us to feel uneasy about our faults and limitations."

These delightful "tutorials" have added weight and significance; we are presented with the finely written expression and vision of life by an important American novelist-turned-critic-and-creative-writing-teacher. In one passage, Gardner offers what I take to be the very soul of his artistic, and esthetic, last will and testament to young writers:

"He makes the scene vivid in the reader's mind; that is, he encourages the reader to 'dream' the event with enormous clarity, by presenting as many concrete details as possible. . . . Good descrip-tion is symbolic not because the writer plants symbols in it but because, by working in the proper way, he forces symbols still largely mysterious to him up into his conscious mind where, little by little as his fiction progresses, he can work with them and finally understand them. To put this another way, the organized and intelligent fictional dream that will eventually fill the reader's mind begins as a largely mysterious dream in the writer's mind."

Too often the characters in unpublished students' efforts, or the first published works of semi-professional writers, are flabby or still-born. The characters lack moments of intense personal and public struggle; they don't live in peril of losing or sacrificing anything of value; we are not caught up in their lackluster quest; and they don't evolve percep-tions worthy of our emotional and intellectual engagement. Gardner shatters this coddled and sheltered fiction:

"No fiction can have real interest if the central character is not an agent struggling for his or her own goals but a victim, subject to the will of others. [Failure to recognize that the central character must act, not simply be acted upon, is the single most common mistake in the fiction of beginners.] We care how things turn out because the character cares—our interest comes from empathy—and though we may know more than the character knows, anticipating dangers the character cannot see, we understand and to some degree sympathize with the character's desire approving what the character approves [what the character values], even if we sense that the character's ideal is impractical or insufficient. Thus, though, we can see at a glance that Captain Ahab is a madman, we affirm his furious hunger to know the truth, so much so that we find ourselves caught up, like the crew of the *Pequod*, in his lunatic quest."

With this posthumous sheaf of essays, Gardner joins a select club of major novelists who wrote of the agony of the creative process. One thinks of Dostoevsky's notebooks for his major novels, or his invaluable *The Diary of the Writer*, Henry James' *The Art of the Novel*, E.M. Forster's *Aspects of the Novel*. Hemingway, Robert Penn Warren, Richard Wright, and Ralph Ellison have also explored, eloquently, the problems and the processes of creating meaningful fiction.

But Gardner—who died in a motorcycle accident in 1983—was the first major novelist of his generation to set down his lectures, notes on literature culled from the firing line of teaching in the university since the Ivory Tower started employing the practicing novelist as a creative writing coach in the mid-1950s. His book maintains the high standards of his literary forebears, even as it speaks to the specific problems of the serious young writer who would attempt to create authentic literature.

After **Barbara Jordan** gave her grand keynote address at the 1976 **Democratic Convention**, the lofty TV commentator, Eric Sevareid, **asked: How do you** explain this phenomenon, where did she come **from?** Sevareid **was vaguely** referring to the genesis of Jordan's vaulting **eloquence, her** accent, her larger-than-life view of America's constant **need to recollect its** separate parts, and its special-interest groups, into **a collective sense** of purpose and nationhood. That Sevareid knows more about ancient Athens than he does about his fellow country-men, the Afro-Americans—"the Omni-Americans" really—typifies the wretched narrowness of supreme white intellectual airs.

Actually people like Jordan's father (a part-time minister and full-time longshoreman) are the easily traceable basis and genesis of the strength within the race, and the backbone of *Drylongso,* a remarkable book by a gifted, black social anthropologist, John Langston Gwaltney. Just as Patricia Roberts Harris, President Carter's Secretary of Health and Human Services, really comes from the "core-culture"; her father was a dining-car waiter, as she had to remind Senator William Proxmire, when she appeared before his Senate committee. Proxmire saw the light-skinned, coiffured woman before him, and got lifestyle and color confused with content and historical memory.

Although both of these Negro women are vastly different in many ways, both came from the striving, respectable, lower middle class; both are full of political savvy, street smarts, eloquence, an unstoppable fury

288

for work, action, achievement, and a keen respect for their elders—the very benchmarks by which Afro-Americans have always measured themselves and their ethos. *Drylongso* unearths the genesis of this ethos, this intelligence, and yes, Mr. Sevareid, this phenomenon.

Drylongso strikes a superior balance between illuminating, entertaining reading and significant, path-breaking research in the best scholarly tradition of social anthropology. Much of its success stems from the author's skill in interviewing forty-three upper-lower-class to lower-middle-class, striving, culturally enriching black survivors, who live close enough to economic collapse and chaos of the streets to know the fire. They are "Drylongso"—or ordinary people—and this book records their uniqueness and their ethos. Gwaltney's technique of apparently asking a highly pertinent, suggestive lead question, then removing himself from the role of interviewer and allowing the richness of the oral story-telling to flow, accounts for part of his success. Gwaltney personally knew the people whose eloquence he recorded in more than a dozen Northeastern urban black communities during the early 1970s. From this base, Gwaltney interviewed *their* friends and relatives, so that a kind of grapevine was established, concerning the underground attitudes of Afro-American witnesses.

Gwaltney's prologue before each interview are brilliant delineations (the pure envy of any novelist). They are never personal assessments, but rather insightful overviews into how the individual is regarded in the community; he doesn't tell us what the people should believe, but allows their stories and lives to reveal the truth, as a basis for celebrating or rejecting values. His witnesses express the chaos of Afro-American life, which they call upon from the ruptured past and the inferno-like present. For example, listen to Hannah Nelson. "Each day that we live like this, with more responsibility than any other people and no authority at all, our people become more disorganized. TV, movies, drugs, and school make our young men into walking disgraces and we can do nothing about it so long as we live among white people."

At the same time these witnesses believe, by and large, that the core of black culture *is the mainstream* and at the heart of the American experience ("sometimes I wonder if there are any other Americans besides us," says one of them, John Oliver, sounding very much like Barbara Jordan).

Gwaltney is something of a black Tiresias, but in his case, the Oracle of Delphi is the conscience of the race, as expressed through the "core culture"-as-chorus of *Drylongso*. This chorus is as rugged on whites as it is on other blacks, believing "that when the wagon (for Justice) comes, everybody's got to go." Recombining the old-time Negro wariness of white duplicity with a mocking of the latest political right-wing adage leads one oracle to remark: "When they say 'America, love it or leave it,' they really mean love them, agree with *them,* or go somewhere else . . . We think white people are the most unprincipled folks in the world, but everybody bears watching."

Nor are the interviewers fooled by the Neo-Afro-Nationalists, as Hannah Nelson admonishes: "Africa is mercifully remote to most of us and that is a good thing, too. Most of our people are remarkably merciful to Africa, when you consider how Africa has used us. . . ."

Gwaltney's study suggests the dynamic evolvement of a furiously complex Negro ethos—a commingling of the spirituals, the blues, urban gospel, street idiom—and the impact upon that ethos from the pressing day-to-day realities of welfare, inflation ("Your cash ain't nothing but trash"), black on black crime, the confusion of values among the young, *all* in juxtaposition with the growing opportunities for the highly skilled black and the declining fortunes of the ill-prepared, the growing gap between the classes within the race, the decomposition of family closeness, even among the core-chorus, who keep ties. As Ellen Saunders says: "My daughter listens to me sometimes, but I listened to my mother all the time."

Perhaps Clifford Yancy described this seething world best. Yancy is a "prudent grandfather in his late forties" who says: "The first thing you have to do is to fight the great enemy out there, the street. That is tough because you have to learn to live with it and pass some of it by and still take some of it in. You have to learn to think for yourself and you have to learn to do that *before* it is too late, not after the bad deal goes down. There is nothing in the drugstore that will mess you up quicker than you can yourself if you are not cool."

Gwaltney's core-chorus is constantly alive to America as "a land of tricksters," as Ralph Ellison once said, and even promising opportunities must be viewed with skepticism and mistrust. Or as Gwaltney describes John Oliver: "Neither Bibles nor Korans nor princes, nor Presidents nor professors are able to convince him that the evidence of his own experience and perception is misleading. He is willing to entertain almost any alternate view of almost anything but his personal experience is far and away his most cogent reality."

For this part, Oliver says: "But I can't see just getting into books, because that's the kind of thing these white folks are going to take all for themselves when old need starts to nudge 'em. I know—I have seen it too often. I want them (his children) to also have something that they can do that white folks think they can't do. Let 'em learn a little napfrying or dietician's work too to go along with that high-class diploma so that they can help themselves when times get tight as Dick's hatband again."

And finally, in sweet juxtaposition to Oliver's advice, are Joseph Langstaff's ennobling words: "If you teach your children to be fair and honest only some of the time and only to some people, you are really telling them that the truth is unimportant."

Several years ago I was given the assignment by a Chicago-based magazine to write an article in which I would attempt to capture the meaning of the moment of ecstasy in the Black Baptist church, employing a novelist's impressionistic overview.

During the course of writing the article—and attending many churches—I found myself struck that, once you moved past the role of preacher as "male envoy from God," so much of the actual day-to-day operation (as well as the church ritual on Sunday) was under the direct control and guidance of women, even as some of these roles were played out in the main, upstage, or off-stage, or as "acolytes." I remember how much of the service evoked the female voice and presence, not only in the choir, but also in the climbing ecstasy of the song-battling divas. Then there was the nurses' cadre, which is there for that moment of a miracle when the faithful become dervishes to a fitful spiritual climb up the ladder of ecstasy and euphoric wonder. The female nurses move in to recharge, to heal, and to bring the faithful back to life. But of course who got you seated in the church in the first place? Well, some women ushers.

Everybody knows that the fortunes of a minister rise and fall by virtue of his capacity to have the strong and sustained backing of his female congregation. These are the people who keep the committees running, set the moral tone, make certain that fund-raising drives are a success. They teach the Sunday school lessons and write the church bulletins. The problem always is to make the males of the church see that these organizational skills of running the infrastructure are a strong training experience for running the highest echelons of pastoral life, or presiding at the levels of spiritual ordination and ministerial investiture. This is the politics of a modern church setting; but it is also a concern for black women writers, filmmakers, and playwrights: how to bring power down front, and even up front.

African-American women have always been the backbone of the Church, because the Church always was the home away from home; the place where we held fast to the dream of making a way out of no way, at every level of our development as a people. It was the social, educational, cultural, and political meeting house, and the emotional and spiritual gathering place, where we met to deal with the issues from slavery to the freedom movement. It is not surprising therefore that behind the names of powerful male leadership, we have Rosa Parks, Fanny Lou Hamer, Ella Baker, to name a few. Indeed, without the leadership of these women in major ritual roles of symbolic action, we would be bereft of a freedom movement.

Nor am I referring here to the larger metaphor of women, in the general commonweal of American life, as reflected by the statement: Behind every successful man stands a woman. Here I am talking about the force and energy of African-American women who, amid the general oppression of their gender, were always in the forefront of our inner struggle and agonies of the culture; always outnumbering the men on the hidden, but real, second and third lines of guidance and direction. They were powerful to us as a people for our nourishment and regeneration; but mainly powerless to command immediate alleviation of their victimization in the larger arenas of political life and economic opportunity.

Now, the white folks simply saw a highly efficient maid or cook, but we blacks saw the same lady, who was "Mrs. Blackburn," who taught Sunday school. This was the woman who taught our aunts (when they were girls) how to sew and knit. Our "Mrs. Blackburns" could make stupendous potato pies; they could do artistic ironing. They led church drives for missions to Africa, and to raise money for those missions. They were the pillars of the various church committees. They were the leading voices amongst the altos in our church choirs. It was our "Mrs. Blackburns" who marched against lynchings, who belonged to the NAACP. They encouraged all of the neighborhood children, particularly the young women, to read and better themselves. These "Mrs. Blackburns" were the heartbeat of the race. The myriad roles taken on by them always outstripped any sociological definition or any artistic attempts to see them, or project them as one-dimensional.

Yet to be sure they were forced to remain in the background, even as they were evolving a most sturdy, angular ethos, forged out of reinvention, even as they were deeply influencing the goals and dreams of black male life and the values of the race. So that one of the artistic charges of the African-American female writer and filmmaker today is to bring the specificity of black female life to center stage, and the issues that they confront down and out of the shadows of their so-called marginality. These filmmakers have the responsibility to project richly dimensional characters and transcend mindless stereotypes of black life.

Heeding the edict "lift up as you pull up" also left some back-breaking memories. Speaking to this new vision on the part of African-American women filmmakers, Carmen Coustaut, has said:

> We all bring out black women characters to the center of the frame, into focus, instead of having the image either misrepresented or depicted as a king of appendage to the central male character.

She goes on to say that

> It's not like we formed a sorority and decided to do that. It is that we see these women have their own agendas, whether they are professors or domestics. They have an existence for themselves.

In African-American literature, I see an attempt in the works of Toni Morrison, Alice Walker, and others to reveal the outline of African-American culture through the range of symbolic roles played by individual black women. I think of Pilate in Morrison's novel *Song of Solomon*, who takes on all roles through self-transformation and reinvention; male/female, tribal mother, African-American frontierswoman, conjure woman, cultural carrier of links back to Africa, cultural motherlode who carries around the bones and skeletons of the patriarch of the family (race); high priestess of the soul of racial memory and mythos in her consciousness; protector of her granddaughter from male victimization. Indeed for Morrison, the slaying of Pilate represents the height of dangers of black-on-black crime. Racial memory is an endangered species when Pilate is murdered by the misdirected gunfire of the radical black nationalist Guitar, who was aiming at one target and ended up assassinating the *motherlode.*

For to silence the "tongue of the motherlode" is to cut off the motherlode of memory of the race from the possible redemption of the psychic powers of regeneration in the oral tradition, and to remove from the nation our ancestral voice, which demands the Republic live up to his highest credo of responsibility. Here I am not simply referring to the power of Harriet Tubman, who led slaves out of bondage at gun-point, but the conscience-bearers of our time like Barbara Jordan, who reminded a nation of its responsibility to the deepest dimensions of freedom in our Constitution, even as that same sacred document had historically denied her existence, as black and female. Or again I think of the eloquent Marian Wright Edelman who continues to instruct the nation about the ways in which we are a country direly neglecting our children, not only poor black, but Hispanic poor, and poor white kids—all of God's children. The mute fervor of her "facts," rendered up out of the smithy of eloquent outrage, is but a part of the high road black women continue to take in this society as ritual conscience-bearers and consciousness raisers of our people and the ethos of the nation. Jordan, Edelman, and other black women manifest their outrage and their petition by transforming memory into the spirit of movement, in a *demonstration* and an *energizing performance,* which pulls at the heart and the mind, thereby forcing the male-dominated institutions of our nation to remember the issues of our day, so often denied. These women understand our national willfulness for wanton forgetfulness.

I believe that in African-American literature the idea of reinvention has been the hallmark of the transformation of those black writers who came after Richard Wright. Many of these writers are black American females, but certainly not all of them. This capacity for reinvention is so abundant and alive in African-American culture. It is epitomized in jazz, and vital in many of the performance arts wherein blacks play a central role. In jazz, in folk music, in the art of the folk preacher's celebratory and ecstasy-reaching moments; in the protest marches as demonstrations and ritual performance of the will for a more demo-cratic union; in rap music, and in signifying; in the magical motions and moves of black athletes.

In oral tradition, so much of what we are and who we are as African-Americans is tied to rituals of affirmation and the mythical language of saga-telling attendant to the ongoing ceremony on the one hand, and the historic ritual of recovering ground from the dislocation spun out by the forces of white supremacy and racism. So often this role of high priestess has been played by black women as taboo-breaking high priestess coming up with new ways to assault the racism of white society, which was always designed to destroy blacks and to keep them fighting each other. So the high priest or high priestess of our culture has to constantly reaffirm the old rituals of experience, and constantly reinvent and come up with new ones to capture the riddled angularity of our experience. Thus, for example, the movement from spiritual to gospel music.

This has also placed a burden on the black female artist to deal with issues of inner group malaise, classism, and color-struck blindness. No matter how much I might extol some of our greatest black male artists, so few have dealt ritualistically or critically with issues of color affliction within the race, which so cripples our condition. Not even *Cane,* that finest of novels of the Harlem Renaissance, which ironically is most sensitive of all novels of the day to the question of color behind the veil. But the author, the fair-skinned Jean Toomer, could never conceive of a black-skinned man as sensitive and eloquent and intellectual as he was. Nor could he conceive of a black woman as an African beauty without large doses of Caucasian blood in her veins.

These issues of class, color, caste, refinement, and basic blackness are so much a part of the materiality of the world of black women. And they are forged in the fires of racial identity, bloodlines, available men, standards of beauty, and therefore were and still are very political. Just to look at some of the titles of works under discussion in this conference suggests that the issues of inner group rejection can be and must be addressed satirically and at the same time in a celebratory way. *Hairpiece: A Film for Nappyheaded People*, or *The Colored Museum*, which satirized many of the foibles and hypocritical standards within the race even as it tackled the problem of our ever estranged identities as a people, and the search for wholeness. Or, conversely, our willingness to celebrate our ranging inwardness as a people via so-called black English, as witnessed in the title of the film *I Be Done Been Was Is*. If white western scholars of James Joyce had read this in *Finnegan's Wake* (and so much of *The Wake* reads like this line), they would be raving over the richness of the broken tongue. Somebody would even be writing a dissertation called "I Be Done Been Was Is." Imagine the fun the deconstructionist would have. Well, I'm not a deconstructionist, I am a Reconstructionist. We need to keep alive the music of our speech patterns. They have surely enriched the American language, even as they are pleasing and fitting and tuneful to tongue and ear.

I am interested in the connection between the film-makers and the novelists and writers. As Debra Robinson (producer of *I Be Done Been Was Is* a documentary about the work and lives of four contemporary black American female comedians) has said:

> I consider black women filmmakers to be at the same point where black women writers were about a decade ago. It took

until the late 1970s for them to get widely published. Black women filmmakers have not been following trends in other films; they have been following a separate voice.

I would hope that African-American women in film will help to make us all aware of this very important development of a separate, life-sustaining voice now enriching the cinemas for us all.

REINVENTION,
ECSTACY, AND
TRANSFORMATION

MICHAEL'S MANDATE

In memory of Arthur White

TRANSFUSION OF THE SOUL

Michael Jordan's mandate (so similar to the artistic demands of the jazz masters and the folk preacher *magna cum laude*) is to come up with something new, something magically different in his free-form furor of reinvention every time he descends upon the set (read *court*), and to do his magic with a euphoric élan. Reinvention, at its zenith, is always nourished upon a disciplined knowledge of skills within a given form; a velocity of free-forming imagination; a certain street savvy; and, as often as not, spiritual zeal.

Audiences expect from Air Jordan specialties, what we expected from the solo flights of Lester Young, Parker, and Coltrane: a moment of uplifting metamorphosis, movements of wonder, self-possession, reinvention and ecstasy, normally not seen or rarely heard of upon this planet. At this heady level of elevation where Air Jordan operates out of with such sweet thunder, we hunger for more than simple entertainment, or mere victory; we thirst for a miracle of momentary self-transformation, in which the soul celebrates the possibilities of the body—even as we are hypnotized by the rhythms of Michael, as he flies, then floats from the free-throw line to do a spin around backwards, triple pump, slam dunk.

TERRITORY OF TRADITION

Remember that our African forefathers originated in cultures wherein even the simple routines of daily living were highly ritualized and that even their cooking utensils were fashioned with forms of symbolism which resonated with overtones of godhead. And though modified, if not suppressed, by the experience of American slavery, that tradition of artistic expressiveness has infused the larger American culture.

> —Ralph Ellison, *Remembering Richard Wright*

For me, Michael Jordan's evolvement is pitched to the rebirth fires of basketball, as *the* sports metaphor for the American Dream of possibility and self-transformation. If my father was a bartender, I can become a novelist, if Jordan's father worked for Commonwealth Edison, Michael can become a millionaire genius on the basketball court. Jordan recreated himself on that court, placed a stamp of style upon this game, and changed it permanently. And he has accomplished this. Heady stuff for a twenty-four-year old. Talent scouts will be going out to college basketball games, in the year 2000, in search of replica Michaels, to row their boats ashore and into championship seasons as Michael perfects his gold stroke in retirement.

The challenges for the basketball player are quite different from those of athletes caught up in the competition on the gridiron, or the baseball diamond. Basketball demands not only that the individual athlete play defense, but he must quite obviously pose some sort of offensive threat. The game is so fast and fluid, bullish, and beefy, sleek, and exhausting, physically as well as emotionally; and you are making these transitions (defense to offense/offense to defense) within seconds. But good offense springs, as it were, from the very rebounding hipbone of good defense. You are on the court in both phases of a game that is always driving your adrenalin to zenith peak gasps for breath. Therefore players are always heard to exclaim about the problem of being able to dig down a little deeper; or to lift their game up a notch higher. Here we are talking about guts, wind, and adrenalin raised to killer-instinct proportions, in a game reputedly known for its grace and poetry of motion, and not for body contact. *To that point I can only howl: in your face, baby, in your face.*

Defense in the lyrically nimble hands of Jordan not only ignites the Bulls' offense, it vaults the adrenalin in the home-town fans. In Chicago, this city of the big shoulders, where the ethnic of hard work is the body and soul to the ethos of our ethnics, the great, soaring genius of Jordan flourishes all the more, in the imaginations of his fandom, by these samples of genuine defensive effort, unselfish enterprise, moxie, and cunning. Not only does Air-Jordan put his burning brand of style and elan upon numerous scoring records, he is also a fleet-fingered pickpocket par excellence. He is the only player in league history to record more than 200 steals, and more than 100 blocked shots in a single session. His 125 blocked shots were the most ever in the NBA for a guard. But it is the scoring and the poetry of those drives that leave his audience breathless, as they climb with Michael, into new imaginative space. . . . *Weaving a silk purse of a move, as he threads his way through the defense, which looks like a bunch of hoggish brawlers and beefy linemen ready to tear the head off of such sweet thunder over Jordan . . . But wait a minute! Michael's elbows are razors; the shoulder blades cliffs of Ali; the flying machine is possessed by the aerialists spring, and the killer instinct (though muted and civilized) of Tyson . . . With spectacular thunder he harpoons the ball down the throat of the hoop.*

AMERICA'S GAME

America's game, indeed. For this sport, like the country, is ever constant in its capacity to reshape itself. Perhaps a dozen black players, along with Bob Cousy, from the Celtics of the 1950s, Jerry West of the Lakers, and Larry Bird of the Celtics, have led the way in this perpetual regeneration of the game over the last thirty-five years. And for all of my admiration for Joe DiMaggio, Ted Williams, Jackie Robinson, Willie Mays, and Roberto Clemente, none of these legends of the diamond, reshaped the *whole* concept of baseball the way Celtic Bill Russell remade basketball from the standpoint of defense in modern basketball. He turned defense into an art form throughout the length of a game. He created a nightmare in the minds of all high scorers with his luminous presence (his long arms and his swatting hands.) Nobody talked about "in your face" around Russell. Indeed, teams sought replicas of Russell, at the center position to terrorize talented shooters. But Jordan seems to be the equivalent of Russell on offense, and he is equally threatening in all facets of defense, as Big Bill was awesome in this category . . . if not as menacing.

The playing-out of basketball is representative of our accelerated pace of life and the swift current of demands, that you must be a specialist, yet a generalist. It symbolizes our willful American drive for immediate attainment of goals; our desperate and highly emotional need for a mingling of rugged manliness and pure poetry of physical expression. For me, basketball suggests the explosive way in which success in this country can reverse itself overnight; how fortune can slip through your fingers, with the flick of an eyelid. In basketball, a twenty-point lead, at half time, often evaporates within the first fleeting minutes of the infamous third quarter. The ability of teams to constantly come back is something akin to our roller-coaster existence, our gambler's psyche, our all-or-nothing way of life. The sudden expiration of the twenty-four-second clock means an immediate do-or-die vignette and *the* constant order of the game in the NBA.

This swift rush of time, this speed clock seems zoned and calculated to the heartbeat of America's competitive furor of the marketplace, or the brain-storming sessions, where the ability to think on one's feet, with lightning-like speed and to come up with creative ideas, is everything. The possibility for all kinds of inventions taking off in this great and consumption-savage culture of ours seems pitched to the dreams of professional ballplayers' hopes to make his mark.

"A Star Is Born", this is the immediate manifestation of the American Dream that basketball holds out for young blacks in the slums of our cities. To have a session on the court, a season in the sun on the concrete, which will in turn allow the individual kid to use his imagination, his savvy, his physical energies, his hunger for some form of male bonding that isn't self-destructive, as he learns teamwork and, at the same time, the art of basketball allows him an identification with a super-star, given the manner in which blacks so completely dominate the game of basketball. You can become Isiah, or Magic, or Dominque, or Michael, by putting on their movements . . . by actually imitating their movements. Nor is any of this too far-fetched, for when one thinks about it the concrete playgrounds are the actual "summer stock" try-out camps for these movements of the spirit to be tried out sun up until the moon places her spell upon the summer's evening. Here these brazen dudes of summer can dream of a brief candle light upon the court, or the high-noon shoot-out with the baddest Brer on this side of town, one on one . . . *mano a mano* . . . and suddenly basketball isn't simply the hoopster's team game, but a sport that is chest for chest, hipbone for hipbone, as much of a male duel as boxing is the ultimate male experience, fist to fist—and the final text of backbone to backbone.

Yet at the same time you can challenge the gods of flight with the aerialist's power of going beyond gravity's laws actually designed to limit man's potential for putting a move on Zeus . . . Even though I have been told man was made in the likeness of God. With all these Michael-spun musings and Jordan-flung halo . . . and playground reinvention . . . try-out camps for round-ball merriment and devil-may-care miracles, as if there were absolutely no harness under heaven to hold them, no wonder Michael has it written in his contract, in blue-black ink, that no man in creation can stop him (not even a beefy Chicago copper) from slamming on the brakes of his chariot and descending upon one of these playgrounds to play a pick-up game, with the berry-brown boys of the slums. He is not the first god to find delight and even instruction by mingling with the common clay of humankind, these who were busy recombining their imitations of the behavior of the gods, with their own imaginative hi-jinks. For it is often in pick-up games where one learns new forms of larcency, audacious bold butt sky-king attempts, and new kniving turns. Upon a summer's afternoon, a gnat can become a knight by getting beside himself and with the song declared: "I decided long ago, never to walk in anyone's shadow /If I fail, if I succeed . . . At least I did as I believe . . . No matter what they take from me . . . They can't take away/ My dignity. . . ."

Yet in basketball (where you really only need two boards and a passion, two hoops and a heart, one leather-bound sphere full of real cool air) our very contemporary alchemists, Magic Johnson and Jordan can soar with stellar newness, for they like Bird have brought together, ironically enough, the old American verities of strict self-discipline, demonic devotion to hard work, fortitude, cunning, precision, personal cleanness, new creativity, the contemporary emotional pitch, the Icarus-like daring of our day, amid a passion for balance. And yet they have recombined all of this yeastiness with shot perfection, defensive deftness, and an especial cold fire for those crunch-close, last-minute, dwindling-down-to-seconds on the clock, when these sacred few (like old Jerry West of the Lakers, and Dr. J. of the 76ers) must have that ball, if their team is to claim the prize of victory.

Jordan alone of these clutch artists, though, has a spirit of movement, which is the special phase of his charisma, and it seems to nourish the fans' need for something beyond a stellar super-star in Chicago, or victory at any price. Michael's talent for magic seems to transform spectators into a state akin to uplifting ecstasy. In a society so hungry for heroes, Chicagoans, all around the city, garner an ecstatic charge out of this risk-taking, enormously ambitious, ebony-skinned American, whose go-for-broke excellence, spun out of reinvention, is but a wonder.

It's as if while stadium fans are watching the lyrical Michael Jordan's swooping rise above the crowd to slam home they are simultaneously hearing a soaring voice-over of Whitney Houston's "The Greatest Love of All," reaching for a climax in the lyrics.

Pitched out of the pedestrian for the moment, Chicagoans are now elevated, with Michael, high above the crowd, and the daily hassle of their living. Here indeed is a zealous transfusion of the soul.

RAINBOW BEYOND THE
BOUNDS OF GRAVITY

The term "off guard" just doesn't settle the score for me in defining Michael Jordan's transforming position on the Bulls, nor the spirit of movement he's creating in the league. For starters, of modern stakes upon the memorable horizon, Jordan reminds me of two great Lakers: the brilliant small forward, Elgin Baylor, and the stellar guard, Jerry West, —*plus* Julius Dr. J. Erving, the recently retired forward for the Philadelphia 76ers. Jordan has the wily, dare-devil moves of a man on a high wire, and the noodle-numbing fakes of Elgin (and Dr. J.); he has a fabulous, last-second creativity, surely scaling the heights of either man.

These sleek, hard-driving forwards would certainly applaud their rhythmic heirs' inside maneuvers, along the baseline, so mean and keen, foxy, then floating, then hanging in air (suspended like a singer who can hold a note without taking a second breath for a record-breaking length of time) and now suddenly ferocious, as juice-jamming Michael slam dunks home! John "Red" Kerr, color man for the Bulls, and the first head coach for the team, told me, "Michael is a much more aggressive player going to the basket than Julius was." It was Kerr who signed Erving to play pro ball in the old ABA league. Michael is a far more dangerous outside shooter than either of these legendary forwards; and his jump shot is probably as sharp as West's on a good night.

Michael Jordan is a kindred spirit of the competitive West, in that when Jordan's team is down ten to twelve points, late in the game, he can turn on the adrenalin with the fury of a man possessed and hit his opponents with a cluster of eight to ten points, providing key steals, along the way. In order to weave the unravelled seam in the Bulls' game back to muster, Michael can mandate himself into a first-rate re-bounder *and* call on his talent for shot blocking. Jerry West had none of these skills. Where West was a fierce competitor, with hoops of cold blue steel in his eyes, Michael is much more of a celebrant of basketball. His game is as blue-flame high with intensity, as was the play of the great guard from West, West Virgina. Michael has a huge appetite for the total fray of the sport, and the potential for leadership, the equal of this *bad* trinity of talented hoopsters. It breaks his heart to lose, even when he sounds as philosophically measured as the articulate Dr. J. himself. In the locker room after the looney 110–109 loss to the Indiana Pacers, which broke the team's four-game break-away streak in the beginning of the 1987 campaign, Michael was heard to say: "You hate to lose this way, but you have to learn from your mistakes. Maybe this loss will force us to come back to earth a little. We just have to get back on track and start up another winning streak." I couldn't help but wonder if Jordan's view of the Bulls' rebounding from the defeat was in anyway linked to the man's personal philosophy that helped bring him back from a devastating foot injury in 1985.

I was told by Elgin Baylor that in the LA locker room, before many a game you always wanted to stay clear of Jerry West, in order to keep your own balance and keel; that this cool-cold-calculated floor leader was a nervous wreck prior to jump-ball game time. Apparently West had that particular kind of intensity known to certain great stage performers, who continually suffer from stage fright; but once revealed in the spotlight, they are all fire-brand business. Jerry was like this when that twenty-four-second clock started. His locker-room fears— and perhaps sense of insecurity—were transformed into competitive aggression and hoops of icy resolve. But Air Jordan, or Such Sweet Thunder, is all steel and deep-ebony silk, wicked wit, and wonder, throughout his forty minutes or so of court time each night out—driving, floating, faking, flying, and defying gravity, as if blessed with a rainbow around his shoulders, which he transforms into a propelling series of kaleidoscopic moves from on high.

* * *

There has been this argument that when a black player is very good he is called a gifted athlete. If it's a white athlete, they say he works very hard. But actually Michael Jordan is a combination of both things. An extremely hard-working dedicated ballplayer—along with great talent. Michael also has moves that were obviously honed on the playgrounds, as well as on the basketball court. Too often coaches try to take the natural ability of black athletes away from the playground *feel* of the game; put them into a kind of constraining professional mode of play. Michael has somehow been able to elude that and has kept his playground furor. The excitement and freedom of the playground, along with the discipline of professional basketball; most athletes can't do that . . . Michael came from a middle-class home, where sound values were taught and instilled. So, his coach at North Carolina, Dean Smith didn't think he had to somehow take the ghetto out of the athlete. Because there was no ghetto in Michael's mentality.

> —Warner Saunders, NBC
> Sports Commentator

I believe that the children are our future Teach them well and let them lead the way . . . Show them all of the beauty they possess inside . . . Give them a sense of pride . . .

> —Whitney Houston, "The
> Greatest Love of All"

PRIOR TO TAKE OFF TIME:
SUCH SWEET THUNDER, HIMSELF

Cut to the Bulls locker room . . . *Now Michael, about those moves . . . where do they come from?*

As with most geniuses, the well-spoken, surprisingly modest Michael Jordan has limited powers to explain his gifts of spirited movement. He says there are no prescriptions. He doesn't try out moves that seem to be working in practice, perfect them, then put them on display in the game; the way a choreographer might script a move out of rehearsals. However, I must say, many a choreographer might pick up on some dazzling ideas by coming to the stadium and observing Michael, for any troupe's renewal of dance patterns, and the potential of the human form to soar in a variety of angles. "The moves come by instinct," Jordan shyly offers.

FORREST: How much did you benefit by having Dean Smith as a coach? JORDAN: Dean Smith was a good coach. He prepared this team well. And he taught me a lot of things related to basketball. That this whole game is a constant learning experience.

Much of the basketball Jordan learned at North Carolina, and particularly defense, has carried over into his game in the pros. Yet because he is known primarily as an offensive threat, Michael has emphatically stated: "Before I retire I want people to see that I'm a good defensive player." Now with the improvement in the Bulls' manpower, Jordan sees his role, almost paradoxically so, as both an assertive leader, *and* a sturdy supporting player. This means he'll be calling on all phases of his game, as the situation demands it.

FORREST: You have said recently that you intend to be the Bulls' team leader. But Michael, how will this new, assertive role be revealed to the players and the fans? JORDAN: I'm talking in terms of my whole approach to the game. I'll play more defense. And I'll be a utility man, if that will do the job.

. . . *Michael Jordan—leader—as utility man?*
Well, what Michael means is this: He wants to deploy his uncanny court awareness, and his ability to move without the ball, as resources to energize all dimensions of the team's nightly offensive production, and the Bulls' defensive cunning. Instead of averaging 37.1 points per game, as he did in last year, Jordan will be down to a mere 30–33 points in the scoring column. Not too shabby. Jordan will be able to "dish-off" more (referring to a situation, common to Michael, wherein a star shooter is surrounded by two or three defensive players and he is then able to hit an open teammate with a quick pass, leading to a clear shot,

and hopefully, an easy basket). This season the Bulls have several fine, pure shooters for Michael to "dish-out" or "kick-out" to in a tight squeeze: guards, John Paxton and Sedale Threatt; forward, Brad Sellers; and center, Dave Corzine, can hit the open shot, consistently. Veteran guard Rory Sparrow adds solid scoring, court stability, and savvy. There is surely a new depth on this team with the confident freshmen Horace Grant and Scottie Pippin. All of this new wingspread of the Bulls' enterprise is buttressed by the inside scoring power and thunderous rebounding presence of perhaps the league's most menacing enforcer, Charles Oakley. Indeed the duo of the fluid, river-flowing Jordan and solid-as-an-oak-tree Charles give the Bulls' fans a nightly display of delightful extremes: poetry in motion *and* a rocking, clearinghouse power.

Meantime, Michael on defense will concentrate more of his furious energy on driving his offensive opponent to distraction, blocking more shots, and turning his talents to Robin Hood thievery down the opponents' passing lanes.

This utility man-cum-leader concept also suggests two other phases of Jordan's admirable character: his modesty and willingness to soar above his own ego and his scoring thrust for a victorious team effort; and his artisan/hard-working man's attitude *about blending his virtuosity of skills into the total machinery of making this team run—as opposed to running the team, as a one-man show, or band . . .* even as he combines for me reflections of the finest qualities of West-Baylor and Julius Dr. J. Erving. But how is all of this working out—thus far?

After the Bulls beat the New Jersey Nets 103–85 for the team's fourth victory of the young 1987–88 season, it seemed to me that Michael's scoring emphasis was not out of proportion to the perspiration he decoded to the other phases of his game. He did score 36 points; yet Coach Doug Collins was able to rest his star; a rare occurrence during the previous year's solo Jordan sagas of soaring time on the court.

Injecting a rested Michael into a line-up at different times during the course of the game when the galloping Bulls suddenly appeared gasping for an Air Jordan special and were fading fast like mock dancing performers running on wooden stilts gave the team desperately needed transfusions.

I asked Coach Collins what he thought of Michael's view of an expanded leadership role? What it meant for the team? How it was going?

"Well I think you can see the answer by the way our young guys are playing. They are working very well. You've got to give Michael a lot of credit. You know he's the heart and soul of this team, and that all the guys look to him," the highly charged coach told me outside the Bulls' locker room.

Bob Sakamoto, that excellent sports writer, who follows the Bulls for the *Chicago Tribune*, has several reflections concerning what Jordan's new role of leadership means for the Bulls.

SAKAMOTO: Leon, in the past when I've talked to Michael about leadership, he's always said: 'Sako, I lead by example. I worry about my own game first of all, and I let that have its effect on the team.' Now what he's doing is pulling back on his own individual game. He's going to worry a little bit more about how John Paxton handles the ball, how Charles Oakley rebounds, what kind of defense Brad Sellers is playing. *And* if they are not quite doing *that*—he's going to go up to them and tell them. He's going to be a little more overt with his leadership. I know in the Atlanta game, Doug Collins said he had never seen Michael Jordan talk as much on the court before. I was covering the game. From the side lines I could hear Michael shouting out to box-out on rebounds; box-out on the free throw line. He was more involved in the total concept of how to win a game, as opposed to how does Michael Jordan beat the Lakers, how does Michael Jordan beat the Celtics. Now it's how do the Bulls beat their opponents.

MICHAEL JORDAN'S RIVALS

If Jordan is to be a true leader in the long run, he must of course provide continual inspiration to his teammates, which is reflected in the victory column. Some of the greatest scorers in the history of this sport had little of this charismatic quality (Wilt Chamberlain and Rick Barry, among them). So that Sakamoto's observations and Coach Collins' "heart and soul" opinion of Michael Jordan are very salient to Chicago's dreams of lifting a championship crown from the Lakers, or the Celtics, or the Pistons . . . and for Jordan's own sense of self-worth as a timeless star.

For the victory that eludes Michael—at this writing in his fourth year with the Bulls—is playing on a championship team. This is the gold ring standard set by his two most worthy rivals in the NBA—Earvin "Magic" Johnson and Larry Bird. Their inspiring leadership has brought on all but total dominance of the Los Angeles Lakers and the Boston Celtics throughout this decade. Because he is a winner and has always played with title-bound teams (in college and in the Olympics), Jordan hungers for an NBA championship season for the Chicago Bulls, as natural to his appetite as leaping off of skyscrapers is for his rival in the world of make-believe—Superman. Of course both Magic and Bird are able to sport gold rings, because each is surrounded by a superb cast of teammates; several of whom are budding super-stars in their own right. In Jordan's first seasons with the team, the players had played with all of the intelligence of a phalanx of baby bulls, butting a deflated, leathery ball about, and not even with red suits adorning their frames. He has fired them out of their lethargy into a rage of energy, worthy of their team name, but not up to the spirit of the city on the make—the hustlers town that Billy Sunday could not put down.

Jordan, of course, always makes his great drives with his tongue hanging out. The joke that floats the lanes is that playing with these guys, where he has to do all the work, Michael can only manifest his naturally tired, inner condition by letting his tongue hang out; and, furthermore, that he is also really sticking his tongue out at his fellow teammates, trying to mock them into the spirit of movement.

But the Bulls are building . . . and if not this year (as we say in Chicago), then surely in the foreseeable future the team should be into the final rounds of the play-offs, driving towards a title. Michael has already shown appetite for the Big Mac of post-season warfare. When the Bulls were pitted against the Celtics, in the first round of the NBA's post-season marathon, last season, Jordan averaged 35.6 points, 7 rebounds, 6 assists, 2 steals, 2.3 blocked shots, while scoring .416 from the field and averaging nearly 90 percent from the foul line, over the course of three games.

"EVERYBODY'S SEARCHING FOR A HERO"

Michael Jordan does not come on the court for the light shoot around, limbering up, prior to the game, which usually lasts 15 minutes . . . "to avoid the hype," he says. Besides, he "wants to see the court clearly" when he and his teammates emerge from the locker room, for their introductions and the tip-off. This makes a lot of sense too, because actually the real practices are held daily for two hours in the morning, when the team is at home. At these rugged drills, nobody works harder than Michael. More to the point, Michael means that the court is surrounded by press people, noise makers, and he wants to avoid the attention that all of them will most certainly drill upon him. (He does take a few shots and lays ups before the actual game starts, however.)

Instead, he prefers to relax before a game, in the locker room, with individual teammates. His is usually at the stadium between five-thirty and five-forty-five. Jordan is very accessible to the working press members who drift in and out of the locker room from six to six-forty-five. His cubicle in the locker room—like an open-faced cell—is perhaps half the width of Jordan's extended arm spread. From this vantage point, he fields questions, usually seated, and jokes, with a fine, signifying wit with his teammates.

Mature yet fun-loving, Michael hangs loose before the game. There is a sense of a man who has an appetite for the tall tale; the intelligence and hearty laughter to enjoy a good story, and the crackling wit to tell a good joke himself. On these occasions his quite handsome, smooth Hershey-bar bronzed face, without a blemish, breaks into that magical

Michael grin. Then there is the youthful smile (that might charm candy from old ladies, and heaven knows what from languishing maidens). But soon we are hearing the deeply rich laughter of young manhood, which well matches Michael's pleasing, deep-tenor-to-light baritone voice.

When Michael Jeffery Jordan emerges from his open cubicle—in short sleeved shirt and slacks—in order to speak with one of the reporters, he reveals a stature and physique of harnessed power. He has long arms, wide wrists, a rock-solid expansive chest, and broad, powerfully sculpted shoulders. He is six foot six inches tall and he weighs in at 200 pounds. Jordan has a dream stature for a heavy-weight prize fighter, or a baseball player. He played all kinds of sports in school; started off playing baseball in the sixth grade. Jordan believes that participating in other sports adds to the skills of movement and grace for the life of a basketball player. After all, basketball—more than any other athletic endeavor—demands that the professional make all kinds of movements with his body on a given night.

You need to remember the authority of Michael's muscular frame; the power in those shoulders and his upper-body strength; for it is this power that supports him and allows him to hang in the air with record-breaking suspension, thus eluding defensive mortals who seek to swat this game away but are forced to come to terms with the laws of gravity Jordan can defy. However, Michael's intelligent execution of his power is ruggedly imperial everywhere, not only in his suspended hang time, but also in his shouldering off of defensive foes, in his tearing the ball away from larger men, with lightning-like deftness; in his soaring, back-over-the-head dunk, when he drives the base line; or when he yanks down a rebound.

Nowhere is the artfulness of the rhythm, grace, invention, and power seen more beautifully expressed concerning the elan of the black ethos and will toward reinvention than in Faulkner's description of the Negro logger's action in "Pantaloon in Black."

Γ⁻ ɔ had done it before—taken a log from the truck onto his

hands, balanced, and turned with it and tossed it onto the skidway, but never with a stick of this size, so that in a complete cessation of all sound save the pulse of the exhaust and the light free-running whine of the disengaged saw since every eye there, even that of the white foreman, was upon him, he nudged the log to the edge of the truckframe and squatted and set his palms against the underside of it. For a time there was no movement at all. It was if the unrational and inanimate wood had invested, mesmerised the man with some of its own primal inertia. Then a voice said quietly: "He got hit. Hit's off de truck," and they saw the crack and gap of air, watching the infinitesimal straightening of the braced legs until the knees locked the movement mounting infinitesimally through the belly's in-suck, the arch of the chest, the neck cords, lifting the lip from the white clench of teeth in passing, drawing the whole head backward and only the bloodshot fixity of the eyes impervious to it, moving on up arms and the straightening elbows until the balanced log was higher than his head. "Only he ain't gonter urn wid dat un," the same voice said. "And when he try to put hit back on de truck, hit gonter kill him." But none of them moved. Then—there was no gathering of supreme effort—the log seemed to leap suddenly backward over his head of its own volition, spinning, crashing and thundering down the incline; he turned and stepped over the slanting track in one stride walked through them as they gave way and went on across the clearing toward the woods.

Jordan achieves all of his artfulness with a rhythmic coordination of movement on the lean, galloping legs of a ballet dancer, moving about, as if his choreographed combinations are performed to a most private, but haunting music, perhaps by Whitney Houston, and the jazz Michael listens to. This sound fusion of balletic grace and vault-slamming, physical power gives Jordan's presence a princely symmetry of seething elegance . . . "I decided long ago/Never to walk in anyone's shadow."

Always behind the phases of Jordan's handsome face, one notes those intelligent, gentle-but-alert, sharply observing eyes. At every turn it is a very intelligent face. The eyes are lively and discerning. So, if Michael Jordan has been mildly amused by my story concerning Jerry West's super-charged-up mood prior to a game—the very antithesis of his own—the reflection suddenly now deepens into stern seriousness when I introduce the problem of drugs in sports and in our general society, and how he can act as a role model for the young. Much of Jordan's disdain of the drug culture has an extra life of its own in this twenty-four-year-old man's devotion to family discipline. This is a young man who hails from a family in the old African-American Southern tradition of tough-love, discipline, perpetual hard work, group up-lift, staying out of trouble, clean living, chores around the house, bring honor to your family and to your race. From this perspective permissiveness was viewed as an oddity of the aristocracy. Self-discipline was valued like an Old Testament commandment. "No matter what they take from me . . . They can't take away my dignity."

JORDAN: My mother and father were strict parents. They really cared about us and our future. And they always encouraged us to think of how we could better our lives.

So that now when our conversation returns to the question of drugs and his role as a model citizen against narcotics, Jordan's face is sabbath serious and his cold stare might be a useful beacon projecting forth from the face of a minister, in his pulpit, looking out upon the young in the congregation, with words of love and warning.

JORDAN: They [the young people] respect me; and they are proud of what I do. They know I play and live in a certain way—without any form of drugs in my life. I hope that this will have a good influence on them, in the long run, to understand that you don't have to do drugs to be important in life and to make a contribution. I certainly do think that I must give a positive image and direction to our youth.

SAUNDERS: Leon, I take the approach that if you are going to clear drugs out of the league—ownership has to say, when you do drugs, you're out. Period.

FORREST: Wait a minute, Warner. Once that athlete got into trouble—that's it. No second chance.

SAUNDERS: There is too much at stake, Leon, the hearts and minds of our children, who see these athletes as heroes. See the youngsters make a jump in logic on this issue. If I'm an athlete and I get high on drugs, then I hit the bottom and I come back up. I write a book, I appear on talk shows. I do community service. I go out and talk to people, kids in grade schools, my message to them is: Don't take drugs, like I did. And the youngster sitting there in the audience says: Well why shouldn't I? Look what happened to this dude. He was a big star. He might have gone down but look how he's come back up? It's the comeback! Why shouldn't I take drugs? he says.

FORREST: For a kid on the street of dreams, the athlete's tale of this drug roller-coaster life paints a very romantic picture of an attractive outlaw-as-hero? Is that your point?

SAUNDERS: *And* instead of that star on the rebound becoming a deterrent to drugs, he actually becomes an ally of the drug culture.

* * *

Michael Jordan gives thoughtful reflection concerning his most fierce competitors. *Bird?* "He's an all-around player. Not known for his quickness; but he uses all of his talents. He's a thinking player." Magic? "At six foot nine inches, he's a trendsetter of the 1980s for a guard." Jordan admires Isiah Thomas of Detroit for his "creative abilities as a small guard." And when we speak of the old man of the mountain, the Lakers' Kareem Abdul Jabbar, Michael says with a gleam in his eyes, perhaps with hopes for a long career for himself: "The word longevity comes to mind." This is Jabbar's eighteenth year in professional basketball; and he commands many of the most highly prestigious scoring records. . . .

"A LONELY PLACE TO BE
SO I LEARNED TO DEPEND ON ME"

Longevity in basketball is spun from endurance and issues from self-discipline (which Michael surely has) and *good luck*. Three seasons ago, Michael suffered an accident in a game that threatened to wipe out his young career. He broke the navicular tarsal bone in his left foot. The impact of Jordan missing sixty-four regular season games in the 1985–1986 season was revealed in the Bulls' unlucky won and lost record. They did manage to hobble into the first round of the NBA's extremely lax elimination tournament. The Bulls played the Celtics; but that was when the daring Jordan returned to the line-up against the judgment of the team's ownership. When Jordan broke Elgin Baylor's record for scoring in one game, Larry Bird himself lavished praise on his rival, declaring: "I know who Michael Jordan is. He's god come to earth disguised as Michael Jordan."

But when I sought out the process by which Jordan came back from this career-menacing injury, Michael was rather mute, and matter of fact; and, as it turns out, this is often the case when it comes to questions that threaten to tap into his personal conquests of will and character, or queries that center too much on the evolvement of his athletic attributes into professional prowess. Muhammad Ali's self-promotion for inner courage, or the vanity of vanities exhibited by certain boorish Bears, seem as foreign to Jordan's spirit as snow in July upon the windshield of a hard-driving Chicago cabbie's taxi. There is the fierce pride in those eyes, however, and a goodly streak of stubbornness, too.

JORDAN: I worked my way back, slowly. Trying to get my confidence and strength back. At first it was difficult, that's true. *But what could I do but prepare myself to make the come back.*

I was talking with Bob Sakamoto about Jordan and that injury, prior to the Bulls game with the Indiana Pacers, at the stadium. As we spoke, I could hear a tape of Whitney Houston in the background.

SAKAMOTO: The injury was serious enough, that for the first time in Michael's career there were doubts cast on his physical ability to ever play again. The more I think about that, the more I realize that if it had happened to you, or I (who don't have one-tenth of the ability he has) we would have been so careful and so tentative, and walked around gingerly. This guy (Jordan) comes back off an injury and he's jumping ten times higher than we do. He's coming down and landing on the same foot, night after night. I think it took a lot of courage to come back that soon . . . to say OK I want to test it out right now and find out if I'm going to be a cripple the rest of my life, basketball-wise, or if I'm going to be able to come back totally 100 percent. Michael told me he spent a lot of time, at home in North Carolina, fighting the feeling and fear that maybe he'd never ever be as good as he once was. That's a scary feeling.

FORREST: Bob, what do you think got Michael through this terrible passage in his life?

SAKAMOTO: Probably an inner fortitude; something that comes from within him. He has a strong character. He's gutsy; he's not afraid of things. I think that's what helped Michael get through that period.

FORREST: What about his parents in all of this capacity to rebound from defeat of injury?

SAKAMOTO: His mom strikes me as being a tough individual. Strict discipline. She may have helped in this road to recovery. But I think it was mainly Michael, *not* being afraid to face the possibility and implications of that injury.

FORREST: This crisis in his life called something out of Jordan's inner will. Demanded yet another stage of development in his manhood, I suspect. Perhaps this is what Michael meant when he told me *"But what could I do but prepare myself."* Not as an interrogative statement, but as a declarative thrust home, like a harpooning dunk.

For me, this is heroic action, the equal to Michael Jordan's achievements on the court; and this too could offer an inspiring transfusion for young people—as any evening of slam dunks and rainbow springs beyond gravity by His Highness.

As I talked with Sakamoto, I could not help but think of the inspiring role the conquering of an athletic injury had upon the character of Santiago in Hemingway's masterpiece, *The Old Man and The Sea.* How Joe DiMaggio's conquest over that still painful bone spur in the heel (and his return to baseball) sparked hope within the old fisherman's soul during the major moment of crisis in his life, when he has gone 85 to 87 days without catching a single fish.

> *Do you believe the great DiMaggio would stay with a fish as long as I will stay with this one? he thought. I am sure he would and more since he is young and strong. Also his father was a fisherman . . . But I must have confidence and I must be worthy of the great DiMaggio who does all things perfectly even with the pain of the bone spur in his heel.*

And then there is the story of how Michael Jordan, himself, didn't make the high-school basketball team, was actually cut from the roster of those who were finally accepted for the team, and had to ask the coach to let him tag along as something of a club manager. No doubt these humbling moments for Jordan, each quite different in the weight and power upon his personality and occurring at completely different times in his career, actually deepened the mettle and the resolve in the man, and made him a more humble person, and a man who can identify with a surprising amount of understanding with the sense of defeat that each of us faces in our daily life.

* * *

FORREST: Michael, in Chicago, you and Walter Payton are the two black athletes who are respected and reverred by white and black citizens of this town. It seems to me that you are both perceived as heroes, across racial lines.

JORDAN: This is good to be judged on the basis of your ability, not your color. To transcend race.

FORREST: Warner, this man Jordan represents a kind of connection between the races, a much-needed one here in Chicago. A bridge over troubled waters. But he achieves this without a boast or a brag.

SAUNDERS: Yes, he does. He does it in an interesting way. He doesn't lose his blackness; but he wasn't burdened with all that baggage of inequality, as we were. All of that was gone when he came along. He doesn't have to see people simply in terms of black and white. That is not in his lexicon. Michael Jordan's always been in a situation where he's been himself as an equal, or even superior. So he doesn't have to be something else, somebody else. He's one of those guys, you say: I hope my son will be like that. An intelligent kid, an athlete as hero.

But what of Michael Jordan on a day-to-day basis? Beyond the loftly gifts? Beneath the scoring records? What about the man behind the famous smile? What of Air Jordan down here on the ground?

SAKAMOTO: I've covered him for four years now. Probably the best break in my life as a sportswriter. I started covering the Bulls the same year Michael Jordan came into this league. We were rookies together you might say. I seen him make every move, and play every single game. I think to myself enjoy it right now because I don't know if I'll ever come across another athlete like Michael Jordan in my sportswriting career, not only his physical abilities, but more importantly, his qualities as a person. He's genuinely a nice person, a down-to-earth person. He's kept his head. He takes time out for people. And I've been around him enough to know that sure he puts on a little bit when he's really tired; and he really doesn't have to deal with the public, but he gives that smile and signs the autographs anyway; yet inside he's really beat. But most of the time when he's out there, his face is lit up and it's genuine, and he really enjoys people and he enjoys life. He's a very special individual.

* * *

Like Bob Sakamota, I'm taken by Jordan's personality and his fabulous court performances. But being a novelist, not a journalist, my drive is to arrest even those heavenly movements of Jordan's to a language that virtually flies off of the page. Michael is a character who is never lost for moves, with those out-lawish movements, so why should I be lost for words, provided from one of my characters, out of *Divine Days* . . . And, out of the voice of St. Peter, no less.

> However, Sugar-Groove detected some whimsy in St. Peter's pitched and whispered baritone: "But tell me how are you—doing it? Particularly the way you do that little sweep around under a cloud pocket, carry up through cross-around corkscrew—outside—in a floating fashion, back hipbone motion transfer over and under super sublime sail, without shaking a tail feather, breathlessly—meantime you are actually going so fast you're threatening to break the sound barrier; meanwhile you are floating backwards and doing it all on the left-hand side of the road, while you seem to be zigzagging right, to the naked eye that is. I can't find the proper words to express the meanings of all your carryings on, your swerving cavorting your—."

It would take Homeric power of vision to capture the epic odyssey of Jackie Robinson's swift, but significant half century of living, in this calamitous land of private and public tribulations. His story was so richly ours, that boys and girls in school should study Robinson's life, in the way you might study symbolic action in great literature.

In the end he was robbed of his life, in a tragically measured manner—in the way life is slowly drawn through the deadly eye of a needle. But the slow extinguishing of his eyesight never snapped Robinson's Epic Vision of our struggle as a people.

In his last public appearance, Robinson was not awed by the streams of garland tardily bestowed upon him by baseball, and the White House, at the second game of this year's 1972 Autumn Classic.

With the snow cap of hair atop his handsome, ebony-rich temple, his blinding eyes squinting in the sun, Robinson on crippled, ricket-ridden legs, spoke out with the lifeforce of an undaunted tragic actor come home to the sport of kings to accept his laurels with dignity, yes, but also to accuse those who would use his garland; and this hour, as a shield for their own outrageous retardation of progress. He would never be satisfied truly with baseball, Robinson admonished millions of viewers, until he saw a black baseball Manager in the game. This note was typical of Robinson's fierce pride, that even in the moment of his glory he should sternly remind his profession and the Republic of its many shortcomings.

Robinson, like the many blacks who came home from World War II, represented a new kind of black man; he set the stage and the tradition among black athletes—professional and amateur—of standing manfully before the lava heat of racism, declaring no matter how many lavish praises are heaped upon me, I know how much further the society must go, and I know what you really think of me off of the field, and I know you are often using my talents at virtual slave-auction conditions.

Behind Robinson, his athletic antecedents are giants, who never had the opportunity to demonstrate their brilliantly sculptured skills under the free skies of an open society. Yet the genius-giants of Negro baseball were the kings upon whose shoulders Robinson, in all of his glory stood. His ten-year stay in the major leagues paid tribute to those past giants, as Robinson turned the athlete's view of himself, and indeed the game completely around.

For the modern black professional baseball players cannot think of stealing bases, running, fielding all infield positions, hitting down either base-line, stealing home, or being a manful leader of men on and off the field, without being deeply influenced by Robinson's shadow.

The epic narrative poem of our fabulous saga in this land really arose in Robinson. His grandmother was a Georgia slave. He was one of five children in a fatherless, Georgia family of bone poverty. His mother was a sharecropper.

The family moved to Pasadena, California, and Robinson sold newspapers and peddled junk to help support his family.

He had rickets as a child, through the malnutrition of his youth. Yet he was to go on to become perhaps the greatest all-around athlete of the century on the fields of track, basketball and football. Ironically baseball seemed to be the lesser of his major sports abilities.

Robinson's great saga may be used by many hustling patriots as an instance of how a black Georgia boy, whose father deserted the family, can make it in this country. But that's not the Robinson story. Exceptions to the ruinous rules of racism and repression and malnutrition only prove the ferociousness of what we face in this country. But it was what Robinson meant to the black man and to his own that really counts.

For like a true epic hero, Robinson's life was riddled with the misfortunes of the least of us. The terrible battle his son had with narcotics, via the Viet Nam experience, and Robinson's inability at first to deal with his son, spoke to a painful dischord in thousands of black families, terrorized in massive dosages by the presence of narcotics, in every pocket and strata of our society.

In the noble reclaiming of his son and the gradual understanding that finally arose between them, something of national significance for us all evolved. And among the awards Jackie Roosevelt Robinson received in his last public appearance was a posthumous award to his son, who had become a director of a drug-abuse center, before his tragic death in an automobile accident.

It was a brutal, yet beautiful melancholy reminder for Robinson—plagued his whole life by chronic diabetes—and his devoted wife, Rachel, standing there on the baseball field in Cincinnati. It was truly our story: all joy commingled with suffering and all suffering touched with spirit of renewal and joy.

Nowhere is that story enriched with more awesome nobility than in the life of Jackie Robinson.

THEATRE OF AGONY AND
CELEBRATION

Our faith in the American possibility is rooted in the opportunity for group progress and particularly individual achievement. The imminence for transformation—the very yeast of our national spirit—in the American Character is born out of the celebrated ethic of enterprise; but it can easily vault from the head (and, yes, the heart) of those with a great appetite for power and economic exploitation.

The genius of the Democratic dogma—that you can be anything you want to be—is as much a riddle as it is a simple platitude.

Transformation of the self is one of the charismatic, sometimes mercurial attributes of the Democratic Character and it is rooted in our frontier-backwoodsman experience; our runaway slave narratives; our migrating innovators, hucksters, travelling salesman, itinerant preachers, populist politicians, hustlers, movers and shakers.

We are always being resettled by immigrants, renewing and shaking up our rickety value system. Even as the new immigrants adapt the language and customs of our national ethos like quick-change artists, digesting a mixed cuisine of words, as they go out to perform in the marketplace . . . 54/40 or fight . . . Manifest Destiny . . . Unionism, bossism, fast buck, sacrifice, honor, freedom, mobism, hard work, thrift, violence, temperance, patriotism, the second change, depression, dislocation, relocation, and, of course, the word signifying the pits of humanity, engrained in our national genesis—*nigger.*

But talk to older generations of European immigrants, recent waves of Asians and Hispanics, or blacks from the South and they all echo themes that fueled their escape: greater freedom of opportunity in the marketplace; freedom from political tyranny. Tyranny for the Europeans, and the others, who came here to escape the repression of dictatorships and Communism; freedom for the Negro, first as slave escaping to the North; and later from Southern-styled racist oppression. Thirdly, for all, the possibility of freedom to express one's deeper dreams, spiritually and intellectually.

In the American Dream—at least—there was always the sense of possibility to move about and the freedom to move up or to move along, if not in one's own life time, then surely the hope of mobility for one's own children.

Inherent in all of this was the ideal of reaching back to help the less fortunate within one's own group, or those fallen by the wayside. The epitome of this extended family was best expressed, I believe in the African-American context, around the turn of the century: One of the slogans of the many middle-class Colored Women's Clubs was "lift up as you pull up."

Middle-class blacks of this ilk learned through slavery and racist repression, Southern and Northern, a searing lesson in continual education and historical continuity: "That it does not matter how far ahead of himself a turtle puts his two front feet, he cannot move his body until he brings up his hind legs." In this specific context, Albert Murray, the essayist, was ironically engaging when in the *Omni-Americans*, he wrote, "Slavery and Oppression may well have made black people more human and more American, while they made white people less human and less American."

Blacks and whites have greatly recreated the American Character, even as they have transformed each other.

Certainly white Americans can't talk, sing, dance, be free, play show tunes, play jazz, protest, preach, sing the blues, dress, walk, gauge the progress of Democracy or the health of the economy, speak of violence, talk of the American family, participate in the major American sports arenas, speak of folklore, tell tall-tale jokes, talk of the self-made man, without being deeply influenced by the impact of the Negro-American Presence, style, and skill within out national culture. And this often occurs at a subconscious level.

Black Americans—as novelists Toni Morrison, Alice Walker, Albert Murray, James Baldwin, Ralph Ellison, and Ernest Gaines have shown—are deeply engrained in the texture of the American Dream and the havoc of its shape-changing value system . . . Forced to forge at every turn a new kind of American, or perish—not a new African . . . To reinvent life and American institutions in order to survive; and driven, as no other Americans are to emboss a stamp of individualism upon these survival contributions—that their very humanity might not remain invisible.

Perhaps the thing that Americans, white and black, don't want to admit is simply this: White Americans don't want to admit how culturally black they are, unless its how brown they can get *vis-à-vis* a suntan. And blacks don't want to admit how white they are. This stubbornness, no doubt, issues from the fact that we as a nation are formed out of a fierce sense of group nationalism. One sees this earnest nationalism in the new waves of Asian immigrants. Meantime they are already transforming and refining the character of our national cuisine, and, of course, being transformed by it.

The ideal of development through transformation is rooted in four dimensions of the American Character: intellectual life, through a better education without limitations, formal and informal, and always shaped by continual self-improvement—which your presence here today so wonderfully celebrates; spiritual and political freedom without dictatorial restrictions; the opportunity in a free and open marketplace; and, finally, individual fulfillment through a constant process of remaking one's life. These are the hallmarks of our promise and a further measure of private and public moral maturity . . . *That I shall be judged solely on my merit—and that I will have something meritorious to offer is also a dimension of the democratic character.*

Dr. Martin Luther King, Jr., who led the movement to transform American to a higher moral and ethical character, expressed this relationship of individual opportunity to Republic best during his March on Washington address, when he declared:

> I have a dream that my four little children will one day live in a nation where they will not be judged by the color of their skin but by the content of their character.

But in our time so much of the content of the American character recreates itself by unbridled killing in the free and open marketplace as *the central dimension* of our national standards.

And as one-hundred-year-old Sweetie Reed, a character in one of my novels, informed me, and President Johnson, in a letter to LBJ, in 1967:

> "Talk about the State of the Union. Why the next thing you know, they'll have somebody peddling steamy air in the helium balloons to the highest bidder proclaiming it was swooped up from hot air in the sleeping room where Miss Elizabeth Taylor snuggled."

I'm troubled how our young people have tossed aside a basic instrument for self-transformation and their American birthright of bold pursuit of Democratic ideals; they don't seem to know any concrete history, or they lack a sense of continuity of past to present. Change and continuity are vital attributes within the felt knowledge we so desperately need as a nation.

White and black students know little about the American Character, as revealed through people like Ben Franklin, Paul Robeson, Susan B. Anthony, and Whitney Young; or the martyred Civil Rights workers, Goodman, Chaney, and Schwerner. Americans who wrought bold change born out of a deep sense of historical preservation and the imperatives for cultural and social change.

The new paganism of personal idolatry of the body, naturally enough, has no spiritual muscle to it but informs that you, too, can be what you want to be—a Number 10—in the line-up of gorgeous, but soulless and mindless clones.

This flabby dimension of our character is not without historical antecedents. It is rooted in the 1970s career craze, tied to our American knee-bone of insecurity in the Depression years, in our great American mythos of rags to riches; in our dread of hydrogen destruction. It springs from a general malaise after the Civil Rights Movement, Viet Nam protests, and Watergate duplicity, concerning the need for winning again in each generation some angle of vision through civic action and virtue, as our ancestral mandate of mission past to present.

The brittle backbone of our family life and our failing educational arteries must share the blight for not finding innovative ways of pumping life into the currents of civic duty, and purifying the language of our political dialogue with a hard-honed poetry.

According to my own judgment, the thinking goes: *I must hurry up and sacrifice everything for me, so that I can swiftly attain all the bounty of the good life for me.*

Dread of economic ruin—or not having attained the thousands of gorgeous material possessions belched up in the marketplace by the time of one's thirtieth birthday—causes a greater psychic spasm in the young body politic than the ultimate spectre of death, as I see the recently unravelling American Character.

In America, it is a disgrace to be moderately comfortable; or to have a rewarding job that does not pay well. Pity it isn't a disgrace in the land of abundance not to do something enterprising about the conditions that keep ever-increasing millions of our brothers and sisters strapped to the jobless poverty cycle and imprisoned in a wilderness of illiteracy; banished from the keys to self-transformation—books, ideas, language, and minimal math skills. And the word itself means nothing unless it is spewed forth from a mindless television commercial. Language is turned back to the border line of learning, to pagan, punk-rock gestures of obscenity; and America goes down on its back.

We may be producing the most gorgeous bodies in the memory of Western man and woman, but our cultural and intellectual growth seems stunted at every dimension. I am reminded of the French essayist La Bruyere, concerning the court of Louis XIV, in this regard:

"Its joys are visible, but artificial, and its sorrows hidden, but real."

Yet what can one expect of our young people when our President (arising early from a late afternoon nap) forgets history and plunders the memory of 6,000,000 Jews in jawboning homilies of healing at a gravesite where sleeps Hitler's most maniacally trained dogs of war? Ah, but then Mr. Reagan had warned us about his lack of felt knowledge concerning the continuities of history long ago, when he stated that he was an adult before he knew there was a racial problem in this country. How was it that a boy from Illinois had not recognized the over-arching nightmare of President Lincoln's agony?

Money as the measure of our spiritual health, as the "bottom line" of "feeling good about yourself" spiritually is being questioned at this very moment across the campuses of our country—among the young and the young at heart—concerning this issue of divestiture. So that the idea of what profit a man (a company or a nation) to gain the whole world and lose the deeper dimensions of its character is raised here by the students protesting Apartheid. What values are we promoting they ask? And can we sleep at night, "feel good about ourselves," as that cliched term beseeches, upon the portfolio of profit based on the suffering of 20,000,000 people languishing in a grievous hell-hole of repression, in order that a white minority can live in luxury and political privilege and continue to flaunt the most essential attributes of Democracy that we Americans hold sacred.

Most of the students participating in these demonstrations are middle-class white Americans. These students are activating a realization of an imperative for recreation that the late Adlai Stevenson addressed twenty-five years ago, when he said:

> The four hundred years of dominance of men with white skin is ending. The vast colored majority of mankind are seeking the opportunity and the respect which white people have been lucky enough to enjoy for so long—sometimes at the colored people's expense. But within this world-wide crisis, we in America, with our colored minority, have a

major role to play—for good or evil. The unfinished work can never be accomplished unless there are enough white men and women who resist to the core of their being the moral evil of treating any of God's children as essentially inferior.

In this regard, I can't help but reflect upon a compelling metaphor for the larger American context, concerning the unfinished work, provided by Faulkner in a chapter of *Light in August*. We are presented with a group of white kids in an orphanage, who are trained by a whispering, satanic grandfather figure to identify the rather subtle differences in skin color of one of God's children amongst their number—therefore his lack of humanity—by the debasing name of Nigger, because the child is slightly less fair than they are. That the children come to call this difference, not in terms of the content of the child's character, but by the quality of skin color, is of course not directly their fault. They echo what they've heard and were told to call the child by, Nigger, before they think to call him by the human name of Joe Christmas. And this verbal mark of cain commences within the soul of the child, as his identification with blackness, and it starts up the sense of self-hatred the child shall carry with him all of his days, as the mocked metaphor of his identity, and of the condition of being a Negro in this world, as an accursed predicament in this world . . . loathing the drops of blackness within the whiteness of the American body politic; and within himself. Singling out the blackness within Joe's whiteness as evil, the white children are marked by hatred before they know Joe's humanity—for before they have learned to think, or know the content of his character, they are bred and nursed on the idea of Nigger, as the image and concept of black inferiority; and this, too, is a dimension of our American Character—to be resisted to the core of our being—"the moral evil of treating any of God's children as essentially inferior." But where do the kids in the white orphanage learn of this verbal badge of inferiority? Well, of course, the ancestral figure, the old white janitor is the one who has passed this identity tag along to the kids. As it turns out, we ultimately learn that the janitor is in fact the grandfather of the five-year-old orphan, Joe Christmas.

So, while I extol the students' efforts—understand where they are coming from—and wish that perhaps more black Americans would make common cause against Apartheid, I cannot help but also reflect upon the line in Stevenson's statement, "we in America, with our colored minority, have a major role to play," as I wonder out loud—isn't it safer to take on the horrors of Apartheid, thousands of miles from our shores, than it is to picket and protest against discrimination in housing that surrounds this very Evanston campus and the racist practices which surround the campuses throughout this country? Isn't it easier for young blacks to march against Apartheid than to ("lift up as you pull up") and set up literacy training programs, and after-school tutoring centers in Cabrini Green or the Robert Taylor homes in Chicago. And why not do both?

Individualism, rooted in the depths of experience, has been the fulcrum of our innovative, national character from the beginning. One thinks, too, of the ingeniousness of our nineteenth-century inventors; of improvisational jazz, as the definitive American artistic expression; of our dynamic drive in the world of cinematic creation; our enterprise from model T to Fleetwood; of those gallant black and white patriots of the Civil Rights Movement, who attempted to transform the Constitution's sacred mandate of liberty and justice for all into an indivisible, living reality; or of the brave young people who dared to make a super-power rethink its heritage and honor in Viet Nam. Or, the furious technological genius set loose by a highly competitive, beloved young President—that we would be first in space by 1970 . . . or, the very renewal of western man's sense of the self-made man, so manifest in the figures of Ben Franklin and Thomas Paine, Frederick Douglass, and Lincoln and in our time James Baldwin, Malcolm X, Caesar Chavez, and Fannie Lou Hamer.

But it must be understood that when we talk about the American Character—the quest for wholeness is rooted in chaos. We are talking about how one deals with chaos, when we use the term, "this person has his or her life together"—he is a "together" individual. This heroic, but often anti-hero, even outlawish spirit and attribute of individualism, springs from those who take the many strands of a diverse personality seething with social, political, spiritual, cultural upheaval and then transforms him- or herself into something that appears like wholeness or "togetherness." Yet the so-called "together" individual always maintains this yeast of content, for change and metamorphosis, at the core of his, or her being, even as we the observer think that at last, thank God, he or she is finally settled. But the unsettled spirit—in this yet-unsettled Democracy of ours—remains the individual's boon, his gift, and our American blessing, and our agony. I would define this quality as the American charisma of personality. Not a fixed radiance or glow of handed-down European aristocracy, but a perpetual appetite for engagement with inner and outer chaos—as the way to self-definition. The new world man or woman is ever reinventing, ever making a new order, as he or she attempts to relocate his spirit in this land.

As a novelist, when I look upon the great American novel, *Huckleberry Finn*, from the standpoint of symbolic action, I am forced to realize that Huck must undergo the process of being brought into the American household, socialized, and civilized by the widow Douglass. Her attempts to refine him, christianize him, and socialize him are linked to the brutalizing he has received at the hands of his father; even as these tough-love forays represent her attempt to refine the American Character, and they are connected to her suspicion of Huck's yeasty, frontier-like spirit, as manifested in the unbridled, angular, raw and rowdy, but redeemable attribute of our American Character. But her attempts must be satirized, and even mocked by Twain. Because for Huck to lose touch with his bad-boy baseness, with his spirit, would be akin to him losing touch with a fundamental quality in the American soul. Her attempts to lift up, as you pull up, to free him from the clutches of his alcoholic and abusive father represent an early portrayal of what we've come to call "child abuse" by an American writer.

Huck Finn, in turn, must make the attempt to free the Nigger Jim from the clutches of slavery, ultimately, for he will never come to known the full maturity of the "free-spirit" that is his as an American until he helps to free Jim. Or, "to steal" the slave out of slavery becomes both a gauge of Huck's humanity and the reader's moral awakening to the contradiction between our Democratic idealism and the existence of slavery . . . And as the opportunity to redeem the past and civilize our nation, as it continued to expand via emigrants journeying west who acted in a most uncivilized manner.

But the Nigger Jim must civilize Huck, too, and he does, through African-American folklore, and his very bodily presence in the imaginative space of Huck's existential search for a big brother and yes, a father. For by virtue of the Nigger Jim's love for his family stolen off into the pits of slavery, Jim ultimately becomes a father-figure, role model for Huck, in ways that young Finn does not consciously understand. But Huck and the reader are made aware of Jim's humanity, not as "Nigger" slave, but as man, by virtue of his enriching connection to the base of all America's quest for freedom, and the language forged upon this continent; and the reenergized moral imperative of setting the captive free. This is why the novel is loaded with black folklore. To get free, Jim must migrate to the territory—ironically go into exile to set his spirit free. Striking out to the territory—relocating his spirit, as it were—is also going out to what was Indian country at the time—the other frontier of America's yet unfinished business with our responsibility toward Democracy. Samuel Clemens, who took his transformed name from a Negro river pilot's expression, *Mark Twain*, did not, of course, create the term Nigger, no more than did his imaginative American cousin of a much later generation, Richard Pryor, but he pounded it home into our national literary sensibility, so that we would not forget who we were and where we came from as a nation—*forevermore*.

Out of the currents of our chaos, and our spiralling diversity, I believe that we must be a people who are forever remaking our country, if we are to conserve consistently what's best and valid in the Democratic spirit and use our rich angularity of character as a springboard for new initiatives of cultural and intellectual fulfillment.

I believe that each new generation must give the body politic this transfusion, as a new birth of freedom, lest a malignancy of self-indulgence enslave the soul and wither away the roots of our imperfect, but worthy, laboratory of Democracy.

TALKING TO GOD

A JOURNEY INTO THE FOREST
OF ROLAND KIRK-COUNTRY

Roland Kirk took on many roles as he turned the surroundings into a kaleidoscopic-paradiso, or a most cooking, wildly electrical kitchen, and before the journey into the high, and ennobling country of his art was climaxed, Kirk—who is a genius—had driven the patrons into the depths and ranges of their psychic night.

In that "Kitchen," wizard-chef-warlock Kirk, with the aid of the following mixing instruments; clarinet, manzello, stritch, flute, tenor sax, celeste, thumb piano, invented up a mighty storm broth and served it up to the patrons.

As he floated his patrons out of The Apartment, Kirk devised his way through the surrealistic landscape, along the country side of his Art, through the forest, through the Jobs' Tear grass; wisteria; cotton fields; patches of maze; magnolia trees . . . Then on through street car tracks, and rivers, screams of the Inferno-like city; back alleys; polluted avenues.

And all along the way, through the labyrinth-odyssey of Kirk's art, the vividness of his sound, the rich harvest of his tonality, the pictures that he draws through his horn hurl the audience into a new vision of the black condition. All of the old sounds, and familiar memories of today are hurled into stark relief, with "blinding sight."

Now Kirk appearing as a Giant behind the wheel suddenly brings the auto to a halt! He leaps from his car and scoops up the body of a little abandoned black girl under a tree. As he stands there he lyrically

341

eulogizes her crumpled form, his sound, and his very own form seem to become transfixed and he appears to become a small child himself, bathed in blissful, lamb-like innocence. And he buried a golden horn inside the improvised coffin for the child that he shaped out of an oak tree; and he buried her high upon a hill.

At another junction, Kirk is a frantic lover, with a whale bone in his throat, and the sun on his spine.

At another burial site, he is the high-priest of the tribe extemporizing on an eulogy to Billie Holiday. (He apotheosized Lady Day's memory.)

Then he is a fairy-tale vulture chasing a lion; then he is Brer Rabbit, and Jack the Fox. Up the stream during a period of massive nostalgia, he becomes John-the-slave.

Heading north in sudden rainstorm, he became an urban guerrilla fighter, blasting from the urban rooftops; then a looted brother in rags, jobless, weeping down his story to his woman in the thunder.

As the many canyons of Kirk's soul were revealed, he swept before our eyes the carved and bejeweled mountains, the erected temples out of his majestic soul searching sojourn.

* * *

Like Giants in the other arts, Kirk not only takes on many roles, he actually becomes all of the characters; stream-of-conscious voices; tears; rages and joy of his chaotic tower of babble that issue from his people, and his soul. He feels that he must deploy the many horns he employs to orchestrate the totality of his massive vision.

The straps yoking his neck leading to the instruments make Kirk appear as a kind of genie bogged down under the toil of discovering the nature of man's existence . . . Like lacerations across his bowed-under body, Kirk seems strapped down to his craft, by a series of whips. But with his jump-diving space suit on, he captures the picture of modern man working through the burden of human problems.

In his attempt to carry everything he sees down the landscape of his Art, Kirk must carry all that is present, all that is ever-green from past wars of survival of black people into today's larger war. All that can hear; and all that he can see with his "blinding sight."

Thus, you hear the foot-stomping from old-time revivals, and the slave field hollers, in his horns and sometimes in the actual howl from Mr. Kirk himself. Then in another "change" Kirk picks up the sounds of the urban scene, with all of the pathos, jagged-dreams, switchblade utterances; deep rock rhythms; haunting hyperbole. Kirk, for instance, could take a phrase like the following splattered across an urban building wall, "Maniac Boss Wolf-Lords," and turn it into a magical storm and a surrealistic dream of a black rebellion.

At the same time he takes phrases like this, and by running them through the ranges of his artistic sweep and memory, Kirk makes these phrases lynching ropes, and sometimes he captures up the memory and the impending terror of bloodhounds chasing an escaping slave, through the high grass . . . for in another way, that "Invisible Whip" that Kirk says drives his art also surges in our racial past.

An inspiring blind genius, Kirk hungers vastly to communicate the whole round mad circus world, that he envisions, and he does.*

---

*Roland Kirk died in 1976.

To the memory of Adeline who
loved the art of Lady Day

Writers are forged in injustice, the
way a sword is forged.
—Ernest Hemingway

SURRENDERING TO THIS LADY

My mother loved Billie Holiday's music, and she had a good feel for what certain vocalists were doing musically, particularly Lady Day. It is possible to say that I was artistically bred more on music than books. And that I was weaned on Billie Holiday's music. For long before I understood very much about what she was doing, saying, or revealing, I was exposed to Billie's long-song. Certainly you have to live, go through a series of changes, metamorphosis before you can commence to benefit from the layers of this hypersensitive singer's wisdom-cutting literature. You must indeed pay your dues to Billie in order to appreciate her work by paying the price of experiencing a broken heart, and you need to have broken a few hearts along the way, as well. In both cases you need to know what it means to surrender to love.

As I think about my own "romance" with Holiday's art and the multifaceted impact she had on me as a novelist. I must confess (because dealing with Billie will force you into a state of confessing, in the way no other singer drives you into doing) that my first novel, *There Is a Tree More Ancient Than Eden,* has at its artistic epicene, a "horrific lynching," which in turn was directly influenced on a primary level by my own attempt to play out Lady Day's most haunting and memorable long-song, and her own creation—"Strange Fruit"—in narrative form. A quotation from this song serves as the epigraph to this novel . . . "Southern trees bearing strange fruit/Blood on the leaves and blood at the root." There are certain dreams turned to nightmares which continue to haunt me concerning Lady Day . . .

I can hear my readers say: "Hush now, Forrest, don't explain, you too were caught up in the magic of her art. Flagrantly unfaithful to your literary Muse. Oh you men! Why can I see the very imprint of Billie's lipstick engrained upon your temple."

ATTRIBUTES OF HOLIDAY'S TRAGIC ART: GOSPEL ACCORDING TO LADY DAY

There are certain attributes of Billie Holiday's art that I'd like to focus on, which comprised for me the body and soul of her work. This artist's canon represents one of the most haunting examples of tragic art, within the American experience, in this century, in which a little girl named Eleanora Fagan Holiday was transformed into Billie Holiday and then into Lady Day.

One major attribute of Billie Holiday's art comes in the form of something that was virtually absent in her musical instrument. I am referring here to the absence of church music upon her art. I believe that in the place of church musical authority—anthems, spirituals, the coming of Gospel songs, hymns, and tabernacle songs—there was the great attention given to a keening intelligence, raw-tone reflection, and intimate personal feelings in her renderings, readings, offerings, and interpretations concerning the mysteries of love and life, race and loneliness. Because she did not have the prop of religion—to "save her soul"—she seemed to know how much the individual is out there on her lonesome when it comes to dealing with matters of the heart, or when the chips are down in the crap shoot that is life. Engagingly enough, she may have been virtually unattached to religious support systems that most other black female singers knew, but this did not mean Lady Day was without spiritual hunger—far from it.

She was personally and artistically attuned to the meaning of the blues; however, Billie was not a blues singer. Nor did she base her art solely upon the fundamental understanding, the accepted folk-wisdom of the blues. This doesn't mean that she would not purloin, or incorporate some measure, line, proverb, axiom, signifying short-rib, or sexually transformed muted cry, stripped from the canon scroll of the blues heritage, into her work. Lady Day infused the blues when she needed it, and where she needed it (in much the way Louis Armstrong used the blues) into her ballads.

Gospel musical tradition came on as a full force in American music much after Holiday's own rather rapid artistic ascent. Like the great American writer Ernest Hemingway, Billie Holiday was already an accomplished artist by the time she was thirty.

The rudiments of the Gospel-sound and shout were there in the Negro religious experience in the South. Certainly the cathartic shout was fundamental to the basic African-American emotional/spiritual moment of ecstasy and release. Negro spirituals were the first examples of the black experience that were taken as expressions of the serious (albeit pristine) stirrings of the consciousness of the race, rendered up artistically. It didn't mean that even sensitive white critics moved past the idea of the Negro as Noble Savage, nor did it mean that they suddenly believed that the New World Africans were capable of producing anything within the serious cerebral sphere of an elevated, intellectual rigor. The spirituals gave voice to a serious side of the Negro-American's evolving soul; these Sorrow Songs provided blacks something in the arts on the American stage that they could feel proud of. Here the Negro was not being presented as grinning in black-faced routines or dancing in minstrel shows or being victimized by deriding comic skits. The Sorrow Songs gave witness to the suffering soul of the race, and for blacks they provide rich illusions to an artistic "otherness" that could be useful down the years, in the way literature continues to instruct. The spirituals were moving—even for certain critics who had grave doubts concerning the New World Africans' capacities in other areas of creative thought and enterprise.

Billie Holiday grew up at a time when many black Americans liked to think of their musical worlds (spirituals and Gospel shouts, on the one hand; and jazz and blues, on the other) as separate. Amid this separation, there was yet another concept: that if you sang blues, you sang blues and you didn't try to play or sing like a jazz artist "sang" out of his musical instrument. If you were a singer of spirituals, then you stuck to that elevated form of religious expression. Spirituals, of course, were originally rendered up a-capella. The emerging Gospel music allowed for instrumentation, and for the singer to give personal invention and witness-bearing. Here was a growing attempt to blend the secular and spiritual worlds. Practitioners of this music were not initially respected in most middle-class churches. It was even thought in certain circles that jazz belonged to the Creole Negroes; and that the blues belonged to the poor Negroes of Mississippi, Alabama, and Georgia. Conversely, Mahalia Jackson—one of the founding mothers of Gospel singing—would never set foot into a dance hall or jazz club to sing. Yet there are times in which you can hardly sit still, without rhythmically rocking, when listening to her sing, "Oh Didn't It Rain," for example, or "Elijah Rock", mainly because of the wonderful driving power of the blues spirit upon her, and the syncopation that comes out of jazz. It is one of the great ironies in American music that Mahalia Jackson and Billie Holiday were influenced primarily by the same two major musical giants: Bessie Smith and Louis Armstrong. Yet no two singers on earth were more different than Lady Day and Mahalia Jackson.

Nearly every major popular black American female singer was musically fashioned by church music; many of them sang in church choirs; or played the church organ, and sang. Among those who immediately come to mind there are Sarah Vaughan, Dinah Washington, Gladys Knight, and Aretha Franklin. Each singer, in different ways, derived a goodly portion of her singing power from the sounding authority of church music, winging through the secular souls. In our time, we have come to understand the idea of soul as being a robust and sensual marriage of blues and Gospel sounds pitched from the throbbing ethos of black America. Most of the great African-American female singers didn't come out of the upper-middle-class churches where Gospel sound was spurned for years. Finis Henderson, who was a professional dancer for over thirty years and Sammy Davis's manager for several decades, told me in an interview: "Billie did not have that Gospel feeling. But it wasn't her. It wasn't there. Her musical interpretation was just a tad different, because she wasn't exposed to the Gospel tradition. So she made up in other areas what the Gospel singers couldn't give to it. Lady Day gave us a different kind of soul. That was her soul; but that was also her exposure."

A sampling from the biography of the great Sarah Vaughan—in conjunction with phases out of Billie's life—might be instructive here, in dealing with this theme of church and family background, versus hard times, and the absence of religious influence. The Divine One was born in Newark, New Jersey, in 1924, and she grew up on music. (Billie was born, April 7, 1915, and from the first page of her "autobiography" we learn: "Mom and Pop were just a couple of kids when they got married. He was eighteen, she was sixteen, and I was three . . . Mom was working as a maid with a white family. When they found out she was going to have a baby, they just threw her out. Pop's family just about had a fit, too, when they heard about it. They were real society folks and they never heard of a thing like that going on in their part of East Baltimore.")

Sarah's mother sang in the Mt. Zion Baptist Church choir and her father, a carpenter, played guitar and piano in his spare time. They were a close family. (*Reputed to be one of the finest guitarists in show business bands, Clarence Holiday—Billie's father—abandoned the family early on, and gave her no fatherly attention nor any financial or emotional support in her growing-up years. Billie ran errands for prostitutes at the local whorehouse when she was six; she was raped by a forty-year-old man when she was ten.*)

At the age of eighteen, and by then a Mt. Zion choir member herself, Sarah Vaughan entered an amateur contest at Harlem's Apollo Theater. She won $10.00 first prize and a week's engagement at this legendary show house on a bill headlined by a superb singer named Ella Fitzgerald. Billy Eckstine heard Sarah there and recommended her to Earl Fatha' Hines, whose band Mr. "B" was then singing with, and Hines took her on as a vocalist.

(*Billie and her mother were about to be thrown out on the streets. Billie ran from joint to joint trying to find a job dancing, or anything, in order to keep from getting dispossessed because they didn't have any rent money. Billie was about sixteen at the time. Billie needed forty-five bucks to keep her and her mother from getting set out on the street.*)

From her "autobiography," *Lady Sings the Blues,* we learn: "Finally, when I got to Pod's Jerry's, I was desperate. I went in and asked for the boss. I think I talked to Jerry. I told him I was a dancer and I wanted to try out. I knew exactly two steps, the time step and the crossover. I didn't even know the word "audition" existed, but that was what I wanted. So Jerry sent me over to the piano player and told me to dance. I started, and it was pitiful. I did my two steps over and over until he barked at me and told me to quit wasting his time. They were going to throw me out on my ear, but I kept begging for a job. Finally the piano player took pity on me. He squashed out his cigarette, looked up at me, and said, 'Girl, can you sing?' So I asked him to play "Trav'lin' All Alone." That came closer than anything to the way I felt. And some part of it must have come across. The whole joint quieted down. If someone had dropped a pin, it would have sounded like a bomb. When I finished, everybody in the joint was crying in their beer, and I picked thirty-eight bucks up off the floor. When I left the joint I split with the piano player and still took home fifty-seven dollars." Eleanora Holiday was commencing the artistic transformation into Billie Holiday that night. She was sixteen years old at the time. Sarah Vaughan recorded one tune with Eckstine, "I'll Wait and Pray," which implies how she was still consciously holding onto church tradition even while launching wings into the world of totally secular music.

One hears in Billie's music very little or any of the cathartic cry that is so essential to the fervor of the religious Gospel utterance and shouting ecstasy. The authority of this voice wails back to the earliest embryos of the blues and back to field cries of warnings and celebrations, and hollers, in slavery. Cries of street vendors were heard in cities after slavery. The uses of this church shout, or cry, as catharsis, reaches its epitome of possibilities when Ray Charles applies and reapplies it through his ever reinventive ways of blending Gospel and blues (country music, too). The ways in which these musical traditions overlap and nourish each other in the art of Ray Charles in one of the great delights and wonders of modern American music. Charles's especially unique voice epitomizes another quality in Negro musical singing expression: the grain or timbre in the African-American singing voice. This attribute of tradition is kept alive in the husky registers and muted ranges of the sophisticated Lady Day's voice. Her singing voice was a blend of the husky and the pure, one overlapping the other; and this gave it a special commingling of refinement and baseness. Holiday does maintain and offer up, in a muted form, this grain in the wood, which works beautifully in songs where she wanted to accent the blues energy, for example, "Please Don't Talk About Me When I'm Gone"; or "Lady Sings the Blues"; "Billie's Blues"; "I Love My Man (and I'm a lie if I say I don't) . . .

FORREST: Finis, what made for that especially memorable quality in Lady Day's songs?

HENDERSON: Billie put so much of herself into a song. It seemed as if she had an innate ability to extract all of the goodies out of a tune and bring them to the surface; the true meaning of what lyricist had in mind. And she was able to because she had a haunting voice. Lady Day didn't have a powerful voice. She couldn't blow you off the stage. When you put "God Bless the Child" together with "Strange Fruit" this tells you what that woman was all about. She loved her blackness. She was aware of what she was. She was also aware of the suffering and pain that *she* had to deal with, in order to become a singer.

SUBTLE, CUTTING CONFIDEN-
TIALITY OF LADY'S LYRICAL READING

Listening and reflecting on Billie Holiday's reading of a lyric as a link of your love life was essential to your mental health. One was struck to the very soul by Lady Day's capacity for, and her willingness to confess in public, and to make this confession seem as intimate and as private an unburdening heartbreak expressed and revealed by your best girl friend seated next to you at your favorite bar. This confidentiality that Billie Holiday revealed and even whispered, too, in a signifying manner, was often a subtle reaching out, in the most understated though cutting manner, about the enormous wretchedness of love. Because she was so understated, you were allowed to think about your own heartbreak, in a much more cool and reflective manner. She didn't wail your heartbreak out of your mind. Rather while she was singing Lady Day created a nonverbal, but real call and response, participatory dialogue between the individual listener's life and her own. (As gorgeous a presence on stage as an opera singer, Lady Day was a muted diva at the microphone even as her private life would have been challenging grist for Verdi or Puccini.) As Holiday was popular with musicians, who also formed her "audience" on the set (for she allowed them to take up their own solos, inspired them to take their own solos, really), so too was she able to conduct her audience into high moments of experience. Their lives in her song were made into a kind of musical metaphor, by this majestic, terribly losted and tormented woman, who became transformed into a supremely precise heart surgeon, upon the stage, which was her operating room.

Hearing, listening, and reflecting on Billie Holiday's reading of a lyric make the song completely new upon reconsideration, as long as you are attuned to reinterpretations of your own love life, or your own life. You must always be open, because Holiday was always trying to bring into the intelligence of her songs all of her continually changing experiences. In this way, too, she was very akin to the view most major jazz men had to their approach to the music. In her greatest readings

("These Foolish Things"; "I Must Have That Man"; "My Man"; "He's Funny That Way"; "You Go to my Head", "I Can't Get Started", "Strange Fruit", "Fine and Mellow"; "Some Other Spring"; "The Man I Love"; "Body and Soul"; "God Bless, Solitude", "I Cover the Waterfront", "Travlin' Light", "Gloomy Sunday"; "I Love My Man"; "Don't Explain"; "You Better Go Now"; "Good Morning"; "Heartache", "No Good Man"; "Embraceable You"; "Every Thing I Have Is Yours"; and "Ghost of a Chance") Lady Day was able to surrender her life completely to the experience of the lyric and the lyric to the experience of her life.

Lady Day could make you understand the misery of love, without making you feel miserable, or so it seems to me, even as she was so often revealing to us the most wrenching situations of love. We are blessed here by two forces. The first was the humor of the blues at nearly all levels (but it was the wit in the blues that Billie found most useful), and if Holiday was hardly influenced by church music, she was surely influenced by the robust pronunciation of the blues that she had heard as a girl in the voice of Bessie Smith.

The literature of Billie's art was nourished at a very early age not in school, or church (like Sarah's) but in a whorehouse, and by the two most eloquent artists of jazz and blues—Louis Armstrong and Bessie Smith. Nourished as she was on the music of these great artists and their high stellar accomplishments, in a whorehouse, refinement and baseness of all kinds became important themes in Billie's art and private life, just as we remember Armstrong for his eloquent fusions of musical forms and his capacity to transform life into an eloquent bridge of the rowdy and the robust—a royal and ripe echo chamber of the affirmation of life. And as Billie recalled the genesis of her artistic development in *Lady Sings the Blues*: "But whether I was riding a bike, or scrubbing somebody's dirty bathroom floor, I used to love to sing all of the time. I like music. If there was a place where I could go and hear it, I went. Alice Dean used to keep a whorehouse on the corner, nearest our place. I used to run errands for her and the girls. When it came time to pay me, I used to tell her she could keep the money, if she let me come up in her front parlor and listen to Louis Armstrong and Bessie on her victrola."

Holiday's own high level of sophisticated wit was shaped by the cabaret singer's art. This wit of her mocking humor, implicit in Billie's artistic IQ, was based upon a superb foundation in all sides and slants of signifying. The art of signifying or using the tongue like a rapier for all kinds of put-downs was advanced to a fine surgical art, when heard crackling at the razor's edge of this honeysuckle rose: an elegant Lady who knew the importance of the high/low wizardry of bitching. For Billie Holiday believed what many modern feminists would as soon as not accept—that in dealing with a man, you must never lose the cutting edge of the bitch's tongue, no matter how sweet the mellowed-down easy times seem to get, with your fine and mellow, sweet-back dude.

> One of the songs I wrote and recorded has my marriage to Jimmy [Monroe] written all over it . . . One night he came home with lipstick on his collar. I saw the lipstick. He saw it and he started explaining and explaining. I could stand anything but that. Lying to me was worse than anything he could have done with any bitch. I cut him off just like that. "Take a bath, man," I said. Don't Explain. That should have been the end of it. But that night stuck in my crop. I couldn't forget it. The words "Don't explain, don't explain" kept going through my system. Soon I was singing phrases to myself. This is one song I couldn't sing without feeling every minute of it. I still can't . . . Many a bitch has told me she broke up every time she heard it. So if anybody deserves credit for that, it's Jimmy I guess—and the others who keep coming home with lipstick on their faces. When that stops happening, "Don't Explain" will be as dated as the Black Bottom. Until then it will always be a standard.

The influence of Lester Young on Lady Day cannot be underestimated. They, renamed each other with the revitalizing titles they were ultimately saluted by: Lady Day and The President. The President's mellow sound and absolute attention to lyrical phraseology gave Lady

Day the artistic assurance, which was almost reverential for every word of a first-rate lyric, as if this was the Word, when superimposed upon by the withering power of experience. They were both poets when it came to meaningful phraseology.

Finis Henderson told me: "I think that she and Prez [Lester Young] had such a beautiful relationship. Because he understood her. He was sensitive to her needs. And he catered to her needs. They were never personally involved. But there was a friendship there. I think there was an awful lot of comfort offered to her in that friendship. Billie needed that kind of friendship."

Their friendship had much resiliency to it because Lady Day also encouraged the President about the richness of his own lyrical style. Of his own self-doubts Lady Day once said: "You know everyone when he first started thought, this man, his tone is too thin . . . Lester used to go out of his mind getting reeds, you know, to sound big like Chu Berry, I told him, 'It doesn't matter because you have a beautiful tone. After a while everybody's going to be copying you.' And so it came to be." No doubt Billie was thinking of her own artistic problem of being influenced by the larger voice of Bessie Smith, an attribute that she didn't have. Yet stylistically Billie had transcended influences and was able to encourage Lester's evolvement of a highly individualistic style. So there was much more to their relationship of mutually encouraging each other than just the simple fact of them enjoying marijuana. On another level, Billie had achieved musically with Lester something akin to what Bessie had with Armstrong, but the relationship between Lady Day and Prez was profoundly deeper. This unconscious psychological quest to achieve in one's artistic life the patterns of one's intellectual parents provides us with at least one success story of fulfillment in Lady Day's saga.

Lady Day's approach to the lyrics reminds me of listening to Sir John Gielgud reading Shakespeare's sonnets or some of the *singing* solilo-quies culled from the great plays of the Bard. For each of these royal artists, the poetry is central to their readings. Though obviously Holiday had a much more difficult job; she had to transform the lyrics of modern songs into art. Gielgud had the greatest material in the history of the English-speaking world to sing about. For all of my respect for Sir John, I am always certain that I am still listening to Shakespeare (which is fine with me). Billie's stamp was so powerful upon a lyric that you soon forgot who her man was who wrote that song . . . or drove her to sing that song:

"I've been told that nobody sings the word 'hunger' like I do. Or the word 'love.' All the Cadillacs and minks in the world—and I've had a few—can't make it up or make me forget it. All I've learned in all those places from all those people is wrapped up on those two words. You've got to have something to eat and a little love in your life before you can hold still for any damn body's sermon on how to behave."

THE EXQUISITE STYLE OF LADY DAY

Like Papa Hemingway, Lady Day was one of the great stylists of modern American twentieth-century art. In both cases, the actual style was extremely deceptive. Simple on the surface, yet rich with colorations, illusions, nuances, and contradictions when you commenced to unveil the layers.

Billie Holiday's fusion of impeccable diction, with just enough of that husky grain of the African-American singing voice, became the hallmarks of her instrument, perhaps even a fusion of male/female. Yet her actual singing voice was a small incandescent lyrical light, reedy and fragile as candlelight illuminating an echo chamber into the solitude and secret prisms of the soul. There was something eerie and haunting about it, and its capacity to hold you in a fixation, as if she was speaking from another world. I feel this particularly in her rendering of "Travalling Light," "Gloomy Sunday," "I Covered the Waterfront," "Solitude," "Embraceable You," "Good Morning, Heartache," and "Lover Man."

Like Sir John Gielgud she could give the most careful introspective, almost scholarly attention to every word of the lyric before her mind, as it was both reproduced and reordered through the agony of her own troubled life, and filtered through the powers of her gifted, tormented, and truth-seeking imagination. Then Lady Day rendered her vision with the most original phraseology. Finis Henderson introduces two aspects of this style. "You could understand everything she said. That clarity of her enunciation." And he goes on to say: "Billie just mesmerizes the English language, that's how exacting she was."

All of this could produce a highly tortured, bewitching, brooding, yet quite frequently jamming, sometimes discordant sound so close to what jazz instrumentalists were trying to produce. Many of her side men were also trying to cut into this good grain, so that the vocalist was really suggestive to them of ways in which they might improvise out of their own lives, might invent phrases of pure power and raw regalness, so brilliantly offered up by the lady with the gardenia in her hair, just a few steps beyond them at the microphone. The jazz critic Leonard Feather expressed this keening relationship best in an article about Billie Holiday in *Down-Beat* in February, 1962. "The rough, tortured edges of the tones, the firm grasp on the note gradually released in a widening vibrato (in later years the grip weakened and the timbre sank), the frequent spontaneous use of flatted thirds and sevenths, the innate sense of syncopation; because of these and other elements she was musically, technically, and emotionally forever a part of jazz."

Billie Holiday could read out "Violets for Your Furs" with a laconic rendering so very close to the cabaret singer's intimacy, her sophisticated, jaded, witty understated manner, yet always alive to bold romantic possibilities.

Recalling a muted line out of Hemingway, the salty and sassy Holiday could sum life up too, and evidence the same bodacious yet understated wit in her husky speaking voice: "A man can leave home one morning, and come home that night whistling and singing to find there ain't nobody there but him. I left two men like that." A fine literary line, too, reminiscent of Hemingway's most believable dialogue, even though one realized upon reflection that people rarely talked the way his characters actually spoke. That was not the point of course. The great stylist was trying to stress or emphasize something about personality in the repetition of phrase, nuance, cunning, voice. In establishing an actualized voice within these characters he rendered up something of the hard-boiled style of their manner. Nobody talked like Holiday, nor did anybody actually sing like her; none possessed a voice like Billie's with its intelligence, all of which made her an American original. Like Hemingway, she cultivated a style, which seemed as natural as breathing; yet each artist created a body of work, which seemed to me, at least, to wear a death mask. The best of the Holiday/Hemingway canon came as close as any American artists (with the exception of Faulkner and O'Neill) to taking us to the borderline of madness, then withdrawing from this precipice in order to render up a tragic vision of life.

MESMERIZING THE ENGLISH
LANGUAGE/AUDIENCE AS LOVER

FORREST: How much do you think the presence of an audience played in her music?

HENDERSON: Well, as you might remember, her audience listened attentively to Billie Holiday. When she spoke nobody even dared breath loud. There wasn't even a murmur, when she spoke. That was just an unwritten law. You came to listen. You might talk when some other artist was on stage. But there was no talking when she was performing. You came to listen to Lady Day. There was no talking when she was on stage.

FORREST: This power that she had over audiences is at is height during the timeframe when the creators of bebop were challenging their audiences to give complete attention to the music, and not to talk, to contemplate.

HENDERSON: Those of us who know music understand that the vocal is on top; and instrumentation comes under. That's the written law and it's the unwritten law. To compete with the vocal you are clashing. A lot of people don't realize that drums have to be tuned. You just don't take a set of drums, prop them up, and start banging on them. Each set of drums have a different tone. And there is a key to tuning them. If you don't know how to tune those drums, you don't know how to enhance the quality of them.

FORREST: Billie's voice was fragile, too.

HENDERSON: Billie didn't have perfect pitch. Dinah Washington had perfect pitch. Sarah had perfect pitch; and it would drive them crazy if you hit a discord. They'd heard it immediately. This didn't bother Billie.

FORREST: Billie didn't know music, in that sense, obviously enough. Sarah, for example, could play the hell out of a piano.

HENDERSON: No, Billie didn't.

FORREST: Possibly a jazz musician might hit a discordant note and she could use it—

HENDERSON: Sure, take advantage of it.

FORREST: What about her stylistic influences on singers, Carmen McCrae for example?

HENDERSON: I don't believe that Billie influenced Carmen. McCrae used to play piano at Killer Johnson's at the Archway Lounge here in Chicago. Played cocktail piano. Now when you think about it none of the singers would have tried to approach Billie's style anyway. Of all of the singers you might want to emulate, you wouldn't dare reach for her. Because she was an institution all of her own.

FORREST: Although her personal life was chaotic, Lady Day's art was one of much discipline and control. I'm talking about Billie when she was at the height of her powers, of course.

HENDERSON: And she didn't waste words. She didn't extend herself beyond a phrase; a phrase went so far and that was it.

FORREST: But was this due, at least in part, to the limits of her own voice range?

HENDERSON: No, I just think that was Billie's interpretation.

FORREST: And none of this riffing and scatting.

HENDERSON: Did not touch her at all. Isn't that interesting. And when you think about singers who came along in that era—Ella and Sarah. Billie was the least touched. Riffing had no consequence for her.

FORREST: As much as she loved the jazz musician's art, too.

HENDERSON: Yeah. Loved them. You might think she would be . . . a scat singer from way out. . . . No, not at all. When you think about Bettye Carter, now you talk about riffing. And there are Sarah and Ella. There are about four or five that really tried.

FORREST: Most of it I don't care for . . .

HENDERSON: No, because most singers don't know where they are going with it.

FORREST: Another facet of Billie's style that I want to get at is the influence of the cabaret singers. Here I am thinking about Mable Mercer. I've been thinking about how Billie's renderings are really rooted in the idea of a reading, or recitation of love . . . And at another level, how a woman may read her man out, in a love quarrel. And that's very close to the art of the cabaret singer. Billie's art was very basic, or based in the common themes of love and death, hunger, pain and loneliness. She is giving us a reading about love; as well as giving us her singing voice. And Billie had the sophistication of a fine cabaret singer, like Mabel Mercer.

HENDERSON: You are talking about an entity, unto herself, when you speak of Mabel Mercer. Nearly all of the singers on the female side of that day pay homage to her. She was second to none. It was her interpretation of a song. That's when they became aware of that delivery and the manner in which the message was delivered. Billie did profit from her exposure to Mabel's singing, in New York.

* * *

An audience is great on certain levels, as substitute lovers, for a certain kind of artist like Billie Holiday, I believe. It can give you an unconditional love, or so it appears. Nothing is demanded, in an extremely intimate basis as night turns into day. For all of the cathartic power of the artist, you really don't take him or her home to bed with you—no matter how much we proclaim a performance of an O'Neill play or Shakespeare's *Hamlet* with Sir John Gielgud in the lead or two sets of listening to Billie Holiday on a night when she was in top form.

If you are that kind of artist, then you need a new audience every night. Like the new attraction that each audience represents, the artist is on the make. You put the make on them. They applaud you; and they fall for you all over again. It's a perfect one-night stand. But it is just this, too: a one-night stand, and as fickle as a one-night stand can be. On another level, the relationship is very dangerous, too, because the audience-as-lover will turn on you, too, if you muck up, or mess up a line, or are just off tune on a particular flight of artistic space; then the audience-as-lover will turn the tables on you. On one level, this has to do with the fact that the individual members of your audience have heard you before, and, therefore, your cutting style must match that of the performance they heard on one of your great solo performances.

An audience's applause never drowns the abuse of an individual lover you are dealing with just now; nor does an appreciative audience's applause that you've just put the make on make up for the rocks in your bed and the absence of a love in your life. Even if that lover is messing with your existence, from miles away. Holiday's voice echoed all of this much more than any artist of our time. Probably the loneliness in Holiday's voice even when surrounded by an audience of lovers implied how for all of the celebration she received from her especially adoring cult of worshippers, there was so often an absence, or pain over love in the immediate terrain of her existence, as well as the long-term historical heartache of her remembering life.

> I don't know why I'm feeling so bad. I long to try
> Something I've never had . . . Never had no kissing . . .
> Look what I've been missing . . .
> Lover Man, where can you be . . . I go to bed with the
> thought that you'll make love to me . . . Strange as it
> seems . . .

There is a passage in *Lady Sings the Blues* that reveals a routine in Billie's apprenticeship years, which is very close to the intimate relationship a cabaret singer establishes with her audience: "In those days they had five or six singers in the clubs and they called them 'Ups.'

One girl would be 'up' and she would go from table to table singing. Then the next one would be 'up' and she'd take over. I was an 'up' from midnight every night until the tips started thinning out, maybe around three o'clock the next afternoon." Change the venue of this ritual and you have something of what the cabaret singer did going from table to table and singing in an intimate, confidential manner.

Lady Day said in her book the following about the evolvement of her style: "Young kids always ask me what my style is derived from and how it evolved and all that. What can I tell them? If you find a tune and it's got something to do with you, you don't have to evolve anything. You just feel it, and when you sing it other people can feel something too. With me, it's got nothing to do with working or arranging or rehearsing. Give me a song I can feel, and it's never work." In her story, as told to William Dufty, Billie also reveals the imperative of the improvisational approach to her singing, which was akin to the jazz musicians' view of invention, as well as a literary axiom that Ernest Hemingway believed in.

Lady Day stated: "No two people on earth are alike and it's got to be that way in music, or it isn't music. I can't stand to sing the same song, the same way, two nights in succession, let along two years, or ten years; if you can then it ain't music, it's close order drill, or exercise, or yodeling, or something . . . But not music." In his acceptance speech for the Nobel Prize, Ernest Hemingway stated: "For a true writer each book should be a new beginning where he tries again for something that is beyond attainment."

Lady Day's singing and phraseology was loaded with skepticism of not only love, men, but of the very words, words, words, she freighted across the landscape of the imagination, with such poignant beauty. There is so often a pity and a bitter irony in her voice. Pascal has said that "true eloquence makes fun of eloquence." The flatness in her style suggests to the audience the down-to-earthiness in her voice. *What of her self-immersion into the body and soul of a song stylistically? For me there was a side of Lady Day that was akin to the art of a superb ventriloquist. She could call up so many of the voices of wrenched-out lovers, who have been stripped of their tongues, and are now only using sign-language, as the Lady, herself, speaks for them, of them to them. Yet like so many great ventriloquists Billie Holiday was limited in certain areas where she could not enter, or which she could not bring to life. Like those singing lovers stripped of their tongues, whose gestures she understood so well, Billie Holiday was almost stripped of everything, so that only the voice of Lady Day could reclaim the edges of their voices, possessed as she was by the similarity of suffering, she saw in their eyes, as she read out their signs. Their signs directed Billie back into her wounds. Thusly Billie's autobiographical relationship to her audience. At the same time the audience was feeling their wounds into her art, by virtue of her way of isolating them into the prison of loneliness, that was her voice. There was wrought a total identification between signers and reader. They were hungry-hearted for her imaginative perceptions of their sensibilities, Lady Day's reflective interpretation of their pain; even as they delighted in hearing the tone of their voices made flesh. Perhaps, in our time, ironically enough, we find ourselves returning to this fifth-grade drop-out, who ran errands for whores (and could surely talk like one off-stage) for illumination, and sustained purification of the tongue, so much have we become the playthings of the whore-merchants of language and language as loose change/chum change, by the advertising junkies. When some one calls out "That was great," in these times, we don't know if the fellow is talking about his sex life, a Jesus Christ-induced spiritual moment, a Mc-Donald's double-burger, mother's milk, the latest supply of felt-tipped condoms, a response to a weather report, or a shake-and-bake move by a college basketball player. One is reminded of the sour critique of our values, and the mutilated language, in the Caporetto scene, in Hemingway's* A Farewell to Arms.

Perhaps there was an indirect relationship between what Hemingway learned from Gertrude Stein ("the abstract relationship of words") and what Billie Holiday gleaned from listening to Mabel Mercer.

JAZZ INTELLIGENTSIA/BASIC BAR ETHOS

Lady Day's musical instrument was embellished by her burnished intelligence and her hypersensitive capacity to surrender to the lyric. She came into the height of her popularity, as well as her powers, around the same time as the bebop school was evolving an authoritative personality and a revolutionary voice. Somewhat mirroring the musical creation of bop's founding fathers (Charlie Parker, Dizzy Gillespie, and Thelonius Monk), Lady Day's music was not for dancing, but contemplation. On certain levels, bop represented a new urban "cry" of jazz, the hieroglyphics of a new Negro consciousness; Billie's "cry" (which transformed her from Eleanora Fagan Holiday to Billie Holiday to Lady Day) magnified a new tortured face of the African-American ethos, even as it sounded out the shape of the new quest for freedom in jazz singing. Just as Parker, Gillespie, and Monk were creating the new frontiers in jazz, Lady Day forged her way with the help of Armstrong's trumpet as the ancestral voice, and Lester Young as the bridge between the traditions of jazz.

Lady Day actually thought of her voice as that of an improvisational instrument, and like that of a jazz musician's echoing chamber: "I don't think I'm singing. I feel like I'm playing a horn. I try to improvise like Les Young, like Louis Armstrong, or someone else I admire. What comes out is what I feel. I hate straight singing. I have to change a tune to my own way of doing it. That's all I know." There were no mountain cries like a mountain cat (or kitchenette kitty). Nor did Holiday try a lot of stylistic embellishments, to wring and to wail.

All of Lady Day's intelligence and art went into her intense concept of phraseology, an the interpretation that nourished that compact phraseology was based in the substance of things seen in her own witness-bearing life. The question of what a quasi-poetic line in a lyric evoked in Billie Holiday was central to what she meant by improvisation. There were actually three kinds of improvisations going on: what a line opened up in Billie; what she opened up in the musicians, by virtue of her interpretation, and what she opened up in her audience, through her poetry of utterance. Yet for all of the decisive power of alchemy, Billie Holiday was probably more dependent on excellent side men than any major singer of her generation. Finis Henderson told me: "Musicians loved Billie; because she didn't interfere with nothing. You could still do your solos; and you weren't competing. You were adding to. And you always wanted to give her something, to see what she would do with it." Perhaps she was also like a beautiful lady who knows better than to ever let you catch her without her make-up on. Yet the make-up she decided upon never was applied to hide the wrinkles she wore (nor to turn her back on her face). *Nor to hide the wrinkles, the rage, the victimization, she had spun out into a spider's web, which draped so much of her art like a grievous, yet wicked veil. Billie Holiday told William Dufty: "Many a time I had the last word in a dressing room argument when I went on stage, threw out the list of songs I was supposed to do, and told my piano player to start off with 'Ain't Nobody's Business If I Do.' This is more than a song to me, it spells the way of life I tried to live, personal freedom, to hell with the what-will-people-think-people, and all that."* This recalls one of Bessie Smith's favorite and most defiant, personal anthems. It was a song that Billie must have listened to scores of times on the victrola at Alice Dean's whorehouse. This rage and contempt for any form of containment of the spirit characterized the life of Billie's intellectual mother, Bessie Smith, even as it became (with her own variations) Lady Day's apostles creed. And Billie heard Bessie singing:

> There ain't nothin' I can do, or nothing I can say, that
> folks don't criticize me.
> But I'm going to do just as I want to anyway and don't
> care if they all despise me.

Lady Day took the essentially Ofay Tin Pan Alley lyrics and made them raw, real, and, on occasion, regal, with her "sulphur-and-molasses voice," as the jazz critic Ralph J. Gleason once described it. She attempted—in the main—to strip these lyrics of their slurpy sentimentality and then polish them down until a deeper grain reflected up in the wood and revealed something of the true relationship between refinement and baseness, culled from her life, and her knowledge of human relations. Where there was a wrinkle of a water mark, then let it be, Baby.

Billie was so often mocking what she rendered up, simultaneously satirizing as she was celebrating romance. She was indeed doing a certain kind of riffing satire that is quite close to signifying. This vocal one-butt shuffle on the sentimental lyrics that Lady Day was simultaneously serving up forms one of the veiled delights of sarcastic slurs and innuendos that lay behind Lady Day's bewitching art. And it was perfectly pitched (though her voice certainly wasn't) to a most ironic view behind the veil from which she observed this hideous and hilarious world. There was often satire that was also on occasion caustic; but it was never a burlesque. Ultimately *to know there; you must go there,* as the saying goes. In fur Lady Day was as much a victim of our American values as she was satirist. "Every night they brought me the satin gown, the white gardenia and the white junk," she has recorded. Yet her work must be read for its social satire and what we've come to call "gender" satire today.

Billie Holiday and the aforementioned bop trinity attempted to move African-American art along in many ways; but one stage that is not cited enough is the role each of these artists (as thinkers) played in attempting to sever the white supremacists' idea that any artful offerings blacks put upon the stage were nourished at their very roots by the gushing naturalness of the Noble Savage. Yet, like Charlie Yard-Bird Parker, Billie Holiday was victimized by the savagery of a world they both sought to satirize and fiercely castigate for its false values. There was a disparagement of artificiality in the work of both Billie and Bird. Each was a victim of personal chaos, which they were able to order into a highly cerebral art upon the stage, but which dominated them more and more off-stage. The furious yeast of personal chaos formed the very nourishing materiality of their creativity. This same chaos was the menacing furor and near madness in which they lived their days; and perhaps it was only on stage that Bird or Billie could have anything resembling control over the furor that drove them. Souls less drawn to chaos like a magnet might create a much more controlled, muted art. But there was an especial beauty that each was able to create of the blood, fever, outrage, loathing, rejection, deep insecurity, absolute nothingness of life, drugs, alcohol, the failures of love, and racism. I am reminded here of what the philosopher Friedrich Nietzsche said, as I ponder the art of Lady Day (and Bird's work, too) . . . "Only the man with chaos within him can give birth to a dancing star."

Lady Day and Bird were outlaws as heroine and hero, most unlikely gun slingers, as it were, given their personal delicacy of soul. There was a muted wail from the soul heard from her voice and his saxophone that weeps over the rail of our age and transforms the nearly nightmarish madness of our contemporary soul into a staggering art—upon occasion. In attempting to escape the nearly criminal attributes of racism, value-hypocrisy, unspeakable materialism, vulgarization of human values of feeling, and the celebration of violence and victimization of all of those one steps over to get to the top (even as we were spiritually crushed on our way to the top) which is the American way to nothingness, we find ourselves coming back to Billie Holiday for illumination about love, and the changes it takes you through precisely because of the impact of these ruinous values upon our souls. She was something of an underground psychiatrist, as much tormented and self-torturing victim as she was oracle-like healer of the outraged heart. A physician who could not heal herself.

Ralph Ellison was writing about Charlie Parker, but he might have been speaking to many of the truths concerning the life of Billie Holiday, as well, the personae she created about her art, and the spiritually blasted, love-struck-down souls who created a cult out of this lyrical lady's lonesome and demon-driven star.

> For the postwar jazznik Parker was Bird, a suffering, psychi-
> cally wounded, law-breaking, life-affirming hero. For them
> he possessed something of the aura of that figure common
> to certain contemporary novels, which R.W.B. Lewis de-
> scribes as the "picturesque saint." He was an obsessed
> outsider—and Bird was thrice alienated: as Negro, as ad-
> dict, as exponent of a new and disturbing development in
> jazz—whose tortured and in many ways criminal striving for
> personal and moral integration invokes a sense of tragic

fellowship in those who saw in his agony a ritualization of their own fears, rebellions and hunger for creativity.

FORREST: Finis, why do you think that so many great artists are self-destructive? Now here we have Holiday and Parker. But I could name several in other arts. Literature for example, Dylan Thomas, Ernest Hemingway. I could go on.

HENDERSON: I couldn't say that so many are self-destructive. But these you've named in music, Lady Day and Bird, were so sensitive to their needs, were the ones who couldn't bear it, without bolstering themselves up with drink or drugs.

FORREST: But what do you think these artists felt that drink or drugs provided them with?

HENDERSON: They *thought* it gave them the strength to go out there and fight—in spite of . . . Otherwise they would have given up.

FORREST: Lester Young, too.

HENDERSON: We are talking about our giants, whose worth is still here.

FORREST: What about those who didn't need the continuous high of addiction in order to bolster themselves up?

HENDERSON: Well, they went on to do whatever it was they did . . . But many of them didn't have the longevity that those we are talking about here possessed.

In 1956, Mike Wallace conducted an interview with Billie Holiday, for his program *Night Beat.* It was shortly before Billie's concert at Carnegie Hall.

WALLACE: You talk with such affection about Bessie Smith and Louis Armstrong. There seems to be a real companionship, Lady, among the greats in the jazz world. Doesn't seem to be as competitive as some others. In some other fields, when you get up there, why its kind of cut-throat. In the jazz field, the greats seem to love one another, and work with one another.

HOLIDAY: You mean like when Dizzy and Louis, myself and Ella—and we all get together? Well, I guess we all suffered. We all had it. So when we get there we appreciate it.

WALLACE: Billie, why is it that so many jazz greats seem to die so early? Bix Beiderbecke, it happened to, Fats Waller wasn't too old; Charlie Parker . . .

HOLIDAY: Well, Mike, the only way I can answer that question is: We try to live one hundred days in one day. We try to please so many people. Like myself, I want to bend this note, and bend that note. Sing this way and sing that way and get all of the feeling, and eat all of the good foods, and travel all over all in one day and you can't do—WALLACE: In your book you wrote, Lady: "You've got to have something to eat and a little love in your life, everything I want out of life goes smack back to that.' Now, when did you discover that. And what does that mean to you, Billie?

HOLIDAY: Well, we all have to eat and we all have to sleep. And I was hungry so long. Now that I do know how to eat and to sleep, and I have travelled——

WALLACE: Actually you like to take life by the forelock and live it while you've got it, and that's why, as you suggested, some jazz performers die young, because they do. Get a little to eat and a little to love——

HOLIDAY: When you get it, you use it——

WALLACE: Life is to use—is the way that you feel.

I was talking with Studs Terkel about the last time he saw Billie Holiday perform on the South Side of Chicago in the mid 1950s.

STUDS TERKEL: I particularly remember her singing "Willow Weep for Me." There was a tragic being there. And the way I put it was—*and we wept*—because Billie was singing not only of her immortality, but the immortality of all of us.

FORREST: Studs, why are many artists so self-destructive? Billie, Bird, Dylan Thomas, Hemingway——

TERKEL: You are talking about artists who *probe in a certain way*. I always say a great artist is not afraid to show his vulnerability. There is a vulnerability streak in us all. But in the case of certain artists that vulnerable streak becomes the subject of that person's art. Think of the Hemingway story. He had that macho streak. Maybe he was insecure about his own masculinity, over the years trying to prove himself . . . So, in his works, this machismo aspect is at the core of his art. With Billie, there is that vulnerability, that gullibility . . . That is being taken by other people. All of which goes back to her childhood.

FORREST: Why the extremes of alcohol, or drugs?

TERKEL: An escape from . . . a surcease daily emptiness.

FORREST: How would you compare Billie Holiday to Ella Fitzgerald, artist to artist, let us say, in terms of these larger-than-life issues?

TERKEL: I once wrote a piece on why I preferred Billie Holiday to Ella Fitzgerald. Ella is a fine performer. The article was called "The Queen's Handkerchief." I felt her work was sometimes automatic. No put-down is intended here. But in the case of Billie Holiday you know at that moment something was happening in her singing that had not happened before. With Ella there was a feeling that it had happened—what she was doing artistically—many times before. Here we are also talking about the difference between a magnificent performer, Ella Fitzgerald, and an artist, Billie Holiday. The artist always reveals himself, or herself, whereas the performer has always a mask. Billie, in revealing her own vulnerability, made you, the listener, aware of your vulnerability. So when Billie sang "Willow Weep for Me" before those ten or twelve people, at two in the morning, at Budland, in this basement (and Ben Webster, the tenor saxophonist, was there) it was not just her mortality she was singing about it was ours, too . . . willow weep for me . . . and we wept.

In reflecting upon Billie Holiday's remarkable style, and its musical sources, T. J. Anderson, one of the leading African-American composers in this country (and a former jazz musician), recently told me: "Billie Holiday's voice quality contained a 'buzz' which we call a 'whiskey' voice, the opposite to the purity and flexibility of Ella and

Sarah. The male counterpart of this quality can be heard in Louis Armstrong and Tony Bennett.

"One night in a club, I heard Billie Holiday sing a song, A-B-A song structure, in which she approached the B section with a note of great dissonance. She held on to this note until it blossomed like a flower. To this date, I don't know whether it was an act of musical genius or whether she was just high. The musical experience proved to be unforgettable. Billie Holiday sang music which fluctuated between despair and optimism, shifted between major and minor modes, and conveyed the depths of blues. Yet the blues constituted very little of her repertoire."

LISTENING, REFLECTING, AND
IMAGINING

NOTEBOOK: Listening, reflecting, imagining out of Lady Day's reading of a lyric could provide you with a clinical reevaluation of your love life, if you were sour of soul, or bruised in the body from a love gone wrong, or upside your head. As in the case with many great healers, Holiday knew havoc of the heart, as the diastole danger, and the systole stigma. One was struck to the mother-wit resources of the very soul by how much her style sounded like a public confession of sheer killing floor muted intimacy, wrought in a conversational tone on the one hand, and on the other there was a divine-demonic sexual fire about Lady Day, which was as dangerous as it was delicious, as my soul danced before the candle of her art, even as my mind sat up to listen to all of the crackling and branching ways her art spoke to me. If you don't believe me, then you'd better listen again to her on "Them There Eyes." Her voice was so often like that of a lady who had just got out of the bed from a very powerful and affirmative sexual encounter, yet she was tired, yawning, and though physically spent, eager to go back again to the place so full of power, ecstasy, wailing, and breathless danger.

Majestic and naughty, and femme fatale, flinty and furious, wicked and too, too flirtatious for words . . . for words, words, words for the flesh of this hamming-up hamlet, who could have benefited by her economy, if he had not been driven to madness by Dylan Thomas, Bird, Shakespeare, and all of the other rapping men starting all of over again Joyce, Poe (your city-mate Billie) . . . But Joyce, one more once . . . ah how "Eveline" would have evoked Billie.

Must I go back to the imperatives of miserable men in her life, as the materiality, fish and bones of her art. "Some men like me cause I'm snappy, some cause I'm happy . . . Some say Billie you're built for speed . . . Put 'em all together, I'm everything a good man needs." Fed on failures. Yet another drug addiction, men who were a drag. Transformed fuck-ups into art, at least on stage. Problem was, very much a female problem, too. There weren't any male Noras for Billie to extend a life-time rage upon and transform his personae into art, while he saved her life in an extended way. Couldn't marry The President, he was gay. Problem for that kind of gal, how does a sexually vibrant woman marry a homosexual who understands her? Talk to Virginia Woolf? Most probably Billie didn't know of her; Lady Day had The President, whom she had named, but she couldn't fuck him; she could only love him. Joyce and Virginia Woolf could have benefited by knowing Billie. Billie them. All three were always searching for a certain mysterious "otherness." Virginia had to inform Leonard that she was not interested in sex on her honeymoon. Mr. Woolf, who was a Jew, had in turn to become the supportive side of his relationship with this genius, who cracked up after the creation of her major works. Hard for a black woman to find this in a man? Both Billie and Virginia's driven mad over their art? Each wrote diaries. Billie wrote diaries into her songs. Both divine ladies were molested as children. How can you be molested as a girl and trust men? Or grow up and develop a "normal" sexual appetite and feeling for men? Both had some lesbian tendencies? Vita for Virginia; or I should say, Virginia for Vita and several others. Bessie and Ma Rainey were bisexual. As for Billie? Rumor has it——Billie "created" "Gloomy Sunday" too late to help Virginia. But would she have listened to the voice of a Negress?

"NO GOOD MAN, EVER SINCE THE
EARTH BEGAN"

FORREST: An interesting kind of phenomenon that I have observed in terms of the psychological subsistence for certain kinds of famous females is this need for comfort and friendship from a gay male. Perhaps he represents something of an uncle/aunt figure—the parents and trustworthy sibling, all rolled into one.

HENDERSON: But it's because they are attuned to a female need. And they serve several purposes, and it's a relationship I never condemned. God made us all.

FORREST: Or, take Ellington, for example, who was about as much of a ladies' man as you can find. There was the dimension of his music and his creativity that was supplied and actually composed by Billy Strayhorn, who was gay, and who introduced the female side within the Ellingtonia of the Duke's musical canon. But now, Finis, here is a question that always comes up. How could a singer know so much about life and love in her songs, and reveal so much about the torments of love gone wrong, and yet be so off-key in her private life about men? Was she a sucker for love, or a sucker for the wrong kind of man?

HENDERSON: If you'll examine our black female vocalists, most of the men attracted to them were players because of the kind of things they sang; the kinds of lines they delivered and the kinds of clubs they worked at . . . Each had her own kind of club setting. Now a lot of the black men didn't approach a lot of black women vocalists, because they felt they were beneath these entertainers. So they never competed for their attention. They figured "I ain't never gonna score with that. I'll just leave that alone." So, consequently, not many of our black females met interesting black men, so they ended up with whites, who could afford to be in their company. These black female singers didn't go that way intentionally. So it was a form of entrapment really, for the black female to be in that situation.

FORREST: Although most of Billie's men were black.

HENDERSON: Yeah, most of her men were black. But most of the women we are talking about had the uncanny ability to end up with players. Those were the ones who had the money to be in their company . . . Those were the ones the singers saw.

FORREST: Then there is the other factor here, too. We as men can leave the gig and go out, from club to club, with little fear of the dangers of the streets, as night hawks. We can make our moves. A lady cannot move about and operate with that kind of freedom as easily as we might.

HENDERSON: That's right. She just can't stroll out. Go hawking. That's an interesting question. Because it wasn't intentional on the part of the female; but she looked up and there it was. And after a while you get tired of getting knocked in the head, and getting your eyes blackened; you got to go on stage. Somebody's got to understand that this is a business.

FORREST: Hard to think of a female who didn't take her share of lumps and abuse. Nancy Wilson, maybe.

HENDERSON: Fortunately, Nancy was never pushed around. But look who she was raised with . . . Cannonball, and his brother. So that was another element that was a protection for her.

There is the problem of loneliness and the perceived beauty of talented female singers. Who had more natural singing beauty than the gifted Sarah Vaughan? Yet she certainly had troubles with men. She was sorely insecure about the powers of her vast orchestra of a voice. The Divine One was also enormously insecure about her presence, because of her looks, and the impact that her "homely" looks had upon her self-esteem. She believed she was "homely" and she was dark-skinned. And on this most crucial and heart-breaking level, Sarah Vaughan, like Dinah Washington, also had to deal with intra-group racism in terms of their Negroid/or African features and color. Then too, so-called decent people didn't like to socialize with show business people, particularly women. Clarice White-Pruitt, who was a professional dancer, for two decades with the Dyerettes recalls the following story about the Divine One:

"Sarah Divine thought she was the ugliest thing going. She didn't think that she could sing. She didn't know that she was sweet. She didn't know that she had this great voice. She took her voice for granted. She was often embarrassed when people would stand up and applaud for her.

"Let me tell you this story. Sarah was getting ready to open up at Basin Street East. And she, and C. B. Atkins and I went to see Lena Horne. Lena had opened at a hotel across the street from the place where Sarah was scheduled to sing. It was a dinner show and Lena was in her glory; and I will never forget Lena's fabulous long black shirtwaist dress. She was so breathtaking, it was unbelievable. What was interesting was to watch the women watch their men watching Lena sing. Among the songs she sang was "Surrey with the Fringe on the Top," which is not a sexy song. Let me tell you, Leon, the way that girl put over that song, it was X rated, it was so sizzling. She would turn around and look at her husband, the band-leader Lennie Haydon; and he'd blush. The thing between them was so dynamic. So we went backstage after the show. And Lena Horne was very black when she talked. Sarah started in telling Lena, 'Oh my God you're so beautiful . . . And I'm gonna open up across the street from you.' And Lena said, 'Shit, they ain't paying for me coming in here looking this good. I got to watch what I eat . . . Look you can go over there, take your shoes off, and stand bare-footed and just sing without a piano player, and you will just jam the place. If I could sing like you, I would never put on any make-up.' And Sarah didn't know that this was a compliment. *She was embarrassed.* And in her private life, as far as her men went, she almost inevitably picked scourgies.''

Dinah Washington apparently found Billie Holiday not only a beautiful idol, but also a goddess to be adored, long before she became a famous singer in her own right. In his book on Dinah called *Queen of the Blues,* Jim Haskins reports the following recollection of Washington's pianist, Jack Wilson: "She told me that when she was a kid going to school in Chicago, she heard that Billie Holiday was coming to Chicago and was going to land at Midway Airport. Dinah skipped school to go to the airport and see Billie get off the plane. This was when Billie was at her height and always wearing ermine and carrying those two little dogs. And Dinah had all her records and just idolized her, and she said that when she saw Billie step off that plane, she thought that Billie was the most beautiful woman she had ever seen." According to Haskins, Dinah imitated Billie consciously during her apprentice years. Apparently Dinah ran into the duality of being very respected by members of the Lionel Hampton band on stage, but they demonstrated an abhorrence of her off-stage, because of her features and dark-skinned complexion. Haskins goes on to observe:

> They allowed as to how she had great talent, but they didn't think much of her looks. Off-stage, Dinah's confidence evaporated. "At that time, it was like a thing about being dark," says Jimmy Cobb, referring to the standard image of light-complected Negro beauty. Dorothy Dandridge and Lena Horne in Hollywood, Billie Holiday on big-band podiums—these were the ideals. Hampton's other girl singers were light-skinned and well-dressed and very attractive. Dinah, although she'd gotten over the adolescent skin problem that had given rise to the nickname Alligator, was not a looker. About five-foot-seven she was plump and top heavy, and her facial features, from eyes to nose to mouth, were over-large and overpowering. "Dinah," says Cobb, "didn't have nuthin'—she was raggedy—and so she went through that kind of number, and I think it kind of stuck to her a little bit."

WALLACE: You've mentioned some of your good friends who are musicians, Billie. But I know some of your good friends who are not musicians. I'd like to get to know them and what it is that you have most in common with them? Their names that I'll give you, Tallulah Bankhead, Charles Laughton, and Orsen Welles.

HOLIDAY: They were brave enough to come up to Harlem when they were starting jazz. I'll never forget the night I met Mr. Laughton. He was looking for his valet. That's how he got wandering around in Harlem. I had no idea he was a movie actor. He always comes around

to see me. And Miss Bankhead, I think she is the end. I love her. I think
of three ladies, Miss Bankhead, Miss Barrymore, and Helen [Forrest].
WALLACE: Now you mentioned these performers, is it that you are all
performers? Is that what you have in common?
HOLIDAY: Miss Barrymore . . . Actresses and artists. I look at them like
wow [some vocal display of awe].
WALLACE: And you don't consider yourself in the same league?
HOLIDAY: My God, No!
WALLACE: Why not? You've worked as hard. You've thought as much
about it. You've developed a style, and technique, just as much as they
have done. You've pleased just as many people, so why aren't you just
as much of an artiste as any one of them?
HOLIDAY: Well, maybe I am, in my little way . . . But they make me cry,
they make me happy. *I don't know if I've ever done that to people, not really.*

LADY DAY AND THE SECULAR
SCRIPTURE

> Had she paints, or clay, or knew the discipline of dance, or
> strings; had she anything to engage her tremendous curi-
> osity and her gift for metaphor, she might have exchanged
> the restlessness and preoccupation with whim for any
> activity that provided her with all she yearned for. And like
> any artist with no art form, she became dangerous.
>
> —The character Sula,
> from Toni Morrison's novel,
> *Sula*

Before the recent rise of those gifted signifying black female writers,
led by Toni Morrison, it was really Lady Day, more than any other
cultural carrier, who spoke in an avant-grade, sophisticated manner—on
the national stage—concerning the themes of heartbreak in romance,
the perils of sentimentality, the ways of men, and the ransom of
heartache, sexual victimization, racism, the wounds of loneliness, all of
which were forged from the injustice engraved upon the black female

perspective. This dimension of Lady Day's art forced you to contem-plate deeply the plight of the condition of the African-American woman's tragic situation, in ways that were both contemplative, intel-lectual, and soul-searching. Lady Day prophetically read out the terrorized terms of the heart, more than any other national black female artist in American culture; and she gave voice to a new consciousness, through the projection of a new voice, an original style of singing. The new sensibility always needs a fresh voice—Lady Day supplied this need. She seemed to create a crossover audience, without particularly plotting to achieve this arching bridge of musical linkage. Holiday's audience was always white, for any number of reasons, among them, economic. Like Morrison in our day, Holiday was revered by a sophisticated audience, which formed a cult of worshippers. Many of these devotees, in both cases, were whites. Many of the white females are not activists in the women's movement. The subject material of Toni and Billie, however, emerges almost totally from the black experience. Still, the times are quite different and the rise in the sensibility of women and race is far more acute; thus, in an audience of, say, 500 people, attending a Billie Holiday set, probably 400 would have been whites, at the height of Billie's powers. Today, at a reading given by Morrison of 1,000, on a university setting, no doubt, you'd have something like 700 blacks and 300 whites. I would speculate that three-fourths of the audience would be female. As the critic Ralph J. Gleason has noted: "Billie's forte was the ballad, the pop tune. That she could take these frequently banal and generally trivial numbers and make them into something lasting, something artistic (most singers, at best, are *artful*) is a tribute to the way she was, for her time, the voice of Woman."

Yet Gleason's statement, and my own speculations and projections need to be buttressed against this whole question of Lady Day's own sense of inadequacy, as a singer. As Holiday's accompanist Bobby Tucker once stated: "There's one thing about Lady you won't believe. She had the *most* terrible inferiority complex. She actually doesn't believe she can sing." This, of course, would not be the first time that the most exquisite sound, painting, poem, sculpture was created by a restless artist preoccupied with his or her own self-doubts in the sphere of the private life; but was able through the rigors of self-discipline, fortitude, and courage to transcend his or her fear and create a living miracle before the altar of the selected art form. Nor would it be the first time that an artist whose work spoke to the riddled chaos of his time through the body of his endeavors was absolutely at loggerheads to deal with it, in the private life; even appeared manipulated by the intricacies of the madness of his day, or changing complexity within an area of life he thought he knew, once upon a time. Those of us who admired many virtues in the art of Faulkner, for example, faced this same intriguing relationship to his art, and certain of his public statements on race. How does Dylan Thomas start off his famous poem: "The force that through the green fuse drives the flower/ Drives my green age; that blasts the roots of trees/ Is my destroyer . . . And I am dumb to tell the crooked rose/ My youth is bent by the same wintry fever."

Billie Holiday's approach was very different from the idea of what T. S. Eliot called: "The process of depersonalisation." By transforming passions without bringing in, or introducing, his own personality upon these passions. Holiday's approach was more akin to that of certain modern writers, like Hemingway, Tennessee Williams, and later Baldwin and Mailer, in the essay form. In her music, Lady recombined her gift for personal metaphor, with the idea of the tribal singer, as high priestess; thus she cast forth the idea in the listener's mind *that what I'm listening to is the living witness of my own life.* Therefore, Lady Day was at once goddess, high priestess, bitch, best girlfriend, signifying barfly, member of the Greek chorus, as she turned your secular life into a litany. Here the high priestess provided the ordering center of your life's chaos. And listeners paid homage to her witness with the reverence and propers pay, in the way that some Holy Ghost Preachers are able to invoke within their congregation. Lady Day was the oracle and you must go to her to get the prophetic word on race, love, heartbreak, abusive men (and even here with a mocking satire). "My

man wouldn't give me no breakfast. Wouldn't give me no dinner . . .
Talked about my supper and put me out doors . . . Had the nerve to
lay a match box on my closes . . . I didn't have so many but I had a
long, long ways to go." You participated fully in her readings and
renderings. This was the form and voice her didacticism took.

In the spring of 1984, I attended a reading given by my former
editor, Toni Morrison, at the University of Illinois at Chicago. There
were probably 750 people in attendance, mostly female. When Finis
Henderson spoke of Billie Holiday mesmerizing the English language,
I couldn't help but remember that spring evening when Toni Morrison
held her audience in the palm of her hand, as she read her mesmerizing prose, in a mesmerizing way. The ladies in the front rows of the
audience—mainly black—nodded in rhythm to Morrison's prose.
They were dazzled and delighted; but it was also very much like a
religious/secular experience for them, it seemed to me. In the
African-American religious experience there are sermons based on the
stories from the Old Testament, which the congregation knows so well,
made new now by this series of sermonettes, based upon the text. Here
Morrison's reading caused within her flock a species of rememory, as
it were. Like Holiday, high priestess Morrison had taken up their
personal grievances concerning the human condition as seen through
the specificity of the black female experience and transformed it into
a haunting art that was spiritual at its base. Although neither Billie nor
Toni is particularly interested in the religious stirrings as, say, Mahalia
or the late James Baldwin of *Go Tell It on the Mountain,* who revealed the
Negro Christian's agony of flesh and spirit. The observing eye of the
main character in Elizabeth Hardwick's highly autobiographical novel,
Sleepless Nights, notes upon an occasion of seeing Lady Day close up:
"The creamy lips, the oily eyelids, the violent perfume—and in her
voice the tropical l's and r's. Her presence, her singing created a large,
swelling anxiety. Long red fingernails and the sound of electrified
guitars. Here was a woman who had never been a Christian."

Listening, reflecting, and learning from Lady Day's reading, one was
struck to the very soul by how much her style wounded as a public

confession of intimacy, wrought in a conversational tone. (That was the highly confidential way too, Toni brought words off the page that night.) It was as if the general audience was being made privy to the unburdening of grief on an individual basis, as expressed and revealed by one's best girl friend, seated next to you at your favorite bar (where they have the best jukebox in town).

Because an aspect of Billie's style was so conversational, she was able to establish an ongoing dialogue with the attuned individuals in her audience. (Morrison oftentime talks about establishing "a hook" within her material and the imaginative world of her reader, and it works quite well. This confidentiality that Billie expressed and even huskily whispered, too, had to do with her reading out, in the most understated way, the enormous wretchedness of love. Because Lady Day was so brilliantly understated, it allowed you to enter forever her very soul, and to think about your own heartbreak in completely new ways. Holiday's voice was small (there were phases, registers, and rasps within it, which were, ironically enough, similar to the witness-bearing of a young girl's utterances, who finds herself trapped in an early adolescence, upon a slippery slab of a crevice, overlooking a bottomless abyss), creating a sound from the fathomless depths of existence; and when we remember that she was raped as a girl of ten, we weep for her in the solitude over the horror of that moment trapped in the sprocket of her mind's eye; you tended to think, as you sat upon that bar stool listening to the person next to you . . . *Not so much, well I could do that . . . Could sing like that but rather you identified with her more, because it meant that your own small voice was being sounded out, and heard. (Made even smaller by all the abuses of this world.) That your grief was being articulated and that the common plight of your ordinariness, and the commonness of your pain was being transformed into the uncommon. That your agony was special—as you really suspected all along—if not remarkable.*

. . . So, as you sat there now at this bar next to your best girl friend, listening to the jukebox, playing Billie's "Good Morning, Heartache", (here we go again), you watched, and saw the barmaid suddenly being transformed before your very eyes into a high priestess. This is the barkeep, who listens to all

of your love-struck heartache, with a confidential ear and a feeling soul. The muted mathematical measurements were in her possession, as she could go from brewing up barmaid to mixologist to high-powered alchemist, evolving your concoction for a hangover of the heartache, just "bad" enough to make you feel good, so that you would never forget just how evil, low-down, but beautiful, too, love can be . . . How love forces you to surrender ("everything that I possess, I offer to you") . . . Or "Love will make you drink and gamble, stay out all night, long." Billie's long-song, which was also her life, has become your solo song for the night. But you must always be open to the light of that candle in the wind, as presented to you through that small echo chamber, because Holiday was always trying to bring you into a higher life of intelligence with her songs and filter through the songs all of her continually changing experiences, masks, moods.

THE ISSUE OF RACE

FORREST: Finis, Billie's autobiography, *Lady Sings The Blues*, with William Dufty, in rereading the book she did I was struck by at least two attributes. There is, on the one hand, a hard-nose, tell it like it is Baby, no-holds-barred broad, who could be a bitch on wheels, mean and evil. On the other hand, there is the innocence, the gullibility . . . Even the little girl operating within her, projecting out of whoever was Billie Holiday.

HENDERSON: But there was all of that in one person.

FORREST: Here we are also speaking of her artistic identity, too. But now the third phase of the work was the very presence of the cruelty of racial prejudice. And how all of that got into their work. . . . I was telling a friend of mine that I was writing an essay on Lady Day. She declared immediately and in no uncertain terms that although she greatly admired Billie Holiday, she could not listen to Billie everyday. Whereas she could play Sarah Vaughan's recordings, night and day. What do you make of her response?

HENDERSON: I think it was the pain that Billie sang out of or spoke of . . . Lot of people couldn't face it. They knew about it but they didn't want to hear it——

FORREST: Even now!

HENDERSON: Yes, even now. The agony that was in her voice. Those songs that we talked about—"Strange Fruit" you could see it, you could picture all that she was thinking about.

FORREST: Of course, at that time lynchings haunted the black experience; and the landscape of the South.

HENDERSON: And it isn't that far removed. They were lynching blacks up into the 1950s.

FORREST: "Strange Fruit" probably reached its zenith of exposure and its greatest force during World War II, when black soldiers were off defending the country in the name of freedom, and couldn't get their rights here at home. Black G.I.'s and African-American citizens, as far as that goes. Billie's life was sorely touched by the plight of her people, she lived that plight.

HENDERSON: She learned a lot of things from the experience with the Charlie Barnett band, too. He was her mentor. Her protector. She was a Lone Ranger out there, in terms of black female singer, singing with a white band, and going into hostile territory. Barnett had to think something of her, to even take her with him and his band, out on the road.

FORREST: Yes, because it wasn't like Branch Rickey with Jackie Robinson, right after World War II, for example. For all of Rickey's progressive boldness in bringing Jackie up to the major leagues, in 1947, there was financial profit to be realized, for sure, in the potential of black talent, and the fan interest having Negro players out on the field would engender in the American baseball public, albeit the hell the black players might catch. Whereas there was no guarantees for Barnett, other than the fact that he was going to catch hell and lose a whole lot of gigs.

HENDERSON: Sure—featuring a black singer, and an attractive black singer, too.

FORREST: The public would say, she's got so much going for her . . . She felt she had nothing going for her . . . She must have had enormous insecurity.

HENDERSON: Well, this allowed for certain people to get in control of her life. They played on that weakness of her drug addiction. When you think about it, that's what happened to Charlie Parker—you can just go on and name them . . . Artists who had to suffer the slings and arrows of prejudice and only now has their true musical worth surfaced. Those of us who were on the inside, we entertainers knew the racism they faced. But the general public didn't know.

NEVER-ENDING DREAM OF
LADY DAY

I have come to this theatre seeking oracle-like advice from the high priestess. She is standing before the microphone, on a small stage, which is darkened, except for the penetrating spotlight upon her. The High Priestess is adorned in her slightly opened secular robe of white mink ermine. Her face is beautifully made up; there is a gardenia in her hair, which she wears in an upsweep. She is wearing her high-heel white slippers. She looks exquisite. Not like the directoress of a sanctuary choir, either.

But a shift in her stance reveals a little too much, and I suddenly realize that beneath the fur that Billie Holiday is gownless, and perhaps even naked. I feel an immediate emptiness in the pit of my soul. I want to rush to her to protect this Lady. Our Lady of Sorrows? Where is your satin gown, Miss Holiday? What do I hunger for? To be her protector? Lover? Father? Brother? Priest? Billie was always so vulnerable, I tell myself. What is it that John Donne said: "There is no exquisite genius without some strangeness in the proportion."

Now she is clearing her throat, slowly opening that sensual mouth of hers, but is it to introduce one of her classic offerings, or to sing, in a stripped-down tongue? I don't see any of her side men providing artistic succor for Lady Day. Billie Holiday singing acapella? Oh no. Then I hear a husky-voiced Holiday somewhere between singing, speaking, and sassying, now revealing:

"Ladies and gentlemen, my text for this twilight is the nothingness of nowhereness . . . " And then Lady Day launches into: "Please don't talk about me when I'm gone . . . though our friendship ceases from now on. And if you can't say anything real nice, just don't talk at all that's my advice. We parting you go your way, I'll go mine. It's best that we do. Here's a kiss, I hope that this brings lots of luck to you. Makes no difference how I carry on . . . Please don't talk about me when I'm gone." Which, of course, is the last thing that any Lady wants in the wake of a break up to be "disremembered." But the cockiness is there. The jauntiness. The upbeat bounce of rebounding is there. Some of the naughty satirical spirit of slyness, akin to the lady who insisted she had never borrowed her neighbor's pots and had, in any case, already returned them.

SUFFER THE LITTLE CHILDREN
AND FORBID THEM NOT, TO COME UNTO
ME.

I am searching the landscape for a little girl named Eleanora Fagan. But I don' see her among those who are playing jacks, pampering dolls, and combing their hair. Nor is she among the ones who are skipping rope, before her very own dollhouse; or scurrying off to ballet lessons. Next I search to find her at the beach, building sand castles in the air. Frantically I return to the neighbor to see if a little girl of her description is playing with building blocks at a given address. Nothing. I feel nowhere. Inside an old building I listen to hear the voice of a grandmother; then I look for a great-grandmother to see if she has a young'un upon her knee, reading the fairy tales, and, in particular, *Little Red Riding Hood* . . . .

Clarence Holiday's light-skinned, upscaled kin thought Sadie too shady for their dicty world. At sixteen he wasn't ready for fatherhood. Baby was three, mother 16, father eighteen when they did marry. Soon Clarence split and went to the army. Clarence's lungs were ruined because of an exposure to poisonous gas; so ended his dreams to become a trumpeter. He turned his musical talents to the guitar. Meantime Sadie supported herself and the baby by scrubbing floors for white folks, all over Baltimore. The white movie star, Billie Dove, provided the tomboy Eleanora with the model of beauty, the glamour of big-screen stardom, and a new identity by transferring the gorgeous Hollywood creature's name and x'ing out her own. She was seduced by a slimy man named Mr. Dick, when she was ten. If modern women hear their agony of violation in Holiday's art, and see it in her story—why wouldn't they? For his rape of the well-developed ten-year-old, Mr. Dick (who was over forty at the time) was sentenced to five years, but the female child was placed in a Catholic institution for girls, where she was condemned to stay until she reached her majority; after all with a body like hers, surely she had enticed the middle-aged man ran the lascivious logic of the court. She did get out when she was twelve, through the intervention of her mother's contacts; but blaming of the victim was already set in place in her psyche, forevermore, as well as the wantonness of men. She heard Bessie Smith and Armstrong in the brothel, over the victrola, where she ran errands and worked as a maid; her intellectual parents, who were themselves great artists and taboo-breakers. Her own parents were victims, taboo-breakers, who lost. But Bessie and Armstrong were taboo-breakers who set their own rules, and "played" by their own set of standards. Each had an original "voice." Each epitomized the soul of the race, too. She was able to separate the beauty and power of the music from the conditions where it was heard. She could think, too: "I guess I'm not the only one who heard her first good jazz in a whorehouse. But I never tried to make anything of it. If I'd heard Louis and Bessie at a Girl Scout jamboree, I'd have loved it just the same. But a lot of white people first heard jazz in places like Alice Dean's, and they helped label jazz 'whorehouse music.' They forget what it was like in those days. A whorehouse was about the only place where black and white folks could meet in any natural way. They damn well couldn't rub elbows in the churches. And in Baltimore, places like Alice Dean's were the only joints fancy enough to have a victrola and for real enough to pick up on the best records."

. . . I found her for a fleeting moment near a junk shop. She was shooting marbles and dice near the junk wagon (next door to where she lived) with some of the neighbor boys . . . Then I observed her roller-skating, boxing, and bike-riding. Then I heard her say: "But whether I was riding a bike or scrubbing somebody's dirty bathroom floor, I used to love to sing all the time. I liked music. If there was a place where I could go and hear it, I went. Alice Dean used to keep a whorehouse on the corner nearest our place, and I used to run errands for her and the girls." But she doesn't seem to know that I am listening to her. Did she believe that she had killed her dear story-telling Great-Grandkin, by laying the old lady's body down? "Grandma's arm was still tight around my neck and I couldn't move it. I tried and tried and then I got scared. She was dead, and I began to scream. The neighbors came running. They had to break Grandma's arm to get me loose. Then they took me to the hospital. I was there for a month. Suffering from what they said was shock." Another shock, too, was Mister Dick. Right name for his violation of the child, called Billie.

Billie Holiday at the microphone now, and I thought I heard her say: "something of a riff on "What did I do to get so black and blue?" She was cracking up, amid her tears of rage and sarcasm.

". . . Or again the craziness of this color shit. Chorus line at the Fox theatre in De-troit projecting the white gals too pale in front of the black males in Basie's black band. We hear tell whole lot of carping goin' down from certain pale parties; got management's lame ass on the grill. Management ups and masks the Miss Anns in black masquerades, like they gonna take off for Mardi Gras, black mask and made them to wear mammy-made dresses. But youalls ain't heard from Heaven, yet. Now I'm gonna tell you the difference between elephant's doo-doo, Ofay's shift, and shit-yellow. Management to the rescue of the lily white sheets. Shiiite. "Lady," these clowns start up real sweet to keep my bitch from boiling. "In order to save your gig and the jobs of the guys in Basie's band, you got to tone down your fair-looking complexion on stage, because we keep getting complaints, again. What are we trying to project? Miscegnation."

"I tell management, yeah I'm a Lady all right so kiss the Lady's royal ass. Now for you white folks out in the audience—cause youall always like to pretend you don't understand these things—I came off too

386

high-yellow, which I surely ain't, with help of them white stage lights, which ain't very mellow . . . too light in my make-up on stage in front of all those black cats in Basie's band. So, Lady Day, you got to blacken up the greasepaint. Swollow the shit. Get rid of your high shit-yellow. Grease down your face to a darker hue. Next they'll be buying stock in Nadnola, and using the money to promote shows. Al Jolson ain't dead yet, Mammy."

A life of withering ironies? Holiday's relationship with her mother was complicated. Her mother never got over being abandoned by Daddy Clarence; or his taking up with another woman; nor his starting up a family with this other woman. (He had abandoned Billie, too.) Billie taught Mom to read. To compensate for the loneliness and emptiness in her mother's life and her sense of rejection, Billie purchased for the talented cook, Sadie Fagan Holiday, a restaurant. Billie easily identified with her mother's sense of rejection. But a whole restaurant, Billie? Bankrolled the whole operation. Maybe Sadie was a great cook, with a big heart, but she had absolutely no business savvy. Her big-heartedness made Mom Holiday's an open invitation for any hungry soul with a story, and a rumbling appetite. She was open season for a sucker with a sop, but so was Billie.

Billie, like many artists, suffered an overidentification with the down and out, the plagued, the wretched, which is fine on stage, before the canvass, or at the typewriter; but perilous to carry over into one's life, as a rule of thumb. Billie went through her own money with about as much common sense as Mom evidenced business sense in running the restaurant. Perhaps Mom felt she could squander, as she pleased, the capital her famous daughter had invested in this restaurant, in much the same way that Billie had handled her own life and her own talent: heedless to the restrictions of disciplined living. In her overidentification with (and no doubt jealousy over) her daughter's success, which Mom probably felt came as a natural gift. Doubtlessly she experienced an easy-come, easy-go attitude—after a lifetime of struggle—with regard to the gift of the restaurant, that it was a stroke of luck, like Billie's talent. But Billie isn't worthy of luck, anymore than I am. After all, if it were not for me, there would be no Billie Holiday.

One day when she was strapped for cash, Billie returned to the restaurant she had bankrolled and created and asked Mom for a loan. Billie didn't need a credit reference here. Sadie couldn't handled the reversal of roles any longer. This was Sadie's restaurant; she needed to show her authority. Mom refused to crank open the cash register. She was trying to reestablish her proprietorship over *her* restaurant and over *her* life, in the face of the gift-giver, who had freed the mother. Billie took this rejection to heart, as a refusal of her mother to open not simply the cash register, but her heart. For Sadie, the daughter had to be put in her place, in order to know who was boss. For Billie: *I couldn't go to you as a child for money, because you didn't have any. So now here's your chance to play out that role of Mom.* Billie felt abandoned. Yet Lady Day's penchant for magnification worked artistically, because out of the mother's rejection, she crafted a song, stripped from scripture, "God Bless the Child That's Got His Own." *Mama may have . . . Papa may have . . . But God Bless the child that's got his own . . . Rich relations give crusts of bread and such, you can help yourself, but don't take too much.*

Later, mother and daughter did make up. When Mom Holiday died young in 1944, Billie was a motherless child, deeply wounded, and abandoned once again. And the little girl we hear in her voice as she sings "God Bless the Child" just now is streaked with abandonments—from mother, father, lovers, great-grandmother, and grandmother, who would not free her fingers from Billie's even in death.

In addition to the long-song Lady Day picked up from the *prima facie* evidence of Jimmy Monroe's infidelities (he stripped Lady Day of her marital bliss and she created "Hush Now Don't Explain" out of the trouble she'd seen, as Billie reveals at the microphone just now), Jimmy also hooked Billie body and soul on drugs. (Of this, she says nothing of course.) The lush gardenia could not hide the growing shadow of her enslavement to the monkey on her back ("the white junk") and during the war she got hooked on the secret, savage powers of the luxuriously expensive, horrific ecstasy of heroine. If the monkey on her back had a savage appetite and need, and slowly grafted his personality over her body and soul, Billie too apparently had an all-consuming need for solace, love, constant spiritual affirmation that she was somebody, which no audience, or man could ever satisfy, so deep was the brooding hunger. "I need your love so badly I love you oh so madly . . . But I don't stand a ghost of a chance with you . . ." This feeling of worthlessness . . ." "I'm nobody/Who are you?/Are you nobody, too." wrote Emily Dickinson.

I thought I heard Lady Day saying in a whispering, husky voice: "I don't have an identity other than what comes out of this voice of mine. But is it mine? Or something that comes out of me? This voice which possesses me too, like the monkey on my back possesses me. Like the men who possessed me in the whorehouse. Like the great-grandfather-slave master who possessed the body of his slave woman, my great-grandmother." Billie was often picked up for possession sometimes set up by the dearest of her misusers. At the microphone she whispered:

"I can never get possession over my life until I'm freed of the power of the Ofay world over me; the white junk upon my back; in possession of my cabaret license to work in New York; in possession of a man, who loves me body and soul . . . Who doesn't try to misuse me." And then she sang "Lover Man."

LITERARY REFLECTIONS OF
LADY DAY

> The one I really liked best, though was my great-grandmother, my grandfather's mother. She really loved me and I was crazy about her. She had been a slave on a big plantation in Virginia and she used to tell me all about it. She had her own little house in the back of the plantation. Mr. Charles Fagan, the handsome Irish plantation owner, had his white wife and children in the big house. And he had my great-grandmother out in back. She had sixteen children by him, and all of them were dead by then except Grandpop. We used to talk about life. And she used to tell me how it felt to be a slave, to be owned body and soul by a white

man who was father of her children. She couldn't read or
write, but she knew the Bible by heart from the scriptures.

Lady Sings the Blues, with
William Dufty

The mythical power of Billie Holiday's life, charged by the immediate abuse by men throughout her life, and the mythical-sexual
victimization by the slave-master of her great-grandmother becomes an
obvious scale model for a most troubling and memorable novel,
Corregidora by Gayl Jones. Her heroine, Ursa Corregidora, is a singer,
whose life as artist is created out of the crucible of cruelties meted out
by her lover, and the terrible, historical weight, out of slavery, she
carries upon her soul, going back to the savage sexual abuses of her
white landowner, great-grand kinsman.

In Lady Day's saga it was her great-grandmother who had suffered
the debauchery of the white slave owner in Virginia. He used her body
like that of a brood mare; while old man Fagan kept his wife in the
luxury of the Big House, he sired sixteen children in his breeding
place "out in back." Billie was made aware of this legendary female
victimization out of the mouth of the family matriarch, who had not
only borne the abuse, but passed it down to her great-granddaughter,
as a witness-bearing, high priestess of the tribe, in the folk manner of
the oral tradition. "And she used to tell me how it felt to be a slave, to
be owned body and soul by a white man who was the father of her
children."

In *Corregidora*, the legend preserved down the matriarchal line, via
the female tongue, goes back to the sexual bestiality of the Brazilian
slave master, Corregidora. Sire of both Ursa's great-grandmother and
her grandmother, Corregidora was also a procurer, a pimp off of the
flesh of slave women, some of whom were the flesh and blood he had
fathered. Pitched to the truths of oral tradition, as memory, the slave
women and their female ancestors must, in turn, keep the Corregidora
mythic memory alive, basically by producing females, who are told of

the historical abuses wrought upon family women by Corregidora. Told with a kind of Faulknerian furor for the primacy of story-telling, cast from the nightmare of history, but never out of its shadow, we come to see that the only way to keep the family truth alive is through the child-bearing of females and passed along verbal retelling of the Corregidora tale until it is riveted into the psyche forevermore. (All of this becomes the opposite of the patriarchial drive to have sons as heirs to the plantation power, or authority over the kingdom.) Jones's universal female obsession here? You simply cannot trust men (who, after all, not only keep the books but write the books, thereby depending upon a lapse of memory) with the charge of telling the truth, which would reveal the depths of their own sexual savagery. Only women *singing* their own tale to their daughters (therefore making it anew with each generation) can keep alive the needful intelligence of memory that the sisterhood must learn to listen to.

Ursa is a woman of the contemporary world, a blues singer, a story-teller's story-teller, who can't flip the weight of the Corregidora saga off of her back, or out of her soul; nor does she try. This legend "records" the Bible of her being. It informs the power of her singing; it also traps her in the past. For the milestone of memory can also be a millstone. Her jealous lover, Mutt, pushes Ursa down the stairs, and she is unable to have children. Mutt's deed becomes as mighty (on a personal level) as that of the demonic patriarch Corregidora. For Ursa is not able to produce any females nor pass on the family saga of Corregidora, so necessary to the intelligence of her sex, in an intimate way. Thus, Ursa is robbed twice of her female possibility beneath the burden of her gender. The powerful white master could destroy the written record, or never write the truth, but Mutt destroys Ursa's future to conceive female life, and shape it up; and by implication, the future of female knowledge—that of women knowing who they are out of the shackled beds of their history. The tragic vision here for females is this: You can't escape the hounding power of male authority in the past, or the present. We are talking about the great difficulty of Ursa with her heritage ever being able to love any man.

Recalling Holiday's life, too, a white great-grandsire (and his kind) started the double victimization of the black female: slavery and sexual debasement; but mainly it was black men who hurt Holiday's heart on the most intimate basis. Reflecting Jones's model of Holiday, Ursa did keep alive the heartbreaking torment of her tale, because of the depths it etched upon her art. (At least this was the attempt of the novelist.) Both were good, hypersensitive listeners. Neither Lady Day, nor Ursa, created children; yet both kept the saga of male usurpation of the female body and soul alive in the tissue and sinewy strength of their singing, passing along certain truths and intelligence to the listening audience of the sisterhood of women.

In creating an audience, Lady Day re-created herself, and the children her body never possessed. Both Holiday and Ursa passed on the bitter cup of their heritages in keeping with the commandment-like utterances of the matriarchs who shaped them up into early awareness at a tender age. But for Ursa, the family saga was more hounding since it was handed down generation to generation with her mother passing it along to her, finally; therefore the saga was enriched and heightened by each new matriarchal revision. Lady Day's capacity to plunge her artistic instrument back into the drowning memory of yesterday's vulnerability and extract from those waters this remnant of life (as she covered the waterfront of life's perils) and through mouth-to-mouth resuscitation breathe life back into the almost spent, ship-wrecked wretch, even as oral tradition gave birth to her conscious-ness, reveals to me the power that memory played upon Lady Day, as story-teller, because not only was she a hypersensitive witness, she was also a very keen listener, with a long memory.

Sterling Plumpp has used the blues as a primal source material for his poetry and as an index into the biographies of the blues people he writes about. Plumpp is in the tradition of writers like the poet Sterling Brown and the playwright August Wilson. There are many fine lines in his poem *Billie Holiday*, a tribute to Lady Day, which evoke the bridge between the blues singer and the jazz singer in this vocalist's art:

Feel and hear.
Her insistence on in
side lore. Personal in
jury. Subpoenaed
by tears dripping in silence.
After each throb
has surrendered.
To epochs of stillness.
She
rises from impulses of
hurt/to sing fine
print on the pain.
Employs
a microscope in her ears.
Crawls a
round in silence.

One paragraph into anything by Papa and you knew it was Hemingway. The first three or four words from any of her masterpieces, and you knew immediately: Lady Day. These were two of the major stylists of our epoch for me. I wanted to get her absolute attention to phraseology; her keening concern for every word into my writing. At her best, Lady Day completely dominated a lyric and the listener's attention. I wanted to be as eloquent on page as she was with her phraseology at the microphone. I wanted to dominate my reader's attention in a similar manner. I was also influenced by Lady Day's way of transforming what was passed along to her by other artists, Armstrong and Bessie Smith, into an art all her own. I was attempting to do this with the writers I had been influenced by. How to wrestle free of the influences, yet keep alive the strengths learned from the lions and the lionnesses of the literary past. How to incorporate what I needed from them into my own art. For, if Billie was dominated by all kinds of unsavory influences in her private life, she certainly dominated and reshaped the voices that inspired her apprenticeship. For all of my respect for Hemingway and Holiday, I was very much aware that each in his or her own way had come to parody the styles they were known for toward the end of their careers. The voice of each artist—so shattered by the impact of too much lush-life living—had wrenched off into self-parody.

There is an old African proverb: When an old man dies, a library burns down. For me the writer Hemingway and the singer Lady Day transcended this superb proverb concerned with the wisdom of oral tradition. We have Hemingway's great short stories and certain of his novels; we will have the recordings of the best of Lady Day forever-more. This fascinated me about the possibility of literacy creation: the permanence that transcends death.

Holiday and Hemingway were very self-destructive, fighting demons that went back to childhood. Hemingway did not possess the grand range of Faulkner, or the massive landscape of Balzac, Proust, or Thomas Mann. Holiday's range was narrow. Yet for me, at the time, each was the epitome of the existential warrior.

In turning these stellar artists into celebrities, the public probably robbed each of an opportunity to develop a sustained, rich inner life for the long haul. Each artist isolated upon certain obsessions.

For Hemingway it was manhood; for Lady Day, loneliness. In the statement Hemingway sent to the Nobel Prize Committee, when he received notice of the Award, Papa stated: "Writing, at its best, is a lonely life . . . He grows in public stature as he sheds his loneliness and often his work deteriorates. For he does his work alone and if he is a good enough writer he must face eternity, or the lack of it, each day." That the appetite of each was so lavish for celebrity, and self-bolstering, based in alcohol and drugs, suggests the close relation-ship between the life force and the death wish, which so haunted each artist's hypersensitive instrument.

When I started writing *There Is a Tree More Ancient Than Eden*, I knew from Holiday's impact upon my writing that not only are "writers forged in injustice, the way a sword is forged," as Papa Hemingway instructed, but that artists are similarly "forged." But more importantly, so are a suffering people. The Jews and the blacks. "Behold, I have refined you, but not like silver; I have tried you in the furnace of affliction," cries out the Old Testament Prophet Isaiah.

Not only does my first novel have at its epicene of "horrific lynching," based on one fundamental dimension of Lady Day's "Strange Fruit," but also the character of Jamestown reveals a keening, haunting engagement with Holiday's song, in the early days of his own evolvement. And Jamestown's sister, Madge Ann Fishbond renders up a monologue about her life, which seems, upon reflection, pitched out of the muted memory of Holiday's remembering art, even as Lady Day speaks to this novelist from another world, in this mock of *Paradise Lost.* But this is not a kingdom where you can have your music for free. You must pay for it by purchasing your experience in the purgatory of pain, where, ironically enough, there is no Christian deliverance.

> Pastoral scenes
> Of the gallant South
> The bulging eyes
> and the twisted mouth . . .
> Scent of magnolias
> Sweet and fresh
> Then the sudden
> Smell of burning flesh . . .

ACKNOWLEDGMENTS

The author would like to acknowlege the following sources and scenes where the essays between these covers were printed or delivered, as speeches.

In the Light of the Likeness— Transformed originally appeared in Volume 7 of *Contemporary Authors Autobiography Series,* 1988. Copyright Leon Forrest 1988.

Souls In Motion. Originally appeared in *Chicago* Magazine. July, 1985. Copyright Leon Forrest, 1985.

Words to *Move Mountain,* copyright 1983 by Margaret Pleasant Douroux, reprinted with permission.

Character Behind the Walls of Residential Segregation Appears here in print for the first time. Essay was an out-growth from a speech given by the author as the keynote luncheon address at the 10th Annual Fair Housing Seminar, at the Palmer House in Chicago, April 23, 1991. Copyright Leon Forrest, 1991.

Elijah appears here for the first time. Copyright Leon Forrest, Summer, 1991.

A Conversation with Ralph Ellison, originally appeared in *Muhammad Speaks,* December 15, 1972 issue.

Luminosity from the Lower Frequencies was originally published in *The Carleton Miscellany,* vol. XVIII, no. 3, Winter 1980. Reprinted in *Speaking For You, the Vision of Ralph Ellison,* edited by Kimberly W. Benston, 1987. Copyright Leon Forrest, 1980.

Going to the Territory, a review of Ellison's collected essays. *Chicago-Tribune,* July, 1987. Copyright Leon Forrest, 1987.

Morrison's Magic Lantern. Previosyly unpublished. Copyright Leon Forrest, 1990.

Brown's Body and Soul. Previously unpublished. Copyright Leon Forrest, 1990.

Faulkner/Reforestation. Originally published in the *Faulkner and Yok-*

napatawpha Series, Faulkner and Popular Culture, 1988. Copyright, 1988.

The Transformation of Grief. Essay delivered at the Fifth Biennial Conference on Southern Literature, at Chattanooga, Tennessee, April, 1989. Copyright, 1989, Leon Forrest.

The Mystery of Meaning was originally delivered as the inaugural address for the Allison Davis lectureship at Northwestern University, October, 1981.

Forged in Injustice. Book review of Allison Davis's book entitled: *Leadership, Love and Aggression. Chicago Magazine,* November, 1983.

A Eulogy to Allison Davis is the speech given for Professor Davis at the memorial service in his honor, December 3, 1983, at Bond Chapel, University of Chicago.

An Indictment of the Soviet System via Rabelaisian Satire. Book review of Alexander Zinoviev's novel *The Yawning Heights.* Published in the *Chicago Tribune,* June 17, 1979.

Graphic Gospel According to James Baldwin. Book review of *Just Above My Head,* a novel by James Baldwin. Published in the *Chicago Tribune,* September 16, 1979.

Evidences of Jimmy Baldwin. A previously unpublished essay. Copyright, 1986.

Borges: Haunting Dreams, Golden Fantasies. Book reviews published in the *Chicago Tribune,* October 9, 1977.

Self-Portrait of Black America. A book review of John L. Gwaltney's *Drylongso,* appeared in the August 31, 1980 issue of the *Chicago Tribune*

Spiritual Flight of Female Fire was the title of the key-note address for the Conference on Independent Black Female Filmmakers, held at Northwestern University, in May of 1991.

A Solo Long-Song: For Lady Day. This essay was published in the Spring, 1993 issue of *Callaloo.*

A Journey into the Forest of Roland Kirk-Country was published in the August 29, 1969 issue of *Muhammad Speaks.*

Michael's Mandate. Previously unpublished. Copyright Leon Forrest November 25, 1987.

Jackie Robinson: His Story, Our Story. Published in *Muhammad Speaks,,* 1972.

Theatre of Agony and Celebration. Convocation address at Northwestern University, June, 1985. Copyright Leon Forrest, 1985.

C O L O P H O N

The text was set in Baskerville, a typeface
designed by John Baskerville (England,
1706–1775). He was a writing master and an
engraver of tombstones before becoming a
printer and type designer. Baskerville re-
worked the old Roman faces into a classic
typeface that has become the standard by
which all serif faces have been compared. The
display face is Melior.

Composed by Alabama Book Composition,
Deatsville, Alabama.